The Great Lakes Economy
Looking North and South

Prepared by the Federal Reserve Bank of Chicago
and the Great Lakes Commission

Published by the Federal Reserve Bank of Chicago
Chicago, Illinois
April, 1991
Edited by William A. Testa

ISBN 0-9614358-3-6

Preface

In 1985, the Federal Reserve Bank of Chicago and the Great Lakes Commission conceived and produced a statistical compendium of the Great Lakes region entitled The Great Lakes Economy: A Resource and Industry Profile of the Great Lakes States. *Those who produced that volume, and those who used it, felt that decision makers and analysts needed a common set of facts with which to better understand the region's economic position and perform- ance. This common set of facts has been used in developing common regional strategies, enhancing understanding, and focusing attention on the region's common concerns.*

This volume, The Great Lakes Economy Looking North and South, *represents a culmination of several years' research which updates and eclipses its predecessor in several important ways. The volume provides analysts of the region the opportunity to interpret the facts surrounding the region's endowments, performance, and changes. In doing so, several authors have chosen to look beyond the states themselves to the closely-linked Canadian portion of the Great Lakes region. With the rise of low-cost transportation and communication, the world has shrunk but regions have grown—often spilling over national boundaries. Finally, the scope of topics has been broadened. Resource and industry trends and performance are still addressed in full but the linkages among the region's resources, people, and industries are also brought to the fore. Further, the region has moved through a series of development strategies so that it is now time to assess the past, to save what is valuable, to discard mistaken avenues, and to plan for the future.*

Silas Keehn
President
Federal Reserve Bank of Chicago

Henry K Hanka
Chairman
Great Lakes Commission

Contents

Development Policy and Outlook

Overview

Nothing remains the same except that changes are continual. So it is, has been, and will be for the Great Lakes economy. Understanding and observing the ongoing process of change helps us to navigate our course rather than merely react to the forces of change.

Like the continent, the region's initial development was motivated by inexpensive exploitation of its abundant natural resources. Timber was cleared and shipped east to build ships, bridges, and buildings. Agriculture was developed to feed a continent's burgeoning population. Minerals were excavated for use as materials for emerging goods-producing industries both here and abroad.

Following a familiar evolutionary pattern, derivative industries were established coincidentally with natural resource activities. The transporting of these resource goods to market led to the building of roads, canals, and railroads. The Great Lakes waterways provided a ready-made transportation system, thereby enhancing the region's profitable exploitation of its natural resources as well as paving the way for the movement of a wider range of commerce.

The need for manufactured goods, especially tools and machines, by natural resource and transportation industries gave rise to manufacturers including makers of farm implements, steel rails, locomotives and ships, and machinery related to lumber, paper, and mining. Later, as the Plains were opened to farming and livestock, the Great Lakes region's economy evolved further. Demands for the region's manufacturing products were boosted by settlers who needed both household goods and farm equipment. With regard to consumer goods, the region's fledgling retail businesses became pioneer "export sectors" by shipping specialized home goods overland to frontier households. Moreover, the region's transportation sector filled a vital need in shipping agricultural products to eastern markets. Emerging metropolises such as Chicago took on enhanced roles as wholesaler and financier to the developing Plains frontier.

These developments molded the region into a manufacturing center. In doing so, a critical mass of skilled workers, industries, raw materials, and transportation was assembled which amounted to an industrial complex that was much greater than the sum of its parts. As both luck and underlying conditions would have it, a second generation of manufacturing industries emerged which were a natural outcropping of the region's original development. As J. Fraser Hart notes in Chapter 3, the manufacture of automobiles began "after local tinkerers got the idea of hitching marine engines to farm wagons". Other industries such as machine tools, consumer appliances, and construction equipment were similarly forged as inventors were able to bring their ideas to profitable fruition within the rich Great Lakes environment.

As evidenced by the region's above-average per capita income, which persisted through the 1970s, the region's intensive development provided a standard of living that had not been previously witnessed on so massive a scale. In hindsight, the erosion of the region's preeminence in the 1970s and early 1980s stands as a mystery—not in why an erosion occurred—but in how this preeminence was sustained throughout the century despite the rapid opening of the remainder of the continent.

The development legacy

The Great Lakes economy of today is the legacy of this past development. Much remains and much has been squandered. According to J. Fraser Hart (Chapter 3), the population of the region apparently peaked around 1990 and is starting to decline. Members of the baby boom and baby bubble have not migrated into the region. Members of the retirement age cohorts have continued to migrate toward warmer climes, although many choose to stay at least for part of the year. Several forces make these moves compelling. Cold weather is not a natural draw for populations. And some of the same industries that have been responsible for the region's development, namely manufacturing and agriculture, have tended to shed workers as their productivity increased. Manufacturing decline has been abetted, no doubt, as world competitors have emerged. So too, many emerging industries have largely bypassed the region because their production process requires neither bulky natural resources nor a large scale surface transportation system.

A labor shortage rather than a labor glut will be the driving force behind the region's future economic welfare. Increased labor force participation has postponed the day of reckoning both in the Great Lakes and in some other regions. But as the birth rate falls below the population replacement level, labor force growth will depend on the region's willingness and ability to attract immigrants to the U.S. Lamentably, many parts of the region have not, so far, met this challenge and, perhaps, this too is a legacy of its past wealth when the region could afford an attitude and policy of cultural isolationism. As one counter-example, Ontario has prospered in part because Canada has long had an open door to immigrants.

The natural resources legacy also presents a wide range of challenges to the region. Many resources have been depleted by overuse or abuse. For example, the region's most economical iron ore deposits have been exhausted, leaving more expensive deposits which need intensive processing (Henry P. Whaley, Chapter 10). In addition, water quality degradation from industrial and residential pollution has only begun to be rectified. Michael J. Donahue (Chapter 6) lays out a framework for understanding the importance of the region's fresh water resources to the region's economy: 1) as a mode of transport, 2) as a factor of production, 3) as a supporting resource (that is, one whose existence is essential to other natural resources), and 4) as a marketable amenity. Efforts to understand the complex institutional environment in managing the region's water resources are difficult but rewarding. Lessons drawn from the governments and institutions involved in managing the region's water resources extend well beyond the scope of the resource itself. Binational and federal-state relations in the management of water resources have often been jumping off points for broad initiatives in regional planning and cooperation. For example, the region's plentiful lakes and rivers have stimulated a resurgence in outdoor recreation and tourism (Stephen J. Thorp and Stephen L. J Smith, Chapter 12). Several binational and interstate cooperative ventures have been launched to build and promote this industry including a region-wide system of scenic routes—the Great Lakes Circle Tour—and an overseas promotion initiative for the region.

Other natural resources are no longer as economically viable because their use instigates problems rather than solves them. As Athanasios D. Bournakis and James P. Hartnett point out (Chapter 7), the region's historical abundance of coal remains intact today—the region holds 29 percent of the nation's reserves. But while the region's industrial wealth was built from these plentiful supplies, the age of coal has given way to the age of petroleum and natural gas of which the region has few reserves. Environmental concerns have further shifted national coal production from the high sulfur Great Lakes variety toward the lower-sulfur Western and Appalachian fields. But the region's energy consumption remains more dependent than the nation on coal, largely for electric power generation. This consumption will be further tested by the recently-amended Clean Air Act which, among other things, promises to significantly cut sulfur dioxide emissions. Provisions of the act will please parts of Canada. Demands for curbing acid rain have been vociferous from the northern side of the Great Lakes. As Larry Leefers notes, some Canadian forests have allegedly been degraded by acid rain, although the process is still not well understood (Chapter 10).

With continued pressures on coal usage, the net energy-importing status of the region will continue to grow. The region has made considerable strides in energy efficiency but the threats of the energy trade imbalance to the region's wealth will occupy much future policy debate.

Much of the enduring resource base of the region is a man-made legacy rather than geological in origin. Stephen J. Thorp and Albert G. Ballert recall that the combination of an in-place transportation system—the Great Lakes and an extensive inland river system—promoted rapid development which, in turn, gave rise to a strong multi-modal transportation system (Chapter 8). Key regional issues for the 1990s include: maintenance of competitive balance among the modes; adequate infrastructure investment at all government levels; review of deregulation effects, particularly for passenger transportation; introduction of new technology and related energy conservation and land use planning.

Research and development taking place in the region are another part of the region's industrial legacy (Randel A. Pilo and David D. Weiss, Chapter 11). The Great Lakes region has not received as much federal support for R&D as other U.S. regions across all broad sectors including the largest, the industrial sector, where some emerging defense and high tech industries have favored locales outside the region. Despite this handicap, the region's great intensity of manufacturing and its attendant R&D compensates to such a degree that the region holds an overall R&D share of the nation that is proportionate to the region's share of the national economy. And as other analysts have shown, neither is the region devoid of high tech industries. Rather, after years of economic travails, the region has begun to recognize and act on a broad array of industrial opportunities; it has diversified. The region's informal development motto has become "high tech, low tech, any tech".

In constructing more formal measures of diversification, Robert H. Schnorbus and David D. Weiss (Chapter 4) find that, although the Great Lakes economy diversified to a greater extent than other regions from 1970 to 1988, its economy remains the least diversified of all. Rather, specialization remains acute in the durable goods manufacturing industries which will determine much of the region's future. Despite declining shares of the region's labor force in manufacturing, Eleanor H. Erdevig (Chapter 2) reports that specialization is especially strong in primary and fabricated metals, machinery, paper and printing, and transportation equipment. Although much has been written about the closure and startup of motor vehicle assembly plants during the 1980s, the overall effect on the Great Lakes area has been to rearrange auto production facilities rather than to lose facilities (on net) to other regions.

The dominant manufacturing sectors should not belie the vibrant service sectors which are partly a legacy of the region's natural resource and manufacturing industries. As Eleanor H. Erdevig illustrates, 47 percent of industrial corporate headquarters can be found in the 8 states stretching from New York to Minnesota. On the Canadian side, Ontario's primary urban area of Toronto has long held the top spot as administrative center for outlying goods-producing industries and in recent years, its role as a world financial center has also been on the rise. Even as the region's large urban areas diversify into services, linkages to the region's goods-producing industries are deeply imbedded.

A documentation of the linkages between Ontario and the Great Lakes states is important in its own right and also suggests the close economic linkages between the states themselves (David R. Allardice and William A. Testa, Chapter 1). Both Ontario and the U.S. Great Lakes regions are the manufacturing centers of their respective nations so that together they form the manufacturing nucleus of the continent. Moreover, there are heavy trade and investment flows between the Great Lakes states and Ontario. Several industries are shared —especially the auto industries—while others are complementary, e.g. Ontario concentrating more heavily in resource industries in exchange for machinery from the Great Lakes states. Canada and the U.S. are each other's largest trading partners. Trade between the six states ranging from Ohio to Minnesota accounts for one-third of total U.S.-Canada trade. And while the focus of foreign direct investment has shifted somewhat from the bi-national corridor in recent years, the existing stock remains paramount.

The close existing integration of the binational region has obscured the impact of the recent Free Trade Agreement (Eric B. Hartman, Chapter 5). Moreover, recessionary pressures have dominated the economies of both countries in 1990 —Canada more so than the U.S. It is perhaps no surprise then that many Canadians perceive the agreement as something less than a success. In coming years, the agreement will deepen bilateral integration. But as of this date, it is difficult to make a definitive assessment of the beneficial or negative impacts.

Development policy

The events of the past and the realities of today's economy have also left their mark on economic development policy. The great wealth of the past, achieved partly through the spoilage of natural resources, gave rise to several practices and attitudes that hindered the region in realizing its full potential. These practices are now being rectified to various degrees.

First, the meteoric rise in standards of living instilled a complacency among the residents of the Great Lakes and, at least on the U.S. side, a degree of cultural and economic isolationism from the rest of the world. To be sure, there have been some countervailing pressures on the region's residents to look beyond their borders, such as the close proximity and more cosmopolitan outlook of Ontario to the north. More recently, the emergence of the global economy and competitive pressures have awakened the region to global realities (Timothy McNulty, Chapter 13). To regain competitiveness, the Great Lakes is now beginning to look in earnest toward world markets and the attraction of foreign skilled workers. In addition to export promotion efforts by individual states and provinces, interstate and state-province cooperative efforts have been initiated, such as joint foreign trade offices and region-wide tourism promotion programs.

The legacy of abundant natural resources, and the open exploitation of their bounty, had also imbued a careless mentality in the region's economic development thinking about conservation. For these reasons, Daniel K. Ray, Madhu Kapur Malhotra, and Christopher A. Baines (Chapter 14) encourage regional policy makers to incorporate the concept of "sustainable development" into their development strategies. (Some are just beginning to do so.) Sustainable development "meets the needs of the present without compromising the ability of future generations to meet their own needs, and that respects the limits imposed by the ability of the Great Lakes-St. Lawrence River ecosystem to absorb the effects of human activities."

A final legacy from the region's bountiful past resulted in the noncooperative and hostile business development strategies adopted by states during the 1960s and 1970s (Timothy McNulty, Chapter 13). The policy of "smokestack chasing" whereby states aggressively competed for new factories by tax and public facility giveaways ran rampant during this era and it is not fully erased today. Perhaps the closing of the Pennsylvania VW plant, which followed the aggressive bidding war in its site selection, galvanized policy action and re-directed it toward interstate cooperative efforts. Regardless, it seems that the states have learned from the errors of the past and are now embarking on a host of cooperative ventures ranging from regional industry promotion to resource conservation and management. If so, residents of the Great Lakes states can look forward to making the claim that the "level of cooperation within the Great Lakes states exceeds that of any other region in the United States".

Growth in the 1990s

While the future is always murky, it appears that future conditions favor the Great Lakes economy in the 1990s (Diane C. Swonk, Chapter 15). The exchange value of the U.S. dollar has now returned to levels that will keep many of the region's products competitive in world markets. The export boom experienced in the late 1980s may continue to buoy manufacturing and agriculture. However, as Gary L. Benjamin concludes in Chapter 9, Great Lakes farmers must also contend with stagnant growth in domestic consumption of red meats and dairy products. So too, the outcome of negotiations over agricultural subsidies in the recent round of the General Agreement on Tariffs and Trade may also play an important role along with any future changes in trade-distorting policies.

Aside from world terms of trade, U.S. domestic spending on defense systems will also be likely to decrease in the 1990s which will tilt the distribution of domestic demand toward Great Lakes products (Diane Swonk). At the same time, cost pressures in the high growth regions of the U.S. during the 1980s have made Great Lakes locales increasingly attractive to business investment.

Even if these favorable factors do not materialize, the region's course lies in a more favorable direction in comparison to yesteryear. As the authors reveal in the following discussions, the region's development policies and public discussion have changed from being reactive to being pro-active, from adversarial to cooperative, and from inward-looking to global. This turnabout, in addition to the region's economic resurgence in the 1980s, have allowed the region's decision makers to make changes work for them rather than against them.

WILLIAM A. TESTA

The Great Lakes Economy

Chapter 1

Binational Economic Linkages within the Great Lakes Region

David R. Allardice, Vice President and Assistant Director of Research, Federal Reserve Bank of Chicago

William A. Testa , Senior Regional Economist and Research Officer, Federal Reserve Bank of Chicago

A comparison of the Canadian Great Lakes region with the U.S. side provides insights from both contrast and similarity. Both regions can be characterized as the manufacturing centers of their nations. Similar industrial structures, along with strong bilateral trade and investment flows, further suggest that the regions are highly integrated and not merely adjacent. By way of contrast, Ontario's economy has outperformed the Great Lakes states over the long term, suggesting that the U.S. region's eroding share of the national economy cannot be easily attributed to climate and location alone.

The authors thank Tirza Haviv, David Olsen, and David D. Weiss for research assistance.

The advent of the so-called "Free Trade" agreement between the United States and Canada in 1989 refocuses attention on the close economic ties between the two countries—especially in the region surrounding the Great Lakes. Here, where much of each nation's economic activity is located, several factors have created a closely integrated and binational region. Man-made infrastructure (especially related to transportation), locational relation to the remainder of the continent, and also natural resources are complements as well as substitutes for each other. Consequently, it is no surprise to find common industries such as farm equipment, steel, and automotive products in both countries. In addition, the Great Lakes themselves are conducive to transporting large bulk products such as coal, iron ore, and agricultural products between the two regions. Finally, man-made barriers to trade and investment are low and were low—even prior to the binational trade agreement. Taken together, these conditions have helped to form a tightly-linked binational economic region.

Of course, there are also significant differences between the Great Lakes economy of Canada and that of the U.S. The linkages between these two have not been so strong as to have resulted in identical economic performances and directions. Owing to the similar location of the two sides, insights are to be gathered because differences in performance derive from differing public policies pursued, and not from location.

The prospects of even lower man-made barriers to economic integration—stimulated by the "Free Trade" agreement—suggest that a greater awareness of the close relationship can help both regions take full advantage of the economic opportunities that lie ahead. In this regard, it is fortunate, and somewhat ironic, that we know *more* about the linkages and ties between Great Lakes states and Canada than we do about ties among the individual states. With this said, all that remains to do is to take a more intensive look at both the close binational relationship surrounding the Great Lakes and the differing economic directions that are evolving.

A greater Great Lakes region

Defining regional boundaries is difficult in that existing political boundaries (and the attendant data collection) never seem to match the best choice of economic boundaries. So it is in defining a binational Great Lakes region. On the Canadian side, the reality of data collection and political organization suggests that the province of Ontario will represent the Canadian Great Lakes region even though there are strong and recognizable economic flows between western Quebec and the U.S. Great Lakes states and between Canada's plains and the U.S. Great Lakes states. Even with this limitation, Ontario's borders *do* span almost the entire northern breadth of the Great Lakes.

The situation becomes more muddled on the U.S. side of the border. Certainly, the six states extending from Ohio to Minnesota cannot be neglected. Just as certainly, however, western Pennsylvania and northwest New York are closely tied with parts of the Ontario economy and the Great Lakes manufacturing belt. Unfortunately, much of the U.S. data are only collected at the state level. As a consequence, the inclusion of the states of New York and Pennsylvania would greatly bias the statistical tables owing to the large influence of metropolitan New York and Philadelphia. Accordingly, much of the data analysis herein will represent the U.S. Great Lakes region by the six states of Illinois, Indiana, Michigan, Minnesota, Ohio, and Wisconsin.

Linkages

In this overview of the Great Lakes economy, we examine the binational economic linkages between Ontario and the Great Lakes states. First, direct linkages can be readily observed by examining the commodity trade and direct investment flows between the Great Lakes states and Ontario (and Canada). According to the evidence presented, these direct linkages are exceptionally strong. Secondly, the industrial structure of the binational Great Lakes region is examined. The most pronounced similarity is that both sides of the border comprise the manufacturing cores of their respective nations. Lastly, the performance and changing industrial structure within the broader region is

TABLE 1

Great Lakes trade with Ontario and Canada, 1989
(millions of Canadian dollars)

	Ontario		Canada	
	Exports to	Imports from	Exports to	Imports from
Illinois	2,687	4,661	5,297	6,972
Indiana	952	2,507	2,165	2,986
Michigan	21,650	15,698	24,713	16,281
Minnesota	671	979	3,174	1,801
Ohio	3,084	7,285	4,343	8,330
Wisconsin	1,058	1,757	2,150	2,321
Great Lakes (6)	30,104	32,886	41,842	38,692
New York	10,003	4,823	14,484	6,510
Pennsylvania	1,702	2,731	3,229	3,592
United States	56,060	65,593	97,930	93,361

SOURCE: External Affairs and International Trade Canada, *Canadian Imports (Exports) from Individual U.S. States 1989, Customs Basis.*

TABLE 2

Exports to Ontario and Canada as a share of overseas exports, 1989
(as percent of total exports)

	Exports to	
	Ontario	Canada
From		
New England	12.5	26.6
Middle Atlantic	18.2	25.0
South Atlantic	10.6	16.5
East South Central	18.3	24.4
West South Central	3.9	6.8
East North Central	46.3	53.6
West North Central	17.5	31.0
Mountain	8.9	15.6
Pacific	4.2	9.4
Great Lakes states (6)	43.4	51.1
Great Lakes states (8)	34.5	41.6
Illinois	28.5	42.6
Indiana	37.6	44.8
Michigan	67.2	69.7
Minnesota	14.1	26.0
New York	15.7	21.2
Ohio	45.6	52.2
Pennsylvania	25.5	33.6
Wisconsin	27.1	35.8
United States	15.2	21.6

SOURCE: External Affairs and International Trade Canada, *Canadian Imports from Individual States 1989*; and U.S. Census Bureau, *Origin of Movement of U.S. Exports of Merchandise by State.*

NOTE: Unreported, not specified, estimated shipments and undocumented exports to Canada are allocated to U.S. states on the basis of state share of documented exports.

geographic proximity between Ontario and the Great Lakes states along with national economic concentration in the Great Lakes region for both countries have conspired to form a most significant binational trading relationship. Trade between the Great Lakes states (6) and Ontario accounted for almost one-third of binational trade in 1989—this excluding the key New York and Pennsylvania areas that legitimately fall within the Great Lakes economic sphere (Table 1). A fairly even balance of trade is maintained, with Ontario shipping 30.1 billion (C$) in goods to Great Lakes states in 1989 in exchange for 32.9 billion (C$) in imports from the Great Lakes states.

This intensive trade relation with Ontario has resulted in Canada as being the Great Lakes region's greatest export market (Table 2). Aside from the

examined and here the parallel abruptly ends. At the same time that most of the Great Lakes states have experienced sharp deindustrialization, Ontario and parts of the western Great Lakes region have continued to industrialize. More broadly, Canada's economy has "imploded" into the Ontario region during the 1980s while, in the U.S., decentralization away from the Great Lakes states has carried over from the 1970s into the 1980s.

Trade flows

Canada and the United States are, respectively, each other's most important trading partner. Exports to Canada from the U.S. account for over one-fifth of total U.S. exports while Canada's exports to the U.S. comprise over two-thirds of its total exports. Trade between Ontario and the Great Lakes states can be characterized as the nucleus of this intensive trading relationship. To be sure, there are several other important north-south trade patterns of note: Both New England and California export significant amounts of electronic computers; Canada exports electric power to New England from the Atlantic provinces; Alberta supplies the Great Lakes states with crude petroleum and natural gas; and Canada exports pulp, paper, and newsprint from British Columbia. However, the

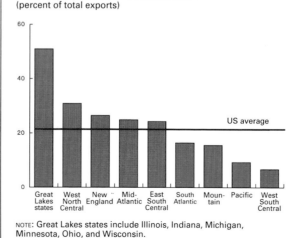

FIGURE 1

Regional exports to Canada, 1989
(percent of total exports)

NOTE: Great Lakes states include Illinois, Indiana, Michigan, Minnesota, Ohio, and Wisconsin.

East North Central region, which the Great Lakes region encompasses, no other U.S. Census region exports a greater share of its world exports to Canada—that being over 50 percent in 1989 (Figure 1). In comparison, according to 1987 figures from the U.S Department of Commerce for the Great Lakes region (which excludes Minnesota), the next largest trading partners accounted for 6.5 percent (Japan), 5.3 percent (Mexico), and 4.8 percent (Great Britain) of exports (Table 3).

The character of binational trade between Ontario and Great Lakes states centers around a

TABLE 3

Destinations of regional manufactured exports, 1987
(percent of regional total)

	Great Lakes	United States
Canada	49.2	23.4
Japan	6.5	10.4
Mexico	5.3	6.2
Great Britain	4.8	6.0
Germany	4.3	4.9
France	4.2	3.3
Netherlands	1.9	3.1
Korea	1.5	2.9
Taiwan	1.4	2.7
Belgium/Luxembourg	1.9	2.5
Total (10 countries)	81.0	65.3

SOURCE: As reported by Tim R. Smith, "Regional Exports of Manufactured Products", *Economic Review*, Federal Reserve Bank of Kansas City, January, 1989, pp. 21-29. The data are compiled from "State of Export Series", Foreign Trade Division, Bureau of the Census, U.S. Department of Commerce.

NOTE: The Great Lakes region includes the states of Ohio, Indiana, Michigan, Illinois, and Wisconsin.

highly significant and bilateral trade in autos, automotive parts, and engines (i.e. comprising 61 percent of Ontario and Great Lakes trade in 1989) (Figure 2). The Auto Pact of 1965 encouraged the tariff-free movement of cross-border trade in new autos and parts while providing for minimum production requirements in Canada. Since its enactment, investment in Ontario by U.S. domestic auto makers, and foreign makers as well, has increased. While automotive trade is heavy between most of the individual Great Lakes states and Canada, much of its focus remains concentrated within the Michigan-Southern Ontario area (See Appendix 1 for detailed state imports and exports).

Aside from the heavy bilateral trade in the automotive sector, the Great Lakes states export heavily in the areas of chemicals, and machinery and equipment to Ontario (Table 4). Great Lakes exports of metals, automotive products, chemicals, and machinery and equipment are also notably heavy to the remainder of Canada.

Great Lakes imports of paper, pulp, lumber, and other forestry products from Ontario amounted to 1.7 billion (C$) in 1989 while imports of machinery and equipment exceeded 2 billion (C$). Great Lakes imports of forestry products from the remainder of Canada exceeded those from Ontario. At the same time, the Great Lakes states imported 4.3 billion (C$) in energy materials from Canada—chiefly petroleum and natural gas.

Foreign direct investment

Throughout this century, foreign direct investment linkages have also bound together Canada and the U.S. As of 1986, the United States accounted for 73 percent of foreign direct investment in Canada as measured by gross book value of capital. As measured by assets and sales, this represents 14 percent of U.S. multinational investment abroad in all countries in 1986.

On the flip side, Canadian companies with affiliates located in the United States accounted for approximately 22 percent of gross book value of foreign direct investment in the U.S.—Canada being one of the top investors along with Great Britain, Japan, and Germany.[1] This latter share is quite large

FIGURE 2

Regional exports and imports with Canada, 1989
(billions of dollars Canadian)

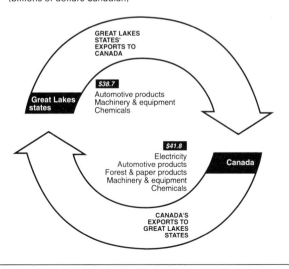

TABLE 4

**Commodity trade by major category, 1989
Great Lakes states (6) vs. Ontario and Canada**
(millions of dollars Canadian)

	Great Lakes states trade with			
	Ontario		Canada	
	Exports	Imports	Exports	Imports
Agricultural	730	986	971	1,016
Forestry	288	1,744	384	4,054
Mining	498	279	581	521
Energy	810	190	874	4,308
Metals	897	1,612	1,081	2,525
Machinery & Equipment	6,296	2,002	8,287	2,568
Automotive	17,155	21,308	18,912	23,138
Other Trans. Equip.	506	699	867	871
Chemicals	1,284	1,074	1,597	1,928

SOURCE: External Affairs and International Trade Canada, *Canadian Imports (Exports) from Individual States 1989*.

relative to Canada's share of the world economy which varies from year to year between 3 and 4 percent of OECD output. From a Canadian perspective, this investment amounts to 71 percent of Canada's total direct investment in all foreign nations.

The United States has been investing in Canada since at least the late 1890s. But during the post-World War II era, especially up to the 1970s, foreign direct investment was especially strong, paralleling the robust U.S. multinational investment that took place throughout the world during that time period. While continuing to grow during the 1970s and 1980s, U.S. investment in Canada eased as Canada instituted policies to discourage U.S. ownership of assets including the establishment of the Foreign Investment Review Agency (now Investment Canada) and the National Energy Program which was subsequently dismantled.

Further adding to a swing in the direction of net capital flows, Canadian direct investment in the United States quickened during the 1970s and 1980s and it has outpaced other nations' investment in the U.S. in recent years. Some have attributed this trend to Canadian companies' desire to assure access to the large U.S. market by establishing branch plants or affiliates in the U.S.[2] If so, the recent Free Trade Agreement can be expected to help stem the outflow of Canadian capital insofar as the agreement assures that the U.S. market can be served from locations in Canada without the specter of future trade impediments. Others argue that U.S. foreign direct investment in Canada will falter because, in the absence of trade tariffs, Canadian product demand can now be served at lesser cost from U.S. factories.[3]

Direct investment linkages that are in place *strictly within* the binational Great Lakes region (e.g. Ohio and Ontario) are somewhat more difficult to document. To be sure, there are strong inter-company linkages especially in the manufacturing sector. To a large extent, the Great Lakes states and Ontario represent part and parcel of the same core manufacturing region of the North American continent. Accordingly, it is not surprising to find that branch plants and affiliates traverse the national boundary along the Great Lakes. The economic similarity and cohesiveness of the larger Great Lakes manufacturing belt quite naturally stimulated cross-border investment and organizational ties. At the same time, periods of increased trade barriers have stimulated direct investment flows as Canadian or U.S. companies have tried to skirt the penalties of tariffs by direct investment abroad.[4] For many industries already headquartered in the Great Lakes, such as the Big Three auto makers, a short jump across the border into the neighboring Canada's manufacturing nucleus resulted in both market and organizational economies.

U.S. foreign direct investment in Ontario

While interregional investment flows are difficult to document aside from scattered reports of individual company transactions, it is possible to observe direct investment from the U.S. to Ontario and, conversely, from Canada to Great Lakes states. Here, by inference, the strong organizational link-ages within the binational region become apparent.

In examining direct investment in Ontario by U.S. companies, industry coverage is not compre-hensive at the provincial level. However, data are available for the manufacturing sector and this sector accounts for by far the largest share of foreign direct investment.[5] The importance of foreign direct investment is best illustrated by the share of man-

TABLE 5

United States affiliates in Ontario, 1976 and 1986

Industry	Total value added				Total employment			
	Level		Share of total		Level		Share of total	
	1976	1986	1976	1986	1976	1986	1976	1986
	(C$ millions)		(%)				(%)	
Manufacturing	11,160	26,099	50.4	44.5	373,970	340,005	43.8	36.0
Food and beverage	997	2,652	39.0	38.3	30,257	27,255	36.4	31.3
Tobacco	d	d	d	d	d	d	d	d
Rubber and plastics	538	1,164	70.6	54.6	22,181	18,570	63.3	46.6
Leather	41	d	22.0	d	2,685	d	20.5	d
Textiles	305	603	53.4	20.7	13,872	8,559	46.4	33.7
Knitting mills	d	d	d	d	d	d	d	d
Clothing	d	207	d	21.0	d	5,942	d	17.0
Wood	34	38	9.9	3.0	2,166	880	10.9	3.0
Furniture	72	273	18.4	22.0	3,406	4,772	14.7	15.0
Paper	410	829	37.9	30.0	16,250	10,770	35.6	26.0
Printing and publishing	127	379	12.0	11.0	5,179	6,581	11.0	10.0
Primary metals	243	457	12.5	11.0	7,888	4,847	11.1	8.0
Metal fabrication	902	1,236	43.2	26.0	32,858	19,565	37.3	22.0
Machinery	815	1,412	60.2	53.0	29,778	20,641	54.7	44.0
Transportation	3,268	8,475	87.5	77.0	88,793	109,665	82.3	70.0
Electrical products	1,122	3,129	61.6	58.0	49,874	41,941	61.8	48.0
Non metallic minerals	275	691	36.0	35.0	9,837	9,716	35.8	35.0
Petroleum and coal	d	488	d	74.0	d	5,149	d	69.0
Chemicals	1,099	3,131	67.2	58.0	26,832	27,148	62.0	54.0
Miscellaneous	492	841	55.2	44.0	18,636	15,576	45.3	37.0

SOURCE: Statistics Canada, publication No. 31-401.

NOTE: Entries market with a "d" signify either suppressed or insignificant data.

ufacturing activity with U.S. influence (Table 5). U.S. affiliates in Ontario comprised 44.5 percent of Canada's manufacturing value added and 36 percent of employment in 1986.

Note also that this higher share of value added than employment implies that U.S.-based manufac-turing tends to be "high value added" or more capital/technology intensive in nature. A look at specific industry foreign direct investment concen-tration bears this out. In 1986, almost one-third of affiliate employment could be found in transporta-tion equipment industries with electrical products, machinery, plastics, and chemicals also comprising significant shares of total foreign direct investment in manufacturing. Nonetheless, a frequent concern

of Canadian observers has been that U.S. affiliates have concentrated in the less creative and more labor intensive activities within industries such as autos while neglecting capital and technology intensive job functions such as research and development.[6]

U.S. company influence in Ontario manufactur-ing has waned as a share of total manufacturing since 1976 (Table 5). However, this erosion reflects not an absolute decline in investment nor a gain in third party control of Canadian manufacturing activity. Rather, Canadian companies have ex-panded more rapidly and now account for a greater share of total activity in Ontario.

TABLE 6

United States affiliates in Ontario and Canada, 1970-1986

Year	Ontario—Total manufacturing		Canada—Total manufacturing	
	Total value added	Total employees	Total value added	Total employees
	(C$ millions)		(C$ millions)	
1970	5,993	373,473	9,145	589,320
1971	n.a.	n.a.	n.a.	n.a.
1972	7,336	372,191	10,730	571,560
1973	n.a.	n.a.	n.a.	n.a.
1974	10,080	397,679	15,062,	609,018
1975	n.a.	n.a.	n.a.	n.a.
1976	11,160	373,970	16,851	576,949
1977	n.a.	n.a.	n.a.	n.a.
1978	13,615	375,211	20,901	574,788
1979	n.a.	n.a.	n.a.	n.a.
1980	15,854	359,446	24,533	547,729
1981	17,869	356,615	26,749	532,089
1982	17,049	328,876	24,828	480,322
1983	20,379	325,191	29,356	469,636
1984	23,922	338,247	33,357	476,836
1985	25,631	344,607	35,265	482,403
1986	26,099	340,005	36,449	475,906

SOURCE: Statistics Canada, No. 31-401.

NOTE: n.a. indicates no data are available.

Canada's foreign direct investment in the Great Lakes

During the 20th century, Canadian manufacturers have invested heavily in the U.S., especially along the Great Lakes, Middle Atlantic, and New England regions. Some analysts believe that the underlying motivation has been to assure access to the large U.S. market for goods. Indeed, the argument has been made that many Canadian manufacturers need a larger American market so as to remain competitive in Canada by producing on a larger scale.[7]

Over the 1977-87 period, direct investment by Canadian firms in the Great Lakes states has not kept pace with other nations' investment as measured by either affiliates' employees or by the gross book value of assets (Table 7). The exceptions are that New York and Pennsylvania have attracted far more foreign direct investment (proportionately) than the other Great Lakes states. The heavy concentration of Canadian foreign direct investment

in New York has historically concentrated in western New York in the Buffalo area.[8]

The slower pace of Canadian direct investment in the Great Lakes reflects not so much a weak capital flow from Canada to the U.S. nor even a weak flow into the Great Lakes. After all, Canadian affiliates were responsible for over 55,000 *more* Great Lakes jobs in 1987 than in 1977. So too, Canadian investment in the U.S. over the same period exceeded the pace of remaining nations combined. Rather, foreign direct investment by Canada has tended to concentrate in the Southeast region including Florida and Georgia; and in the Southwest and California. At the same time, foreign direct investment by all nations in the Great Lakes states has progressed rather well in light of the region's overall "emptying out" of its manufacturing base. In part, the foreign direct investment surge in the Great Lakes over the 1977-87 period has been influenced by heavy Japanese participation in transplant auto assembly and auto parts plants and also through heavy investment in the steel industry.[9]

In looking at the *cumulative stock* or investment position of Canada in the Great Lakes rather than at recent investment *flows*, it can be seen that lagging Canadian investment is only a recent phenomenon. As of 1987, the proportionate gross book value of Canadian affiliates in the region exceeded the U.S. (Figure 3). This from a foreign direct investment indicator that tends to undercount the value of investments made in the distant past and whose "book value" understates today's market value.[10] So too, employees of Canadian affiliates in the Great

TABLE 7

Canadian and other countries' investments in the Great Lakes states, 1977-87

	Gross book value, 1987		Employees, 1987	
	Level	Change 1977-87	Level	Change 1977-87
	($US millions)	(%)		(%)
Illinois				
Canada	2,288	473.4	25,300	97.3
Other	10,369	375.0	140,800	130.8
Indiana				
Canada	502	162.8	14,300	169.8
Other	3,262	381.1	51,500	105.3
Michigan				
Canada	2,121	66.5	18,700	50.5
Other	5,440	383.1	75,800	164.0
Minnesota				
Canada	2,383	42.9	9,900	(10.5)
Other	1,909	458.2	31,100	379.0
Ohio				
Canada	1,277	483.1	19,400	149,9
Other	9,131	326.1	112,800	134.8
Wisconsin				
Canada	922	147.2	12,700	59.3
Other	1,691	311.4	40,700	80.6
Great Lakes (6)				
Canada	11,006	275.2	100,300	121.8
Other	31,802	362.0	452,700	135.8
New York				
Canada	5,203	588.2	39,000	177.2
Other	17,343	730.2	261,100	142.9
Pennsylvania				
Canada	2,711	739.3	34,700	353.5
Other	8,001	358.8	133,800	135.2
U.S.				
Canada	73,241	532.3	590,500	212.0
Other	272,971	394.5	2,569,200	149.6

SOURCE: United States Department of Commerce, Bureau of Economic Analysis, *Foreign Direct Investment in the United States, Operations of U.S. Affiliates of Foreign Companies (1977-1986), 1987 Benchmark Survey*, Table 8.

Lakes region fall only slightly short of the national average as a share of total foreign direct investment employment.

Industry structure

Comparing the structure of employment by industry in Ontario with the Great Lakes states sheds some light on the similarities and differences

TABLE 8

Employment by industry sector in the Great Lakes, 1990Q1

	Canada	Ontario	Great Lakes (6)	U.S.	Rest of Canada	Ontario	Great Lakes (6)	Rest of U.S.
	000s of jobs				% of total			
Mining & forestry	200.1	36.9	56.1	748.3	2.7	.9	.3	.8
Construction	519.8	221.7	858.2	5,445.0	4.9	5.3	4.1	5.1
Manufacturing	1,835.8	914.5	4,612.8	19,410.0	15.5	21.8	22.1	16.6
Retail trade	1,311.8	530.7	3,856.9	19,800.3	12.9	12.6	18.5	17.8
Wholesale trade	560.8	222.7	1,224.3	6,335.3	5.6	5.3	5.9	5.7
F.I.R.E.	648.9	296.9	1,188.5	6,911.3	5.8	7.1	5.7	6.4
Services[a]	5,175.0	1,976.7	9,103.6	51,570.3	52.7	47.0	43.6	47.5
Total	10,268.3	4,198.9	20,892.8	110,699.0	100.0	100.0	100.0	100.0

SOURCE: *Employment, Hours, and Earnings*, Statistics Canada; and *Employment and Earnings*, Bureau of Labor Statistics, U.S. Department of Labor.

NOTE: See Appendix 2 for individual states. Sum of individual industry employment levels may not total because each industry sector (including total) was seasonally adjusted (by the Federal Reserve Bank of Chicago) as a separate series.

[a]Includes government, transportation and public utilities, and services. Data are seasonally adjusted by the Federal Reserve Bank of Chicago.

in the respective regional roles of Ontario and the Great Lakes states which are jointly situated on the northern part of the continent.

Comparing data covering different nations and derived from two different statistical agencies is a difficult task. Data are often reported as a by-product of public program monitoring rather than constructed as an analytical tool. Even when designed for research and monitoring, the data covering a subject will rarely match in definition and category. After some careful thought followed by reorganizing of data to achieve compatibility, employment shares by industry sector are presented for both countries in Table 8.[11]

Generally speaking, Ontario and the Great Lakes states are similar in employing larger shares in manufacturing and lesser shares in services than their respective national averages. Manufacturing employment exhibits the most striking similarity between Ontario and the Great Lakes states. Both regions host a very similar percentage in manufacturing at 22 percent of employment in 1990, first quarter, although this varies widely from state to state (Appendix 2). More importantly, both Ontario's and the Great Lakes states' manufacturing share significantly exceeds that of the remainder of their respective nations. This again characterizes the binational Great Lakes as the manufacturing nucleus of the continent.

Mining and forestry employment was far less concentrated in Ontario relative to the rest of Canada; and the share was far less in the Great Lakes states than in the remainder of the U.S.

The remaining goods sector, construction, trailed far behind in the Great Lakes states while Ontario's share exceeded Canada. Ontario's strong overall economic growth performance during the 1980s contributed much to this sector as construction reflects investment behavior in being highly responsive to rapid growth and capacity saturation. Some indicators of regional growth in Canada, particularly population migration, suggest that investment growth has reversed its regional pattern of the late 1970s and early 1980s when peripheral regions, especially in Western Canada, were growing more rapidly than Ontario.[12] As energy and mineral prices have ebbed, centralization of growth favoring Ontario has resulted.

Both the employment shares of wholesale and retail trade fall short in Ontario relative to Canada while the Great Lakes exceeded the U.S. However, in one very important business service area, finance, insurance, and real estate (FIRE), Ontario employment concentration was very high while the Great Lakes states tend to employ a lesser share. In part, this reflects the Toronto area's stature and recent ascendancy as the center of finance in Canada. Toronto's strength as a center of finance and corporate headquarters is largely based on service linkages with mining and manufacturing activity in outlying areas. To a similar extent, the Chicago area serves as the premier regional financial center and headquarters for the Great Lakes states. Here, service linkages are largely based on the region's manufacturing and agricultural industries.

Manufacturing structure

In examining individual manufacturing industries, Ontario and the Great Lakes states are similar in hosting high concentrations of jobs in the core "metal bending" industries including primary and fabricated metals and transportation equipment—mostly automotive (Table 9). Outstanding differences between Ontario and the Great Lakes states lie in the nondurable textile, apparel, and leather products industries in which Ontario is more highly concentrated.

One useful way of grouping manufacturing industries is by the intensity of the key input in their manufacturing production process, be it technology,

FIGURE 3

Stock of Canadian investment in the Great Lakes, 1987
(percent of total)

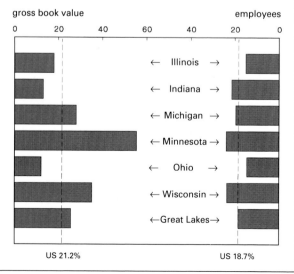

TABLE 9

Employment in manufacturing, 1986
(index of concentration)

	Thousands of jobs		Index of concentration[a]	
	Ontario	Great Lakes states	Ontario	Great Lakes states
Food and kindred products	84.2	327.9	1.43	1.07
Textile mill products	36.2	18.8	.96	.14
Apparel and other textiles	22.7	67.6	.82	.31
Lumber and wood products	20.1	95.7	.95	.70
Furniture and fixtures	21.4	101.3	1.60	1.04
Paper and allied products	43.5	162.7	1.56	1.21
Printing and publishing	47.3	343.5	1.13	1.20
Chemicals and allied products	45.7	216.8	1.29	1.09
Petroleum and coal products	9.7	26.0	1.17	.80
Rubber and plastics	35.5	264.8	1.33	1.75
Leather and leather products	11.9	18.3	2.34	.61
Stone, clay, and glass	25.5	131.7	1.25	1.19
Primary metals	71.9	300.8	2.09	1.99
Fabricated metals	85.4	528.9	1.54	1.81
Nonelectrical machinery	54.1	700.5	.62	1.83
Electric and electronic equipment	74.0	431.4	1.07	1.06
Transportation equipment	113.1	647.2	2.13	1.73
Instruments and related products	14.8	133.3	.71	1.10
Miscellaneous products	25.3	72.6	1.63	.92

SOURCE U.S. Dept. of Commerce, Bureau of the Census, *County Business Patterns;* and Statistics Canada, *Census of Manufactures.*

[a]Defined as the industry's share of total employment in the geographic area as a ratio to the industry's share of total employment in Canada plus the U.S.

capital equipment, labor force, or natural resources (Table 10).[13] Here it is seen that Ontario and the Great Lakes states' economies alike tend to concentrate in technology intensive industries —transportation equipment, chemicals, machinery, instruments, and electronics. Substantial differences arise, however, in that Ontario's concentration in both labor intensive industries and resource intensive industries exceeds that in the Great Lakes where capital and technology intensity tend to characterize the production processes. Ontario's labor and resource intensive industries lie chiefly in paper and allied products, furniture and fixtures, lumber and wood, textiles and apparel, leather, and petroleum products.

Performance

To the extent that they diverge, trends in employment performance between Ontario and the Great Lakes states can provide useful insights into policy questions. This is so because public policies affecting business, industry, and labor force may differ markedly across national borders. Yet, the locational and climate considerations in the broader Great Lakes region are much the same. Accordingly, the effects of policy may be more easily discerned from the effects of climate and location. Of course, in drawing the locational parallel between Ontario and the Great Lakes states, it is well to remember that, from the Canadian perspective, southern Ontario is Canada's Sunbelt in a manner of speaking, although the ready accessibility of Canadian business owners to the U.S. Sunbelt makes the locational analogy of southern Ontario as a Canadian Sunbelt far less than perfect.

Over the long term, comparisons of total employment and/or industry sector employment between the two Great Lakes regions are not advisable. In addition to differences in methodology of data collection and construction between the two countries at any one point in time, Canada's primary labor force survey, "the employment, hours, and earnings" program, has changed dramatically over time.[14] For this reason, our comparisons begin in the first quarter of 1983, this being a time when both Canada and the U.S. were near the trough of the 1979-82 slowdown or recessionary years.

In examining growth in total employment, Ontario and the Great Lakes states have grown by similar rates from 1983 to 1990 (Figure 4). In fact, there is little difference between the larger Great Lakes region and the remainder of Canada and the U.S. In part, the strong performance in the states reflects the deep employment trough into which the region had fallen over the 1979-83 period. Still, as the length of the current expansion extends on into

TABLE 10

Employment in manufacturing, 1986
(index of concentration)

Industry by factor intensity	Thousands of jobs		Index of concentration*	
	Ontario	Great Lakes	Ontario	Great Lakes
Technology	358.3	2,129.3	1.22	1.43
Capital	280.0	1,456.8	1.05	1.44
Labor	104.7	260.0	1.26	.62
Resource	191.9	744.7	1.32	1.02
Total	934.9	4,590.8	1.22	1.26

SOURCE: Statistics Canada, *Census of Manufactures* (manufacturing jobs) and *Employment, Earnings, and Hours* (total jobs); U.S. Department of Commerce, Bureau of the Census, *County Business Patterns,* and U.S. Department of Labor, Bureau of Labor Statistics.

*NOTE: Defined as the industry's share of total employment in the geographic area as a ratio to the industry's share of total employment in Canada plus the U.S. Technology intensive producers include chemicals and allied products, nonelectrical machinery, electric and electronic equipment, transportation equipment, and instruments and related products. Capital intensive producers include textile mill products, printing and publishing, rubber and plastics, and primary and fabricated metals. Labor intensive producers include apparel and other textile products, furniture and fixtures, leather and leather products, and miscellaneous manufacturing products. Resource intensive producers include food and kindred products, tobacco, lumber and wood products, paper and allied products, petroleum and coal products, and stone, clay and glass products.

the 1990s, the somewhat arbitrary choice of base year 1983 wears thin as an explanation of Great Lakes economic strength during the 1980s because the effect of using the trough year is averaged over many years.

The finance, insurance, and real estate industries were growth engines in both the U.S. and Canada during the 1980s. The Great Lakes employment base continued to erode in this area, however, underperforming this sector's performance in the rest of the U.S. In contrast, Ontario's already strong

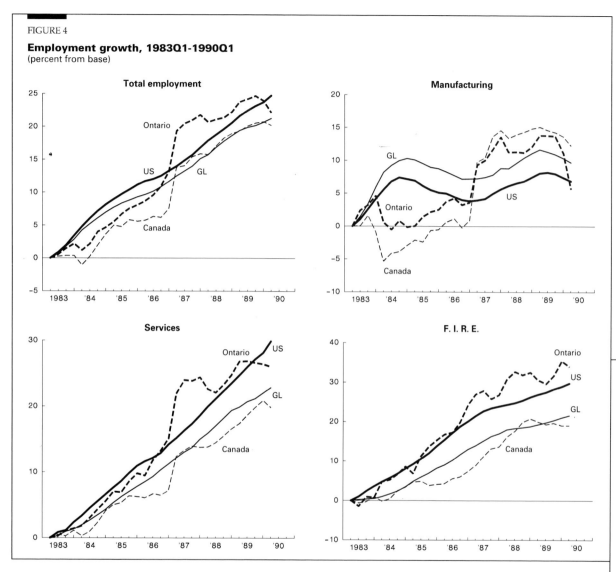

FIGURE 4

Employment growth, 1983Q1-1990Q1
(percent from base)

have "hollowed out" what was the continent's manufacturing core as illustrated by the region's declining share of manufacturing output. As we have already seen from the employment data, the Great Lakes states have been losing their premier share of manufacturing. Table 11 displays real output shares in manufacturing and shows that, from 1970 to 1986, the Great Lakes' share of U.S. real output in manufacturing declined from just over 30 percent to just over 25 percent. This drop would undoubtedly have been larger with the inclusion of western New York and Pennsylvania both of which declined sharply over the period. At the same time, Ontario's share of Canada's output had been climbing from 50 percent to over 54 percent.

One hypothesis for the Great Lakes decline has been that the high concentration of manufacturing served as an economic "agglomeration" for the first half of this decade.[16] That is to say that the high spatial concentration of manufacturing in the "core area" produced synergies or cost savings which derive largely from geographic proximity of related

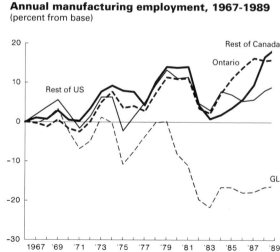

FIGURE 5

Annual manufacturing employment, 1967-1989
(percent from base)

SOURCE: Staff estimates by Federal Reserve Bank of Chicago using data from Bureau of Labor Statistics, *Employment and Earnings;* and Statistics Canada, Industry Division, #31-203, *Manufacturing Industries of Canada: National and Provincial Areas;* and Statistics Canada, *Employment, Earnings and Hours.*

concentration in these areas continued to lengthen as growth exceeded the remainder of Canada.

Both Ontario and the Great Lakes states were led by manufacturing as one strong engine of recovery. Great Lakes states' growth in manufacturing exceeded the rest of the U.S. (again, partly the trough effect) while Ontario matched the rest of Canada. Into the year 1990, however, disturbing

signs of a sharp drop-off in Ontario's manufacturing employment were emerging.

Over the longer term, manufacturing performance in Ontario has easily eclipsed the remainder of the Great Lakes region (Figure 5). Since 1966, growth in Ontario, the remainder of Canada, and the non-Great Lakes U.S. have expanded by more than 10 percent while the Great Lakes states have lost manufacturing employment.[15] These trends

industries to each other and, equally important, from a transportation/distribution system that was, before trucking and air freight, largely dependent on rail lines for shipment. One argument posits that rail distribution encouraged centrality in production location because the costs of radial shipment from a central nexus (i.e. the Great Lakes manufacturing belt) are not much different from disbursed shipment from remote branch plants (by rail). This is so because the costs of shipment from distant branch plants by rail, though perhaps closer in distance to peripheral markets, entails costly terminal transfer of goods within the rail network. As truck transport came to the fore, with its relatively lower costs of terminal transfer and its flexible shipment in smaller bundles, the economies and cost savings of the core manufacturing belt were no longer enough to hold the Great Lakes manufacturing agglomeration in place. Branch plants and decentralization of U.S. manufacturing was thereby encouraged by construction of the interstate highway system and increasing technological improvements in truck transit such as refrigeration.

This particular line of reasoning receives some support from observing the differing intraregional patterns of growth. From Table 11, it is clear that not all Great Lakes states have experienced erosion in manufacturing share to the remainder of the U.S. In particular, Wisconsin's and Minnesota's shares have been on the upswing over the 1970s and 1980s, as have other states in the West North Central regions.[17] Along with Ontario's experience, this lends credence to the paradigm that decentralization of manufacturing is occurring as the continent develops over time (i.e. other regions merely lag the development of the Great Lakes core) rather than from any fundamental factor cost or policy mistakes being practiced in the Midwest.[18]

Another set of reasons offered for the Great Lakes states' decline centers on the Great Lakes' relative cost differences (i.e. disadvantages) in relation to the developing South and Southeast states for such factor costs as wage, energy, and land prices. Such low-priced factors of production may have become accessible to U.S. manufacturers as construction of the U.S surface transportation system opened up new territories for expansion.

FIGURE 6

Employment growth, 1983Q1-1990Q1
(percent from base)

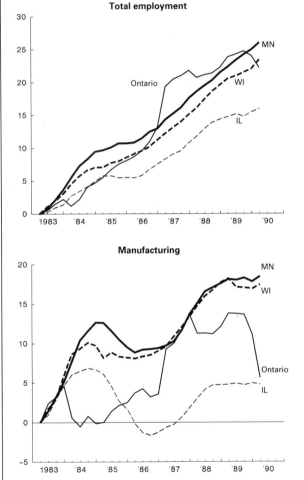
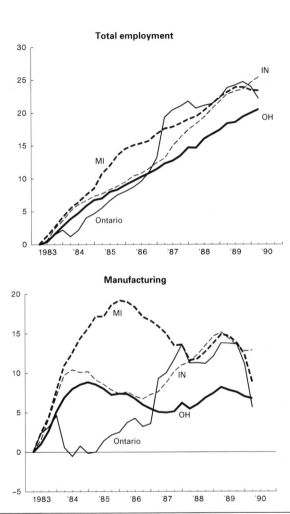

Favorable climate is also often included as contributing to the Sunbelt cost advantage by resulting in fewer transportation and production delays. At the same time, the advent of air conditioning during the 20th century overcame the down side of warm climate for office and production workers.

In opposition to factor costs, an alternative explanation centers on differing industry mix as new industries, often high technology and defense, emerged in Sunbelt and later New England regions rather than in the Great Lakes manufacturing belt.[19]

In an important sense, Ontario's employment growth provides a powerful backdrop for examining the latter two sets of theses of Great Lakes manufacturing decline—industry mix versus competitiveness, primarily because Ontario's climate and location are similar to the Great Lakes, thereby eliminating at least a few of the competing

TABLE 11

Manufacturing output as a share of national output in manufacturing

	Ontario as a percent of Canada	Great Lakes as a percent of United States						
	$1986=100	Great Lakes	Illinois	Indiana	Michigan	Minnesota	Ohio	Wisconsin
		$1982=100						
1970	n.a.	30.3	7.5	3.9	6.9	1.6	7.9	2.5
1971	50.1	30.6	7.4	4.0	7.4	1.5	7.9	2.5
1972	50.6	30.6	7.3	4.0	7.3	1.5	7.9	2.5
1973	51.1	31.4	7.3	4.1	7.7	1.6	8.0	2.6
1974	50.4	30.6	7.4	4.0	7.0	1.6	8.0	2.7
1975	50.0	29.3	7.1	3.7	6.7	1.6	7.5	2.7
1976	50.3	30.0	6.9	3.8	7.5	1.6	7.4	2.8
1977	50.2	30.1	6.7	3.8	7.9	1.6	7.4	2.8
1978	49.6	29.9	6.7	3.7	7.6	1.6	7.4	2.8
1979	49.9	28.8	6.5	3.6	6.9	1.7	7.2	2.8
1980	48.0	26.9	6.3	3.4	6.0	1.7	6.8	2.7
1981	48.8	26.1	6.0	3.3	5.6	1.8	6.8	2.7
1982	49.4	24.9	5.8	3.1	5.0	1.9	6.4	2.7
1983	50.9	24.9	5.5	3.1	5.3	1.9	6.4	2.7
1984	52.6	25.4	5.5	3.1	5.6	2.0	6.4	2.8
1985	53.5	25.6	5.4	3.1	5.9	2.1	6.4	2.8
1986	54.3	25.5	5.3	3.1	5.8	2.1	6.3	2.8

SOURCE: Statistics Canada, Input-Output Division; and U.S. Department of Commerce, Bureau of Economic Analysis.

NOTE: Original dollar values are deflated by industry. n.a. indicates data not available.

reasons for the Great Lakes states' loss of production share. Further, by performing "shift-share" analysis on the manufacturing employment data, we can discern whether lagging manufacturing job performance for the Great Lakes as compared to Ontario arises from differences in industry mix or from competitive effects.

Competitive effects may be more closely related to public policy differences and/or factor cost disparities so that the results can offer guidance in focusing on the importance of public policies in influencing economic development and regional growth. In contrast, a region whose development has faltered because of its industrial mix might be more concerned with determining the directions for industrial diversification of its economy.

There is another reason why the analysis using Ontario can be helpful. "Shift-share" is typically applied to the Great Lakes states versus the U.S. However, many industry classifications (here we

use "two-digit" SIC codes) differ greatly in the Great Lakes from the U.S. but they are similar between Ontario and the Great Lakes. For example, transportation equipment translates into autos in both Ontario and the Great Lakes states but tends to mean aircraft and missiles for the remainder of the U.S. Accordingly, shift-share performed on the Great Lakes versus U.S. tends to mistakenly attribute employment underperformance in the Great Lakes to "competitive problems" rather than real underlying industry mix differences.

Applying shift-share to the "two-digit" manufacturing categories for the 1977-86 period suggests that the Great Lakes states lost over 1.25 million jobs relative to what it would have lost if the Great Lakes states had been:

1) a microcosm of Ontario in 1977—that is having an employment distribution identical to Ontario and

2) experienced the same growth rates as each Ontario industry from 1977-86.

Decomposing this hypothetical loss (the Great Lakes states *actually* lost over 700,000 jobs over the period), the data show that almost the entire job loss can be attributed to competitive effects, i.e. to differences in industry-by-industry growth rates and not to differences in industry mix (Table 12) [20] The largest contributor was the transportation equipment industry during this period in which employment grew by 39 percent in Ontario while employment fell by 16 percent in the Great Lakes states. Nonetheless, industry-by-industry underperformance was pervasive with only minor exceptions.

To be sure, the effects of many underlying differences in industry mix are not accounted for in using this shift-share analysis because the industries are only disaggregated to the two-digit SIC level. Still, the stark differences in employment suggest that there is much to be learned about the Great Lakes economy in terms of its different performance as compared to its Canadian neighbor to the north. [21] Of course, many competing explanations remain to be sorted through as to whether, for example, performance differences are due to such possible influences as factor costs, exchange rates, national policies, or regional policies.

Restructuring in manufacturing

In assessing the future of the Great Lakes states, another question is whether the regional economy is restructuring away from manufacturing and into services and other bases of economic growth. The Midwest economy has been whipsawed by fluctuations in American manufacturing fortunes stemming from such forces as foreign competition, exchange rate fluctuations, and the business cycle. In forecasting the longer term outlook, one would like to know whether the most recent basis of growth, manufacturing, is being replaced with others. If not, signs of lagging regional manufacturing productivity or changing consumer tastes for Midwest manufactured goods will dim the prospects of the region's future growth and well being.

In addressing this question, nominal rather than real output is chosen to reflect manufacturing's importance to the region. The nominal dollar value

TABLE 12

"Shift-Share" decomposition of relative employment loss in manufacturing of Great Lakes states in relation to Ontario

	Great Lakes employment ,1986	Growth 1977-86		"Relative Loss" due to			
		Great Lakes	Ontario	Total	Competitive	Industry Mix	Combination
	(000s)	(%)		(000s)			
Food and kindred products	291.6	-16.0	3.2	-71.1	-94.0	-4.6	27.5
Textile mill products	18.2	-13.0	-29.9	60.3	35.7	56.7	-32.1
Apparel and other textiles	65.0	-28.8	52.9	-96.3	-108.2	-21.7	33.5
Lumber and wood products	93.4	-.6	28.6	-34.0	-34.2	-6.6	6.8
Furniture and fixtures	96.4	6.3	43.7	-48.8	-46.7	-14.8	12.7
Paper and allied products	153.7	-7.0	-4.7	.5	-5.7	4.2	2.0
Printing and publishing	326.5	15.6	34.6	-51.3	-52.3	2.4	-1.3
Chemicals and allied products	163.0	-8.5	10.9	-44.4	-51.9	-9.6	17.2
Petroleum and coal products	20.2	-19.4	-22.9	8.1	2.0	7.3	-1.1
Rubber and plastics	244.3	3.2	12.1	-17.5	-18.5	3.7	-2.7
Leather and leather products	17.7	-43.1	16.2	-24.6	-41.1	-6.2	22.7
Stone, clay, and glass	118.3	-20.5	7.5	-41.6	-41.6	(-)	(-)
Primary metals	293.1	-35.7	-13.2	-107.5	-94.3	-4.9	-8.3
Fabricated metals	511.7	-11.1	4.0	-84.3	-75.5	3.1	-11.9
Nonelectrical machinery	634.5	-20.4	-13.2	-121.0	-22.5	-63.9	-34.5
Electric and electronic equipment	391.2	-19.1	17.0	-166.0	-155.8	9.0	-19.2
Transportation equipment	575.2	-15.7	38.9	-363.8	-360.1	9.2	12.9
Instruments and related product	111.6	-.2	14.7	-13.0	-12.9	3.7	-3.8
Miscellaneous product	67.8	-27.2	9.5	-38.1	-49.5	-4.0	15.3
Total	4,194.7	-14.6	10.9	-1,252.8	1,231.4	-35.2	13.8

SOURCE: *Census of Manufactures 1977 and 1986*, Statistics Canada; and *County Business Patterns*, Bureau of the Census, U.S. Department of Commerce.

NOTE: "Relative Loss" is a hypothetical equal to the difference between actual growth in the Great Lakes and a hypothetical as if the 1977 Great Lakes economy composition by industry was equal to Ontario and its subsequent growth by industry had matched Ontario's. Thus, in the above table, actual Great Lakes job loss is less than "relative loss". Relative loss can be decomposed into three parts: competitive loss is that attributable to differences in industry growth rates only; industry mix component measures the loss (or gain) attributable to differences in industry shares only (holding growth rates equal); and "combination" effect reflects the loss (for example) attributed to a combination of the Great Lakes rapidly growing industries beginning from a low employment base as well as its slow-growth industries starting from a relatively large employment base. Note that the U.S. figures exclude auxiliary employees in both part and total. Total does not add to sum because small industries are excluded.

both the activity of manufacturing firms but also the activity of the region's service firms which sell business services to manufacturers or who transport and wholesale their goods.

Secondly, along with Ontario, both Wisconsin and Minnesota are maintaining their nominal share within the manufacturing sector even as the remainder of the region has not. We have seen that these same parts of the region have performed well in manufacturing which may suggest that the decline in the remainder of the region reflects a period of temporary underperformance rather than a permanent restructuring. These data do not reflect the manufacturing surge taking place in the Great Lakes during 1987 and 1988 as U.S capital investment rose and as exports surged. Toward the future, the robust defense spending on high tech goods which characterized the early 1980s may well give way during the 1990s, tending to benefit the Great Lakes relative to other regions.

Finally, it is well to take note that the remainder of the U.S. has also experienced a declining manufacturing share along with the remainder of Canada. As a consequence, the larger Great Lakes region —both the states and Ontario alike—will remain relatively more concentrated in manufacturing and

of manufacturing activity comprises payments to the region's factors of production—especially wage payments to the region's labor—that give rise to manufactured output. In this way, manufacturing activity reflects this sector's ties to the well-being and incomes of the region's residents.

Manufacturing's share of output has declined in the Great Lakes states and in the remainder of the U.S., and also in Canada outside of Ontario (Table 13). Within Ontario, however, the declines have been much less, if at all. As a consequence, Ontario's manufacturing share of total output came to

surpass the Great Lakes in 1984 and it has remained so (Figure 7), although several individual states including Indiana, Michigan, Ohio, and Wisconsin actually surpass Ontario in manufacturing intensity.

At least two other caveats must be made before concluding that the Great Lakes depends less on manufacturing and more on the service sector. First, no one has yet confirmed that the block of service industries that have displaced manufacturing in the Great Lakes do not themselves arise from manufacturing.[22] After all, the value of manufactured goods shipments from a region may include

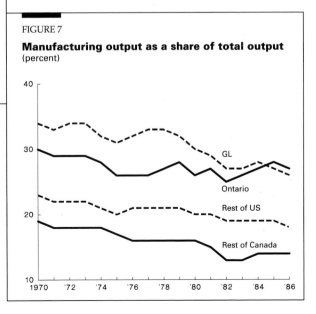

FIGURE 7

Manufacturing output as a share of total output
(percent)

TABLE 13

Manufacturing output as a share of total output in the Great Lakes region, 1970-1986

	Ontario	Rest of Canada	Rest of US	Great Lakes	Illinois	Indiana	Michigan	Minnesota	Ohio	Wisconsin
1970	n.a.	n.a.	.23	.34	.29	.38	.39	.22	.37	.32
1971	.29	.18	.22	.33	.28	.38	.40	.21	.36	.31
1972	.29	.18	.22	.34	.29	.39	.39	.21	.37	.32
1973	.29	.18	.22	.34	.29	.38	.40	.20	.36	.32
1974	.28	.18	.21	.32	.28	.37	.36	.20	.34	.32
1975	.26	.17	.20	.31	.27	.35	.35	.21	.35	.32
1976	.26	.16	.21	.32	.27	.36	.39	.21	.36	.33
1977	.26	.16	.21	.33	.27	.37	.41	.21	.36	.33
1978	.27	.16	.21	.33	.27	.37	.39	.21	.35	.33
1979	.28	.16	.21	.32	.26	.35	.37	.22	.33	.32
1980	.26	.16	.20	.30	.26	.34	.33	.21	.33	.31
1981	.27	.15	.20	.29	.25	.33	.32	.21	.33	.31
1982	.25	.13	.19	.27	.23	.31	.29	.21	.30	.29
1983	.26	.13	.19	.27	.22	.31	.30	.22	.30	.29
1984	.27	.14	.19	.28	.22	.31	.32	.22	.31	.30
1985	.28	.14	.19	.27	.21	.31	.32	.21	.30	.29
1986	.27	.14	.18	.26	.20	.30	.31	.21	.29	.28

SOURCE: Statistics Canada, Input-Output Division; and U.S. Department of Commerce, Bureau of Economic Analysis.

NOTE: Original data were expressed in nominal dollars. n.a. indicates data not avalible.

therefore more sensitive to the vicissitudes of manufacturing fortunes.

Conclusion

The economic linkages between Ontario and the Great Lakes states are tight, both in terms of trade and the organizational linkages of foreign direct investment. In addition, both regions maintain the role as the manufacturing core of their respective nations. The similarity in manufacturing industry mix is close enough to suggest that the there is a broader Great Lakes manufacturing belt that encompasses both sides of the border. Freer trade, lower barriers to investment, and greater communication and understanding will be beneficial to the broader binational region.

Still, there are enough significant differences in composition, direction, and performance so that further binational analysis will shed light on the efficacy of selective public policies. Ontario, largely Toronto, is moving toward being the financial core of Canada while the Great Lakes has, to date, continued to look to New York City and emerging Los Angeles as financial centers. With regard to the most important feature of the Great Lakes economic base, manufacturing, disturbing differences in direction have emerged. Ontario continues to industrialize through a superior performance and centralization within its nation. On the U.S. side, most of the region continues to experience a declining share of the U.S. manufacturing base. Climate and location do not provide the easy answer to the Great Lakes fall from preeminence. Even within the Great Lakes states themselves, some states such as Minnesota and, to a lesser extent Wisconsin, have continued to thrive on a strong manufacturing base.

The answers to the manufacturing puzzle are not academic to the peoples of the Great Lakes states. Relative to the remainder of the nation, the Great Lakes economy continues to strongly rely on manufacturing for the livelihoods of its residents despite a sharp restructuring toward services. Even here, it is unclear whether a service industry base can support the Great Lakes economy of today's size independently of manufacturing and agriculture.

NOTES

[1]The percentage is moderately less when affiliates "controlling" 50 percent or more of companies are considered rather than the BEA 10 percent inclusion.

[2]For example, see David F. Burgess, "A Perspective on Foreign Direct Investment", *Perspectives on a U.S.-Canadian Free Trade Agreement*, Robert M. Stern, Philip H. Trezise, and John Whalley eds., The Brookings Institution, Washington D.C., 1987, pps. 191-216.

[3]For a discussion of this issue and of the Free Trade Agreement's provision with respect to foreign direct investment, see A.E. Safarian, "The Canada-U.S. Free Trade Agreement and Foreign Direct Investment", *Trade Monitor*, No. 3, May, 1988, C.D. Howe Institute, Toronto.

[4]For example, Britain's return to the gold standard in 1925 raised the cost of British imports into Canada, causing Canada to look to other suppliers especially the U.S. Later, the Ottawa trade agreements of 1932, designed to stimulate trade within the British Commonwealth, served to stimulate U.S. direct investment in Canada. See Lawrence D. McCann, *Heartland and Hinterland: A Geography of Canada*, Prentice-Hall, Scarsbourough, Ontario, 1987.

[5]According to U.S BEA data for nonbank affiliates of U.S. companies for 1988, the manufacturing sector comprised 50.1 percent of total U.S. foreign direct investment employment activity in Canada. This share falls short of the 64.7 percent share to manufacturing activity by U.S. affiliates in the world. See Raymond J. Mataloni, "U.S. Multinational Companies: Operations in 1988", *Survey of Current Business*, Bureau of Economic Analysis, June, 1990, pps. 31-44. The provincial data for manufacturing are of Canadian origin and are not compatible with U.S. data.

[6]For a discussion, see Meric S. Gertler, "Industrialism, De-Industrialization, and Regional Development in Central Canada", *Canadian Journal of Regional Science*, VIII:3 (Autumn 1985), pps. 353-75 and Lawrence D. McCann, *Heartland and Hinterland: A Geography of Canada*, Prentice-Hall, Scarsbourough, Ontario, 1987, p. 144.

[7]See survey work by Isaiah A. Litvak and Christopher J. Maule, *The Canadian Multinationals*, Butterworth Press, Toronto, 1981.

[8]For example, see Andrew Solocha, Mark D. Soskin, and Mark J Kasoff, "Canadian Investment in Northern New York: Impact of Exchange Rates on Foreign Direct Investment", *Growth and Change*, Winter 1989, pps 1-16, which also provides an excellent literature review of foreign direct investment by Canada in U.S. regions. See also James W. Harrington, Jr., Daren Burns, and Man Cheung, "Market-Oriented Foreign Investment and Regional Development: Canadian Companies in Western New York", *Economic Geography*, April, 1986, pps. 155-166.

[9]See Alenka S. Giese, "The Opening of Midwest Manufacturing to Foreign Companies: The Influx of Foreign Direct Investment", *Regional Science Perspectives*, 1989.

[10]Data covering foreign direct investment have received much criticism of late. For U.S. data as reported by the Bureau of Economic Analysis, critics have pointed out that data are inadequate because investors fail to report transactions, because book value does not reflect current economic value especially subsequent to inflationary periods, and speculative or portfolio investment is mistakenly counted as direct investment. For a discussion see Lois E. Stekler and Guy V.G. Stevens, *The Adequacy of U.S. Foreign Direct Investment Data*, Board of Governors of the Federal Reserve, Washington D.C., 1990.

[11]On the U.S. side of the border, employment data are taken from the BLS Employment and Earnings or "790" survey. These employment data record nonfarm payroll employment from a survey of establishment records. See Bureau of Labor Statistics, *Handbook of Methods*, U.S. Dept. of Labor, Bulletin 2134-1, U.S.G.P.O., Washington D.C., December 1982.

On the Canadian side, employment data from the Survey of Employment Payroll and Hours program of Statistics Canada are used. The basis of coverage is similar to the BLS survey in surveying nonfarm payroll employment. In both surveys, multi-establishment firms are disaggregated into establishments and classified by primary industry activity for the purposes of reporting employment. For Canada, see "Concepts and Methods", *Employment earnings and hours*, Catalogue 72-002, Statistics Canada (monthly). The countries do differ in their industry classification schemes and definitions. However, at the very highest level of aggregation, the narrow categories can be combined from similar industry sectors. The most significant methodological difference is in the treatment of government employment. To a greater extent, Statistics Canada places, for example, elementary school teachers or transit drivers employed by the government into a service and transportation and public utilities category while BLS places such workers into a "government" category. For this reason, three categories were combined in Table 8 into an augmented "service" industry which includes services, government, transportation, and public utility employment. Despite this correction, the reported employment shares are not strictly comparable.

[12]See Steven G. Cochrane and Daniel R. Vining, Jr., "Recent Trends in Migration Between Core and Peripheral Regions in Developed and Advanced Developing Countries", *International Regional Science Review*, Vol. 11, No. 3, 1988, pp. 215-243.

[13]These categories were originally created by Robert Z. Lawrence, *Can America Compete?*, The Brookings Institution, 1984.

Canada's employment series for manufacturing is derived from their *Census of Manufactures* while U.S. data derive from Bureau of the Census *County Business Patterns* (CBP). Industry definitions are not strictly compatible for the two data bases. A reconciliation was made by assigning Canadian industries to U.S. Standard Industrial Classification codes. The most significant rearrangement of Canadian categories involved splitting Canada's miscellaneous industries apart and creating an equivalent category for U.S. SIC 38—Instruments and Related Products. A detailed accounting of the transformation will be provided by the authors on request. For the U.S data base, one difference is that, for individual industries, employment at corporate headquarters-type and other auxiliary establishments of multiestablishment firms is excluded from industry totals while it is included in the Canadian data. To move the U.S. data in a more comparable direction with Canadian data, we added or allocated "auxiliary" or "CAO" employment back into *County Business Patterns*. In those instances when CAO employment was undisclosed, we apportioned the state's residual auxiliary employment according to industry shares of total (nonauxiliary) employment.

[14]Most significantly, a profound change in sample and methodology of the payroll employment survey occurred in 1983.

[15]The data in Figure 6 will not be strictly comparable to Figure 4 wherein quarterly are plotted rather than annual.

[16]This thesis has been developed by Leonard F. Wheat, "The Determinants of 1963-77 Regional Manufacturing Growth: Why the South and the West Grow", *Journal of Regional Science*, Vol. 26, No. 4, pps. 635-659.

[17]See also Federal Reserve Bank of Chicago, *The Iowa Economy: Dimensions of Change*, 1987.

[18]Note that factor costs and public policy explanations of Great Lakes decline are not necessarily distinguishable from the "age" or "vintage" theories of regional development and related hypotheses. For example, Michael Kendix argues that factor cost and productivity disadvantages (e.g. arising from punitive government regulation) can themselves arise from the "institutional sclerosis" that sets in at a later stage of economic development in older regions such as the Midwest. In such "mature" regions, special interest groups have had the time and resources to institute policies that protect their own interests while stifling competitiveness. See Michael Kendix, "Institutional Rigidities as Barriers to Growth: A Regional Perspective", Working Papers of the Federal Reserve Bank of Chicago, June 1990, WP-1990-6.

[19]For a review, see Advisory Committee on Intergovernmental Relations, *Regional Growth in Historical Perspective*, A-74, Washington D.C., 1980. One shift-share analysis has also been used to posit that the core manufacturing region has been moving through a "product cycle" whereby the "seedbed" function or innovative capacity role of regions has moved from the core to outlying regions over time. See R.D. Norton and John Rees, "The Product Cycle and the Spatial Decentralization of Manufacturing", *Regional Studies*, Vol. 13, pps. 141 -51, 1971.

[20]For a discussion of methodology see Esteban-Marquillas, J.M., "Shift and share-analysis revisited", *Regional and Urban Economics* 2: 1972, pps. 249-261.

The identical Great Lakes shift-share as calculated against the U.S also displays a dominant competitive effect for the 1977-86 period. However, the industry mix is actually positive for the Midwest.

[21]For a discussion of this issue with reference to the Toronto and Chicago metro areas see David R. Allardice "Tracking by the North Star", *Chicago Fed Letter*, Federal Reserve Bank of Chicago, Number 38, October 1990.

[22]For a discussion see William A. Testa, *Manufacturing's Changeover to Services in the Great Lakes Economy*, Federal Reserve Bank of Chicago, WP-1989/21.

APPENDIX 1

Top exports and imports between Great Lakes states and Canada (and Ontario), 1989

ILLINOIS

Exports to Ontario	Level	Share
	(C$ 000s)	(%)
Passenger automobiles and chassis	775,684	16.6
Motor vehicle parts, except engines	305,231	6.5
Electronic computers	170,838	3.7
Rlwy, and street rlwy rolling stock	160,908	3.5
Other telecom. & rel. equip.	133,418	2.9
Motor vehicle parts	132,604	2.8
Front end loaders	93,140	2.0
Books and pamphlets	88,704	1.9
Electric generators and motors	88,330	1.9
Other chemical products	79,319	1.7
Newspapers, mag. & periodicals	70,404	1.5
Special transactions, trade	66,903	1.4
Top 12	2,165,483	46.5
All exports	4,660,612	100.0

Imports from Ontario	Level	Share
	(C$ 000s)	(%)
Trucks, truck tractors and chassis	506,600	18.9
Rlwy, and street rlwy rolling stock	332,689	12.4
Motor vehicle parts, except engines	249,338	9.3
Newsprint paper	226,877	8.4
Other inorganic chemicals	200,827	7.5
Organic chemicals	69,561	2.6
Plastics basic shapes and forms	53,020	2.0
Plate, sheet and strip, steel	51,739	1.9
Passenger automobiles and chassis	44,277	1.6
Metal fabricated basic products	39,430	1.5
Zinc, including alloys	37,709	1.4
Other equipment and tools	37,083	1.4
Top 12	1,849,150	68.8
All imports	2,687,117	100.0

ILLINOIS

Exports to Canada	Level	Share
	(C$ 000s)	(%)
Passenger automobiles and chassis	1,392,851	20.0
Motor vehicle parts, except engines	344,379	4.9
Electronic computers	190,923	2.7
Rlwy, and street rlwy rolling stock	184,354	2.6
Motor vehicle parts	177,995	2.6
Front end loaders	166,549	2.4
Other telecom. & rel. equip.	155,180	2.2
Tractor engines and tractor parts	134,021	1.9
Newspapers, mag. & periodicals	122,883	1.8
Other excavating machinery	115,689	1.7
Other chemical products	112,594	1.6
Electronic generators and motors	99,624	1.4
Top 12	3,197,042	45.9
All exports	6,972,226	100.0

Imports from Canada	Level	Share
	(C$ 000s)	(%)
Crude petroleum	1,118,576	21.1
Trucks, truck tractors and chassis	514,891	9.7
Newsprint paper	474,575	9.0
Rlwy, and street rlwy rolling stock	344,454	6.5
Motor vehicle parts, except engines	266,978	5.0
Other inorganic chemicals	244,266	4.6
Aluminum, including alloys	170,354	3.2
Organic chemicals	161,904	3.1
Lumber, softwood	149,716	2.8
Office machines and equipment	146,227	2.8
Zinc, including alloys	103,706	2.0
Fertilizers and fertilizer material	91,070	1.7
Top 12	3,786,717	71.5
All imports	5,297,142	100.0

INDIANA

Exports to Ontario	Level	Share
	(C$ 000s)	(%)
Motor vehicle parts, except engines	920,335	36.7
Motor vehicle parts	223,452	8.9
Other motor vehicles	78,739	3.1
Air conditioning & refrig. equip.	66,484	2.7
Motor vehicle engine parts	65,791	2.6
Miscellaneous equipment and tools	49,824	2.0
Other metal fabricated basic prod.	45,046	1.8
Aluminum, including alloys	43,472	1.7
Other telecom. & rel. equip.	43,448	1.7
Plastics materials, not shaped	34,729	1.4
Special transactions, trade	32,523	1.3
Other general purpose indust. mach.	30,708	1.2
Top 12	1,634,551	65.2
All exports	2,507,375	100.0

Imports from Ontario	Level	Share
	(C$ 000s)	(%)
Motor vehicle parts, except engines	223,169	23.4
Aluminum, including alloys	64,010	6.7
Newsprint paper	63,685	6.7
Zinc, including alloys	38,661	4.1
Organic chemicals	36,217	3.8
Metal fabricated basic products	31,222	3.3
Lumber, softwood	22,020	2.3
Other gen. purpose industrial mach.	21,754	2.3
Plastics ind. mach. and equipment	21,297	2.2
Television, radio sets & phonographs	20,243	2.1
Other motor vehicles	20,064	2.1
Other equipment and tools	18,541	1.9
Top 12	580,883	61.0
All imports	952,414	100.0

INDIANA

Exports to Canada	Level	Share
	(C$ 000s)	(%)
Motor vehicle parts, except engines	950,710	31.8
Motor vehicle parts	254,758	8.5
Other motor vehicles	121,860	4.1
Aircraft engines and parts	86,981	2.9
Air conditioning & refrig. equip.	73,692	2.5
Miscellaneous equipment and tools	71,331	2.4
Motor vehicle engine parts	69,528	2.3
Other metal fabricated basic prod.	52,810	1.8
Other telecom. & rel. equip.	46,536	1.6
Aluminum, including alloys	46,293	1.6
Plastics materials, not shaped	40,488	1.4
Special transactions, trade	39,136	1.3
Top 12	1,854,123	62.1
All exports	2,986,222	100.0

Imports from Canada	Level	Share
	(C$ 000s)	(%)
Crude petroleum	660,237	30.5
Motor vehicle parts, except engines	226,767	10.5
Newsprint paper	118,566	5.5
Aluminum, including alloys	96,305	4.4
Zinc, including alloys	94,518	4.4
Lumber, softwood	74,802	3.5
Metal fabricated basic products	40,882	1.9
Organic chemicals	39,765	1.8
Iron ores and concentrates	39,461	1.8
Fertilizers and fertilizer material	29,788	1.4
Aircraft, engines and parts	28,624	1.3
Other telecom. & rel. equip.	27,005	1.2
Top 12	1,476,720	68.2
All imports	2,165,089	100.0

MICHIGAN

Exports to Ontario	Level	Share
	(C$ 000s)	(%)
Motor vehicle parts, except engines	6,528,869	41.6
Passenger automobiles and chassis	2,214,334	14.1
Trucks, truck tractors and chassis	647,696	4.1
Motor vehicle parts	605,699	3.9
Motor vehicle engine parts	487,008	3.1
Air conditioning & refrig. equip.	381,672	2.4
Auxiliary elec. equip. for engines	308,072	2.0
Other general purpose indust. mach.	249,812	1.6
Special transactions, trade	217,407	1.4
Crude petroleum	205,565	1.3
Misc. meas. and controlling instr.	197,454	1.3
Furniture and fixtures	151,039	1.0
Top 12	12,194,627	77.7
All exports	15,697,969	100.0

Imports from Ontario	Level	Share
	(C$ 000s)	(%)
Passenger automobiles and chassis	8,373,487	38.7
Trucks, truck tractors and chassis	5,079,885	23.5
Motor vehicle parts, except engines	2,978,703	13.8
Motor vehicle engines and parts	2,047,781	9.5
Whisky	555,551	2.6
Other motor vehicles	192,430	0.9
Metal fabricated basic products	189,250	0.9
Plate, sheet and strip, steel	172,892	0.8
Wood pulp and similar pulp	145,906	0.7
Other gen. purpose industrial mach.	128,202	0.6
Newsprint paper	120,231	0.6
Petroleum and coal products	118,913	0.5
Top 12	20,103,231	92.9
All imports	21,650,603	100.0

MICHIGAN

Exports to Canada	Level	Share
	(C$ 000s)	(%)
Motor vehicle parts, except engines	6,562,002	40.3
Passenger automobiles and chassis	2,300,086	14.1
Trucks, truck tractors and chassis	745,882	4.6
Motor vehicle parts	618,939	3.8
Motor vehicle engine parts	488,457	3.0
Air conditioning & refrig. equip.	384,399	2.4
Auxiliary elec. equip. for engines	318,951	2.0
Other general purpose indust. mach.	253,340	1.6
Special transactions, trade	228,817	1.4
Crude petroleum	205,565	1.3
Misc. meas. and controlling instr.	200,915	1.2
Furniture and fixtures	158,668	1.0
Top 12	12,466,021	76.6
All exports	16,281,116	100.0

Imports from Canada	Level	Share
	(C$ 000s)	(%)
Passenger automobiles and chassis	10,073,445	40.8
Trucks, truck tractors and chassis	5,091,881	20.6
Motor vehicle parts, except engines	2,994,974	12.1
Motor vehicle engines and parts	2,049,523	8.3
Wood pulp and similar pulp	277,605	1.1
Natural gas	275,754	1.1
Newsprint paper	256,760	1.0
Metal fabricated basic products	202,098	0.8
Other motor vehicles	193,336	0.8
Petroleum and coal products	192,906	0.8
Plate, sheet and strip, steel	173,278	0.7
Lumber, softwood	163,987	0.7
Top 12	21,945,547	88.8
All imports	24,712,615	100.0

APPENDIX 1

Top exports and imports between Great Lakes states and Canada (and Ontario), 1989

MINNESOTA

Exports to Ontario	Level	Share
	(C$ 000s)	(%)
Electronic computers	118,156	12.1
Trucks, truck tractors and chassis	92,706	9.5
Iron ores and concentrates	84,800	8.7
Other telecom. & rel. equip.	45,235	4.6
Oil seed cake and meal	30,900	3.2
Motor vehicle parts, except engines	25,139	2.6
Misc. meas. and controlling instr.	20,497	2.1
Other basic hardware	17,661	1.8
Oth. plastics basic shapes and forms	16,884	1.7
Special transactions, trade	16,427	1.7
Other motor vehicles	15,941	1.6
Medical, ophthalmic & ortho. suppl.	14,998	1.5
Top 12	499,344	51.0
All exports	978,614	100.0

Imports from Ontario	Level	Share
	(C$ 000s)	(%)
Newsprint paper	131,956	19.7
Wood pulp and similar pulp	99,233	14.8
Motor vehicle parts, except engines	83,350	12.4
Office machines and equipment	78,144	11.6
Plate, sheet and strip, steel	23,794	3.5
Oth. measur. cont. lab. med. & opt. eqp.	19,569	2.9
Metal fabricated basic products	17,017	2.5
Other agric. mach. and equipment	12,009	1.8
Other equipment and tools	11,136	1.7
Abrasive basic products	10,385	1.5
Syn. rubber and plastic materials	9,921	1.5
Elec. lighting & dist. equipment	9,292	1.4
Top 12	505,806	75.3
All imports	671,496	100.0

MINNESOTA

Exports to Canada	Level	Share
	(C$ 000s)	(%)
Trucks, truck tractors and chassis	322,460	17.9
Electronic computers	146,327	8.1
Iron ores and concentrates	84,870	4.7
Other motor vehicles	81,917	4.5
Oil seed cake and meal	68,625	3.8
Other telecom. & rel. equip.	54,480	3.0
Motor vehicle parts, except engines	40,064	2.2
Misc. meas. and controlling instr.	36,430	2.0
Special transactions, trade	32,957	1.8
Medical, ophthalmic & ortho. suppl.	29,297	1.6
Paper and paperboard	27,764	1.5
Other basic hardware	24,556	1.4
Top 12	949,747	52.7
All exports	1,801,171	100.0

Imports from Canada	Level	Share
	(C$000s)	(%)
Crude petroleum	1,192,485	37.6
Natural gas	288,401	9.1
Wood pulp and similar pulp	250,255	7.9
Fertilizers and fertilizer material	179,744	5.7
Newsprint paper	152,078	4.8
Office machines and equipment	106,826	3.4
Lumber, softwood	94,681	3.0
Motor vehicle parts, except engines	91,819	2.9
Other cereals, unmilled	73,122	2.3
Petroleum and coal products	56,594	1.8
Live animals	53,840	1.7
Plates, sheet & strip, steel	40,687	1.3
Top 12	2,580,532	81.3
All imports	3,173,756	100.0

NEW YORK

Exports to Ontario	Level	Share
	(C$ 000s)	(%)
Aluminum, including alloys	475,060	9.8
Electronic computers	316,116	6.6
Motor vehicle parts, except engines	272,744	5.7
Other photographic goods	206,166	4.3
Oth. metals in ores, conc. and scrap	179,442	3.7
Other telecom. & rel. equip.	175,739	3.6
Books and pamphlets	128,866	2.7
Special transactions, trade	127,486	2.6
Electronic tubes & semi-conductors	118,089	2.4
Unexposed photo. film, plates & paper	110,433	2.3
Paper and paperboard	102,890	2.1
Other end products, inedible	92,125	1.9
Top 12	2,305,156	47.8
All exports	4,823,332	100.0

Imports from Ontario	Level	Share
	(C$ 000s)	(%)
Passenger automobiles and chassis	4,544,854	45.4
Precious metals, including alloys	856,187	8.6
Trucks, truck tractors and chassis	566,411	5.7
Motor vehicle parts, except engines	261,728	2.6
Aluminum, including alloys	245,741	2.5
Petroleum and coal products	220,084	2.2
Photographic goods	217,362	2.2
Office machines and equipment	173,605	1.7
Printed matter	156,610	1.6
Newsprint paper	152,374	1.5
Aluminum ores, concentrates and scrap	140,537	1.4
Oth. telecom. & rel. equip.	131,907	1.3
Top 12	7,667,400	76.7
All imports	10,002,496	100.0

NEW YORK

Exports to Canada	Level	Share
	(C$ 000s)	(%)
Aluminum, including alloys	481,612	7.4
Other telecom. & rel. equip.	456,452	7.0
Electronic computers	387,498	6.0
Motor vehicle parts, except engines	279,634	4.3
Other metals in ores, conc. and scrap	223,693	3.4
Other photographic goods	214,881	3.3
Special transactions, trade	196,874	3.0
Electronic tubes & semi-conductors	179,784	2.8
Other end products, inedible	140,068	2.2
Books and pamphlets	137,794	2.1
Paper and paperboard	128,033	2.0
Unexposed photo. film, plates & paper	113,381	1.7
Top 12	2,939,704	45.2
All exports	6,509,796	100.0

Imports from Canada	Level	Share
	(C$ 000s)	(%)
Passenger automobiles and chassis	4,545,802	31.4
Precious metals, including alloys	955,627	6.6
Aluminum, including alloys	770,200	5.3
Newsprint paper	608,129	4.2
Trucks, truck tractors and chassis	580,971	4.0
Natural gas	440,702	3.0
Petroleum and coal products	372,021	2.6
Crude petroleum	369,960	2.6
Wood pulp and similar pulp	340,328	2.4
Motor vehicle parts, except engines	281,225	1.9
Oth. telecom. & rel. equip.	280,040	1.9
Printed matter	254,872	1.8
Top 12	9,799,877	67.7
All imports	14,484,053	100.0

OHIO

Exports to Ontario	Level	Share
	(C$ 000s)	(%)
Motor vehicle parts, except engines	1,329,165	18.2
Passenger automobiles and chassis	1,051,081	14.4
Motor vehicle parts	746,573	10.2
Coal	467,708	6.4
Trucks, truck tractors and chassis	209,761	2.9
Motor vehicle engine parts	133,300	1.8
Plate, sheet and strip, steel	131,893	1.8
Air conditioning & refrig. equip.	111,467	1.5
Plastics materials, not shaped	104,079	1.4
Miscellaneous equipment and tools	103,494	1.4
Other transportation equipment	93,213	1.3
Special transactions, trade	81,039	1.1
Top 12	4,562,773	62.6
All exports	7,284,871	100.0

Imports from Ontario	Level	Share
	(C$ 000s)	(%)
Motor vehicle parts, except engines	1,098,598	35.6
Newsprint paper	137,634	4.5
Other inorganic chemicals	130,713	4.2
Bars and rods, steel	90,036	2.9
Metal fabricated basic products	84,857	2.8
Plate, sheet and strip, steel	79,188	2.6
Other equipment and tools	71,837	2.3
Motor vehicle engines and parts	71,471	2.3
Passenger automobiles and chassis	65,076	2.1
Nickel and alloys	64,434	2.1
Other gen. purpose industrial mach.	59,712	1.9
Other transportation equipment	59,352	1.9
Top 12	2,012,908	65.3
All imports	3,083,849	100.0

OHIO

Exports to Canada	Level	Share
	(C$ 000s)	(%)
Motor vehicle parts, except engines	1,366,703	16.4
Passenger automobiles and chassis	1,231,318	14.8
Motor vehicle parts	751,213	9.0
Coal	471,555	5.7
Trucks, truck tractors and chassis	250,745	3.0
Plate, sheet and strip, steel	136,918	1.6
Motor vehicle engine parts	134,273	1.6
Plastics materials, not shaped	125,583	1.5
Other transportation equipment	119,705	1.4
Air conditioning & refrig. equip.	119,413	1.4
Miscellaneous equipment and tools	117,291	1.4
Electronic computers	101,564	1.2
Top 12	4,926,281	59.1
All exports	1,366,703	100.0

Imports from Canada	Level	Share
	(C$ 000s)	(%)
Motor vehicle parts, except engines	1,111,676	25.6
Newsprint paper	280,172	6.5
Wood pulp and similar pulp	162,594	3.7
Other inorganic chemicals	157,690	3.6
Petroleum and coal products	149,246	3.4
Lumber, softwood	127,289	2.9
Metal fabricated basic products	115,710	2.7
Zinc, including alloys	106,394	2.5
Bars and rods, steel	96,803	2.2
Other equipment and tools	86,358	2.0
Plate, sheet and strip, steel	81,159	1.9
Organic chemicals	80,479	1.9
Top 12	2,555,570	58.8
All imports	4,343,390	100.0

APPENDIX 1

Top exports and imports between Great Lakes states and Canada (and Ontario), 1989

PENNSYLVANIA

Exports to Ontario	Level	Share
	(C$ 000s)	(%)
Motor vehicle parts, except engines	256,999	9.4
Electronic computers	114,395	4.2
Plastics materials, not shaped	105,978	3.9
Organic chemicals	72,385	2.7
Auxiliary elec. equip. for engines	69,185	2.5
Plate, sheet and strip, steel	65,235	2.4
Trucks, truck tractors and chassis	52,310	1.9
Books and pamphlets	48,880	1.8
Lumber	48,694	1.8
Televisions, radio sets & phonographs	47,830	1.8
Other chemical products	47,619	1.7
Clay bricks, clay tiles & refract.	45,323	1.7
Top 12	974,833	35.7
All exports	2,730,732	100.0

Imports from Ontario	Level	Share
	(C$ 000s)	(%)
Trucks, truck tractors and chassis	109,562	6.4
Lumber, softwood	97,955	5.8
Nickel and alloys	95,716	5.6
Wood pulp and similar pulp	80,537	4.7
Newsprint paper	74,489	4.4
Other iron and steel and alloys	74,451	4.4
Motor vehicle parts, except engines	73,487	4.3
Office machines and equipment	69,676	4.1
Other equipment and tools	48,586	2.9
Passenger automobiles and chassis	47,298	2.8
Metal fabricated basic products	42,787	2.5
Bars and rods, steel	38,121	2.2
Top 12	852,665	50.1
All imports	1,702,307	100.0

PENNSYLVANIA

Exports to Canada	Level	Share
	(C$ 000s)	(%)
Other end products, inedible	292,207	8.1
Motor vehicle parts, except engines	271,347	7.6
Electronic computers	131,174	3.7
Plastics materials, not shaped	120,430	3.4
Organic chemicals	83,253	2.3
Plate, sheet and strip, steel	74,360	2.1
Auxiliary elec. equip. for engines	70,777	2.0
Other chemical products	67,421	1.9
Special transactions, trade	62,373	1.7
Other telecom. & rel. equip.	62,298	1.7
Clay bricks, clay tiles & refract.	61,004	1.7
Other materials in ores, conc. and scrap	60,831	1.7
Top 12	1,357,475	37.8
All exports	3,591,843	100.0

Imports from Canada	Level	Share
	(C$ 000s)	(%)
Newsprint paper	374,646	11.6
Aluminum, including alloys	241,071	7.5
Lumber, softwood	212,173	6.6
Wood pulp and similar pulp	145,699	4.5
Trucks, truck tractors and chassis	137,426	4.3
Iron ores and concentrates	127,664	4.0
Nickel and alloys	107,813	3.3
Other iron and steel and alloys	93,318	2.9
Motor vehicle parts, except engines	77,990	2.4
Office machines and equipment	74,299	2.3
Other equipment and tools	73,746	2.3
Zinc, including alloys	71,484	2.2
Top 12	1,737,329	53.8
All imports	3,229,095	100.0

WISCONSIN

Exports to Ontario	Level	Share
	(C$ 000s)	(%)
Passenger automobiles and chassis	228,825	13.0
Motor vehicle parts, except engines	116,552	6.6
Motor vehicle parts	94,262	5.4
Miscellaneous equipment and tools	74,481	4.2
Paper and paperboard	58,955	3.4
Newspapers, mag. & periodicals	48,673	2.8
Other general purpose indust. mach.	41,062	2.3
Marine engines and parts	35,536	2.0
Trucks, truck tractors and chassis	30,232	1.7
Electronic computers	27,457	1.6
Other meas., lab equip., etc.	27,315	1.6
Pulp and paper industries machinery	23,416	1.3
Top 12	806,766	45.9
All exports	1,756,473	100.0

Imports from Ontario	Level	Share
	(C$ 000s)	(%)
Wood pulp and similar pulp	334,709	31.6
Motor vehicle parts, except engines	208,768	19.7
Newsprint paper	93,899	8.9
Other chemical products	30,945	2.9
Syn. rubber and plastic materials	30,904	2.9
Metal fabricated basic products	20,102	1.9
Cereal preparations	16,398	1.5
Other equipment and tools	16,108	1.5
Other agric. mach. and equipment	15,676	1.5
Other iron and steel and alloys	15,464	1.5
Plate, sheet and strip, steel	13,879	1.3
Other paper	11,465	1.1
Top 12	808,317	76.4
All imports	1,058,438	100.0

WISCONSIN

Exports to Canada	Level	Share
	(C$ 000s)	(%)
Passenger automobiles and chassis	229,067	9.9
Motor vehicle parts, except engines	125,276	5.4
Motor vehicle parts	108,497	4.7
Miscellaneous equipment and tools	106,984	4.6
Paper and paperboard	73,425	3.2
Newspapers, mag. & periodicals	58,308	2.5
Other general purpose indust. mach.	54,844	2.4
Tractor engines and tractor parts	50,024	2.2
Wheel tractors, new	44,375	1.9
Other meas., lab equip., etc.	41,161	1.8
Pulp and paper industries machinery	40,634	1.8
Marine engines and parts	38,917	1.7
Top 12	971,512	41.9
All exports	2,320,631	100.0

Imports from Canada	Level	Share
	(C$ 000s)	(%)
Wood pulp and similar pulp	783,823	36.5
Motor vehicle parts, except engines	215,780	10.0
Newsprint paper	127,810	5.9
Crude petroleum	113,731	5.3
Lumber, softwood	72,269	3.4
Other cereals, unmilled	51,670	2.4
Syn. rubber and plastic materials	41,383	1.9
Other paper	38,845	1.8
Other chemical products	35,470	1.6
Other paper for printing	32,759	1.5
Aircraft complete with engines	31,112	1.4
Metal fabricated basic products	26,368	1.2
Top 12	1,571,020	73.1
All imports	2,150,410	100.0

TOTAL GREAT LAKES

Exports to Ontario	Level	Share
	(C$ 000s)	(%)
Motor vehicle parts, except engines	9,225,291	28.1
Passenger automobiles and chassis	4,270,917	13.0
Motor vehicle engines	1,802,844	5.5
Trucks, truck tractors and chassis	985,779	3.0
Motor vehicle engine parts	732,966	2.2
Air conditioning & refrig. equip.	631,077	1.9
Electronic computers	499,740	1.5
Coal	473,132	1.4
Special transactions, trade	437,465	1.3
Other general purpose indust. mach.	408,293	1.2
Auxiliary elec. equip. for engines	373,176	1.1
Other telecom. & rel. equip.	365,990	1.1
Top 12	20,206,670	61.4
All exports	32,885,914	100.0

Imports from Ontario	Level	Share
	(C$ 000s)	(%)
Passenger automobiles and chassis	8,490,175	28.2
Trucks, truck tractors and chassis	5,596,573	18.6
Motor vehicle parts, except engines	4,841,926	16.1
Motor vehicle engines and parts	2,144,957	7.1
Newsprint paper	774,282	2.6
Wood pulp and similar pulp	589,425	2.0
Whisky	567,572	1.9
Rlwy. and street rlwy. rolling stock	422,277	1.4
Other inorganic chemicals	407,082	1.4
Metal fabricated basic products	381,878	1.3
Plate, sheet and strip, steel	356,150	1.2
Oth. general purpose industrial mach.	255,113	0.8
Top 12	24,827,410	82.5
All imports	30,103,917	100.0

TOTAL GREAT LAKES

Exports to Canada	Level	Share
	(C$ 000s)	(%)
Motor vehicle parts, except engines	9,389,134	24.3
Passenger automobiles and chassis	5,156,853	13.3
Motor vehicle engines	1,912,186	4.9
Trucks, truck tractors and chassis	1,371,991	3.5
Motor vehicle engine parts	754,726	2.0
Air conditioning & refrig. equip.	679,199	1.8
Electronic computers	521,721	1.3
Special transactions, trade	477,022	1.2
Coal	467,425	1.2
Other general purpose indust. mach.	459,690	1.2
Other telecom. & rel. equip.	412,210	1.1
Auxiliary elec. equip. for engines	399,645	1.0
Top 12	22,001,802	56.9
All exports	38,691,615	100.0

Imports from Canada	Level	Share
	(C$ 000s)	(%)
Passenger automobiles and chassis	10,191,449	24.4
Trucks, truck tractors and chassis	5,639,192	13.5
Motor vehicle parts, except engines	4,907,994	11.7
Crude petroleum	3,214,042	7.7
Motor vehicle engines and parts	2,152,224	5.1
Wood pulp and similar pulp	1,480,185	3.5
Newsprint paper	1,409,961	3.4
Lumber, softwood	682,744	1.6
Natural gas	564,155	1.3
Other inorganic chemicals	516,538	1.2
Syn. rubber and plastic materials	500,851	1.2
Metal fabricated basic products	477,350	1.1
Top 12	31,736,685	75.8
All imports	41,842,402	100.0

APPENDIX 2

Employment by industry sector in the Great Lakes region, 1990Q1
thousands of jobs (and percent of total)

	Mining & forestry	Construction	Manufacturing	Retail trade	Wholesale trade	Transportation & public utilities	Finance, insurance & real estate	Services	Government	Services (3)[a]	Total
Illinois	19.8 (.4)	218.9 (4.2)	981.0 (18.8)	906.7 (17.4)	377.3 (7.2)	306.7 (5.9)	374.3 (7.2)	1,294.9 (24.8)	744.3 (14.3)	2.,345.8 (44.9)	5,221.9 (100.0)
Indiana	7.9 (.3)	1,22.3 (4.9)	636.2 (25.4)	476.9 (19.1)	125.0 (5.0)	132.4 (5.3)	123.9 (5.0)	520.0 (20.8)	361.3 (14.4)	1,013.7 (40.5)	2,504.0 (100.0)
Michigan	10.4 (.3)	141.8 (3.6)	942.2 (23.7)	726.6 (18.7)	201.7 (5.2)	151.9 (3.9)	191.5 (4.9)	913.0 (23.4)	635.4 (16.3)	1,700.3 (43.6)	3,896.9 (100.0)
Minnesota	8.2 (.4)	83.9 (3.9)	400.5 (18.8)	394.5 (18.5)	130.1 (6.1)	108.7 (5.1)	122.6 (5.8)	551.6 (25.9)	331.4 (15.6)	991.7 (46.6)	2,130.3 (100.0)
Ohio	17.9 (.4)	1,99.4 (4.1)	1,113.8 (22.9)	928.4 (19.0)	269.3 (5.5)	218.8 (4.5)	256.5 (5.3)	1,160.4 (23.8)	715.4 (14.7)	2,094.6 (43.0)	4,875.0 (100.0)
Wisconsin	2.3 (.1)	91.8 (4.0)	557.0 (24.5)	423.8 (18.7)	120.6 (5.3)	100.3 (4.4)	119.7 (5.3)	520.5 (22.9)	336.7 (14.8)	957.5 (42.2)	2,269.8 (100.0)

SOURCE: *Employment, Hours, and Earnings*, Statistics Canada; and *Employment and Earnings*, Bureau of Labor Statistics.

[a]Includes government, services, and transportation and public utilities.

APPENDIX 3

Manufacturing employment, 1986
thousands of jobs (and concentration index)

	Food and kindred products	Textile mill products	Apparel and other textile	Lumber and wood products	Furniture and fixtures	Paper and allied products	Printing and publishing	Chemicals and allied products	Petroleum and coal products	Rubber and plastics
Illinois	91.6 (1.19)	3.3 (.10)	16.9 (.31)	11.5 (.33)	18.8 (.76)	34.8 (1.02)	111.4 (1.54)	60.3 (1.20)	11.5 (1.40)	48.9 (1.28)
Indiana	34.0 (.95)	.8 (.5)	8.3 (.33)	20.2 (1.26)	22.0 (1.93)	13.0 (.83)	32.8 (.98)	29.5 (1.27)	3.4 (.90)	38.5 (2.18)
Michigan	43.5 (.74)	3.1 (.12)	20.5 (.50)	14.2 (.54)	27.8 (1.48)	21.4 (.83)	43.1 (.78)	39.7 (1.04)	2.2 (.36)	47.3 (1.62)
Minnesota	48.1 (1.59)	1.8 (.13)	3.4 (.16)	13.2 (.97)	5.7 (.59)	13.8 (1.04)	43.8 (1.55)	10.6 (.54)	1.7 (.52)	15.5 (1.04)
Ohio	56.7 (.79)	5.7 (.18)	13.7 (.27)	16.4 (.51)	17.2 (.71)	33.9 (1.07)	71.8 (1.07)	66.2 (1.42)	6.4 (.84)	94.3 (2.66)
Wisconsin	54.0 (1.67)	4.2 (.30)	4.8 (.21)	20.3 (1.41)	10.7 (1.04)	45.8 (3.23)	40.6 (1.35)	10.5 (.50)	.8 (.24)	20.2 (1.27)

	Leather and leather products	Stone, clay, and glass	Primary metels	Fabricated metals	Nonelectrical machinery	Electric and electronic equipment	Transportation equipment	Instruments and related products	Miscellaneous products	Total
Illinois	3.8 (.51)	29.2 (1.04)	53.8 (1.41)	115.4 (1.57)	160.9 (1.66)	133.6 (1.29)	45.3 (.48)	39.5 (1.30)	23.9 (1.20)	1018.4 (1.10)
Indiana	2.1 (.60)	19.5 (1.51)	70.6 (4.00)	55.7 (1.64)	65.6 (1.47)	84.8 (1.78)	76.3 (1.75)	11.4 (.8O)	10.0 (1.08)	597.5 (1.40)
Michigan	1.8 (.31)	17.2 (.81)	55.2 (1.89)	128.6 (2.29)	134.0 (1.82)	38.6 (.49)	322.9 (4.49)	14.5 (.63)	8.9 (.59)	995.8 (1.42)
Minnesota	1.8 (.59)	9.4 (.86)	6.0 (.40)	34.4 (1.19)	85.3 (2.26)	32.2 (.80)	7.3 (.19)	32.8 (2.75)	6.5 (.83)	371.9 (1.03)
Ohio	2.0 (.29)	48.6 (1.87)	93.0 (2.62)	143.0 (2.09)	158.0 (1.76)	96.9 (1.01)	162.4 (1.86)	24.1 (.85)	14.8 (.80)	1123.7 (1.31)
Wisconsin	6.9 (2.20)	7.8 (.67)	22.1 (1.39)	51.8 (1.68)	96.7 (2.40)	45.3 (1.05)	33.1 (.84)	10.8 (.85)	8.6 (1.04)	494.1 (1.28)

SOURCE: U.S. Bureau of the Census, *County Business Patterns*.

NOTE: Excluding SIC 21. Auxiliary employees included or allocated.

Chapter 2

An Overview of the Economy of the Great Lakes States

Eleanor H. Erdevig, Economist,
Federal Reserve Bank of Chicago

The eight states bordering on the Great Lakes are a substantial segment of the United States economy with almost one-third of the nation's population. The region is centrally located with a well diversified and integrated economy and increasing international connections. Agriculture and manufacturing are major contributors to the area's output and the region is an important source of exports, particularly to Canada. The area's location and resources—people, institutions, and natural resources—have been important to its economic development in the past and will continue to be so in the future.

FIGURE 1

The Great Lakes states

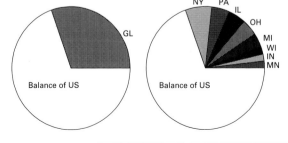

Eight states border on the five Great Lakes —namely, Minnesota, Wisconsin, Illinois, Indiana, Michigan, Ohio, Pennsylvania, and New York. These states are located mainly in the east north central area of the United States and represent a centrally located, diversified, and integrated economy with increasing international ties (Figure 1).

Structure of the Great Lakes economy

The region of the eight Great Lakes states is a significant segment of the United States' economy. Its population of about 76 million amounts to almost one-third of the nation's total. With about 12 percent of the total land area, the population density of the area considerably exceeds the nation's average.

The population of individual states ranges from 18 million in New York to 4.4 million in Minnesota (Figure 2). The large industrial states of New York, Pennsylvania, Illinois, Michigan, and Ohio have an above average percentage of their population living in metropolitan areas. Only in Indiana, Minnesota, and Wisconsin are there smaller proportions of the population in metropolitan areas.

Per capita personal income is currently about equal to or above the U.S. average in four of the states—New York, Illinois, Minnesota, and Michigan. New York is considerably above the U.S. average, with Illinois just slightly above (Figure 3). The income trends in individual states between 1986 and 1989 have been mixed, although there appears to have been a slight downward trend in most states. New York, Illinois, and Pennsylvania appear to be exceptions, with incomes rising there. Rising levels of personal income in New York City are partly attributable to the financial services industry which grew rapidly in the 1980s.

In general, the overall sources of personal income in the Great Lakes states are similar to those in the U.S. About 56 percent of personal income comes from wages and salaries, 17 percent from dividends, interest, and rent, and 14 percent from transfer payments in both areas.

Manufacturing has been a very important source of employment for Great Lakes states, but

FIGURE 2

Population of the United States and Great Lakes states, 1989

FIGURE 3

Per capita personal income
(percent of U.S. average)

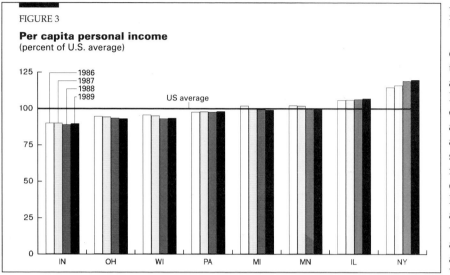

FIGURE 5

Major manufacturing industries in the Great Lakes states, 1989
(location quotients relative to U.S.)

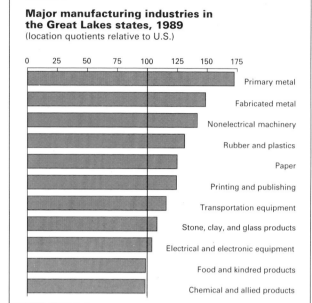

pared to 17 percent in the U.S. (Figure 4).[1]

Manufacturing's share of employment in each of the individual states has also been declining. However, the rates of decline relative to the U.S. average have varied among the states. The steepest declines in manufacturing's share of employment have been in New York, Pennsylvania, and Illinois. This contrasts with rates of decline that are slower than the U.S. average in Minnesota and Wisconsin.

has been gradually decreasing in importance. This has also been true in the nation, but its decline in manufacturing's share of employment has been slower. This largely reflects the fact that manufacturing's share of employment was previously higher in the overall Great Lakes states area than in the U.S. (35 percent vs. 30 percent in 1966). As manufacturing's share of employment has declined in the Great Lakes states, it has gradually converged toward that of the nation and is now at 20 percent com-

While manufacturing's share of employment has been decreasing, private services' share of employment has been increasing. In this case, private services includes transportation and utilities; wholesale and retail trade; finance, insurance, and real estate; and personal and business services.

The Great Lakes states are major industrial states. As a measure of the importance of various manufacturing industries in these states relative to the national average, a concept known as the

location quotient is used. The location quotient compares an industry's share of total employment in an area to the industry's share in the nation with the ratio multiplied by 100. If an industry's ratio is above 100, that industry is more important in the area than it is in the U.S.

FIGURE 4

Employment: manufacturing
(percent manufacturing)

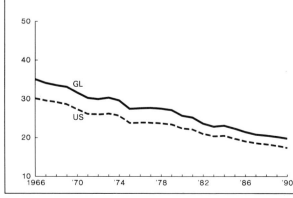

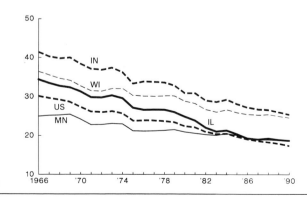

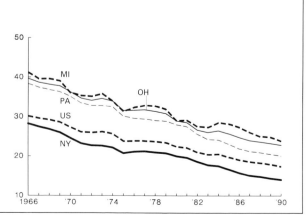

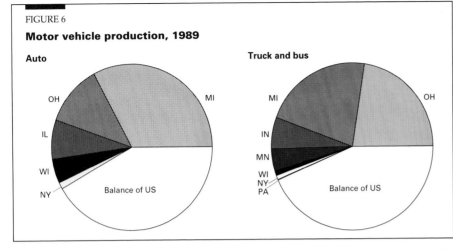

FIGURE 6

Motor vehicle production, 1989

Auto

Truck and bus

According to the location quotients for the various manufacturing industries, heavy industry engaged in producing primary and fabricated metal products and nonelectrical machinery is substantially above average importance in the Great Lakes area. Other industries with above average shares of employment include those producing rubber and plastics, paper, printing and publishing, and transportation equipment (Figure 5).

One of the more important industries in the Great Lakes area is the production of motor vehicles. In 1989 about 58 percent of all autos produced in the country were assembled in five of the Great Lakes states. Michigan alone produced one-third of all autos in the U.S. Similarly, about 56 percent of all trucks and buses were manufactured in the Great Lakes area. Ohio and Michigan are the major truck and bus producers with 44 percent of the nation's total (Figure 6).

Not only are domestic motor vehicle assembly plants located in the area, but the majority of newly established foreign-owned assembly plants (known as transplants) have also been established in the area. Of the 31 domestic auto assembly plants, 17 (or 55 percent) are located in these states and three of the five transplants and two of the three jointly-owned auto plants have also been established here (Figure 7). About half of the domestic and transplant truck assembly plants are also in the area (Figure 8).

Although much has been written about the closure and startup of motor vehicle assembly plants during the 1980s, the overall effect on the Great Lakes area has been to rearrange production facilities rather than to lose facilities to other regions. During the 1980s in the U.S. 17 car and truck assembly plants were closed and 17 were opened. In the Great Lakes states, 8 plants were closed and 9 were opened, for a net gain of one plant. This represents a significant reduction of old facilities and the expansion of new plants and technology.

The Great Lakes states are also an important area for agricultural production. Just over one-fifth of the nation's cash receipts from farm marketings comes from these states. Major commodities are

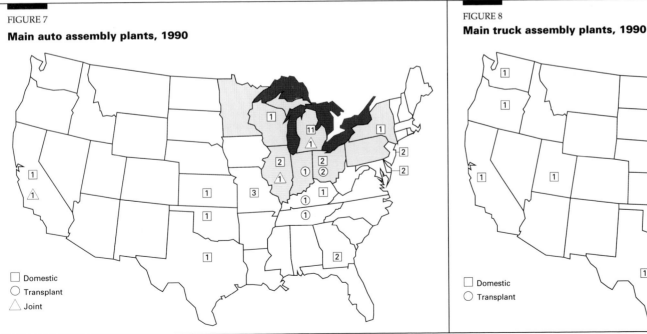

FIGURE 7

Main auto assembly plants, 1990

☐ Domestic
◯ Transplant
△ Joint

FIGURE 8

Main truck assembly plants, 1990

☐ Domestic
◯ Transplant

corn, soybeans, milk, and hogs. About half of the corn, soybeans, and milk and about two-fifths of the hogs produced in this country come from just these eight states.

As might be expected, inasmuch as the area is an important producer of agricultural products, it is also a major source of exports of agricultural products. In 1989 just over one-fifth of all agricultural exports came from the Great Lakes states. This amounted to some $8.9 billion.

Not only is the area important for agricultural exports, but it is also important for manufactured exports. In 1986, the most recent year for which data are available, approximately 2.3 million manufacturing employees in the U.S. were involved, either directly or indirectly, in producing goods for export. Of this total 38 percent or 900 thousand employees were located in Great Lakes states. Most of the individual Great Lakes states have an above average percentage of their manufacturing employment involved in producing goods for export. This is especially true in the states of Minnesota, Ohio, Michigan, and Indiana (Table 1).

In addition to employment in manufacturing plants that are producing exported products, either directly or indirectly, part of the employment in nonmanufacturing industries is also related to manufactured exports. Major industries are trade,

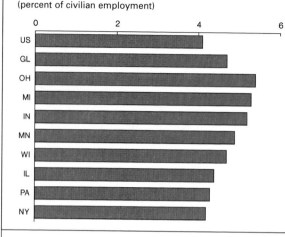

Employment relevant to manufactured exports in the Great Lakes states, 1986
(percent of civilian employment)

business services, and transportation, communication, and utilities. In the Great Lakes states, except for New York, an above average proportion of employment is engaged in manufacturing. As a result the ratio of total employment that is related to manufactured exports to civilian employment is above the national average in all of the Great Lakes states (Figure 9).

methodology which has resulted in a reduction in the amount of exports that are not accounted for. Another way of looking at it is to consider just the amount that is accounted for. Great Lakes states represent about 30 percent of the manufactured goods exported where the state of origin is identified.

Even after adjusting for changes in data methodology, however, export growth currently underpins much of the forward momentum of the Great Lakes economy.[2] Exports of manufactured goods are estimated to have increased 14 percent in the Great Lakes states compared to an increase of 7 percent in the rest of the U.S. during the first 6 months of 1990 compared to the same period a year earlier. All of the Great Lakes states, except New York, showed an increase in exports greater than the U.S. average. The greatest increases have been in Wisconsin, Ohio, Indiana, Illinois and Pennsylvania (Figure 10).

Canada is the major trading partner of the U.S. but it is even more important to the Great Lakes region. About 23 percent of U.S. manufactured exports are bound for Canada, while roughly 40 percent of such exports from the Great Lakes area are destined for Canada. As a result the primary factors influencing Canadian imports from the U.S.—exchange rates and the rate of Canadian economic growth—have a disproportionate impact on the economy of the Great Lakes states.

Economic strength in the region relates partly to the importance of exports to the area. As the country's exports have increased, the Great Lakes area has benefited. During the first six months of 1990, one-fourth of the exports of manufactured goods from the U.S. came from the Great Lakes states. This appears to be up from the 22 percent in 1989, but a large part of the increase may be the result of a change in data

TABLE 1

Employment related to manufactured exports, 1986

	Manufacturing employment	Export related employment			% of manufacturing employment
		Direct	Supporting	Total	
	(000s)				
Illinois	988.9	45.2	78.7	123.9	12.5
Indiana	575.1	32.3	43.7	76.0	13.2
Michigan	942.8	56.2	69.1	125.3	13.3
Minnesota	357.5	25.6	28.4	54.0	15.1
New York	1,267.5	74.9	86.0	160.9	12.7
Ohio	1,086.7	63.0	88.4	151.4	13.9
Pennsylvania	1,042.6	52.4	79.6	132.0	12.7
Wisconsin	486.1	22.7	33.8	56.5	11.6
Great Lakes states	6,747.2	372.3	507.7	880.0	13.0
United States	18,371.2	1,060.9	1,257.3	2,318.2	12.6

SOURCE: U.S. Department of Commerce, Bureau of the Census, *Exports From Manufacturing Establishments: 1985 and 1986*, Analytical Report Series (AR86-1), Issued January 1989, Table 5a, pp. 26-42.

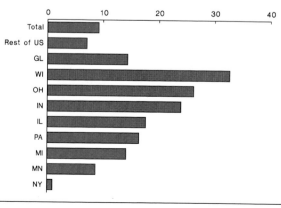

FIGURE 10

Exports of manufactured goods
(percent change, 1989-90, 6 months)

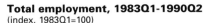

FIGURE 11

Total employment, 1983Q1-1990Q2
(index, 1983Q1=100)

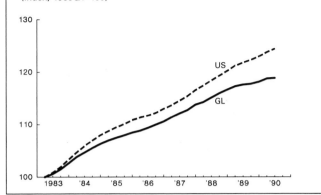

Trade between the Great Lakes states and Canada is best characterized by its large and balanced relation. Goods traded amount to about $90 billion each year (both exports and imports) and account for roughly one-half of all U.S. trade with Canada.

Recent trends

During the economic recovery that began at the end of 1982 in the U.S., the Great Lakes economy has grown, but total employment growth has lagged

that of the nation (Figure 11). Part of this slower growth reflects the severe effects of the back-to-back recessions in the early 1980s on some of the region's major industries. Part of the slow growth reflects the structural changes in Great Lakes' industries that have enabled them to compete more effectively in an increasingly international economy.

Overall, manufacturing employment growth in the Great Lakes states has been slower than in the nation during the recovery. Smaller states have been able to add manufacturing jobs faster than the

larger industrial states. The so-called older industrial states have been more affected by industrial restructuring, especially New York and Pennsylvania (Figure 12).

Foundations for the future

The region's location and resources have been important to the development of the area in the past and will continue to be so in the future.

Many of the major companies in the United States have found the Great Lakes states the ideal

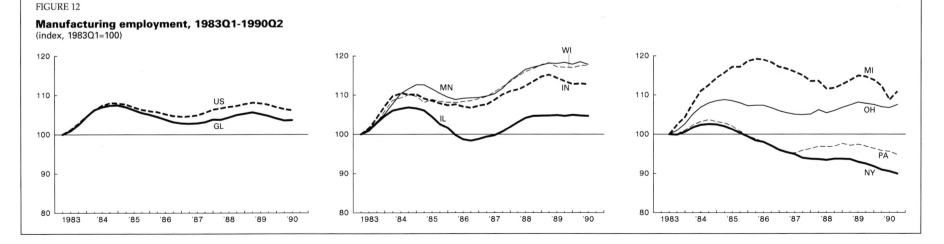

FIGURE 12

Manufacturing employment, 1983Q1-1990Q2
(index, 1983Q1=100)

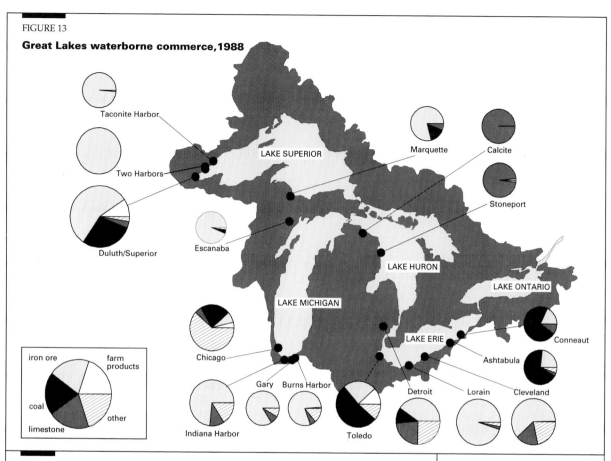

FIGURE 13

Great Lakes waterborne commerce, 1988

(Map showing locations: Taconite Harbor, Two Harbors, Duluth/Superior, Escanaba, Chicago, Gary, Burns Harbor, Indiana Harbor, Toledo, Detroit, Lorain, Cleveland, Ashtabula, Conneaut, Marquette, Calcite, Stoneport, with lakes labeled LAKE SUPERIOR, LAKE HURON, LAKE MICHIGAN, LAKE ERIE, LAKE ONTARIO)

Legend pie chart: iron ore, farm products, coal, limestone, other

TABLE 2

Fortune 500 companies: industrial and nonindustrial

	Industrial		Nonindustrial	
	Number	% of US	Number	% of US
Illinois	48	9.6	34	6.8
Indiana	11	2.2	8	1.6
Michigan	19	3.8	15	3.0
Minnesota	15	3.0	16	3.2
New York	59	11.8	71	14.2
Ohio	40	8.0	25	5.0
Pennsylvania	34	6.8	19	3.8
Wisconsin	11	2.2	4	0.8
Great Lakes states	237	47.4	192	38.4
United States	500	100.0	500	100.0

SOURCE: *Fortune*, April 23, 1990, pp. 346-364; and *Fortune*, June 10, 1990, pp. 304-330.

location in which to develop and expand. Of the Fortune 500 largest industrial companies in the country, almost half (or 237) have their company headquarters within the eight Great Lakes states. Of the 500 largest nonindustrial companies, about two-fifths (or 192) are in this area (Table 2). Nonindustrial companies include diversified service companies, commercial banking companies, diversified financial companies, savings institutions, life insurance companies, retailing companies, transportation companies, and utilities.

A major advantage of the area is its central location which enables it to serve as a transportation center. Early transportation was by water and today waterborne commerce on the Great Lakes remains an important means of integrating the economies of the states bordering on the Great Lakes. Duluth, Chicago, and Toledo are important ports for shipments of farm products both to other lake ports and overseas. But the largest volume of shipments are of iron ore, coal, and limestone to support the steel industry and its customers (Figure 13).[3]

Seven of the top 30 airports in terms of revenue passengers enplaned are located in the Great Lakes states. These include the airports at Chicago (O'Hare), New York (LaGuardia and Kennedy), Detroit, Pittsburgh, Minneapolis/St. Paul, and Philadelphia. Of these the busiest airport in the country is O'Hare in Chicago where 27 million passengers enplaned in 1988. International connections are expanding with Chicago's O'Hare Airport only 4000 airline miles from London and 6300 miles from Tokyo.

The Great Lakes states currently have almost one-fourth of the interstate highways in the country. These highways are located on just 12 percent of the land area of the country and support an extensive trucking industry.

The Great Lakes are the largest body of fresh water in the world. The five lakes in the aggregate represent 94 thousand square miles or 244 thousand square kilometers of water surface with a total shoreline of about 10,000 miles or 17,000 kilometers (Table 3).[4] In total, about three-fourths of the world's fresh water is contained in the Great Lakes.

Finally, among the resources of the area are the banking facilities which provide access to capital. The area has about 19,000 domestic commercial banking offices, i.e., banks and branches, about 30 percent of all such offices in the U.S. Foreign banks have also established offices in the area. Of the approximately 565 U.S. offices of foreign banks, 320 (or 56 percent) are in Great Lakes states (Figure 14). The largest concentration of foreign banking offices is in New York City, with Chicago a distant second.

FIGURE 14

Banking facilities in the Great Lakes states, 1989

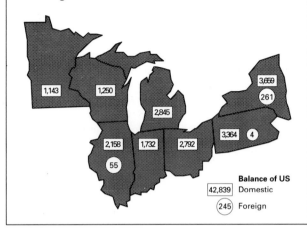

Employment trends indicate that the overall recovery in the area has lagged that of the nation, but performance varies widely from state to state. Manufacturing employment in the area since the first quarter of 1983 has expanded somewhat more slowly than in the U.S. following more severe losses during the back-to-back recessions in the early 1980s.

The long-term outlook for the area depends partly on its resources—people, institutions, and natural resources. Among those that were highlighted were the large number of headquarters of major industrial and nonindustrial companies, its extensive transportation network, its population, its water resources, and its domestic and foreign-owned banking facilities which provide access to capital.

NOTES

[1] Employment figures based on those provided by the Bureau of Labor Statistics, U.S. Department of Labor, *Employment and Earnings*.

[2] The decrease in "unaccounted for" from 1989 to 1990 was distributed to states in 1989 based on 1989 export proportions.

[3] *Waterborne Commerce of the United States, Part 3, Waterways and Harbors, Great Lakes*, 1988, Department of the Army Corps of Engineers, WRSC-WCUS-883.

[4] *The Great Lakes: An Environmental Atlas and Resource Book*, U.S. Environmental Protection Agency, Chicago, Illinois, and Environment Canada, Toronto, Ontario, 1987

Conclusion

The intent of this overview was to emphasize that the Great Lakes area is a centrally-located, diversified, and integrated economy with increasing international connections. Agriculture and manufacturing are significant segments of the region's economy and the area is an important source of exports, particularly to Canada.

TABLE 3

Great Lakes physical features

		Superior	Michigan	Huron	Erie	Ontario	Total
Volume	*(cu. mi.)*	2,900	1,180	850	116	393	5,439
	(cu. km.)	12,100	4,920	3,540	484	1,640	22,684
Area:							
Water	*(sq. mi.)*	31,700	22,300	23,000	9,910	7,340	94,250
	(sq. km.)	82,100	57,800	59,600	25,700	18,960	244,160
Land drainage area[a]	*(sq. mi.)*	49,300	45,600	51,700	30,140	24,720	201,460
	(sq. km.)	127,700	118,000	134,100	78,000	64,030	521,830
Total	*(sq. mi.)*	81,000	67,900	74,700	40,050	32,060	295,710
	(sq. km.)	209,800	175,800	193,700	103,700	82,990	765,990
Shoreline length[b]	*(miles)*	2,726	1,638	3,827	871	712	10,210[c]
	(kilometers)	4,385	2,633	6,157	1,402	1,146	17,017[c]

[a] Land drainage area for Lake Huron includes the St. Marys River. Lake Erie includes the St. Clair-Detroit system. Lake Ontario includes the Niagara River.

[b] Including islands.

[c] These totals are greater than the sum of the shoreline length for the lakes because they include the connecting channels (excluding the St. Lawrence River).

Chapter 3

Population and the Labor Force

John Fraser Hart, Professor of Geography,
University of Minnesota

The population of the Great Lakes region apparently peaked around 1990, and is starting to decline. The basic pattern of cities in the region has hardly changed for a century or more, but the central cities of metropolitan areas are losing population, while their suburbs continue to gain.

Suburbanization has coincided with increased employment in professional services. Employment in retail trade has been shifting up the urban hierarchy, from smaller to larger places, but employment in manufacturing has been trickling down the hierarchy. Small towns have continued to gain population because they have been transformed from farm service centers into minor cogs in the national manufacturing system.

Increased female participation in the labor force has postponed the day of reckoning with the labor shortage as the "baby bubble" follows the baby boom through the population pipeline. Older people have been migrating to the Sunbelt or to the recreation, resort, and retirement belt along the southern margin of the Great North Woods, which, like the suburbs, is enjoying continuing population growth.

Reproduction rates in the region have fallen below the replacement level, and its future population growth will depend on its ability to compete with better situated coastal regions in recruiting immigrants from Latin America and from Asia.

The Great Lakes are too far north. The Wilderness Line, officially so designated by the government of Canada, is closer to Lake Superior than the Ohio River is to Lake Michigan (Figure 1). A line drawn from Fargo to Minneapolis, and thence to Green Bay, Muskegon, and Ottawa, divides the Great Lakes region into a productive and urbanized south and a sparsely populated north that is appreciably less developed and less prosperous. Nature is niggardly north of this line. The rocks were scraped bare by glaciers, the summers are too short and too cool for most crops, the soils are sour and thin, much of the land is poorly drained marsh and bog, and the floor of the coniferous forest is littered with needles that acidify percolating rainwater enough to leach essential plant nutrients from the soil, which already has far too few.

The Great North Woods are a tough place to have to try to make a living. The difficult natural environment frustrates attempts at farming. The original forests of pine and spruce made fortunes for early lumber barons, who reaped the growth of scores of decades in a few brief years and then moved on, taking their profits with them and leaving millions of acres of barren cutover waste. The spindly second growth of birch and aspen is a sorry replacement for the splendid primeval forests, but it provides the raw material for pulp and paper mills. The tough old crystalline rocks of the north secreted lodes of iron and other valuable metallic

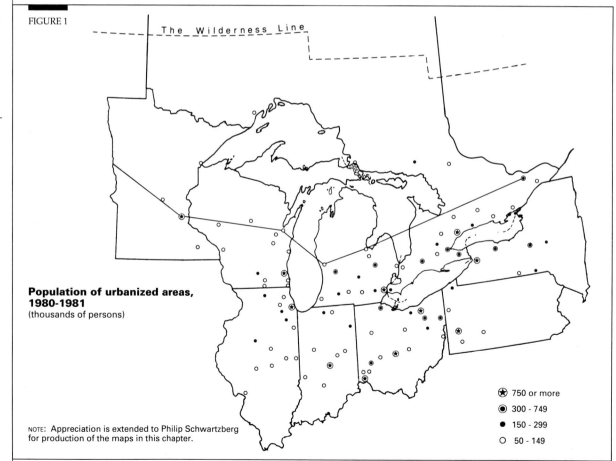

FIGURE 1

The Wilderness Line

Population of urbanized areas, 1980-1981
(thousands of persons)

NOTE: Appreciation is extended to Philip Schwartzberg for production of the maps in this chapter.

★ 750 or more
◉ 300 - 749
● 150 - 299
○ 50 - 149

TABLE 1

Population, 1950-1981, and estimates, 1990-2010
(thousands of persons)

	1950	1960	1970	1980	1990*	2000*	2010*
UNITED STATES	151,326	179,323	203,302	226,546	249,891	267,747	282,055
Illinois	8,712	10,081	11,110	11,427	11,612	11,580	11,495
Indiana	3,934	4,662	5,195	5,490	5,550	5,502	5,409
Michigan	6,372	7,823	8,882	9,262	9,293	9,250	9,097
Minnesota	2,982	3,414	3,806	4,076	4,324	4,490	4,578
Ohio	7,947	9,706	10,657	10,798	10,791	10,629	10,397
Wisconsin	3,435	3,952	4,418	4,706	4,808	4,784	4,713
Six states	33,382	39,638	44,068	45,759	46,378	46,235	45,689

	1951	1961	1971	1981
CANADA	14,009	18,238	21,568	24,343
Ontario	4,598	6,236	7,707	8,625

* estimates

SOURCES: *1980 Census of Population.* Volume I, Chapter A, Part 1, Table 8; *Statistical Abstract of the United States, 1990*, Table 29; *Canada Year Book 1990*, p. 2-19.

ores, but mining camps had no reason for existence once the ore had been removed, and they have been almost as impermanent as the lumber camps. The towns, such as they were, have existed mainly to process and ship the products of mines and forests, and the northern part of the Great Lakes region has been able to support few cities.

The cities, the people, and the economic development of the Great Lakes area are concentrated in the south, but the southern boundary of the region is hard to identify. Michigan is the only state or province that is completely within the watershed of the Great Lakes, but the watershed was breached early on by easy portages and canals, later by all other modes of transport, and to most modern traffic it means little or nothing. For convenience the Great Lakes region is here defined as the six states of Minnesota, Wisconsin, Michigan, Illinois, Indiana, and Ohio, as well as the province of Ontario, even though parts of all but Michigan quite clearly are outside the region, whereas western Pennsylvania and western New York just as clearly are part of it.

Roughly one-fifth of the people of the United States live in the six Great Lakes states, whose population has been increasing, but at a decreasing rate, since World War II (Table 1). Official estimates prepared by the U. S. Bureau of the Census indicate that the population peaked in each state except Minnesota around 1990, and they may already have begun to lose population. The summer of 1990 truly is a tricky time to be trying to talk about population in the United States, however, because the most recent census from which results are available was taken ten years ago, and all population estimates will have to be recalibrated when the results of the 1990 census become available.

The province of Ontario, which has just over one-third of the people of Canada, has been gaining population almost twice as fast as any of the six states, but its rate of growth also has been decreasing. Statistical comparisons of Canada and the United States often are awkward, because the Canadian census of population is taken every five years, in the years ending in -1 and -6, but the United States census of population is taken only once a decade, in the years ending in -0, and the two censuses use definitions and classifications that differ, sometimes quite sharply, sometimes more subtly.

Furthermore, the Great Lakes states and Ontario are topheavy statistically; each is so dominated by one or two major metropolitan areas that statistical aggregates conceal much of their internal diversity. Two-fifths of the people of the region live in only seven metropolitan areas (Chicago, Detroit, Toronto, Minneapolis-St. Paul, Cleveland, Milwaukee, and Indianapolis), and another third live in smaller metropolitan areas

(Figure 1). Less than one of every four residents of the region lives outside a metropolitan area, where some trends run counter to metropolitan trends.

It is easy to become confused about the population of metropolitan areas in the United States, because the census reports different figures for the population of the central city, the urbanized area, and the Metropolitan Statistical Areas (MSA) (Table 2). For example, the population peaked in many major cities around 1950, and it has been declining spasmodically ever since, because people have been moving to the suburbs, but the population of their urbanized areas and their MSAs has continued to increase.

To begin with, a metropolis must have an incorporated central city of at least 50,000 people, but metropolitan areas have been defined because most cities have sprawled far beyond their incorporated limits. The MSA includes the entire county in which the central city is located, plus all other counties that have close economic and social ties to the central city. Government agencies collect and publish a prodigious amount of information about MSAs, and some people even confuse MSAs with cities, but some MSA counties have extensive tracts of land that could not be considered metropolitan, or even urban, by the wildest stretch of anyone's

TABLE 2

Population of gateway cities, 1980
(thousands of persons)

	Metropolitan area	Urbanized area	Central city
Chicago	7,937	6,780	3,005
Detroit	4,753	3,809	1,203
Cleveland	2,834	1,752	574
Pittsburgh	2,423	1,810	424
Minneapolis	2,137	1,788	371
Cincinnati	1,660	1,123	385
Milwaukee	1,570	1,207	636
Columbus	1,244	834	565
Buffalo	1,243	1,003	358
Indianapolis	1,167	836	701

SOURCES: *1980 Census of Population.* Volume I, Chapter A, Part 1, Tables 30, 34, and 27.

imagination. The urbanized area consists of the central city and the densely built-up fringe areas with 1,000 or more people per square mile. The urbanized area (Figure 1) is the real geographical city. Unlike the central city and the MSA, which are defined by fixed political boundaries, the urbanized area keeps changing as the city changes, but it is defined only once each decade, when the decennial census is taken.

The basic pattern of cities in the Great Lakes region has persisted with remarkably little change for a century or more (Figure 1). From census to census the population of individual places has grown chaotically (or stochastically, depending on your point of view), but over the long run most cities have retained their relative positions in an urban system that has been expanding. Some have risen or fallen a few notches in the standings, but the list of cities ranked by size in 1980 looks very much like the list for 1880.

The first places founded in the Great Lakes region are still the largest, and they have evolved into the economic capitals of their areas. They were port cities—Toronto, Buffalo, Cleveland, Detroit, Chicago, and Milwaukee on the lakes, Pittsburgh at the head of the Ohio River, and Minneapolis-St. Paul at the head of the Mississippi. The port cities were the gateways to the region. They were the jumping-off places, the outfitting centers where the early settlers could equip themselves with the tools and implements they would need to tame the frontier.

When they prospered and began to produce a marketable surplus, the gateway city was the principal link between the settlers and the older cities of the east. It was the collecting center where the surplus of the land was assembled for shipment eastward, and the distribution center for goods from eastern factories. Some of the products of the land had to be processed to reduce their bulk before they were shipped, and the gateway city became a manufacturing center, first for the processing of farm products, then for the manufacture of farm machinery, and eventually, in the eastern part of the region, for the manufacture of automobiles, after local tinkerers got the idea of hitching marine engines to farm wagons.

The gateway cities soon added banking, financial services, and a whole range of other professional and human services to their repertoires of activities, and they have evolved into the economic capitals of their sections of the region. They are the command and control centers of a postindustrial world in which the transfer of numbers, words, and ideas has become as important as the transfer of goods and people, few workers make things, and most jobs involve processing information, making decisions, and doing things for others. The principal engines of modern metropolitan growth are no longer housed in factories and stores, but in office buildings, in hospitals, and on college campuses. The gateway cities have retained their preeminence because they are the best locations for the quaternary economic activities on which contemporary society depends.

Manufacturing also played a major role in the growth of the second and third order metropolitan centers that sprouted in the gaps between the gateway cities, especially at lake ports that enjoyed special advantages for assembling raw materials, or on rivers where falls or rapids could be harnessed for power. The second order centers are older and larger. They are in the eastern part of the Great Lakes region, which has been dominated by the iron and steel industry in western Pennsylvania and northeastern Ohio, and by the automobile industry in Michigan, Ohio, and Indiana. Detroit is the headquarters of the automobile industry, but the manufacture of components and final assembly have been farmed out to plants in smaller cities.

Some of the smallest, fourth order, metropolitan centers of the Great Lakes region are also manufacturing centers, but some are specialized in other types of activities, such as education and public administration, which have been major growth activities since World War II. The growth of state capitals and university towns to metropolitan size is ironic, because our forebears did their best to protect the most easily corrupted members of society against the snares and pitfalls of the big, wicked, and sinful city by locating the capital and the university as far from it as possible in a setting of rural purity.

American metropolitan centers have been turning themselves inside out since World War II,

and so have smaller towns, although on an appropriately reduced scale. Retail businesses that once were downtown now flourish in suburban shopping malls or on expressway strips, which also have the most prestigious new office buildings. Many of the best new jobs are in outlying business centers rather than downtown. Residential areas have sprawled far and wide, some in compact blocks, some in leapfrogging subdivisions, and some in the farflung homes of people who commute distances that seem unconscionable even when you remember that their jobs are at the edge of the city rather than downtown.

The flight to the suburbs and the increasing importance of skilled employment have abandoned large parts of many central cities to people with low skills who are snared in a web of unemployment, poverty, senseless violence, hopelessness, and despair. The massive in-migration of poorly educated people from the rural South to northern cities during and after World War II has been blamed in part for the flight of many lower middle income people to the suburbs. With them they took their jobs and their incomes, leaving the central city with a greatly reduced tax base just when it had to grapple with almost intractable social problems. Some of the lowest rates of school completion and the highest rates of unemployment, poverty, infant mortality, and crime in the Great Lakes region are in some of its larger central cities.

In contrast, the wealthiest counties in the region in 1985 were in the metropolitan suburbs (Figure 2). Only the largest metropolitan areas, plus a few specialized smaller places, exceeded the national average, and most of the counties within nine-tenths of the national norm were in north central Illinois, eastern Wisconsin, southern Michigan, and northern Ohio. The poorest counties were in the North Woods areas of northern Minnesota, Wisconsin, and Michigan, in the Appalachian Uplands of central Pennsylvania, and on the flanks of the Adirondack Mountains in northern New York. Some people might argue that differences in the cost of living, about which we have little information, might blunt the impact of some of these disparities.

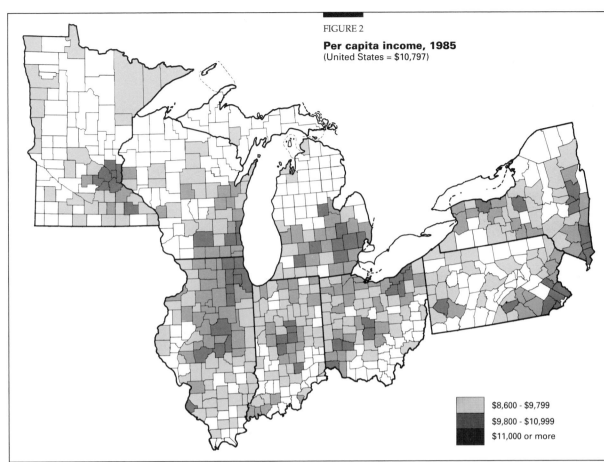

FIGURE 2

Per capita income, 1985
(United States = $10,797)

$8,600 - $9,799
$9,800 - $10,999
$11,000 or more

In sharp contrast, employment in manufacturing has been trickling down the urban hierarchy, from larger to smaller places. It has also been moving from the central city out to the metropolitan

FIGURE 3

Employment by industry group, six Great Lakes states and Ontario, 1950-1981
(millions of workers)

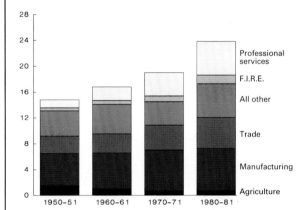

suburbs, because manufacturing is no longer a smokestack industry. Many of the great hulking factories in the grimy old industrial districts along the waterfront and the railroads are derelict, and their smokestacks have long been still. They have been supplanted by lowslung new structures on neatly landscaped grounds with ample parking space in planned industrial parks near major highways and expressways, often close to the airport. The new factories reflect the shift from mass production of long runs of standard items to more specialized production that is flexible enough to switch product lines quickly in response to changing demand. Monolithic manufacturing processes have been broken down into specific tasks, and many tasks have been hived off to subcontractors or moved to less expensive sites.

The reorganization of production has helped to disperse employment in manufacturing (Figure 4). The percentage of the labor force employed in manufacturing declined between 1950 and 1980 in metropolitan areas and in the older industrial areas

Suburbanization has coincided with significant changes in employment by industry sector. Employment data in the United States and Canada are not strictly comparable, but the trends in the six Great Lakes states and Ontario have been so similar that the data can be combined in a single graph despite their lack of comparability (Figure 3). The number of persons employed in the traditional city-building sectors, such as manufacturing and trade, increased only slightly between 1950 and 1981, and the percentage of the labor force employed in manufacturing actually declined, but employment increased more than fourfold in professional services, such as health care and education. Some people have argued that the services sector of the economy is recession-proof, because employment and wages in

this sector seem to keep growing no matter what, but the best evidence indicates that this sector merely responds to recessions more slowly than other sectors.

Employment in trade and manufacturing has increased only slightly, but these modest aggregate changes mask major geographical changes. Retail trade has been shifting up the urban hierarchy, from smaller to larger places, ever since the automobile replaced the horse and buggy, and since World War II it has been moving out to the edge of town from the old central business district. In many urban areas today "downtown" is little more than a convenience shopping area for those who work there, and recent attempts to resuscitate it have been unsuccessful.

in the eastern part of the Great Lakes region, but it increased dramatically in smaller places and throughout the western part of the region. Some of the new manufacturing establishments in small towns and rural areas are branch plants of companies seeking lower taxes and cheaper floor space in places where they can tap the cream of a nonunionized labor supply, but some have been started by local entrepreneurs. The new small-town manufacturing plants are not dominated by any particular industry or type of industry. Some, predictably, make food products or process other local raw materials, but others make metal goods, rubber goods, or virtually any other manufactured product you can think of.

Too many of the new factories in small towns and rural areas were attracted by the availability of cheap labor, and they can decamp just as abruptly as they arrived. They have been a welcome first step in the shift away from agriculture, but they do not provide a satisfactory basis for sustained economic growth, and leaders in rural areas should use the transition period to educate a labor force in marketing, accounting, finance, and other modern business skills. The people of the Great Lakes states have always believed in the importance of education, and at state levels the percentage of high school graduates exceeds the national average. Educational attainment is highest in suburban counties, as one might expect, and lowest in the more remote and less accessible areas that need economic development the most (Figure 5). Of course an educated labor force does not guarantee economic development, but an inadequately trained labor force is virtually guaranteed to forestall it.

The spread of employment in manufacturing has been the salvation of many small towns, whose population has continued to increase, however slowly and fitfully, despite the dire predictions of those who seem determined to ignore all evidence that they are growing. They have been transformed from farm service centers into minor cogs in the national manufacturing system, because there is precious little farm population left to serve, and the modern farm families who remain demand more and better goods and services than most small towns can provide.

Perhaps no other sector of the economy has changed so drastically since 1960, or is so poorly understood, as agriculture. The number of persons employed in agriculture has been decreasing (Figure 3), and so has the number of farms, but not nearly so calamitously as many people think, because the official census definition of a farm includes large numbers of hobby, weekend, part-time, and other undersized operations that are best described as "nonfarm farms." The successful modern family farm has become a family farm business that sells at least $100,000 worth of farm products each year, and even then one or more members of the family may have to take an off-farm job to maintain a satisfactory cash flow.

Farm wives who have taken off-farm jobs have helped to swell the ranks of the female labor force. They seem to have played an especially important role in the growth of manufacturing in small towns, although the percentage of women in the labor force still is slightly lower in agricultural than in metropolitan areas. One of the greatest changes in American society since World War II has been the steady increase in the number of women employed outside their homes. In 1950 women comprised only 28 percent of the labor force in the six Great Lakes states, but by 1980 their share had risen to 46 percent (Table 3). The increased number of working women and two-income families is increasing demands for quality day-care facilities, and it will

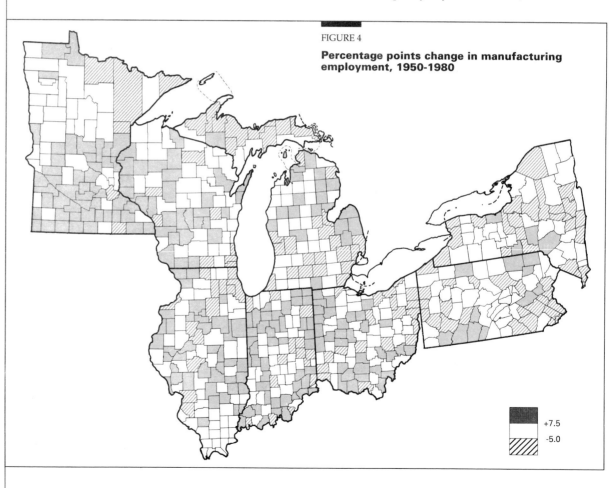

FIGURE 4

Percentage points change in manufacturing employment, 1950-1980

+7.5

-5.0

probably reduce long-distance migration, because both spouses will be less likely to be able to move to the same place at the same time.

Increased female participation in the labor force has merely postponed the necessity of facing up to the labor shortage impending in the Great Lakes region when the "baby bubble" enters the labor force pipeline. In 1980 the age groups 20-24 and 15-19 had more than five million people each, but the groups aged 5-9 and 0-4 had only four million (Figure 6). The number of new workers who will enter the labor force will drop from a million a year, which was the norm in the 1980s, to only 800,000 a year in the 1990s unless the region attracts significant numbers of in-migrants.

Estimates of migration in the United States can be based on census survival techniques, on "components of population change," or on previous state of residence, but all three point in the same direction: the six Great Lakes states are losing more migrants than they are gaining.

The census survival technique is based on the assumption that people will be ten years older when a census is taken ten years later. For example, the number of people aged 25-29 in a given area in 1980 should be the same as the number of people aged 15-19 in the same area in 1970 unless some of these people had moved away or died, or unless people of this age group had moved into the area. This technique indicates that the six Great Lakes states actually

TABLE 3

Women as a percentage of the employed labor force, Great Lakes states, 1950-1980

	1950	1960	1970	1980
Illinois	30.2	34.6	39.7	45.9
Indiana	27.0	32.8	38.8	45.5
Michigan	26.8	32.8	38.3	46.5
Minnesota	27.4	33.3	39.8	45.4
Ohio	28.2	32.9	38.0	44.9
Wisconsin	27.3	32.4	39.1	45.6
Six states	28.2	33.3	38.9	45.6

SOURCES: *Census of Population: 1950.* Volume II, Part 1, Table 73; *Census of Population: 1960,* Volume I, Part 1, Table 119; *1970 Census of Population. General Social and Economic Characteristics. United States Summary* (PC(I)_CI), Table 161; *1980 Census of Population,* Volume I, Chapter C, Part 1, Table 240.

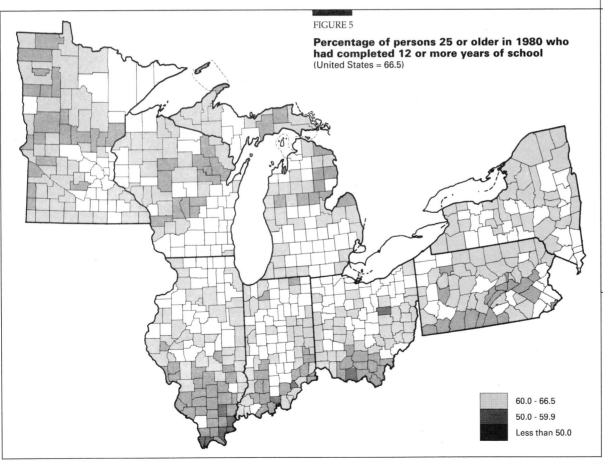

FIGURE 5

Percentage of persons 25 or older in 1980 who had completed 12 or more years of school
(United States = 66.5)

60.0 - 66.5
50.0 - 59.9
Less than 50.0

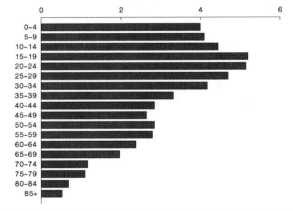

FIGURE 6

Number of persons in the Great Lakes region in five-year age groups, 1980-81
(millions of persons)

did enjoy a net in-migration of 25,000 to 30,000 young adults aged 25 to 34 each year in the 1950s and 1960s, but this stream has dried up since 1970.

In response to popular demand, the Census Bureau uses the best data available to prepare annual estimates of the components of population change (births, deaths, and net migration) for each state and county in the United States, perhaps against its better judgment, because many of the data are not as good as one might wish, and some

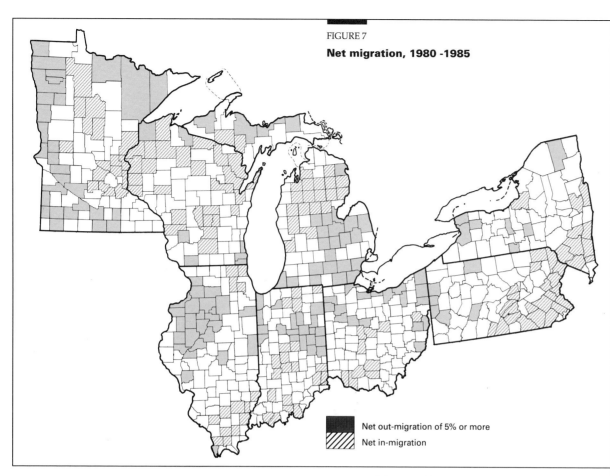

FIGURE 7

Net migration, 1980 -1985

■ Net out-migration of 5% or more

▨ Net in-migration

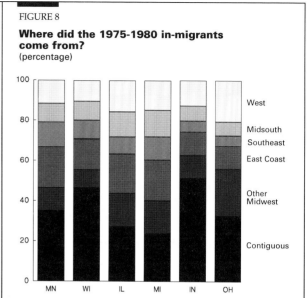

FIGURE 8

Where did the 1975-1980 in-migrants come from?
(percentage)

West

Midsouth

Southeast

East Coast

Other Midwest

Contiguous

MN   WI   IL   MI   IN   OH

are little better than educated guesses. These estimates indicate that the six Great Lakes states suffered a net out-migration of 1,556,000 people, or 3.4 percent of their 1980 population, between 1980 and 1985. Most counties in these states lost outmigrants during this period, and scattered groups of counties lost more than five percent (Figure 7). The counties that lost most heavily are in older industrial areas as well as in agricultural areas, and apart from heavy out-migration they seem to have little in common. The counties that attracted migrants are mainly in retirement areas, although a few suburban counties also did very well.

Data on previous place of residence are based on a question on the long form of the census questionnaire (which is completed by only twenty percent of the population) that asks people where they lived five years ago. The resulting state of previous residence data indicate that 2.6 million residents of the six Great Lakes states in 1980 had lived in another state in 1975, and 3.8 million people had moved from these six states to another state since 1975, for a net loss of 1.2 million people. Most migrants to the Great Lakes states between 1975 and 1980 were homegrown, so to speak, because they came from contiguous states or from other states in the Midwest (Figure 8). Chicago, Detroit, and the cities of Ohio attracted migrants from the East Coast and the South; many of the migrants from the South were black.

More than half of those who migrated out of the Great Lakes states between 1975 and 1980 moved to retirement areas in Florida, Texas, the rest of the South, California, Arizona, and the rest of the West (Figure 9). People from the eastern Great Lakes states were more likely to head for the South, those from the western Great Lakes states for the West. It seems that members of the baby boom and baby bubble age groups are not migrating to the Great Lakes states, while out-migration is depleting the older age groups.

The age groups of the Great Lakes region in 1980-81 seem to fall into three fairly distinct size categories (Figure 6): the seven groups under 35 had four to five million people each, the four groups between 40 and 60 had two-and-a-half to three million each, and the groups over 60 tailed off rapidly. These categories are related to the four major stage-of-life moves made by most middle-class Americans. The first move, and perhaps the most traumatic, is when they leave home and go off to college or to military service. The second is when they move to the city and take their first job. The third is when they move to the suburbs, buy a house, and start raising a family. The fourth is when they retire and move to the Sunbelt or to "the lake." Between the ages of 30 and 60 they seem to stay put; individuals often move, of course, but there are no massive migrations comparable to the four major stage-of-life moves.

By 1990 most of the baby boom generation had moved to the suburbs, where presumably they have settled down until they retire. They have bought and furnished their first homes, which they may have trouble selling when they decide to trade up, because the smaller numbers of people in the baby bubble age groups behind them will probably soften the demand for starter homes. The baby boomers should keep automobile dealers happy, however, because they are in the peak years for buying cars, and they are also at the age when most Americans traditionally start saving more of their income.

It seems rather journalistic to talk about an "aging" population when the baby boomers are just reaching maturity and half the people of the Great Lakes states are still under 30, but nevertheless the median age in the six states, as in the nation, is slowly inching upward. In most of the six states the median age is within two years of the national norm, and the exceptions are a fairly mixed lot (Figure 10). They include counties in areas that are perceived to lack economic opportunities for young people, such as older industrial areas, coal-mining areas, and agricultural areas where the size

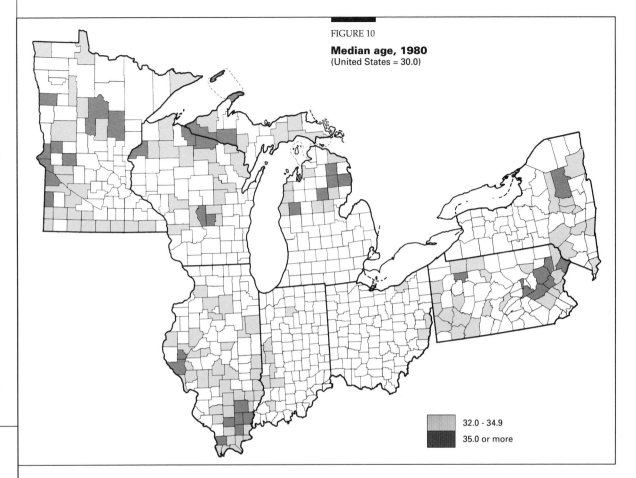

FIGURE 10

Median age, 1980
(United States = 30.0)

32.0 - 34.9

35.0 or more

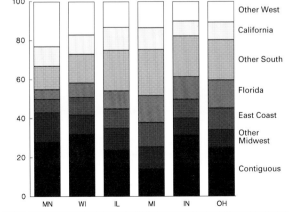

FIGURE 9

Where did the 1975-1980 out-migrants go?
(percentage)

of farms is increasing rapidly, but they also include many counties in the recreation, resort, and retirement belt along the southern margin of the Great North Woods.

Recreation has been one of the major growth industries of the Great Lakes region since World War II, thanks to shorter work weeks, longer vacations, more disposable income, and the environmental movement. Better highways and better automobiles have made distant areas more easily accessible, and water bodies have been especially attractive, whether rivers in Michigan, the innumerable glacial lakes of Wisconsin and Minnesota, or the Great Lakes themselves. The southern margin of the Great North Woods has become one of the

nation's premier recreation, resort, and retirement areas (Figure 11). The developing resort areas have attracted entrepreneurs and people of above average income, and these areas boast a host of new jobs in hotels and motels, eating places, gift shops, amusement parks, and a variety of recreational activities. Many of these are service jobs that employ young people and women, and they do not pay very well.

The resort season, which once lasted only from Memorial Day to Labor Day, has been stretched by the development of winter sports activities, such as snowmobiling and skiing. Lengthening the resort season has been a boon to resort area businesses, which no longer have to make their entire year's income in a mere fourteen hectic weeks, but it has brought them into head-on collision with semester-system colleges, which must start classes before Labor Day in order to schedule exams before Christmas, thereby depriving resort areas of much of their cheap labor just before one of their busiest weekends.

Many recreation and resort areas have also become havens for retired people, whose numbers have burgeoned because of the greater longevity of the population and increased early retirement. Many retired people are "snowbirds;" they can afford a summer place in the Great Lakes region and a winter place in a milder clime to which they flee before the first flakes start to fly. Establishing resident status in another state also enables them to avoid some of the highest state income tax rates in the nation. The decennial census of population greatly underestimates the number of retired people of the Great Lakes region, because it is taken on the first of April, when the snowbirds are still in the South. A tally of Social Security beneficiaries in December also gives a poor estimate of the number of retired people, because many snowbirds have already fled for the winter, but even so some of the highest percentages of Social Security beneficiaries are in the resort and retirement belt along the southern edge of the Great North Woods (Figure 12). Not surprisingly, the percentages of beneficiaries are highest where the median age also is highest (Figure 10).

The pensions of retired people "import" income that generates jobs in construction, real estate, retail trade, legal services, health services, social services, water supply, sewers, and garbage collection. Even when they are soaking up the southern sun retired people must employ caretakers and maintenance people. The jobs generated by retired people have enabled retirement areas to retain their own young people, who hitherto have had to move to cities in search of work, and to attract young people from other areas. These new jobs have had an important multiplier effect, and this multiplier effect has helped to improve the quality of health services and social services, which are notoriously poor in most rural areas.

Preliminary results from the 1990 census of population seem to verify estimates that the

population of the six Great Lakes states has stabilized and is starting to decline. Since World War II population growth has been concentrated in three types of areas: the suburbs, retirement areas, and towns that have state universities. The metropolitan fringes and retirement areas probably will continue to grow, but they attract people mainly from within the region rather than from outside it. The cities of the region traditionally have grown by recruiting young people from the surplus in rural areas, because the fertility of the urban white majority has been below the replacement level, but the size and fertility of the rural population now has fallen so low that the cities will have to look to other sources for their future growth. Much of their growth will

depend on the higher fertility levels of minority groups and on immigration, and they must compete for new immigrants with areas that are better situated to recruit them.

During the 1980s the United States admitted even more immigrants than in the peak years of European immigration between 1900 and 1910, but most of the new Americans in the 1980s were Hispanic and Asian rather than European. The majority have remained in interceptor areas along the west, east, and Gulf coasts, although some have moved to large metropolitan areas in the interior. Ontario has prospered in part because Canada has long had an open door to immigrants, and because the province of Quebec is Francophone. Toronto at-

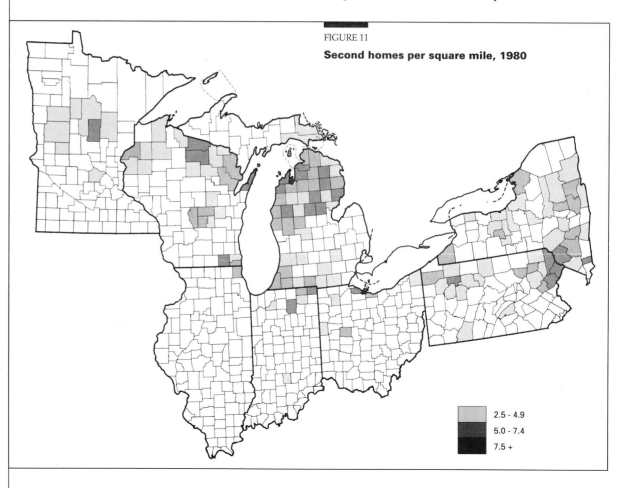

FIGURE 11

Second homes per square mile, 1980

2.5 - 4.9

5.0 - 7.4

7.5 +

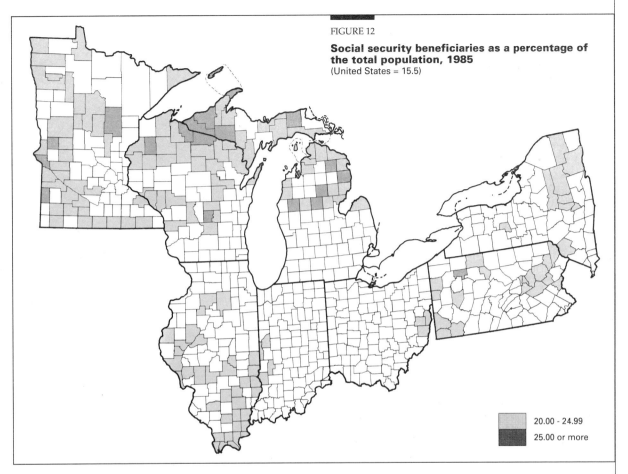

FIGURE 12

Social security beneficiaries as a percentage of the total population, 1985
(United States = 15.5)

20.00 - 24.99

25.00 or more

of the economic preeminence and political clout they once enjoyed. The old manufacturing belt has become the rust belt, the frost belt, and it has lost much of its comparative advantage to areas on the coasts that are perceived as nicer places to live, especially by skilled workers in high technology industries.

The future growth of the population of the United States will depend on immigration more than on natural increase, and many of the immigrants will be people from Asia and Latin America who fracture English in a different way than Midwesterners. The growth of population in the Great Lakes states will depend on the ability of their people to cope with their new reduced status. They have long assumed that their region was the continental heartland, but now they will have to learn how to sell it, and they will have to recruit the immigrants and the entrepreneurs who will help them to improve on what it has been and to dream of what it might become.

REFERENCES

Calvin L. Beale, *The Revival of Population Growth in Nonmetropolitan America*, ERS 605 (Washington: U. S. Department of Agriculture, Economic Research Service, 1975).

_____, "Americans Heading for the Cities, Once Again," *Rural Development Perspectives*, Vol. 4, No. 3 (July 1988), pp. 206.

Gerald Carlino, "From Centralization to Deconcentration: Economic Activity Spreads Out," *Business Review* (Federal Reserve Bank of Philadelphia), May/June 1982, pp. 15-25.

Theodore M. Crone, "The Aging of America: Impacts on the Marketplace and Workplace," *Business Review* (Federal Reserve Bank of Philadelphia), May/June 1990, pp. 3-13.

John Fraser Hart, "The Changing Distribution of the American Negro," *Annals of the Association of American Geographers*, Vol. 50, No. 3 (September 1960), pp. 242-266.

_____, "Facets of the Geography of Population in the Midwest," *Journal of Geography*, Vol. 85, No. 5 (September/October 1986), pp. 201-211.

_____, "Small Towns and Manufacturing," *Geographical Review*, Vol. 78, No. 3 (July 1988), pp. 272-287.

William J. Kahley, "Measuring Interstate Migration," *Economic Review* (Federal Reserve Bank of Atlanta), Vol. 75, No. 2 (March/April 1990), pp. 26-40.

Steven Strongin, "Services Also Slow Down," *Chicago Fed Letter*, No. 36 (August 1990), pp. 1-3.

William A. Testa and David R. Allardice, "Bidding for Business," *Chicago Fed Letter*, No. 16 (December 1988), pp. 1-3.

tracts many newcomers who leapfrog Montreal to get to the largest English-speaking city in Canada. The municipality of Toronto routinely sends out property tax notices in six languages—English, French, Chinese, Italian, Greek, and Portuguese.

If one may be so bold as to generalize about the values and beliefs of more than forty million people, the residents of the Great Lakes states consider themselves superior to other people, especially foreigners, but they can no longer afford that luxury. The region's rich endowment of soil, mineral, and forest resources helped it to prosper for more than a century. The people who settled it had to work diligently to develop these resources, to be sure, but they have taken the prosperity of the region as a tribute to their own diligence, and they

have complacently accepted full credit for the rich resource base that nature provided.

Hard work virtually ensured success. People have had to take few risks, and they have been wary of risk-takers, whether they be called speculators, gamblers, developers, or entrepreneurs. Sons have taken over the family farm or the family business from their fathers, and they have continued to do things in the ways that have worked so well. They have eagerly latched onto technological innovations that have lightened their labors and loaded their pockets, but they have been cautious and conservative about accepting new ideas.

The people of the Great Lakes region have been comfortable with themselves and their region, and it is hard for them to realize that they have lost some

Chapter 4

Interregional Competitiveness and Diversification

ROBERT H. SCHNORBUS, SENIOR BUSINESS ECONOMIST AND RESEARCH OFFICER, FEDERAL RESERVE BANK OF CHICAGO

DAVID D. WEISS, ASSOCIATE ECONOMIST, FEDERAL RESERVE BANK OF CHICAGO

The Great Lakes economy has been strengthened in the 1980s by the reemergence of manufacturing as a driving force in the U.S. economy and by the increasing competitiveness of those industries in the Great Lakes, relative to other regions. In the process of becoming more competitive, the structure of the Great Lakes economy has evolved into a more diversified economy than existed in prior years. Yet, compared to other regions, the Great Lakes remains the least diversified of any regional economy.

The role of the Great Lakes region as the industrial heartland of the nation has been diminishing at an alarming rate for many years. Since the beginning of the 1970s, the region has lost nearly one-quarter of its once commanding 37 percent share of the nation's production of goods. Even within the Great Lakes economy, the importance of manufacturing to the total output of goods and services has been declining in every state except Wisconsin (Figure 1). This trend toward deindustrialization, whether measured by the importance of the region's manufacturing sector to the nation or to the regional economy, is a serious concern to policy makers responsible for stimulating regional industrial growth. At a time when the Free Trade Agreement will be opening the Great Lakes to increased competition from Canadian manufacturers, policy makers must weigh the merits of attempting to expand the region's dependence on manufacturing against nurturing new industries outside of the manufacturing sector. If the right choices are made, the region's slow spiraling decline may finally end. Unfortunately, policy makers seldom have an analytical framework on which to base their choices.

Some insights into how the Great Lakes economy is changing and, thus, how policy makers might shape development strategies can be gained by comparing structural change and diversification of the Great Lakes economy relative to other regions of the nation. The Great Lakes is not alone in experiencing deindustrialization. New England and the Mideast regions have also shared in a trend away from a manufacturing-based economy. However, even regions that are industrializing their economies share one thing in common with the Great Lakes—their industrial structures over time are becoming more like the nation's. While each region has a distinctive economy, regions are diver-

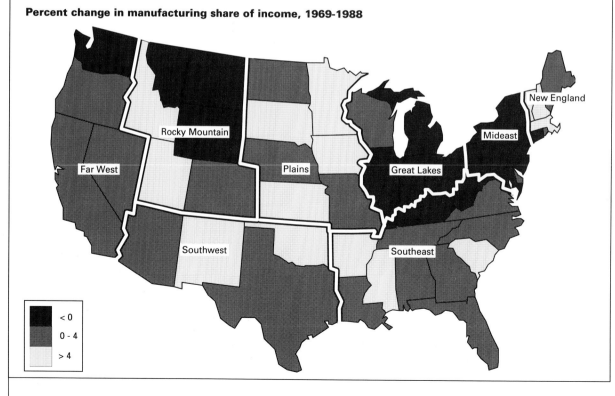

FIGURE 1

Percent change in manufacturing share of income, 1969-1988

sifying their economies. How have the Great Lakes' industrial structure and competitiveness of individual sectors shaped the direction and pace of structural change and diversification?

Structural differences among regions

As the image of an "industrial heartland" would suggest, the structure of the Great Lakes economy has been dominated by manufacturing activity. Although this concentration in manufacturing conceals a diversity of economies among the states within the region, there is far greater diversity among regions. Using nonfarm income shares of

TABLE 1

Sectors of specialization by state

1970	Illinois	Indiana	Michigan	Ohio	Wisconsin
Agricultural services					
Mining					
Construction					
Nondurable goods	S			S	HS
Durable goods	HS	HS	HS	HS	HS
Transportation and public utilities	S				
Wholesale trade	HS				
Retail trade					S
Finance, insurance and real estate	S				
Services					
Government					

1988	Illinois	Indiana	Michigan	Ohio	Wisconsin
Agricultural services					
Mining					
Construction					
Nondurable goods	S	HS		HS	HS
Durable goods	S	HS	HS	HS	HS
Transportation and public utilities	HS	S			
Wholesale trade	HS				
Retail trade					
Finance, insurance and real estate	HS				
Services					
Government					

Key: S = less than 10% above U.S. average.
HS = 10% or more above U.S.

TABLE 2

Sectors of specialization by region

1970	New England	Mideast	Great Lakes	Plains	Southeast	Southwest	Rocky Mountain	Far West
Agricultural services				HS	HS	HS	HS	HS
Mining					HS	HS	HS	
Construction	S			S	S	HS	HS	
Nondurable goods	S	HS			HS			
Durable goods	HS		HS					
Transportation and public utilities		S		HS		S	HS	
Wholesale trade		S		HS		HS	S	
Retail trade				HS	S	S	HS	S
Finance, insurance and real estate	S	S						
Services	HS	HS						HS
Government					HS	HS	HS	HS

1988	New England	Mideast	Great Lakes	Plains	Southeast	Southwest	Rocky Mountain	Far West
Agricultural services	HS			S	S		S	HS
Mining					HS	HS	HS	
Construction	HS				S	S		S
Nondurable goods		S	HS	HS	HS			
Durable goods	HS		HS					S
Transportation and public utilities				HS	HS	S	HS	
Wholesale trade	S	S	HS					
Retail trade	S				S	S	S	S
Finance, insurance and real estate	HS	HS						
Services	S	HS						HS
Government					HS	HS	S	

Key: S = less than 10% above U.S. average.
HS = 10% or more above U.S.

the eleven major industrial sectors in 1988 (most recent data available), structural differences among regions can be identified. Regional specialization of a sector occurs when the share of a particular sector in a regional economy is greater than that sector's share of the national economy.

The Great Lakes economy is currently specialized in two major sectors—durable and nondurable goods manufacturing. Both sectors might be characterized as representing a high degree of specialization, that is, the shares of income in these two regional sectors are more than 10 percent higher than the sector's share for the nation as a whole. Of the two sectors, durable goods manufacturing is by far the most important. For example, over 20 percent of the region's income is derived from this sector, compared to only 13 percent nationwide. Put in a somewhat different perspective, 13 percent of the region's income comes from producing the durable goods needed by the region (using the nation as the norm). Thus, the difference between what is consumed internally and produced in total (i.e., the remaining 7 percent) can be attributed to producing durable goods that are exported to other regions and nations. The 7 percent coming from exports is larger than the share of income derived from half of the remaining sectors in the region and almost as large as the total share of the nondurable goods sector. Manufacturing activity, especially in the production of steel, autos, and capital goods, clearly defines the Great Lakes economy.

With the exception of Illinois, industrial structures of the Great Lakes states deviate little from the regional average (Table 1). Led by Michigan, with 28 percent of its income generated in that sector alone, each of the five states displays a specialization in durable goods manufacturing. Michigan's high degree of concentration in durable goods leaves little room for the state to be specialized in any other sector. The other four states show additional specialization in nondurable manufacturing, but surprisingly little else. Among the five states, only Illinois has managed to develop an economic specialization outside of manufacturing.

Illinois has an economic specialization in transportation and public utilities, wholesale trade, and finance, insurance and real estate. Largely due to its transportation network, warehousing infrastructure, and commodity markets, Chicago serves the role of "merchant" to the rest of the region, exporting its business-related services throughout the Great Lakes states. Indeed, Illinois has an industrial structure more similar to New England—the epitome of the Yankee trader—than to the Great Lakes region.

In fact, every other region of the nation has a broader base of specialization than the Great Lakes (as shown in Table 2). Each region of the nation has at least two industries in which it is highly specialized, and each has two or more additional industries in which it has at least some degree of specialization. For example, both New England and the Southeast have a high degree of specialization in four industries and a low degree of specialization in three additional industries. Even the sparsely populated Plains and Rocky Mountain regions have avoided having their economic fortunes concentrated in such a narrow range of industries as the Great Lakes.

Despite greater diversity than the Great Lakes, all regions have retained distinctive economies. The Mideast, reflecting the dominance of New York City

and (to a lesser extent) Philadelphia, is clearly a service economy, with a high degree of specialization in financial institutions and services industries. Still the Mideast retains some specialization in nondurables and wholesale trade. The Far West has a high degree of specialization in sectors on both the goods- and the service-producing sides of its economy, as well as two sectors with low levels of specialization. Both New England and the Southeast have above-average concentrations of income in seven of the eleven industrial sectors. However, New England has more sectors with specialization in the service-producing side of its economy, while the Southeast has more specialization on the goods-producing side of its economy. The Plains tends to be linked to agriculturally related activities, ranging from agricultural services to food processing. Finally, the Southwest and Rocky Mountains reflect both regions' rich oil and other mineral resources.

The specialization at the sector level fails to reveal the scope of diversity that exists among regions at the more detailed industry level. The durable goods sector in the Great Lakes, for example, is entirely different from the durable goods sector in New England. Yet, one need not display a mountain of detail in order to identify a region's key industries. By going down to the two-digit level of industrial classification, the regions can be well defined by their top five industries of specialization (Table 3). In the Great Lakes region four of its top five specialties can be found in durable goods manufacturing, which essentially defines its in-

dustrial complex of steel, autos, and machine tools. The Far West's distinct association with Hollywood, Boeing, and mineral resources can also easily be identified in this fashion. The Plains' resources are directed towards the processing and handling of food. Both the Southwest and the Rocky Mountain regions are heavily focused on natural resources, reflected in their specialization in mining. The Southeast centers on the nation's tobacco, textile, and furniture industries. And the presence of Wall Street and Washington, D.C. is reflected in the Mideast specialization in security brokers and museums. Only New England, which hosts so many specialized sectors, fails to be suitably represented by its top five industries (however, the presence of Hartford, Connecticut emerges with the region's sixth most specialized industry—insurance carriers).

TABLE 3

Industrial specialization by region: Top 5 rankings

New England

Fisheries
Leather and leather products
Misc. manufacturing
Instruments and related products
Educational services

Mideast

Securities & commodities
  brokers and services
Local and interurban passenger transit
Educational services
Museums, botanical, zoological gardens
Other financial, insurance, & real estate

Great Lakes

Motor vehicles and equipment
Primary metals
Fabricated metal
Rubber and misc. plastics
Machinery except electrical

Plains

Pipelines except natural gas
Railroad transportation
Metal mining
Leather and leather products
Food and kindred products

Southeast

Tobacco manufacturers
Textile mill products
Coal mining
Forestry
Furniture and fixtures

Southwest

Oil and gas extraction
Pipelines except natural gas
Metal mining
Petroleum and coal products
Heavy construction contractors

Rocky Mountains

Metal mining
Coal mining
Nonmetallic minerals except fuels
Oil and gas extraction
Railroad transportation

Far West

Motion pictures
Transportation equipment
  except motor vehicles
Fisheries
Forestry
Lumber and wood products

For virtually every region, the top five industries have dominated since at least the beginning of the 1970s. If regions have not lost their historical identity, how have they been changing over time? Have they been building on their economic strengths and becoming more specialized, or have they moved toward a more balanced economy?

Structural change in the 1970s and 1980s

Industrial structures of regions are not etched in stone; economic forces from within and from outside the region change how the region's resources are allocated in the production of goods and services for both internal consumption and for export. Fundamental changes to structure can take decades or more to occur. But minor shifts are continuously occurring as an essential part of the evolutionary process of change. Patterns of change among regions provide some insights into the future structure of regions.

The structure of the Great Lakes economy has hardly gone untouched by the forces of change. In some respects, the region has been following a pattern similar to all regions. Consider, for example, how the Great Lakes' industrial structure of 1970 differs from what it is today. Twenty years ago, durable goods manufacturing was not only the largest sector in the Great Lakes region, but the only sector in which it held any kind of economic specialization. Even now that the services industry has surpassed durable goods manufacturing as a share of total income, the region is still not specialized in services. However, the region has seen the emergence of its second sector of specialization—nondurable goods manufacturing.

A broadening specialization of the region's industrial base to include both durables and nondurables would seem an obvious direction for the Great Lakes region to take—the region has built upon its historic strengths. But, while some regions have followed a similar pattern of altering their structures by building on their strengths, others have changed in entirely different ways. For example, while the Great Lakes was expanding within manufacturing, the Southeast was adding a new specialization in transportation and public utilities, perhaps reflecting the emergence of Atlanta

as a major airline hub. At the same time, the Far West was shifting from service-related sectors to goods-producing sectors. As the Far West has grown rapidly (it now represents roughly one-sixth of the national economy), it appears to have become less dependent on government services, while developing a specialization in construction and durable goods production in the 1980s compared to the 1970s. New England made the biggest adjustment, however, developing new specializations in both manufacturing and service-related sectors. In

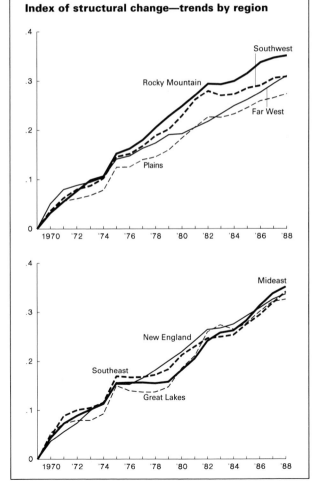

FIGURE 2

Index of structural change—trends by region

1970, New England was highly specialized in only two sectors (durables and services) and had some degree of specialization in three other sectors. But by 1988, New England was highly specialized in four sectors and had some degree of specialization in three others.

Among the four remaining regions, two—the Rocky Mountains and the Southwest—substantially reduced the number of sectors in which they had previously developed specializations. In 1970, the Rocky Mountains had a high degree of specialization in six sectors—three in both goods-producing and service-producing activities. By 1988, the region had lost its specialization in nondurable goods manufacturing and wholesale trade. And of the remaining five sectors, it was reduced to only two (mining and transportation) that qualified as highly specialized sectors. The Southwest also began 1970 with specialization in seven of the eleven sectors, with five having a high degree of specialization. By 1988, the region had lost two of its specialized sectors (one in both the goods-producing and service-producing activities), and of its five remaining sectors only two were highly specialized. In both cases, the high-growth years during the "energy boom" of the 1970s appear to have given way to the "energy bust" years of the 1980s, accompanied by a decline in resources devoted to construction and trade activities relative to the nation.

The pace of structural change

Industrial transformation among regions proceeded at different rates, which seems to bear little relationship to their structures in 1970 (Figure 2). For example, the two fastest changing regions, Mideast and Rocky Mountains, could not have been more different in their structural makeup. The Mideast region in 1970 was highly specialized in nondurable goods manufacturing and services, while the Rocky Mountains specialized in natural resources. The slowest changing region, the Plains, would seem to have far more in common with the Rocky Mountains region than with the Southwest region, which had the second slowest rate of change over the period. The Great Lakes ranked about in the middle (fifth out of eight regions). Interestingly,

TABLE 4

Rate of structural change—ranking by region

	1969-79	1979-88	1969-88
New England	5	3	3
Mideast	7	1	1
Great Lakes	8	2	5
Plains	6	7	8
Southeast	3	4	4
Southwest	2	8	7
Rocky Mountain	1	5	2
Far West	4	6	6

however, much of its structural change occurred in the 1980s, which was a period that began with two severe back-to-back recessions. Indeed, recessions have always been a catalyst for change.

Three regions experienced marked accelerations in their rates of structural change in the 1980s, relative to their rates in the 1970s—the Great Lakes, New England, and Mideast regions (Table 4). Among these three, New England's ranking shifted the least, moving from fifth in the 1970s to third in the 1980s, while the Great Lakes and Mideast regions shifted the most, moving from the bottom two positions to second and first places respectively among the eight regions. In general, the more mature and recession-vulnerable regions of the nation generated the greatest amount of internal change during the last decade. New England's sensitivity to recession was less obvious than in the Great Lakes because of its rapid growth in "high-tech" industries, where cyclical factors were swamped by a strong growth trend derived partly from the federal policy to re-arm the military.

These three regions were also the same regions that were undergoing deindustrialization within their own economies. In contrast, those regions that were in the process of industrializing appear to have slowed their rate of change during that decade. Moreover, the rate of change seems to be independent of the degree or type of economic specialization in the region at the beginning of the 1970s. In general, it would appear that industrialization is a much slower process than deindustrialization, and recessions could retard the one and accelerate the other.

At the more disaggregated industry level of activity, the underlying sources of structural change are surprisingly similar among regions. In virtually every state, the share of income from business services and health services made the greatest absolute contribution to structural change, increasing in every region between 1970 and 1988. Beyond those two industries, most regions altered their industrial structures by lowering their concentrations in their industries of specialization. The Great Lakes region, for example, sharply decreased its concentration in the industries that comprise its durable goods sector. A similar pattern was followed by each of the states in the Great Lakes region and by other regions as slow growing manufacturing industries were supplanted by faster growing service-related industries. Thus, while some regions have been able to build on past strengths, most regions were experiencing the same forces of economic change that have been shifting the national economy away from manufacturing and towards service-related industries over time.

Structural change within the Great Lakes region shows almost as much variety as the comparison among regions (Figure 3). Illinois and Ohio underwent the most structural change since 1970, well ahead of the other three states. But it was Illinois and Michigan, two states with different industrial structures, that showed the most acceleration in the rate of change from the 1970s to the 1980s. Wisconsin and Indiana, both of which typically had the strongest growth in employment and output among the Great Lakes states, experienced the least amount of structural change. In contrast, Illinois and Michigan were the two states with the weakest overall employment and output performance in the Great Lakes (and even the nation), particularly in the 1980s.

Structural change seems to be more a condition of economic weakness and decline than of economic vitality. But to what end is all this structural change directed? Clearly, from the above data, regional economies are not falling back on their historical strengths but are developing new specializations. But is this broader specialization making each region uniquely different in terms of its industrial structure, or is it making regions more homogeneous?

Diversification trends among regions

Diversification is a measure of income distribution relative to a national norm. The more like the nation the region is, the more diversified its economy is considered to be. The underlying assumption here is that the national economy has a "perfect" balance of industries in order to meet all its internal needs for goods and services. Diversification measures the difference between an industry's share of a regional economy and the national economy—the bigger the difference summed over all industries, the less diversified the region.

The single most striking feature among all the regions of the nation is their persistent trend toward diversification (as shown by the downward trend in the index of diversification, Figure 4). All eight regions ended the 1980s with more diversified

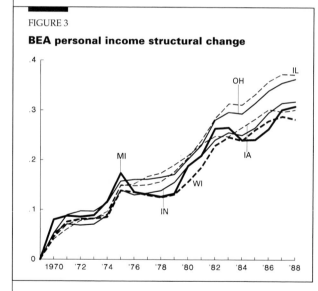

FIGURE 3

BEA personal income structural change

economies than the ones they started with in 1970s. The Great Lakes region began the 1970s as the least diversified economy in the nation and remained the least diversified throughout the 1970s and 1980s (Table 5). However, the Great Lakes region had the distinction of undergoing among the most diversification of any region. The Plains started the 1970s as the most diversified regional economy, but underwent the least amount of diversification of any region over the entire period of the 1970s and 1980s. The Southwest ended the 1980s with the most diversified regional economy. Although the Great Lakes underwent about as much diversification as the Southwest over the period, the Great Lakes region started with the least amount of diversification and thus remained less diversified than most other regions.

While the trend among regions was definitely toward diversification, three different patterns were followed. Some regions, such as the Great Lakes,

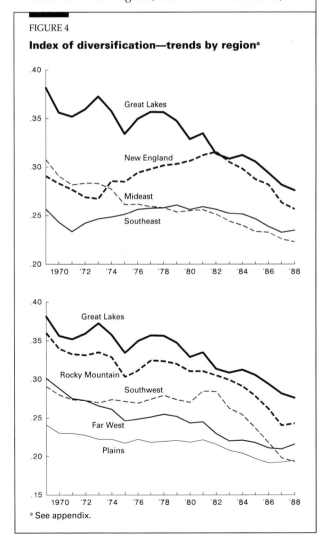

FIGURE 4

Index of diversification—trends by region[a]

a See appendix.

followed a fairly steady trend toward greater diversification. Some regions, notably the Southwest and Plains, seem to have flattened out during the late 1970s and early 1980s, but these were regions that began with relatively more diversification than most other regions. Finally, some regions, particularly New England and the Mideast, were actually moving towards less diversified economies for an extended period in the late 1970s and the early 1980s.

New England was perhaps an anomaly from the general trend toward diversification. The industries that appear to be contributing the most to the move toward increased specialization during the early 1980s were concentrated in construction and government. Given the rapid growth that New England was experiencing during that period, the growth in these two sectors may represent unbalanced or excessive growth. The demand for construction and greater government services may have been generated by real economic growth, but its rapid pace was not sustainable. Many of the current problems in the region may have begun during this period. Weakening property values in the 1990s may be the result of overbuilding and unsustainable levels of government spending in the 1980s.

The source of much of the Great Lakes' diversification can be found in two states—Ohio and Michigan (Figure 5). Michigan began the 1970s with by far the least diversified economy in the region. While it also ended the 1980s with the least diversified economy within the region, Michigan had moved most rapidly toward diversification. Michigan's high degree of specialization in durable goods manufacturing would seem to make it a logical candidate for substantial diversification. But Michigan is interesting because its rate of structural change was not that distinctive. What change did occur was in the right industries to generate diversification in the region, relative to the structural changes that were occurring at the national level.

Although much less extreme than Michigan, Ohio was a major contributor to the region's diversification. Ohio was about average for a Great Lakes state with respect to its degree of diversification in 1970. By the end of the 1980s, the state had moved toward the lower end of the ranking in terms of diversification. Thus, while it was less heavily

TABLE 5

Comparisons of diversification—ranking by region[a]

	Degrees of diversification		Rate of diversification
	1969	1988	1969-88
New England	5	2	2
Mideast	7	4	1
Great Lakes	1	1	7
Plains	8	7	3
Southeast	3	5	4
Southwest	6	8	6
Rocky Mountain	2	3	8
Far West	4	6	5

[a]1 represents the least diversified or the least change in diversification.

specialized in manufacturing industries than Michigan, Ohio was able to accomplish as much improvement in its diversity as Michigan.

At the other extreme, Wisconsin started the 1970s with an economy almost as diversified as Ohio's, but retained the same degree of diversity throughout the 1970s and 1980s. Its structural change was slow, changing in lock step with changes in industrial mix at the national level. Structural change had a neutral effect on the

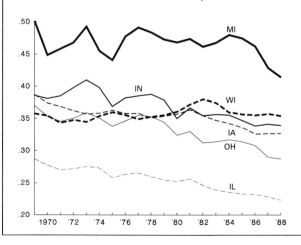

FIGURE 5

Index of diversification—trends by state

Wisconsin economy, leaving it as much different than the nation as in 1970.

Of the final two states, Illinois remained highly diversified and Indiana remained relatively specialized. That Illinois should retain its broad base of specialized industries over the period is less surprising than the fact that Indiana has failed to diversified away from its historic specializations of steelmaking and auto parts supplier. Despite impressive growth of service-related industries in the Indianapolis area, Indiana has made little progress in diversifying its economy relative to the nation. Part of the reason may be found in the decision to invest heavily in modernizing steel mills in the Gary area, thereby concentrating the industry's production capacity in the central part of the nation. Whether Indiana will be better off being tied to the steel and auto industries than by being more broadly diversified will depend on how successful those industries are in capturing market share against global competitors. If these industries fail to keep pace with market growth, their importance to the state economy will fade and other more competitive industries will take their place. Ultimately, it is the competitive advantages that determine how much and how quickly a state or regional economy will diversify over time.

Competitive advantage and the diversification process

In order for structural change to lead to diversification in every region, some movement away from historical specializations must occur. The income growth from service-related industries in regions with below-average concentrations in service-related industries must grow at faster rates than in regions with high income concentrations in service-related industries. Similarly, regions with high concentrations of income from manufacturing industries, as in the case of the Great Lakes, must have lower rates of growth in their industries of specialization than in regions that are not specialized in manufacturing industries. Thus, some regions must be industrializing while others are deindustrializing—which is exactly what has been happening in the last two decades.

The key to a regional industry's growth performance relative to its national counterpart is its competitive advantage. Historically, competitive advantage in manufacturing has been associated with such factors as location of natural resources and high transportation costs. Such locational advantages explain much of the Great Lakes specialization in the durable goods industry, especially steel with its access to iron ore in Minnesota and coal in West Virginia and Pennsylvania. Over a shorter time horizon, competitive advantage may be associated with relatively low labor costs or high productivity, access to expanding markets, and desirable amenities (such as warm climate, good schools, and cultural activities). Agglomerations of manufacturing industries lowered the transportation costs of acquiring intermediate components and basic materials.

Both long-term and short-term competitive advantages can gradually deteriorate. While low labor costs may have at one time attracted manufacturing industries to the Great Lakes, high labor costs today are contributing to the decline in the region's manufacturing sectors. Similarly, the introduction of new technologies can weaken historical competitive advantages. For example, the introduction of cheaper forms of transportation, such as interstate highway systems, can reduce the advantage of locating near markets or natural resources. Less is known about competitive advantages among services. Certainly, climate has benefited the development of retirement centers in Florida and the growth of the health and personal service industries to serve that population. But service-related industries, such as insurance and banking, have also sprung up in Indianapolis, Indiana, and Columbus, Ohio, which offer no self-evident advantage over a host of comparably sized cities around the nation. Nevertheless, above-average growth itself can serve as a measure of competitive advantage of a region and can serve as a guide to how competitiveness is contributing to diversification. Identifying the net contributions of competitive advantage from all industries to a region's growth, as distinct from industrial mix, reveals a pattern of negative contributions in the deindustri-

alizing parts of the nation and positive contributions in the industrializing parts of the nation (Table 6).

In the Great Lakes region, a lack of competitiveness has been detrimental to the growth of income. On average, over 80 percent of its industries were growing more slowly than their industry counterparts in other regions both in the 1970s and 1980s. In the 1970s, income losses due to competitive disadvantages offset the gains from having a favorable industrial structure. This cost the region $21 billion (not adjusted for inflation) in income that could have been earned in 1979 if only the region's industries had grown at the same rate as their counterparts nationally. Income would have been 6 percent higher than it was actually was in 1979 with the shortfall attributed to competitive disadvantages. Somewhat surprising, however, was the fact

---

TABLE 6

Net contributions to regional growth

	1970s		1980s	
	Competitive effects	Industrial mix effects	Competitive effects	Industrial mix effects
New England	--	-	++	+
Mideast	--	+	+	+
Great Lakes	--	+	--	-
Plains	+	-	--	-
Southeast	++	-	++	-
Southwest	++	+	-	-
Rocky Mountain	++	+	--	-
Far West	++	+	++	+

Key: +, - = Net contribution (positive or negative) less than 10%.
++, -- = Net contribution 10% or more.

---

that primary metals and transportation equipment other than motor vehicles showed competitive strength during this period. By 1988, competitive disadvantages over the previous eight years cost the Great Lakes $57 billion (not adjusted for inflation). Otherwise, income would have been 11 percent higher than it was in 1988. The only industry to retain its competitive advantage from the 1970s was the relatively small apparel industry. Most of the other industries with a competitive advantage in the 1980s were linked to transportation services.

During the 1970s, only two other regions experienced income losses due to competitive disadvantages—New England and the Mideast. Both regions share with the Great Lakes some of the heaviest deindustrialization in the nation during the 1970s. The Mideast region was hardest hit, with income in 1979 20 percent below what it would have been if the region's industries had grown at the same pace as their national counterparts. Certainly, part of that loss was the rapid decline of the steel industry in Pennsylvania (particularly Pittsburgh) and its supporting industries, such as fabricated metals, machinery, and mining. In contrast to the Great Lakes, however, only about half of the industries in the Mideast region were hurt by competitiveness factors. Many industries on the service side of its economy managed to equal or exceed the growth achieved nationally by those industries. A good example may be the transformation of the Pittsburgh economy from a steel town to a regional financial center. While not as large as it once was relative to other cities in the nation, Pittsburgh has found a way to offset some of the loss of its steel exports by exporting financial services.

New England was an exception during the 1970s in that its overall competitive disadvantages were amplified by an unfavorable mix of industries. New England's income in 1979 would have been about 10 percent higher without its competitive problems and another 1 percent higher if its mix of industries had not been weighted towards the more mature, slow growing industries nationally. With over 75 percent of its industries suffering competitive problems, it is interesting to note the major sources of competitive strength in the New England economy—insurance carriers, instruments, electronic components, and transportation equipment excluding motor vehicles. The insurance carrier industry has been the traditional strength of the region. But in the remaining three industries were the underpinnings of the "Massachusetts Miracle"—the emergence of the defense and "high-tech" industries. Even in these industries, the contribution of the region's competitive advantage was small compared to the contribution that industrial mix made. In other words, much of the industries' growth in New England must be

attributed simply to the fact that those industries were growing rapidly in the nation and New England was able to keep up with that growth.

As the nation took on the image of a bi-coastal economy in the 1980s, the Plains and Rocky Mountain regions joined the Great Lakes as the only net losers from competitive disadvantage. However, the role of competitiveness diminished substantially from the 1970s for most regions (Table 7). For example, the Rocky Mountain region had nearly 90

TABLE 7

Proportion of regional industries with competitive advantage

	1970s	1980s
New England	21 %	70 %
Mideast	4	50
Great Lakes	18	17
Plains	49	24
Southeast	84	30
Southwest	88	43
Rocky Mountain	89	36
Far West	79	24

---

percent of its industries growing faster than their national counterparts in the 1970s, but less than 40 percent in the 1980s. The exceptions were the New England and the Mideast regions, which went from among the weakest in overall competitiveness to among the strongest.

For the Great Lakes, virtually all of the industries that were competitively weak in the 1970s continued to be weak in the 1980s (Table 8). Among the industries that were competitively strong in the 1970s, only apparel in the nondurables sector and transportation services continued to show competitive strength in the 1980s. Other industries that emerged with competitive strengths were concentrated in two sectors: first, the nondurables sector, with lumber, leather, textiles, and furniture (consistent with the rise of the nondurables sector as an area of specialization) and second, the transportation sector, with air, water, and pipelines. In contrast, industries that lost their competitive advantage in the 1980s were from virtually every

sector of the region's economy—from health services to primary metals.

Within the Great Lakes region, Wisconsin was a notable exception to the dominance of competitive disadvantage among industries. Half of all of its industries were growing faster than their national counterparts during the 1970s and one-third were competitively strong in the 1980s. Moreover, one-third of the competitively strong industries in the 1980s carried their competitive strength over from the 1970s. Indeed, during the 1970s, Wisconsin was the only Great Lakes state where competitiveness made a positive contribution to economic growth.

Linking diversification with regional policy making

The role of a region's industrial competitiveness in diversifying its economy is intuitively straightforward. Holding everything else constant, if an industry in which the region is specialized is growing slower than its national counterpart, its share of the regional economy would decline relative to the industry's share of the national economy resulting in the region's economy being more diversified. Eventually, if the poor competitive performance continued, the industry could lose its specialization status. Similarly, if the region is nonspecialized in a particular industry that is growing faster in the region than in the nation, its share of the regional economy would rise relative to the nation. As the industry's share of the regional economy rises, it would also have the effect of diversifying the regional economy.

TABLE 8

Net contributions to state growth

	1970s		1980s	
	Competitive effects	Industrial mix effects	Competitive effects	Industrial mix effects
Illinois	--	+	--	+
Indiana	-	-	-	--
Michigan	-	+	--	--
Ohio	--	+	-	+
Wisconsin	+	+	-	-

Key: +, - = Net contribution (positive or negative) less than 10%.
      ++, -- = Net contribution 10% or more.

The process is more complex than suggested because both competitiveness and industrial mix interact to determine what industries contribute the most to a region's overall growth performance. In the case of the 1970s, the distribution of competitive advantages among regions was so skewed toward southern and western regions that competitive advantages *per se* could play only a minor role in regional diversification. That is, in the northeast quadrant of the nation, most industries were growing slower than their national counterparts. Whether an industry was highly specialized or highly nonspecialized, it was likely to be growing slower than the same industry in other regions. While below-average industry growth among specialized industries would move the region's industrial structure toward diversification, its nonspecialized industries, also with below-average growth, would be moving away from diversification. Regardless, whether the region achieved a more diversified economy would depend on relative competitive performance, that is, whether the slow-growing specialized industries were contributing less growth to the region than the slow-growing nonspecialized industries.

For policy makers seeking to diversify their regional economies, the primary objective is straightforward. Find ways to improve the competitive strengths of regional industries. The improvement can come from a direct subsidy that reduces operating costs, such as tax breaks or low-interest loans. Or, the improvement can come from an indirect subsidy, such as better roads and other infrastructure improvements. Although in both instances higher taxes to finance the subsidy can be detrimental to all firms in the region, the second case has the potential advantage of being accessible to many firms. Essentially, a competitive environment is created for everyone in the region. However, the benefits created by such a policy in terms of additional jobs and earnings become difficult, if not impossible, to measure. The first case has the advantage of being delivered only to selected firms where the returns to the policy can be measured in terms of additional jobs and earnings. The problem is to determine how to choose what firms are to receive the targeted benefits, or perhaps to find better ways of measuring indirect benefits.

To many regional policy makers, the widely touted goal of diversification means to move away from declining industries of the past and toward high-growth industries of the future. What can easily be lost in the process is the possibility that future growth industries may not have a competitive advantage in a particular region and will require heavy subsidization to survive, much less attain a competitive advantage against regions with a natural competitive advantage. And even that assumes that the policy makers are successful at forecasting what the high-growth industries of the future are going to be.

The goal of diversification itself is debatable. In its truest sense, diversification improves the chances of the region to grow at the national average. If a region already has a favorable mix of industries that on average are growing faster than the nation, diversification will mean moving toward slow-growth industries and slower overall growth for the region. Even regions with an unfavorable mix of industries may find high-growth industries bring undesirable traits with them, such as higher cyclical vulnerability for the region.

Thus, the objective of the policy maker must be shaped by multiple criteria that can rank the attractiveness of an industry. National growth rates of industries is one criterion by which industries can be ranked. Cyclical sensitivity is another criterion. Relative competitiveness within the region is a third possibility. Other criteria exist, but these three can illustrate how the selection process can work. Suppose that the policy maker wants to maximize growth, but also wants to minimize cyclical swings in the region's economy. The best combination of industries to target will be determined by a new ranking of industries derived from a weighted combination of each industry's rank by growth and cyclical sensitivity. The weights can vary subjectively, according to how much importance the policy maker places on a "recession-proof" economy. Or a policy maker can try to select competitively strong industries that are relatively cycle free. Again, it would be some weighted average of industries in the region with competitive strength and low cyclical sensitivity. Any number of separate criteria can be used to make the final selection of industries that will best meet the long-term objectives of the policy maker.

The structural change and diversification of a regional economy is a complex process with limited opportunities for intervention by policy makers. Each region is unique, undergoing its own internal changes leading to a common end—more balanced and self-sufficient regional economies. In the process of structural change and diversification, competitiveness is a critical element that must be factored into any policy consideration. The key to successful policy making is identifying and understanding a region's competitive advantages and trying to build upon those advantages.

APPENDIX 1

Diversification index

This is an annual income based diversification index. There are three subscripts, representing, location, industry and time:

$$\sum_i \left| (INC_{rit}/INC_{rTt}) - ((INC_{USit} - INC_{rit})/(INC_{USTt} - INC_{rTt})) \right|$$

Where INC = Income
       r   = region
       US   = United States
       i   = 2 digit SIC industry
       T   = total nonagricultural sector
       t   = year

The region is subtracted from the United States numbers so as not to bias the index towards large regions.

This index relates each industry's share of income to the national average. Having a share 1% below the industry's national average has an equivalent effect on the index as a share 1% above the national average. So if many of a region's industries are highly specialized or non specialized, then the index will be large. If most of a region's industries have a share of income close to the national average, then the index will be small. The possible range of the index is zero to two.

Location quotient

The location quotient is an annual measure of the concentration of a region's income relative to the United States. The three subscripts identify region, industry and time.

$$(INC_{rit}/INC_{rTt})/(INC_{USit}/INC_{USTt})$$

Where INC = Income
       r   = region
       US   = United States
       i   = industry
       T   = Total nonagricultural sector
       t   = year

If an industry's share of income is equivalent to the national share then the location quotient is equal to one. If an industry is concentrated in a region, its share of income in the region is larger than the industry's share of national income, then the location quotient is greater than one. If the industry is not concentrated in the region, then the location quotient is between zero and one.

Shift share analysis

Relative gain or loss is the actual change in jobs for an industry within a region minus the change that would have occurred if the industry had the same share of income and same growth rate as it did at the national level.

$$\text{Relative Loss} = GR_{ri} * INC_{ri0} - GR_{USi} * INCH_{ri0}$$

Where INC   = Income
       GR   = growth
       r   = region
       US   = United States
       i   = industry
       T   = total
       0   = beginning of period
       1   = end of period
       INCH = hypothetical income
       $INCH_{ri0}$ = $INC_{USi0} * (INC_{rT0}/INC_{UST0})$

Relative loss can be divided into three categories, competitive effect, industry mix effect and allocative effect, which sum to relative loss.

Competitive effects = $(GR_{ri} - GR_{USi})\, INCH_{ri0}$
Mix effect   = $(INC_{ri0} - INCH_{ri0}) * GR_{USi}$
Allocative effects   = $(GR_{ri} - GR_{USi}) * (INC_{ri0} - INCH_{ri0})$

In percentage growth rate terms

Relative loss   = $GR_{ri} - INCH_{ri0}/INC_{ri0}$
Competitive effect   = $(GR_{ri} - GR_{USi})\, INCH_{ri0}/INC_{ri0}$
Mix effect   = $(INC_{ri0} - INCH_{ri0}) * GR_{USi}/INC_{ri0}$
Allocative effect   = $(GR_{ri} - GR_{USi}) * (1 - INCH_{ri0}/INC_{ri0})$

Index of structural change

The structural change index is a cumulative measure of change based on 2 digit SIC income. The index is region specific and has two subscripts, the industry and year.

$$\sum_i \left| (INC_{it}/INC_{Tt}) - (INC_{i69}/INC_{T69}) \right|$$

Where INC = Income for the region
       i   = 2 digit SIC industry
       T   = total nonagricultural sector
       t   = year
       69   = base year

This index compares an industry's share of total income to its share at the beginning of the period (1969). The larger the absolute change in the share of income, the larger will be the industry's effect on the index. Both increases and decreases in the share increase the index.

Chapter 5

The Free Trade Agreement with Canada and the Great Lakes Economy

ERIC B. HARTMAN, SENIOR POLICY ANALYST, NORTHEAST-MIDWEST INSTITUTE

Two years into the Free Trade Agreement (FTA) between the United States and Canada, it remains hard to define the agreement's overall impact on the bilateral economic relationship. FTA implementation has gone fairly smoothly but has coincided with slowing growth and incipient recession in both countries. Many benefits of the agreement are prospective, since the phase-out of tariffs and some trade barriers will not be completed until 1998. So far, businesses on both sides of the border have responded favorably to the agreement, even seeking a speedup of the schedule for tariff removal. But the agreement comes in for criticism from Canadians who blame many economic dislocations on the FTA and from Americans who believe it has left substantial Canadian trade barriers intact.

The U.S.-Canada Free Trade Agreement (FTA), as it nears its second birthday, presents a paradox.

At the institutional, nuts-and-bolts level of tariff reduction, dispute settlement, and follow-up negotiations, the agreement that came into force on January 1, 1989, by and large appears to be a success. Canada's trade minister has noted that 99 percent of trade between the two countries since the FTA took effect has flowed unimpeded by trade disputes.[1] The U.S. trade negotiator responsible for most follow-up talks says the agreement "continues to work well."[2]

Yet neither government can demonstrate that the FTA so far has had the beneficial impact on bilateral trade that was confidently forecast when the agreement was signed. No one foresaw that the FTA's initial implementation and elaboration would coincide with a steep increase in Canadian interest rates, a commensurate rise in the value of the Canadian dollar versus the U.S. dollar, and the onset of an economic slowdown that was heading toward a full-blown recession in both countries during the latter half of 1990. With these fundamental economic forces skewing production, consumption, and investment decisions, the effect of the FTA, whether for good or ill, has been difficult to trace.

This difficulty has posed a problem for the agreement's supporters, especially in Canada. Critics of the current Canadian government's trade policy have been quick to condemn the agreement based on anecdotal evidence of economic hardship allegedly related to the FTA's implementation, and the government has not been able to marshal convincing macroeconomic evidence to show net economic benefits for Canada flowing from the FTA.

Meanwhile, on the American side, questions linger about the balance of benefits achieved in the agreement, given the substantial U.S. deficit in merchandise trade with Canada that persists under the FTA. This imbalance is concentrated in Canada's merchandise trade with the Great Lakes states, particularly in the motor vehicle industry, which is a mainstay of the regional economy.

Deepening bilateral integration

Although the agreement's advocates deserve some blame for overselling the FTA's potential as a short-term tonic for the North American economy, doubts about the agreement's impact should be kept in context.

The Free Trade Agreement comes on top of a bilateral economic relationship that was already the largest and one of the most open in the world. The United States and Canada are each other's largest trading partners. Bilateral merchandise trade in 1988, the year before the FTA took effect, already exceeded $150 billion, with U.S. exports of $71.6 billion and imports of $81.2 billion. U.S. bilateral exports were up 19.7 percent over the 1987 level, and Canadian exports rose 14.5 percent; total two-way trade was up 16.9 percent. Canada absorbed more than a fifth of U.S. exports; the United States absorbed about 70 percent of Canada's exports. Three-quarters of this bilateral merchandise trade was duty-free by 1988, even before the FTA began the phased elimination of all bilateral tariffs by 1998.

The first year under the FTA saw continued growth in U.S.-Canada trade, albeit at a slower pace than in 1988. U.S. exports to Canada rose 10 percent in 1989, to $78.8 billion; U.S. imports from Canada rose 8.4 percent, to $88.0 billion. Strong growth in U.S.-Canada trade helped propel Canada by the end of 1989 from ninth place (in 1979) to seventh place worldwide in both imports and exports and helped the United States retain its top global ranking in both categories.

In the first half of 1990, U.S. exports to Canada continued to increase, although at a much reduced rate of 5.5 percent. As growth in Canada's economy slumped sharply, U.S. imports from Canada stagnated, with preliminary reports for the first half of 1990 showing an actual decline of -0.2 percent. However, by September, monthly trade data began to show that the U.S. economy also was slowing down sharply and that Canada was beginning to benefit from the increasing price of its oil and gas exports due to the crisis over the August invasion of Kuwait by Iraq. The combined effect of recession-induced shrinkage in Canadian demand for imports and the upward surge in energy prices gave Canada a September merchandise trade surplus of $1.27 billion; Canada's September trade surplus with the United States alone was $1.78 billion.

Such ebbs and flows in trade can only be seen in their true proportion against the backdrop of the sheer size of the economic entity created by the FTA. With a combined GNP approaching $5.7 trillion (of which Canada produces nearly $500 billion), the United States and Canada add up to a market larger by $1.5 trillion than the 12-nation European Community.

How the FTA is changing U.S.-Canada trade: Key features of the agreement

It was the competitive opportunities presented by that huge North American market that inspired President Ronald Reagan and Prime Minister Brian Mulroney to propose a bilateral free-trade agreement in 1985.

Tariff reduction

The centerpiece of the agreement that resulted from their initiative is the commitment to ratchet down all remaining bilateral tariffs to zero by 1998. Tariffs on some items were eliminated entirely on January 1, 1989. Others are to be cut in five equal annual slices, with total elimination by January 1, 1994. The remainder, encompassing the most import-sensitive products on both sides of the border, will be cut in ten equal annual stages, ending on January 1, 1998.

The length of the phase-out for these import-sensitive goods means that the trade-liberalizing impact of eliminating tariffs will not be felt significantly for some years. But the agreement does permit a speed-up of the rate of tariff removal at the request of businesses in Canada and the United States, if no strong objections are lodged by the affected industries. One such follow-up agreement on accelerated tariff cuts already took effect in 1990. This acceleration pact affected U.S. imports and exports worth $3 billion each. Goods covered included chemicals, pharmaceutical products, electric motors and engines, and diesel engines. Most of the 400 products affected became duty-free immediately upon implementation of the tariff-cut acceleration agreement in May 1990. Other products will become duty-free on January 1, 1991. The rest will move from the ten-year to the five-year phase-out schedule. A second annual acceleration

agreement is expected to be reached early in 1991 and to take effect by July.

Investment review eased

The FTA removes significant obstacles to bilateral direct investment. It commits both countries to provide national treatment for the establishment, acquisition, sale, and operation of businesses. By 1992, Canada will end its review of indirect acquisitions of Canadian businesses by U.S. companies; by 1994, Canada will raise to $150 million (in constant 1992 Canadian dollars) the threshold for review of direct acquisitions. (The threshold for 1991 will be $75 million Canadian.) The agreement also prohibits virtually all performance requirements on new investments, including domestic-content requirements and requirements that investors export a certain percentage of their output.

Through 1989, U.S. direct investment in Canada totaled $52 billion, having risen $1.4 billion in the FTA's first year. Canadian direct investment in the United States was $30.1 billion, up $2.7 billion in the FTA's first year.[3]

Government procurement

Of special value to small businesses will be the FTA's easing of access to central-government purchasing across the border. Federal government procurement by designated agencies is open to both U.S. and Canadian suppliers without discrimination on contracts valued at more than $25,000, so long as the supplier uses goods with at least 50 percent U.S. or Canadian content, as measured by direct manufacturing costs. The comparable threshold under the General Agreement on Tariffs and Trade, the 99-nation global trade agreement, is $171,000, so that U.S. and Canadian suppliers will have a competitive edge over suppliers from other countries. However, none of these nondiscrimination rules apply to governmental entities below the national level.

Services trade

Under the FTA, no new discriminatory regulations may be applied to service providers in more than 150 sectors. The essential feature of the agreement is that service providers from across the border must be treated the same as domestic service providers, giving them the right to sell their services without having to establish a local pres-

ence, unless the same requirement is imposed on domestic providers.

In financial services, where regulatory structures and rules in both countries are complex, some special provisions apply. For instance, U.S. nationals are no longer subject to a Canadian regulation forbidding more than 25 percent of a bank's equity to be foreign-owned. Similarly, U.S.-controlled financial entities are exempt from a cap of 16 percent foreign ownership of total Canadian domestic bank assets. Any further liberalization of financial regulations on either side will be extended to both Canadian- and American-controlled banks without discrimination.

Energy

The FTA prohibits most import and export restrictions on energy supplies. Most bilateral energy trade involves exports from Canada to the United States; in the event of short supply, Canada could reduce exports to the United States only to the same extent as it reduced supplies to domestic users.

Dispute settlement

On top of these significant steps to liberalize bilateral trade and investment, the FTA also establishes precedent-setting institutions and procedures for the settlement of bilateral disputes.

One of these mechanisms fulfills a key objective of the Canadian government in the FTA talks, which was to protect Canadian exporters from the arbitrary application of U.S. laws penalizing the subsidization or below-cost dumping of products in the U.S. market. The FTA takes away from U.S. and Canadian courts the power to review administrative antidumping and countervailing-duty rulings imposed by trade agencies on each other's companies. Instead, these rulings are now reviewed by binational dispute-resolution panels, drawn from rosters of Canadians and Americans, with the power to determine whether the ruling in a given case conforms to the law of the country that issued it. So far this mechanism has been used in 14 cases with little complaint about its fairness on either side of the border.

A second mechanism addresses other disputes concerning implementation or trade liberalization under the FTA. In these cases, if consultations between trade ministers of the two countries fail to produce a settlement, the two sides can refer disputes to a binational panel for binding arbitration. Such panels have convened in two cases to date, but in neither did the panel's ruling achieve closure of the trade dispute. In one case, concerning access for U.S. processors to Pacific salmon and herring caught in Canadian waters, the two nations' trade ministers had to negotiate a settlement after an inconclusive ruling by the binational panelists. In the other, which upheld a U.S. law regulating the size of lobster that can be sold in the U.S. market, a settlement was negotiated but then rejected by the Canadian government on the advice of their fishing industry; the case remains unresolved.

Unfinished business

The dispute-settlement provisions of the FTA represent an acknowledgment that the agreement is not a finished transaction but a dynamic arrangement, with much depending on its further implementation and elaboration. Also built into the FTA are a series of commitments to ongoing negotiation and consultation on implementation issues, such as harmonization of product standards, customs administration, and extension of liberalization in services, government procurement, and business travel and tourism.

Automotive trade

The ongoing consultation of greatest consequence for the Great Lakes states concerns the future of the North American automotive industry. The FTA left important issues unresolved in this sector, which accounts for more than a third of Great Lakes trade with Canada (see further discussion below) and for nearly 30 percent of all bilateral merchandise trade. One of the central issues outstanding concerns the level of U.S. or Canadian value added that a vehicle or part must have in order to qualify for duty-free handling at the U.S.-Canada border.

A binational panel of experts appointed by the Canadian trade minister and by the U.S. Secretary of Commerce and U.S. Trade Representative has had the task of making a recommendation on this issue. The panel also will assess and report on the fit between the rules governing bilateral automotive

trade and the global competitive environment facing the North American industry.

The two assignments are closely connected. The value added requirement determines which products are counted as U.S. or Canadian and hence eligible for duty-free treatment under the FTA "rule of origin." If automotive parts and vehicles with relatively little U.S. or Canadian manufacturing content can qualify for duty-free bilateral treatment, the U.S. and Canadian automotive-parts industries will come under intensified competitive pressure from suppliers based in third countries such as Japan and South Korea.

Like the Big Three vehicle-manufacturing companies themselves, the parts industry in both countries is besieged by Asian competitors, which have made inroads in Big Three procurement while continuing to enjoy preferential ties to their traditional customers, the major Asian vehicle assemblers. A key FTA negotiating issue was how to adapt bilateral arrangements made when the North American market was isolated to the new situation of global automotive competition.

The FTA's automotive provisions are superimposed on the requirements of the 1965 Auto Pact between Canada and the United States. Under that 1965 agreement, Canada agreed to end certain subsidies on exports to the United States but gained the right to impose performance requirements on the Big Three in exchange for the privilege of selling vehicles in Canada. As applied by Canada, the Auto Pact allows the Big Three to import vehicles and parts duty-free not only from the United States but from anywhere in the world, so long as they produce one vehicle in Canada for every one sold there and produce at least 60 cents worth of Canadian automotive parts or vehicles for every dollar's worth sold there.

These requirements led the Big Three to establish a large production base in Canada, both to sell into the Canadian market and to get the benefit of duty-free sourcing (estimated to be worth $300 million in 1987).[4] As enforced on the American side, the Auto Pact limited some of the potential losses for American parts makers by requiring that at least 50 percent of the invoice cost of automotive

goods had to be U.S. or Canadian in order to qualify for duty-free entry into the United States.

The arrival of Asian vehicles and Asian vehicle makers in North America, which accelerated rapidly in the 1980s, led the Canadian government to develop comparable incentives for their use of Canadian content and for the siting of production in Canada, including a new version of the export subsidy that the Auto Pact was intended to eliminate. Canada held out the prospect as well that these Asian companies could eventually qualify for global duty-free sourcing, as under the Auto Pact, by steadily increasing their procurement and production in Canada.

The FTA terminates Canada's direct subsidy of exports to the United States by these newcomers to the North American market. However, subsidies based on their attainment of gradually increasing production targets in Canada will be allowed to run their course, terminating only in 1996, with significant residual subsidization possible after that date owing to the lag between meeting production targets and receiving the reward. (These subsidies take the form of remission, or rebate, of duties paid on import of automotive products from third countries, in proportion to the amount of Canadian procurement or production achieved by the auto maker.) Since the Asian producers in Canada aim to sell the bulk of their output in the U.S. market, these production incentives are de facto export incentives as well.

The FTA also closes membership in the Auto Pact, so that no companies other than the Big Three will be allowed the privilege of global duty-free sourcing of vehicles and parts. In addition, even the Big Three are required to meet a more demanding value added requirement for duty-free shipments to the United States from their Canadian subsidiaries. Under this new rule of origin, 50 percent of the direct cost of manufacturing (not including overhead and profits) must be incurred in the United States or Canada in order for automotive products to qualify for duty-free entry.

Even this standard does not ensure that the major components (engine and drivetrain) of a vehicle must be produced in North America in order for it to count as a Canadian or U.S. product and hence come in duty-free. The binational automotive panel therefore recommended in August 1990 that the automotive value added requirement be increased to 60 percent, with a phase-in period if necessary to ease the strain on the auto makers. However, the Canadian government has balked at implementing the recommendation, disputing the Canadian parts industry's contention that the step would be to the mutual advantage of both Canadian and U.S. parts suppliers.

This rule-of-origin issue, along with the problem of policing Canada's obligation not to expand the scope of its production-based incentives for the Asian auto makers, remains near the top of the FTA implementation agenda for U.S. negotiators. The issue is also a high priority for many members of the U.S. Congress from the Great Lakes region. These lawmakers remain very concerned that the Auto Pact's artificial tilt of bilateral automotive trade in Canada's favor has not been righted under the FTA, and they fear that it will be aggravated by Canada's continuation of duty-free sourcing for the Big Three and of duty-rebate incentives for production by Asian auto makers that have set up shop north of the border.

Provincial compliance

Also high on the implementation agenda is the issue of compliance by Canada's provinces with some of the liberalization commitments contained in the FTA. The prime cases in point are in the alcoholic beverage sector, where Canadian law gives sweeping power to the provinces to limit the sale and distribution of beverages from other provinces as well as other countries.

Canada agreed under the FTA to remove discriminatory mark-ups by provincial governments on the prices charged for U.S. wines. (For distilled spirits price discrimination was to end January 1, 1989.) However, the provinces have been slow to comply with the phase-out, and U.S. wineries have seen new forms of provincial discrimination take the place of those being eliminated under the FTA. For example, Quebec's liquor board decreed that American wines could be sold only on consignment, with a minimum yearly sales quota of more than $120,000; failure to meet the quota would make the winery liable for a prohibitive handling fee. Such

new barriers have been erected on top of provincial laws allowing only a limited number of officially "listed" wines to be sold. Nearly two years into the implementation of the FTA, consultations between the U.S. and Canadian governments over these non-compliance questions had not resolved the problem.

Canada did not undertake to liberalize its similar provincial restrictions on the marketing of imported beer, but the FTA does bar any worsening of the treatment of imported American beer. Nonetheless, Ontario's liquor control board in 1989 instituted a new, higher processing fee for carrying American brews in government stores, claiming that the fee merely reflected increased handling costs.

TABLE 1

Great Lakes merchandise trade with Canada, 1989
(in millions of U.S. dollars)

State	Imports	Exports	Balance
Illinois	4,474.7	5,614.0	1,139.2
Indiana	1,825.6	2,486.6	661.0
Michigan	20,781.2	13,381.3	-7,399.9
Minnesota	2,689.8	1,470.3	-1,219.5
New York	12,196.8	4,707.6	-7,489.2
Ohio	3,664.0	6,897.8	3,233.8
Pennsylvania	2,736.1	2,872.0	136.0
Wisconsin	1,808.5	1,918.6	110.1
Great Lakes total	50,176.7	39,348.2	-10,828.5
United States total	82,780.0	73,934.5	-8,845.5

SOURCE: U.S. Department of Commerce, Office of Canada.

Such discriminatory practices have been challenged by the U.S. Trade Representative under the General Agreement on Tariffs and Trade (GATT); Canada has already lost a GATT case brought by the European Community over its similar discrimination against European alcoholic beverages. In addition, U.S. brewers Stroh (headquartered in Detroit) and G. Heileman (based in LaCrosse, Wisconsin), have filed petitions against Canada's discriminatory practices under Section 301 of U.S. trade law, which permits retaliation for violations of international trade agreements. The U.S. Trade Representative has accepted these petitions as the basis for an unfair-trade-practice investigation.

Subsidies

While the FTA establishes a dispute-settlement mechanism for review of antidumping and subsidy rulings by national authorities in Canada and the United States, it does not alter the relevant laws of either country. The FTA contains a mandate to negotiate for up to seven years on a new regime for the control of subsidization and dumping that distort bilateral trade. The United States has long been concerned about the extent of subsidies provided by various levels of government in Canada in the name of industrial policy or regional economic development. Canadians have had some mirror-image concerns about U.S. practices but mainly have been eager to limit their liability for subsidization under U.S. law. Bilateral consultations on this major item of unfinished business have occurred, but no serious negotiation is anticipated until the shape of any new global agreement on subsidies and dumping emerges from the current round of talks to reform the GATT Subsidies Code. If no new GATT subsidies agreement is reached, then the subsidy issue could become a focal point of intense controversy over trade policy between the two parties to the FTA.

Regional predominance in U.S.-Canada trade

The resolution of these and other outstanding bilateral issues matters profoundly to the eight states of the Great Lakes region, because they account for the lion's share of U.S. trade with Canada—nearly $90 billion of the $156.7 billion total merchandise-trade volume allocated state by state in a U.S. Department of Commerce compilation of bilateral trade data (Table 1).

The Great Lakes states claimed 53.2 percent of all U.S. exports to Canada in 1989, 60.61 percent of U.S. imports from Canada, and 57.1 percent of total trade volume. Imports to the Great Lakes states ($50.18 billion) from Canada substantially exceeded export ($39.35 billion), producing a 1989 regional trade deficit with Canada of -$10.83 billion. This deficit actually was larger than the overall U.S. trade deficit with Canada for 1989 (-$8.85 billion, using the Commerce Department's state-by-state compilation; -$9.2 billion according to the official Commerce Department figure for the bilateral merchandise-trade balance, which takes into account residual trade volume not allocated to particular states.)

Both the region's large share of total trade volume and its disproportionate share of the overall U.S. trade deficit with Canada stem from the heavy concentration of the U.S. motor vehicle industry in the Great Lakes states. As noted above, since 1965 North American motor vehicle production has developed as an integrated whole on both sides of the U.S.-Canada border under the incentives created by the bilateral Auto Pact. The Big Three are now being joined in Canada by transplant producers from Japan and South Korea (such as Toyota, Honda, Suzuki, and Hyundai), which have received similar incentives from the Canadian government to produce in Canada and which also aim to sell much of their output in the huge American market.

The upshot of these special factors affecting motor vehicle trade is a big bilateral trade deficit for the United States in the automotive sector. This deficit of -$11.022 billion in 1989 (Table 2) actually exceeded the overall U.S. trade deficit with Canada. Also notable was the development of a small 1989 deficit (-$167 million) for the United States in vehicle-parts trade, where the historical pattern has been a U.S. surplus partly counterbalancing the overwhelming Canadian advantage in finished vehicles.

The concentration in the Great Lakes states of the industry affected by this special imbalance explains why the region's trade with Canada, although robust, is also markedly unbalanced. The Great Lakes region's trade balance in vehicles and parts in 1989 was a deficit of -$8.95 billion, with exports of $13.53 billion outweighed by imports of $22.48 billion (Table 3).

State merchandise trade profiles

ILLINOIS ranked fourth among the Great Lakes states in total trade volume with Canada in 1989, with merchandise exports and imports of more than $10 billion. Exports exceeded imports by $1.139 billion (see Table 1 for this and other states' bilateral trade balances with Canada). The state accounted for 14.3 percent of Great Lakes exports to Canada and 8.9 percent of the region's imports from Canada.

TABLE 2

U.S. motor vehicle trade with Canada, 1989
(in billions of U.S. dollars)

Exports to Canada

Motor vehicles	8.691
Parts	9.895
Combined	18.586

Imports from Canada

Motor vehicles	19.713
Parts	10.062
Combined	29.775

Motor vehicle trade balance

Motor vehicles	-11.022
Parts	-0.167
Combined	-11.189

SOURCE: U.S. Department of Commerce, Office of Automotive Affairs.

Illinois owed its positive trade balance with Canada in 1989 largely to substantial sales of industrial equipment, which accounted for nearly 30 percent of the state's $5.614 billion in exports to Canada. Automotive vehicles and parts were almost as important, accounting for more than 28 percent of Illinois exports to Canada. The next largest share of Illinois exports, 8.6 percent, came in the category of electrical machinery and parts.

Illinois' merchandise imports from Canada reached $4.475 billion in 1989, with mineral fuels such as crude petroleum contributing 22.7 percent to the total. Vehicles and parts came in second, accounting for 15.5 percent. Also significant were imports of paper and paper products (11.2 percent of imports), industrial equipment (7.2 percent), and locomotives and parts (6.6 percent).

INDIANA also enjoyed a positive trade balance with Canada in 1989, and the amount —$661 million—was substantial considering the relatively small volume of trade involved (imports of $1.826 billion, exports of $2.487 billion, total volume of $4.313 billion). Indiana shipped 6.3 percent of the region's exports to Canada and took in just 3.6 percent of Canadian imports. Leading the export list were motor vehicles and parts, accounting for 35.7 percent of total export value. Next in importance were

exports of industrial equipment (27.4 percent) and electrical machinery (8.8 percent.)

Nearly two-thirds of Indiana's imports from Canada in 1989 came under just five headings: mineral fuels (32.13 percent), vehicles and parts (11.8 percent), industrial equipment (8.1 percent), paper and paper products (6.8 percent), and aluminum and aluminum products (5.9 percent).

MICHIGAN trades more with Canada than any other state in the Great Lakes region—more than any other state in the country, for that matter. Michigan's share of Great Lakes exports to Canada is 34 percent, and its import share is even larger, at 41.4 percent. Total trade volume of $34.16 billion is divided between exports of $13.38 billion and imports of $20.78 billion, yielding a 1989 trade deficit of -$7.4 billion.

Two-way trade in motor vehicles and parts dominates the economic relationship between Michigan and Canada. In 1989 Canada imported vehicles and parts from Michigan valued at $7.6 billion. Michigan in turn imported vehicles and parts worth $15.2 billion, resulting in an automotive trade deficit with Canada of -$7.6 billion. This one product category accounted for 57 percent of Michigan's exports and 73 percent of Michigan's imports.

Other significant Michigan exports were industrial equipment (17 percent) and electrical machinery (8 percent). Notable on the import side, in addition to vehicles and parts, were industrial equipment (10.9 percent) and mineral fuels (2.6 percent).

MINNESOTA also had a sizable trade deficit with Canada in 1989, although on a scale much smaller than Michigan's. The state recorded a deficit of -$1.22 billion on total trade volume of $4.16 billion, with imports of $2.69 billion and exports of $1.47 billion.

Minnesota's top exports to Canada were motor vehicles and parts (26 percent), industrial equipment (20 percent), electrical machinery (8 percent), and measuring (e.g., optical) instruments (5.4 percent). Major imports from Canada were mineral fuels (49.6 percent), wood pulp (8 percent), industrial equipment (6.4 percent), paper and paper products (5.7 percent), and fertilizers (5.6 percent).

NEW YORK ranks second only to Michigan in the region as a trading partner with Canada. The state's total volume of $16.9 billion in bilateral trade is tilted heavily in Canada's favor, with imports of $12.2 billion and exports of $4.7 billion yielding a deficit of -$7.5 billion for New York. New York takes in 24.3 percent of Great Lakes imports from Canada and accounts for 12 percent of the region's exports to Canada.

New York exports to Canada in 1989 were diverse. Leading categories of exports were electrical machinery (14.7 percent), industrial equipment (13.3 percent), aluminum and aluminum products (8.9 percent), motor vehicles and parts (6.2 percent), measuring instruments (5.7 percent), precious stones and metals (5.3 percent), and printed materials (4.7 percent). Top categories of imports from Canada were motor vehicles and parts (38.1 percent), mineral fuels (9.6 percent), precious stones

TABLE 3

Great Lakes motor vehicle trade with Canada, 1989
(in millions of U.S. dollars)

State	Imports	Exports
Illinois	693.3	1,596.8
Indiana	216.1	887.5
Michigan	15,181.0	7,604.4
Minnesota	379.0	101.8
New York	4,644.7	292.3
Ohio	944.4	2,370.8
Pennsylvania	239.0	279.5
Wisconsin	184.1	396.8
Great Lakes total	22,481.7	13,529.8
Great Lakes balance	-8,951.8	

SOURCE: U.S. Department of Commerce, Office of Canada.

and metals (7.1 percent), aluminum and aluminum products (6.5 percent), and paper and paper products (5.6 percent).

OHIO ranked third, behind Michigan and New York and just ahead of Illinois, in trade with Canada in 1989. Total trade volume was $10.56 billion, with exports of $6.89 billion and imports of $3.66 billion giving Ohio the region's best trade balance with Canada, a surplus of $3.23 billion. One reason for

the surplus is Ohio's strong positive trade balance in vehicles and parts; exports in this category exceed imports by $1.43 billion.

Ohio's exports of vehicles and parts account for 34.4 percent of total exports to Canada. Other major export categories are industrial equipment (24.9 percent), mineral fuels (6.3 percent), and electrical machinery (4.8 percent).

Motor vehicles and parts are also the leading category of Ohio imports from Canada, accounting for 25.8 percent. Also significant are imports of industrial machinery (10.5 percent), paper and paper products (8.3 percent), and iron and steel (5.6 percent).

PENNSYLVANIA enjoyed a trade surplus with Canada in 1989, albeit a modest one of $136 million on total trade volume of $5.6 billion. The state's $2.87 billion in exports came from diverse categories, led by industrial equipment (17.7 percent), electrical machinery (10.4 percent), motor vehicles and parts (9.7 percent), and plastics and plastic products (7 percent).

Top items among Pennsylvania's imports of $2.74 billion from Canada were paper and paper products (15.5 percent), motor vehicles and parts (8.7 percent), aluminum and aluminum products (8.1 percent), wood and wood products (8.1 percent), and industrial equipment (6.9 percent).

WISCONSIN traded less with Canada than any other Great Lakes state, with total trade volume of $3.73 billion, made up of $1.92 billion in exports and $1.81 billion in imports, producing a slight surplus of $110 million. Wisconsin's major exports were industrial equipment (36.2 percent), motor vehicles and parts (20.7 percent), electrical machinery (7.2 percent), and paper and paper products (5.1 percent). Leading imports from Canada were wood pulp (36.7 percent), motor vehicles and parts (10.2 percent), paper and paper products (9.7 percent), industrial equipment (5.9 percent), and mineral fuels (5.8 percent).

Assessing the impact and the prospects of the FTA

Canadian and U.S. news reports and studies have cited many cases of business expansion in Canada in response to the tariff cuts and other

market-opening measures of the FTA, with new production capacity developing in everything from baked goods to billion-dollar gas pipeline projects, from plastic food containers to bath soap. At the same time, there have been Canadian job losses due to consolidation of production in the United States, causing shutdowns of Canadian factories making items such as Gillette razor blades, Whirlpool appliances, and Gerber baby food. But consolidations are working the other way, too, as in the case of General Motors' electric-locomotive engines, which are now built in Ontario instead of Illinois.

Canada's opposition parties, which made the FTA their prime target in the 1988 parliamentary election but lost, now blame virtually every job loss in Canada on the FTA. But these Canadian foes of the agreement tend not to dwell on the creation of new jobs, nor on the export-inhibiting role played by Canada's high interest rates, the high value of the Canadian dollar, and the slowdown in U.S. economic growth. Much of the Canadian public seems to share their critical view of the FTA, nonetheless; in an October 1990 public-opinion poll by Canadian media, only 7 percent of Canadians agreed that the FTA had helped Canada's economy, while 49 percent said the FTA had hurt and 32 percent felt the FTA had made no difference.[5] (According to the same poll, Canadians take a similarly negative view of the proposal by their government that Canada join in new free-trade talks with the United States and Mexico, which began preliminary discussions of a bilateral FTA of their own in 1990.) However, the FTA in 1989 and 1990 was a lower priority for Canadians than the political crisis caused by the failure of a constitutional reform effort that would have settled the relationship between the "distinct society" of francophone Quebec and the rest of the Canadian federation.

On the U.S. side, trade with Canada has never been a preoccupation of the American public. Negotiation of the FTA did attract considerable attention and kindled concern in Congress over the persistence of a sizable bilateral trade deficit. However, with an economy ten times the size of Canada's and with less dependence on exports for their prosperity, Americans continue to attach far less importance to the bilateral economic relationship than do Canadians, even though Canada is the nation's largest trading partner and the U.S. economy does depend increasingly on exports for its growth.

In the end, Canada and the United States have much to gain by following through on the FTA to make trade and investment within the bilateral market secure by keeping the rules stable and predictable. This was, in fact, the chief impetus behind creation of the FTA; the mutual advantage that results remains the best reason for retaining the agreement and implementing it conscientiously.

NOTES

[1] External Affairs and International Trade Canada press release, "International Trade Minister Crosbie Comments on the Free Trade Agreement," (Ottawa, Canada: January 19, 1990), p. 1.

[2] Statement of Charles E. Roh, Jr., Assistant U.S. Trade Representative for North American Affairs, before the U.S. Senate Committee on Finance, Subcommittee on International Trade (Washington, D.C.: September 28, 1990), p. 1.

[3] U.S. Library of Congress, Congressional Research Service, *U.S.-Canada Free Trade Agreement: Assessment and Implications for a U.S.-Mexico Free Trade Agreement*, by Arlene Wilson, September 12, 1990, p. 5.

[4] U.S. Library of Congress, Congressional Research Service, *The Effect of the Canada-U.S. Free Trade Agreement on U.S. Industries*, by Arlene Wilson and Carl E. Behrens, July 22, 1988, p. 7.

[5] Christopher Waddell, "Nation's major concern is deteriorating economy," *Toronto Globe and Mail*, October 29, 1990, pp. A6-A7.

Resources and Industry

Chapter 6

Water Resources and Policy

MICHAEL J. DONAHUE, EXECUTIVE DIRECTOR,
GREAT LAKES COMMISSION

The Great Lakes-St. Lawrence system lends not only geographic definition to this region, but helps define its distinctive socio-economic, cultural and quality of life attributes as well. Water is the region's life-blood; the foundation of an immense yet fragile ecosystem. It is also a critical link between North America's industrial and agricultural heartland and destinations throughout the world.

The "institutional ecosystem" for Great Lakes-St. Lawrence management rivals the physical eco-system in complexity. A multitude of governmental jurisdictions and non-governmental interests establish or influence water policy—an exercise complicated by the vastness of the resource, its binational character, and its multiple-use properties. Reconciling political and hydrologic boundaries is the essence of the management challenge. Long regarded as the world's greatest laboratory for scientific experimentation, the Great Lakes-St. Lawrence system is now developing a reputation as the world's greatest laboratory for institutional experimentation and management innovation.

Those who share stewardship responsibility for the economic and environmental well being of the Great Lakes-St. Lawrence region are confronted with a management challenge of monumental, yet largely unseen dimensions. The challenge is monumental because it is as complex, as dynamic and as perva-sive as the Great Lakes-St. Lawrence system itself. The challenge is largely unseen because it is not a challenge posed by the physical system and its many components. The challenge is that of policies, programs and institutions; the question of how this region—as a collectivity of political jurisdictions —organizes itself to manage shared resources for the common benefit.

Water is the universal medium in the Great Lakes-St. Lawrence system, and its impact is pervasive. It influences not only the region's environment, economic base and quality of life, but its system of governance as well. An investment in its informed use, management and protection is an investment in the overall future of the region. Water is not an interesting sidelight to the Great Lakes economy; it is woven into the very fabric of that economy.

The following discussion explores the impor-tance of Great Lakes-St. Lawrence water resources from a policy and institutional standpoint. Physical and institutional ecosystems are examined and the role of water resources in the region's economy is documented. Roles and responsibilities in water policy are reviewed from the local to binational arenas, with a special emphasis on U.S.-Canada relations and the pivotal role of regional, multi-jurisdictional institutions. A series of trends and their implications for water resource policy and management are presented, with suggestions on policy directions to manage and protect the world's greatest freshwater resource—the Great Lakes.

The physical ecosystem: Expansive yet fragile

A descriptive statement of the physical attri-butes of the Great Lakes-St. Lawrence system demands the frequent and almost tiring use of superlatives. It is a system of virtually unfathom-able expanse and corresponding complexity. Its myriad characteristics are inextricably linked to—and in large part the determinants of—the region's environmental health, economic well being and overall quality of life. Yet, the expansiveness and complexity of the resource belies its fragility. Even minor stresses—whether they be physical, biological or political—can have lasting impacts upon the sustainable use, development and protec-tion of the resource.

Expansive and intensively used, the Great Lakes-St. Lawrence system enjoys global promi-nence. It contains some 65 trillion gallons of fresh surface water; a full 20 percent of the world's supply and 90 percent of the United States' supply. Its component parts—the five Great Lakes—are all among the fifteen largest fresh water lakes in the world. Collectively, the Lakes and their connecting channels comprise the world's largest body of fresh surface water. They lend not only geographic definition to the region, but help define the region's distinctive socio-economic, cultural and quality of life attributes as well (see Figures 1 and 2).

An international resource shared by the United States and Canada, the Great Lakes-St. Lawrence system encompasses 95,000 square miles of surface water and a drainage area of almost 300,000 square miles. Extending some 2,400 miles from its western-most shores to the Atlantic, the system is compa-rable in length to a trans-Atlantic crossing from the east coast of the United States to Europe.

According to the Great Lakes Basin Framework Study, the U.S. portion of the Basin alone contains almost 250 species and subspecies of fish; over 180,000 acres of coastal wetlands; almost 40 million acres of forested land; and 32 million acres of agricultural land.[1]

Lake Superior is the largest of the five Great Lakes and, by surface area, is the largest freshwater lake in the world.[2] Extending over 350 miles from the northeast shores of Minnesota to the northwest shores of Ontario, Lake Superior is 160 miles in breadth at its widest point, encompassing 31,700 square miles of surface water within a coastline approaching 3,000 miles in length. The deepest of the Great Lakes (1,333 ft.) with an average depth of 489 feet, Superior contains almost 3,000 cubic miles of water. Due to this volume and its relatively constrained outlet (St. Marys River to Lake Huron), Superior has a retention time of 191 years; twice that

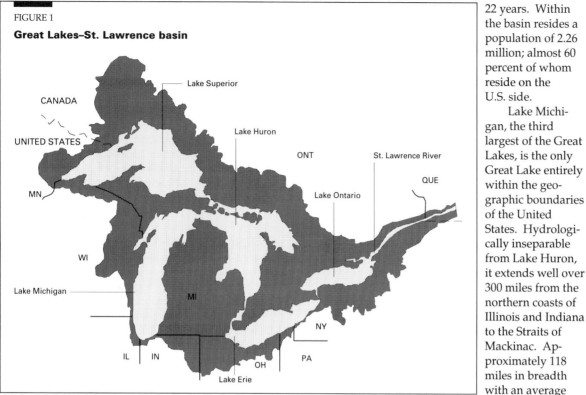

FIGURE 1

Great Lakes–St. Lawrence basin

22 years. Within the basin resides a population of 2.26 million; almost 60 percent of whom reside on the U.S. side.

Lake Michigan, the third largest of the Great Lakes, is the only Great Lake entirely within the geographic boundaries of the United States. Hydrologically inseparable from Lake Huron, it extends well over 300 miles from the northern coasts of Illinois and Indiana to the Straits of Mackinac. Approximately 118 miles in breadth with an average depth of 279 feet

(923 ft. maximum), Lake Michigan contains approximately 1,180 cubic miles of water. The land mass within the basin is approximately twice as large as the 22,300 square miles of water surface it drains and includes portions of Illinois, Indiana, Michigan and Wisconsin, collectively accounting for 1,660 miles of shoreline. A population of 14 million resides within the Lake Michigan drainage basin—far more than that of any other Great Lake. Retention time for Lake Michigan's water volume is just under 100 years.

Bordered by four states and a province, Lake Erie is the fourth largest of the Great Lakes. Despite its size (length—236 miles, breadth—57 miles) and relative shallowness (average depth of 62 feet), it yields the smallest volume of the five Great Lakes (116 cubic miles). Its retention time is but 2.6 years. The Lake's surface area is just under 10,000 square miles and is surrounded by 856 miles of shoreline.

The most densely populated of the five Lake basins, almost 13 million U.S. and Canadian citizens reside in the Lake Erie drainage basin. The preponderance (88.8 percent) reside on the U.S. side.

Lake Ontario, the smallest of the Great Lakes in terms of surface area, is bordered by the province of Ontario on the north and west and New York on the south and east. While similar to Lake Erie in length and breadth (160 and 53 miles respectively), Lake Ontario's greater average depth (283 feet) yields almost four times Erie's volume (393 cubic miles) and three times its retention time (six years). Lake Ontario's surface area is 7,340 square miles; its drainage area is approximately four times as large. A population of just over six million resides in the basin; approximately two-thirds of these residents are located on the Canadian side. Lake Ontario's coastline is approximately 726 miles in length.

Also of significance in characterizing the physical attributes of the system are the connecting channels. The St. Marys River is the northernmost of these, a 70 mile-long waterway providing an outlet for Lake Superior and contributing an average of 75,000 cubic feet per second (cfs) of its waters to the lower four lakes. The St. Clair and Detroit Rivers—and Lake St. Clair between them—form a 77 mile long channel connecting Lakes Huron and Erie. At its outlet, the Detroit River flows at an average rate of 186,000 cfs into the western basin of Lake Erie. The Niagara River, linking Lakes Erie and Ontario, continues on for 35 miles, with an average flow of 50,000 cfs over the Niagara Falls. The St. Lawrence River, in providing the linkage between the Lakes proper and the Atlantic, is one of the world's premier waterways, extending some 383 miles as it carries an average of 240,000 cfs of water to the ocean.

By any measure, the Great Lakes-St. Lawrence system is of global significance, an expansive and interconnected system of lakes and connecting channels that collectively define one of the most dominant physical features on the face of the earth. The size, configuration and biological diversity of this system give rise to its multiple use properties, its environmental and economic significance, and the complexity and gravity of public policy issues concerning its use, development and protection.

of Lake Michigan and almost two orders of magnitude longer than Lake Erie. The drainage basin totals 81,000 square miles and encompasses portions of Michigan, Minnesota, Wisconsin and Ontario. Approximately 700,000 citizens of the United States (79 percent) and Canada (21 percent) reside within the drainage area.

Lake Huron is the second largest of the Great Lakes and one of two shared (on the U.S. side) by only a single state (in this case, Michigan). Extending over 200 miles from the Straits of Mackinac to the headwaters of Lake St. Clair, Lake Huron is 183 miles across at its widest, with an average depth of 195 feet and a maximum depth of 750 feet. Its shoreline totals 3,180 miles in length. The Lake Huron basin has a large land to water ratio relative to the other Great Lakes; its 74,800 square miles of land are approximately three times the total surface water area. Lake Huron's retention time is just over

FIGURE 2

Great Lakes–St. Lawrence River system

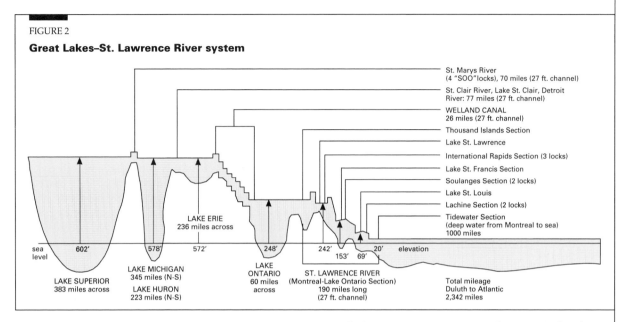

St. Marys River
(4 "SOO"locks), 70 miles (27 ft. channel)

St. Clair River, Lake St. Clair, Detroit
River: 77 miles (27 ft. channel)

WELLAND CANAL
26 miles (27 ft. channel)

Thousand Islands Section

Lake St. Lawrence

International Rapids Section (3 locks)

Lake St. Francis Section

Soulanges Section (2 locks)

Lake St. Louis

Lachine Section (2 locks)

Tidewater Section
(deep water from Montreal to sea)
1000 miles

LAKE ERIE
236 miles across

sea level   602'   578'   572'   248'   242' 20' elevation
153' 69'

LAKE SUPERIOR
383 miles across

LAKE MICHIGAN
345 miles (N-S)

LAKE HURON
223 miles (N-S)

LAKE ONTARIO
60 miles across

ST. LAWRENCE RIVER
(Montreal-Lake Ontario Section)
190 miles long
(27 ft. channel)

Total mileage
Duluth to Atlantic
2,342 miles

Water and the economy

The role of the Great Lakes-St. Lawrence system in advancing regional, national and binational economic development has been recognized (but not fully appreciated) for many decades. The mere physical presence and geographic configuration of the system and its attendant attributes were, and continue to be, a determinant of locational decisions for business and industry. Much of the early economic activity during settlement of the region was directly attributable to resource exploitation potential (e.g., fisheries, trapping, mining, forestry) and the availability of water-based transport. While the current industrial base is more diversified, the Basin's water resources continue to exercise a substantive role in the attraction and retention of industry. Growing concerns over depletion of the Ogallala aquifer in the West, as well as water shortages in Southwest regions of the United States, have prompted some researchers to predict a dramatic resurgence of water-dependent industry in the Great Lakes-St. Lawrence Basin. While such predictions are based as much on speculation as fact at the present time, they do illustrate the economic utility of the water resource, and the attendant need

to devise water management and economic development strategies sensitive to that utility.

The regional economic impact of the Great Lakes-St. Lawrence system is pervasive but can generally be attributed to its standing as a mode of transport; a factor of production; a "supporting resource"; and a "marketable amenity".

Great Lakes-St. Lawrence system potential as a mode of transport has long been recognized and actively pursued by both the United States and Canada. Historical analysis indicates that development of the system's transportation potential was a driving force behind numerous physical infrastructure decisions and helped shape development of many regional resource management institutions and practices.

In the United States, a federal interest in the Great Lakes-St. Lawrence system was initially articulated in the Northwest Ordinance of 1787, which declared the navigable waterways into and between the St. Lawrence and Mississippi Rivers to be common highways and forever free.[3] That same year, Congress authorized payment for construction of lighthouses, beacons, public piers and related facilities, an action that further established the federal interest in water resources. Ten years later,

the first navigational improvement to the system was recorded when the North American Fur Company constructed a small lock on the St. Marys River at Sault Ste. Marie. Further recognition of the system's transportation potential was demonstrated in 1822, with Congressional authorization of a canal to connect the Illinois River with Lake Michigan. Two years later, the Congress enacted the first of an extensive series of River and Harbor Acts authorizing physical improvements to the navigation system. An extensive history of such improvements by both countries is highlighted by the intensive development of the Welland Canal in the late 1920s and early 1930s, the construction of the St. Lawrence Seaway in the 1950s and the completion of the Poe Lock at Sault Ste. Marie in 1969, among others. A review of the developmental history of the Great Lakes transportation system over the past two hundred years, including the many significant events not identified here, yields a portrait of a regional economy born of and shaped by the presence of the Great Lakes-St. Lawrence system.

The transportation potential of the Great Lakes-St. Lawrence system was also a catalytic force in the early development of regional resource management institutions. Dworsky and Francis observe that the initial call for a permanent, international body to address Great Lakes-St. Lawrence issues was an outgrowth of continuing negotiations between Secretary of State Elihu Root and Canadian Prime Minister Sir Wilfred Laurier in the final decade of the 19th century.[4] In 1895, the two countries established a Deep Waterways Commission to investigate the feasibility of constructing a seaway to permit transportation access to the Atlantic. This entity later developed into the International Joint Waterways Commission (1903), a precursor of the International Boundary Waters Treaty of 1909 and its implementing agency, the International Joint Commission. More recently, the formation of the Great Lakes Commission was prompted by an emerging sense of regionalism among Great Lakes states brought about in large part by the impending opening of the St. Lawrence Seaway. Numerous other regional organizations —both public and private—have emerged as well, aided by the existence of a waterborne transportation system that demonstrated the interconnectedness of the Great Lakes and the jurisdictions that surround them.

The continuing contribution of this transportation system to the region's economy is very capably summarized by Thompson and Johnson in their examination of grain transportation on the Great Lakes-St. Lawrence Seaway.[5] The authors conclude: "with adequate long-range planning the Seaway will continue to serve as an important contributor to the well-being of both the national and Lake State economies." Schenker, Mayer and Brockel, in their exhaustive analysis of the Great Lakes transportation system, elaborate further: "The major advantage of the Great Lakes-St. Lawrence Seaway System is the proximity of large industrial and resource areas to Great Lakes ports, and the complementary of certain basic movements.... The locational decisions of many iron and steel manufacturers were based upon the economies of water transportation. The System will continue to serve the resource demands of the major industries in the Great Lakes region."[6]

According to the St. Lawrence Seaway Development Corporation, well over a billion metric tons of cargo, with a value of more than $200 billion, have moved through the Seaway to and from ports in North America, Europe, Asia, Africa and the Middle East.[7] The cumulative impact of Seaway usage on local economies has been established at over $3 billion per year.

A second means of examining the economic aspects of the Great Lakes-St. Lawrence system is from the perspective of water as a factor of production, including both consumptive and non-consumptive uses. As determined by the International Joint Commission, the seven principal consumptive use sectors in the Basin, in descending order of magnitude, include manufacturing, municipal, power generation, irrigation, rural-domestic, mining and rural stock.[8] Non-consumptive uses include instream use, cooling water and any other use where the water withdrawn is returned to the Basin.

According to the Regional Water Use Data Base Repository maintained by the Great Lakes Commission, water use in 1988 (instream and withdrawals) totaled 985 billion gallons per day.[9] Almost 60

percent originates from Great Lakes-St. Lawrence system proper, with the balance drawn from tributaries and groundwater. The largest single category by far is self supply—hydroelectric, an instream use that represents more than 94 percent of the total water usage per day. Of the 56 billion gallons actually withdrawn from the Basin each day, almost 97 percent is returned. Consumptive uses account for approximately 18 billion gallons per day, but are expected to increase in future years, largely in the manufacturing, irrigation and power generation sectors. Such increases have captured the attention and concern of the International Joint Commission, with measurable impacts upon lake levels and competition/conflict between water users identified as potential scenarios.

The Great Lakes-St. Lawrence system as a "supporting resource" is a third means of categorization that broadens understanding of its economic importance. For purposes of this discussion, a "supporting resource" is one that has not only an economic value unto itself, but by virtue of its characteristics, supports the existence of other natural resources with an economic value (e.g., the fishery, waterfowl populations, wetland resources, and regional climate).

The economic importance of these and other lake-based natural resources is not to be underestimated. The Basin's substantial waterfowl population, for example, is due largely to the existence of the Basin's water resources and is responsible for generating substantial economic benefits through hunting related revenues alone. The Basin's wetlands serve important functions in groundwater recharge, flood and erosion control, thermal exchange, sediment and nutrient traps, and fish and wildlife habitat. While the value of such functions is difficult to quantify in economic terms, the contribution of wetlands to recreational/commercial activities (e.g., hunting, fishing, nature observation) is significant, conservatively estimated by the House Merchant Marine and Fisheries Committee at $10 billion nationwide.[10] Great Lakes wetland resources contribute substantially to this figure. Finally, the "lake effect" characteristics of the region's climate have a tempering impact upon seasonal temperatures. The impact is economically favorable, with

specialty crop production and overall agricultural productivity benefiting.

Water as a "marketable amenity" provides a fourth and final perspective on the economic value of the Great Lakes-St. Lawrence system. Of concern here are non-consumptive, in-Basin, and essentially non-manipulative uses of the water resource that generate regional and international economic benefits. Examples include, among others, water-based recreation, quality of life factors and, in a more general sense, the aesthetic value of the resource.

Water-based recreation is an exceedingly broad category encompassing the more obvious recreational activities (e.g., boating, fishing, swimming) as well as those where the presence of the Great Lakes-St. Lawrence system plays a more subtle, yet significant role (e.g., nature observation, hiking, sightseeing). Individually and collectively, the contribution of these activities to the regional economy is staggering. For example, sport fishing, recreational boating and water-based tourism are all multibillion dollar industries in the Great Lakes states.

The attributes of the Great Lakes-St. Lawrence system also factor significantly into "quality of life" considerations. The presence of these resources influences locational decisions (business and residential), recreational preferences and, in a more general sense, overall living patterns. The economic implications of a favorable "quality of life" environment are difficult to quantify but are unquestionably substantial.

The aesthetic value of the system is a subset of this "quality of life" consideration. An individual places a value on the resource, not as a function of its present or potential economic utility, but its contribution to their personal enjoyment and overall sense of well-being. The aesthetic value of the Great Lakes system is shaped in large part by the magnitude of its physical dimensions and diversity of attributes. The extent of the aesthetic appeal of the resource can be measured only imperfectly by approximate "shadow-pricing" methods (e.g., property values, tourism patterns), but is nonetheless an indicator of the contribution of the Great Lakes-St. Lawrence system to the regional economy.

Water policy and United States-Canada relations

William G. Milliken, former governor of Michigan and past chairman of The Centre for the Great Lakes, once stated that "The attitude of some is that the Lakes should be treated as just another body of freshwater... and that it is no longer important to treat the Great Lakes as something special. That attitude is akin to saying that the Mona Lisa is just another painting, the Eiffel Tower just another structure or an eagle just another bird."[11]

It would be equally misleading to characterize binational Great Lakes-St. Lawrence policy as "just another" set of issues among myriad U.S.-Canada diplomatic exchanges. The Great Lakes-St. Lawrence system possesses a number of unique attributes that elevate the importance of such issues in Canada-United States relations.

First and foremost, the Great Lakes and St. Lawrence River form an international boundary. For purposes of governance, the Lakes have historically been perceived as convenient lines of demarcation between adjacent political jurisdictions, rather than as hydrologic units that bind those political jurisdictions together. All substantive issues aside, the binational character of the Lakes has prompted concerted (though sometimes sporadic) attention from the two governments and their various jurisdictions.

Second, the sheer immensity of the resource also speaks to its stature as a touchstone for Canada-United States relations. The Great Lakes Basin encompasses well over a quarter million square miles of land and water in the two countries and envelops almost one third of the entire Canada-United States border.

The Great Lakes Basin is the industrial heartland of the United States and Canada and is home to many of the factors of production, transportation centers, distribution systems and markets so critical to the viability of both their economies. Coupled with long established trading partnerships and interlinked economic activity, the Basin and its shared resources have long been a focal point for binational relations.

The systemic nature of the resource offers a fourth reason for its unique binational status. The Great Lakes-St. Lawrence system consists of a series of large retention basins with relatively minor connecting channels that permit a continuous but constrained flow from the upper to lower Lakes and then on to the Atlantic Ocean via the St. Lawrence River. Retention times may be substantial, but the Lakes do indeed comprise a single, interconnected system. Riparian interests in the lower lakes are subject to the physical and environmental manipulations and stresses occurring in the upper lakes. Similarly, each country is subject to the consequences of the use or abuse of the resource by its counterpart. Hence, mutual interest in avoiding the "tragedy of the commons" has raised binational sensitivity to Great Lakes management needs.

Finally, the Canada-United States boundary within the Great Lakes Basin has long been the locus for extended experimentation in political/diplomatic/institutional endeavors. In simple terms, it constitutes a barometer for binational relations. The origin of diplomatic agreements and joint institutions focusing on Great Lakes boundary and resource usage issues is found in the earliest years of U.S. constitutional history and relations with Great Britain. Joint discussions dating back to the mid-nineteenth century gave rise to the International Boundary Waters Treaty of 1909 and its implementing agency, the International Joint Commission.[12] Even today, despite their failings, binational arrangements for Great Lakes management continue on as "grand experiments" and, in many respects, as international models.

As the physical and socio-economic attributes of the Great Lakes Basin gain recognition as national and international assets, developmental decisions will experience a corresponding rise in complexity and political notoriety. The binational governance structure will serve an increasingly critical role as the Great Lakes-St. Lawrence policy process maintains its status as a touchstone for Canada-United States relations.

The "institutional ecosystem": A perspective on the Great Lakes policy process

David Allee of Cornell University once observed that "the dynamics of interorganizational relationships in river basin management can be compared in their complexity to the dynamics of the hydrology of a river basin".[13] This astute observation is confirmed by the evolution and current status of institutional arrangements for governance of the Great Lakes-St. Lawrence system.

"Institutional ecosystem" is a term that describes the multitude of public and private entities that set or influence Great Lakes policy as well as the various formal and informal linkages and interactions among them. In fact, many of the laws that govern the natural ecosystem also have corollaries for the institutional ecosystem. Concepts such as "survival of the fittest"; interdependency; competitive exclusion and functional specialization all apply.[14] Institutions are dynamic, living organisms with behaviors and traits as complex as those of the physical and biological resources they are charged with managing. Understanding them—and learning how to manipulate them for the benefit of the resource—is an essential component of the policy process.

Historically, the Great Lakes policy process—and the institutions involved in it—have been taken for granted. The preponderance of attention has been directed at questions of *what* is managed rather than questions of *how* it is managed. With few exceptions, the Great Lakes policy process has long been viewed as a mysterious "black box". A regional resource management or economic policy problem is inserted at one end, mixed with relevant laws, programs and funds, and somehow transformed into rational policy that exits the other end of this "black box".

This characterization has begun to change in recent years with the realization that public institutions (at any level of government) are not merely vehicles for operationalizing policies formulated by legislatures or officials of a given administration. Great Lakes institutions themselves provide an environment in which policies can be devised, altered, interpreted, advocated or otherwise transformed. In essence, the institution can determine not only the success or failure of a given policy, but the very existence of that policy and its impact upon the resource base and economy.

As a shared, multi-purpose resource, the Lakes are intensively used and managed at every level from the local to international arena.[15] Eight states and two Canadian provinces share the Basin. Literally hundreds of governmental entities are charged with management of some aspect of the resource, including municipalities, county health boards, state and provincial departments of natural resources, planning and conservation districts, over a dozen federal agencies (American and Canadian) and several international bodies as well. Most are limited in management authority to a defined political jurisdiction and/or a specific management function (e.g., water supply, flood control, water quantity). Yet, singly and collectively, they contribute to the status of the resource and therefore, influence binational relations. Further, a constellation of research institutes, citizen groups, business/labor organizations, policy centers, foundations, and special interest coalitions have flourished as well, using the various access points to government institutions to influence the direction of Great Lakes policy and management activity.

Treaties, agreements, memoranda of understanding and diplomatic exchanges between and among state, provincial and federal governments in the United States and Canada have frequently been employed in the Great Lakes policy process. For example, a series of treaties dating back to the Treaty of Paris in 1783 have been employed to address binational issues between the United States and Canada. The International Boundary Waters Treaty of 1909 emerged as the culmination of early joint initiatives, and remains today as the principal guide for Canada-United States relations on Great Lakes water quality and quantity issues.

The Canada-United States Great Lakes Water Quality Agreement, signed by the two federal governments in 1972 and subsequently amended in 1978 and 1986, provides for the development and implementation of programs to control municipal and industrial water pollution sources; work toward elimination of toxic substance discharges; identify various non-point sources of pollution; improve monitoring and surveillance; and carry out other functions. At the inter-state/provincial level, the Great Lakes Charter (1985) and Great Lakes Toxic Substances Control Agreement (1986) are examples of cooperative agreements among the Great Lakes governors and premiers.[16,17]

Memoranda of understanding are a "step down" from an agreement in terms of formality and political consequence. They are available to (and among) federal, state and provincial governments. At the federal level, for example, an August, 1980 Memorandum of Intent established a joint Canada-United States approach to investigating the acid rain issue. At the state level, examples include transboundary air pollution Memoranda of Understanding between Quebec and New York, Quebec and Vermont and Minnesota and Ontario. While Article I of the U.S. Constitution prohibits these devices from being binding agreements unless ratified by Congress, they serve as "good faith agreements" between two or more jurisdictions seeking remedy to a shared problem or as a consultation device for a shared issue.

The two governments frequently exchange diplomatic notes or otherwise communicate on resource management issues of shared concern. These exchanges are as varied as the seemingly infinite array of transboundary issues that arise. John Carroll refers to this as "adhockery";[18] a more appropriate term might be "creative diplomacy". These exchanges can be used as a precursor to the development of an agreement, treaty or other mutual understanding. They can also be used as something of an "end run" around an institutional structure that is not always as responsive as it should be.

The complexity of this Great Lakes "institutional ecosystem" is a well-documented and readily observable phenomenon. Not surprisingly, charges of organizational inefficiency and redundancy have been leveled at the Great Lakes policy process over time. While justified in some cases, such charges fail to recognize that complexity is not a "de facto" consequence of an inefficient process. Rather, institutional complexity is a fact of life defined by the nature of the resource and the diversity of its uses.

By virtue of its expansiveness alone, a complex, multi-jurisdictional management approach is assured. Until the rather recent emergence of the ecosystem management concept, the five Great Lakes and St. Lawrence River were considered to be, and therefore managed as, discrete hydrologic units. Consequently, the various management

functions associated with the water and related land resources of the Basin were assigned in a piecemeal, issue-specific manner to the many established political jurisdictions.

Unlike most other major bodies of fresh surface water in North America, the Great Lakes-St. Lawrence system possesses certain properties that lend themselves to intensive multiple uses. The system provides, for example, a tremendous volume of high quality fresh water; accessibility by population and industrial centers; and a hydrologic configuration suitable for commercial transportation. Despite the long-standing diversity of resource uses, however, resource management at the governmental level tends to be compartmentalized and geographically confined. Within a given state or province, for example, separate departments or ministries may address water quantity, water quality, transportation, economic development or tourism concerns. The complexity increases by an order of magnitude when the management issue is a binational one.

The interface between hydrologic and political boundaries also breeds complexity. Water bodies have historically been perceived as convenient lines of demarcation between adjacent political jurisdictions rather than as shared and unifying resources. The Great Lakes-St. Lawrence system has, until rather recently, been viewed in such a light. As a result, for decades management institutions developed essentially independently on each side of the border before even the most rudimentary binational efforts were instituted.

The ecosystem management concept is being increasingly embraced, in some manner, by the various units and levels of government in the Basin. Developing for over a century, yet not formally recognized in Great Lakes management until the 1978 Great Lakes Water Quality Agreement, this concept recognizes the interdependency of the physical, chemical, biological, and human processes within the Great Lakes system. As explained by the International Joint Commission's Water Quality Board, the concept "provides the philosophical framework and scientific rationale to grasp the notion that everything in the basin is related to and affects, to some degree, everything else in the basin."[19]

In application, the ecosystem management concept rejects a structured, compartmentalized management approach for one that recognizes and accommodates the interdependency between all components and uses of the Great Lakes Basin and its resources. While this notion has been accepted conceptually, application has been problematic. Established units of government typically resist any initiative that results in a loss of their autonomy or authority to manage the resource base in their accustomed manner. Canada-United States relations must contend with this.

Finally, institutional complexity typically increases as the institutional framework adapts to "new" knowledge. Increased scientific understanding of the Great Lakes-St. Lawrence system, changing social issues and preferences, and a changing political climate all generate "new" knowledge that must be assimilated by a management institution. In such cases, the institutional framework will adapt in one of three ways: internal re-ordering and/or expansion of management processes within existing institutions; formation of inter-institutional linkages to address implications of "new knowledge"; or creation of new institutions to address unmet management needs. In each case, increased institutional complexity is the observed outcome. Given that the Great Lakes-St. Lawrence system is a vast "freshwater frontier" and its experiments in bilateral relations constitute a "political frontier", the continuing trend toward institutional complexity in Canada-United States relations is not surprising.

Governments also possess some inherent tendencies when operating in a multi-jurisdictional resource management setting. The political science literature, specifically that relating to organizational theory, provides a series of explanations for the evolving structure, function and authority associated with binational resource management efforts. Most obvious is the fact that the United States and Canada maintain distinct governmental structures, political philosophies and perspectives on the bilateral management of the Great Lakes. Bureaucracies of any kind must also contend with tendencies toward institutional inertia; "crisis response" management; political pressures for creating new institutional mechanisms rather than refining

existing ones; the perception of regional and binational institutions as rather "weak" bodies constrained by the prevailing political will of member jurisdictions; and the experimental nature of regional and binational resource management.

Roles and responsibilities in water policy

In his review of domestic and binational Great Lakes-St. Lawrence management approaches, Munton observes, "The similarities in Canadian and American institutions and legislation are hardly surprising, given the common social roots, historical experiences, and political and philosophical traditions as well as the extraordinary level of communications and exchanges across the border between the two countries."[20] Despite these similarities, however, Munton goes on to note that, "It is ... the differences which are the more interesting and the more revealing." These differences must be acknowledged and addressed in the pursuit of viable regional mechanisms for Great Lakes-St. Lawrence water resource policy and management. In the ensuing discussion, the respective roles of the various levels of government in Great Lakes-St. Lawrence water policy will be described, and their interrelationships highlighted.

The United States federal government

The U.S. federal government is well represented in the complex Great Lakes-St. Lawrence management framework, both in terms of institutional presence and power. Francis explains: "The federal government exercises considerable influence, especially through its fiscal dominance and extensive use of conditional grant funding to states. In many areas of resource and environmental policy and programs, the federal role is paramount, although wide use is made of federal-state cooperative programs which are jointly funded."[21] Caldwell elaborates, explaining that "the salient feature of environmental legislation in the United States is its federal intergovernmental character—federal financial assistance, standard setting and specific regulation, with state and local responsibility for implementing and enforcing environmental provisions subject to federal approval."[22] Accountability for Great Lakes management efforts lies at the

federal level, where policies and programs are either dictated directly or relegated to the states with the retention of oversight authority.

The U.S. federal role is firmly established under the Constitution, reaffirmed in a series of major pieces of federal legislation, and reinforced operationally though policies and programs. Buttressed by statutory and case law, these various clauses provide the federal government with broad powers in resource management at the interstate and international level.

The constitutional separation of the executive, legislative and judicial branches of the U.S. federal government—and its attendant system of "checks and balances"—ensures each branch an important role in water resource management. Within the executive branch, the President has the power to negotiate treaties with Canada, issue executive orders to shape institutional and policy frameworks, establish directives for federal agencies involved in resource management, and influence the budgetary process upon which federal efforts rely. At the legislative level, the U.S. Congress has the power to ratify treaties with Canada, consent to interstate compacts, pass federal laws with far-reaching resource management implications, and approve the federal budget. The power of the federal judiciary is the third balancing force in this tripartite system. The U.S. Supreme Court is empowered to determine the constitutionality of federal laws and actions, interpret legislative intent, and intervene and settle interstate disputes.

As early as 1787, with the approval of the Northwest Ordinance, the Great Lakes region was formally recognized under federal domain. Soon thereafter, with the adoption of the U.S. Constitution in 1789, the federal government was granted broad authority under the commerce, property, general welfare, war, treaty and compact consent powers. The Rush-Bagot convention of 1817—limiting naval armaments in the Great Lakes—was perhaps the first recognition of the Great Lakes system as a regional (i.e., international) resource demanding a strong federal presence. A series of U.S.-Canadian agreements addressing mutual navigation rights followed, as did the establishment of various binational waterways commissions in the 1880s and 1890s.

A series of landmark federal laws—most of which were passed in the early decades of the 1900s—also explain the evolution of the federal role in water resource policy and management. The Rivers and Harbors Act, first enacted in 1827 and subsequently amended on numerous occasions, established the U.S. Army Corps of Engineers as the developer and protector of the nation's navigable waters (including the Great Lakes), and asserted Congressional jurisdiction over those waters.

Passage of the federal Public Health Service Act of 1912 was an initial step in formalizing a federal role in environmental management matters.[23] The federal Flood Control Act, first enacted in 1917, empowered the federal government to improve navigable waterways and watersheds, which include many of the Great Lakes rivers and tributaries.

Any lingering doubts as to the constitutional authority of the federal government to legislate on environmental/resource management issues were essentially negated with the signing of the National Environmental Policy Act of 1970 (NEPA).

The "new federalism" philosophy, prevalent in the United States since the early 1980s, involves an effort to relegate traditional federal resource management responsibilities and associated programs to state jurisdiction. While this trend has already had a pronounced impact upon the Great Lakes-St. Lawrence management effort, it is yet unclear as to what the long-term consequences will be.

The U.S. federal system in characterized below in summary fashion, reflecting in part the work of Francis and Caldwell.[24] Drawing upon their investigations, the following key characteristics and attendant implications for Great Lakes-St. Lawrence management are noted:

■ The separation of powers among the executive, legislative and judicial branches of government, and the resultant system of "checks and balances". Each branch of government has a significant role in the development of water policy: it can emerge from executive action (e.g., abolishment of the Title II River Basin Commission system); the Congressional legislative process (e.g., passage of the Clean Water Act); or a judicial decree (e.g., water quantity management/water diversion implications of the *Sporhase v. Nebraska* decision of 1982). The system is a dynamic one, and the action of one branch is subject to investigation or refutation by another.

■ The tradition of bipartisanship. The political allegiance of elected officials lies first with the constituent and second with party affiliation. The Congress recognizes the need for consensus building among often diverse groups when their interests coalesce on a given issue. This tendency is reflected in the bipartisan support that has become a hallmark of regional cooperation on Great Lakes issues.

■ The openness and accessibility of the federal policy-making process. Individuals and interest groups can access a number of avenues to introduce or influence resource management policy. Members of Congress have long been receptive to legislative initiatives from constituents. Political sensitivities in the executive branch exist as well, and agencies susceptible to constituent pressures can respond with emphasis/deemphasis on specific issues. Finally, the judicial system grants citizens and interest groups standing in the courts, and litigation is increasingly used as a policy-making device.

■ The legislative and fiscal dominance of the federal government vis-à-vis state and regional governments. Landmark federal legislation in the early decades of this century, coupled with other initiatives in more recent years, has affirmed the leadership role of the federal government in most areas of resource management. While the "new federalism" philosophy has increased state roles in designing, funding and implementing regional programs, strong oversight functions have been retained by the federal government. Further, federal fiscal resources—and the dependency of the states upon them—have given rise to conditional state grants and federally supported cooperative arrangements where the federal government serves as the "senior member" in the "partnership" approach.

The Canadian federal government

The role of the Canadian federal government in Great Lakes-St. Lawrence management is markedly different than that of its United States counterpart. The origin of such difference is found in the British North America Act of 1867 which allocates legislative powers between the provincial and federal governments. The Act grants provincial governments jurisdiction over the management and sale of public lands, property and civil rights and "matters of merely local and private nature within the province." Section 92 is key in that it emphasizes the provincial right to the use of resources within its boundaries on the basis of its ownership of them.[25]

The federal government has certain broad powers which influence the use and development of water resources. These include the general power to legislate for "peace, order and good government," as well as regulation of banking, taxation, the public debt, and defense and criminal law. Munton elaborates, "Provinces have clear constitutional authority in the areas of natural resources such as land and forests, intra-provincial commerce, property and civil rights, municipal governments and matters of a local or private nature. The federal government ... has clear jurisdiction over federal lands, coastal and inland fisheries, oceans, navigation and shipping; and various matters of a national or extra-provincial nature, including transportation and international commerce." He adds that "agriculture and health are matters of concurrent jurisdiction."[26]

Federal responsibilities for environmental protection and resource management are embodied in a series of legislative acts, cabinet directives, federal-provincial agreements, orders-in-council and international treaties and agreements. A common theme running throughout them is recognition of the stature of the provincial role in resource management and the necessity for intergovernmental devices to address multi-jurisdictional (domestic and international) issues. In an examination of such issues, MacNeil states: "Effective management strategies in any one of these jurisdictional situations necessarily concerns both orders of government. This appears to be an almost inescapable conclusion.... It flows not only from the fact that environmental problems are dominated by spillovers. It flows also from four characteristics that stand out in each part of the analysis: ecological interdependence; physical interdependence; problem interdependence; hence, jurisdictional interdependence. The overriding corollary of this, of course, is intergovernmental cooperation at all levels and in all possible forms. It is difficult if not impossible to visualize any political or institutional structure, or any system of powers, that would reduce the importance of such cooperation or that would work without it."[27]

The basis for specific Canadian federal involvement in Great Lakes-St. Lawrence management is embodied in a limited number of federal statutes that have been broadly interpreted over the years. Principal among them is the Fisheries Act, the first version of which was enacted in 1868. A key provision prohibiting the discharge of deleterious substances into waters "frequented by fish" has, over time and via amendments, become a potent federal device for pollution control. Since its passage, it has also provided the foundation for promulgation of an extensive series of guidelines and regulations.

Three acts warrant additional attention by virtue of their implications for federal-provincial and Canada-United States relations. The first of these is the Canada Water Act, passed in 1970 following a number of years in development. The Act, in seeking explicit definition of the federal role and intergovernmental relationships in water resource management, provides for: federal-provincial consultative arrangements and cooperative agreements in the development and implementation of water management plans; the establishment of federal-provincial agencies to plan and implement approved water quality management programs; water quality control regulations designed to address eutrophication problems; public information programs; and inspection and enforcement programs.

A second federal statute of particular interest is the Canada Clean Air Act, designed to protect Canadian citizens from dangerous pollutants, while setting minimum ambient air quality standards and establishing air quality monitoring programs. Significantly, 1980 amendments to the Act included a reciprocity clause allowing U.S. representation with respect to transboundary air pollution effects.

A third act, the Canadian Environmental Protection Act of 1988, provides a comprehensive approach to the life cycle management of chemicals and fills gaps in federal toxic substances legislation. In establishing a national chemicals assessment program, the act will generate information that can strengthen efforts to develop binational Great Lakes water quality objectives.

Francis and Munton characterize the Canadian system of government as follows: [28]

■ The concentration of power in the majority party, and more specifically in the executive branch. In Canadian government, party loyalty among legislators is paramount; coalition government is not a standard. Because the majority party forms the entire Cabinet, the executive branch tends to concentrate power and, in effect, controls the legislature. The opposition party is decidedly impotent. Hence, the "pressure points" for effecting change in water policy are found not in the legislative branch but in that of the executive.

■ The relative stability of the executive branch. Both the federal and provincial governments tend to be more "stable" than their U.S. counterparts. Recent developments aside, majority parties have been known to retain office for decades. This form of entrenchment can be positive in the sense that longer-term programs and goals can be pursued with some modicum of continuity. Conversely, perceived inadequacies in a given area are less likely to be addressed or policies reversed in the absence of a change in power.

■ The stature of the civil service in policy development. The characteristics identified above, coupled with a "tradition of professionalism" in the civil service, tends to concentrate policy-making power and influence in the upper echelons of departmental management as opposed to elected officials. Consequently, the civil service serves as the origin for many of the government's legislative initiatives and policy directives.

■ The emphasis on broad interpretation and application of statutes. Canada is much less prolific than the United States in legislative matters, preferring to address emerging issues with broad interpretation and application of relatively few statutes. Such interpretation is vested in the executive branch via promulgation of rules and guidelines. This discre-

tionary authority further strengthens that branch's role as the locus of governmental policymaking.

■ The separation of powers and attendant "checks and balances" is not observed within the federal or provincial government, but within federal-provincial relations. In water policy and all other areas of government activity, the division of authority between the federal and provincial governments is seldom well defined, and their respective viewpoints are seldom uniform. Hence, intergovernmental relations tend to provide the "checks and balances" lacking within a single jurisdiction.

■ The power of the province relative to the federal government. The Canadian Constitution grants the provinces extensive authority and self-determination in the area of resource use and management, among others. This authority is fairly well defined in intraprovincial matters but significantly less settled when transboundary issues (domestic and international) arise.

Great Lakes states

Although the riparian states exercise substantial authority in water policy, such authority is not intrinsic. It is largely derived from, and therefore subject to, a preemptive federal authority. Federal dominance is a function of the political and hydrologic attributes of the Great Lakes-St. Lawrence system: it is a navigable waterway, an interstate resource, and it has an international character. Further, the several constitutional powers vested in the federal government, coupled with the evolution of statutory and case law, have preserved and strengthened that intergovernmental relationship. The Great Lakes Basin Commission explains:

"In view of the construction that the Supreme Court has given the 'commerce clause' in conjunction with the 'necessary and proper clause' and the 'supremacy clause,' it can be said that the federal government may interpret the power to manage water resources almost completely if the Congress chooses to do so."[29]

Historically, it has been the policy of the Congress that water resources management should be a primary responsibility of the state under the broad rubric of federal authority. In fact, prior to the signing of the National Environmental Policy Act of 1970 (P.L. 91-190), "many legal scholars doubted the constitutional authority of the United States government to legislate on environmental issues".[30] Such issues were viewed as regional or local concerns, and, hence, not under the purview of the federal government. The Great Lakes states have long maintained broad responsibility in the areas of water supply; waste disposal; water quality; fish and wildlife; recreation and scenic preservation; shoreland and floodplain management; land management; mineral, oil and gas extraction; standard setting; investigation and enforcement; planning; and others.

Three observations clarify the nature of federal-state relations in the context of Great Lakes water policy The first is the grantor-grantee relationship. While the Great Lakes states do enjoy some autonomy in developing Great Lakes water policy, the preponderance of their activity is delegated by the federal government under statute. In most cases, federal funding assistance provides an incentive for compliance. As the National Research Council and Royal Society of Canada explain in their analysis of the Great Lakes Water Quality Agreement:

"Although federal policy generally seeks delegation of authority to the states under the approximately dozen applicable major laws, delegation depends on state compliance with federal requirements. Each law establishes a distinct program under which a different state-federal program plan for each state is negotiated annually to specify program objectives and federal and state funding contributions."[31]

Second, the Great Lakes states have historically been regarded as "second-class citizens" in binational Great Lakes water policy issues. Article XI of the Great Lakes Water Quality Agreement states that the "parties commit themselves to seek the cooperation of the State and Provincial governments in all matters relating to this Agreement." In practice, the progress realized under the Agreement is largely attributable to the extensive involvement and considerable investment of the states and provinces. Yet, the states had no formal role in the formulation, review and renegotiation of the 1972 Agreement. While the states do have an active

operational role in meeting binational commitments, the federal government has been historically reluctant to provide an expanded (much less equal role) at the policy-setting level. This historical pattern is gradually changing, as indicated by state involvement in the 1987 protocol to the Great Lakes Water Quality Agreement and new mechanisms for federal-state consultation, such as the U.S. Policy Committee established by the U.S. Environmental Protection Agency.

Third, federal-state relations have been characterized by the use of an array of coordinative mechanisms. While the federal-state hierarchy in binational relations is jealously guarded, an historical emphasis on coordinative arrangements between the two attests to their interdependence. Many generic institutional forms for regional resource management provide some mechanism for state-federal coordination; this is most assuredly the case in the Great Lakes Basin. While the federal government has an aversion to formal binding agreements with the states on binational issues (e.g., lack of a U.S. equivalent of the Canada-Ontario Agreement under the Great Lakes Water Quality Agreement), it has participated actively in various intergovernmental forums (e.g., member of Great Lakes Basin Commission, observer to Great Lakes Commission).

Great Lakes provinces

The British North America Act grants Canadian provincial governments primary management authority over the natural resources within their boundaries. Section 92 of that Act places under provincial auspices the management and sale of public lands, property and civil rights, and "matters of a merely local and private nature within the province." When the resources at issue are of a regional and binational nature, however, jurisdictional questions arise.

Environment Canada, in an examination of Canadian institutional arrangements for water resource management, notes:

"In the constitutional history of Canada, problems of jurisdiction have often plagued the achievement of an integrated definition of the renewable resources problem, and with regionalism given primary importance in Canadian federalism, a

more fluid and problem oriented approach to jurisdictional matters is necessary."[32]

The analysis further noted that the definition of water itself has evolved over the last fifty years and, in so doing, has exacerbated the jurisdictional problem. Once considered a proprietary resource owned and controlled by the provinces, it came to be defined in relation to the nature of its use. "Consequently, water which flows across provincial boundaries or which takes on differing or multiple functions is subject to changing and conflicting jurisdictions with the result that a purely proprietary administration of water resource use is now regarded as inefficient by both levels of government." The Canadian Environmental Law Research Foundation adds:

"The combination of indirect reference to water in the constitution and limited guidance from the courts makes it impossible to define precisely the respective roles of the federal-provincial governments in water management."[33]

It is perhaps this shared authority and omnipresent jurisdictional uncertainty that has given rise to extensive use of federal-provincial management agreements. In Ontario, principal among these are the Canada-Ontario Environmental Accord and the Canada-Ontario Agreement Respecting Great Lakes Water Quality. The former recognizes "a federal role in developing national baseline pollution standards, the need for cooperation on implementation, and a primary provincial role in enforcement". The latter provides the federal-provincial arrangements necessary to fulfill the terms of the Canada-U.S. Great Lakes Water Quality Agreement. A third agreement—the Canada-Ontario Strategic Plan for Ontario Fisheries—provides a similar mechanism for implementing the terms of the Joint Strategic Plan for Management of Great Lakes Fisheries, adopted in 1981. Additional agreements have addressed a variety of other resource management topics.

Beyond the broad powers vested in the province by the British North America Act of 1867, a series of statutes guide Ontario's involvement in resource management. The earliest of these in terms of water quality is the Public Health Act of 1884, requiring approval of water supply systems by the provincial government and, further, making the discharge of wastes into such an offense. Statutory authority was broadened and made more explicit by the 1957 Ontario Water Resources Commission Act which "provided substantial authority regarding ground and surface water supplies, sewage disposal, and pollution abatement, and the setting of water quality standards and effluent standards for both municipal and industrial sources."[34] An omnibus Environmental Protection Act was passed in 1971 with special emphasis on air quality and hazardous waste management. The 1975 Environmental Assessment Act is the Canadian counterpart to the U.S. National Environmental Policy Act.

Regional, multi-jurisdictional institutions

State, federal and provincial agencies have always had important water resource policy and management functions, and almost exclusive responsibility for standard setting and regulation/enforcement activities. However, there is a second layer of governance, comprised of regionally oriented institutions. In the broadest of terms, they serve to transcend the parochialism of the "traditional" political boundaries and focus instead on hydrologic boundaries.

Among the regional institutions, the International Joint Commission and Great Lakes Fishery Commission are the principal ones operating at the binational level, where the use of treaties, conventions and agreements between the United States and Canada comprise the more formal mechanisms for cooperative approaches to shared problems. The former, created via the International Boundary Waters Treaty of 1909, has monitoring, surveillance, and quasi-judicial functions relating to water quality and quantity issues arising along the common frontier of the two countries. The latter, created by convention in 1954, directs its efforts at maximizing the sustained productivity of the Great Lakes fishery through control of the sea lamprey and the conduct and coordination of fisheries research.

At the U.S. domestic regional level, principal public institutions include the Great Lakes Commission and the Council of Great Lakes Governors. The Commission, created by joint legislative action of the eight Great Lakes states, was established in 1955

to promote the informed use, development, and protection of the Great Lakes via information sharing, interstate coordination, and advocacy on a wide range of regional economic development and resource management issues. The Council was established in 1982 as a forum for discussion and action by the Great Lakes governors on pertinent regional issues. In Canada, various inter-provincial and federal-provincial agreements are in force, as well as the Interdepartmental Committee on Water with representation from twenty federal departments and agencies.

Regional organizations play a pivotal role in Great Lakes-St. Lawrence management: they provide the forum in which all the "players" at all levels of government can coordinate their shared implementing roles and focus them on common problems and opportunities. They provide a framework for nurturing new ideas and management innovations, while providing a buffering capacity to temper the impact of change. As essentially voluntary arrangements among traditional jurisdictions, they have limited autonomy and power, thereby posing little threat to their membership. Yet, by coordinating actions and promoting consistency among these members, they do facilitate subtle yet substantive change in resource management practices.

While the various regional, multi-jurisdictional institutions involved in Great Lakes policy share many goals and common interests, distinct priorities, constituents and methods reflect the nature of their respective mandates. There are, however, several common characteristics that all such entities exhibit. Such institutions are responses to the multi-jurisdictional, multiple-use resource management requirements of the Great Lakes Basin: in essence, an acknowledgment that management by hydrologic rather than political boundary is a fundamental tenet of sound water policy. They are also "creatures" of their signatory parties, being fully accountable to them and, necessarily, highly flexible and adaptable to emerging needs and the changing political climate in member jurisdictions. "Soft management" is a term that best describes such institutions, which generally lack regulatory and enforcement capability, focusing instead on coordi-

nation, policy development and advocacy. One primary value is found in their ability to promote the "strength in numbers" concept: providing a unified regional front for advocating policies to federal governments and legislatures.

Sub-state/provincial institutions

Resource management institutions at the sub-state/provincial level consist of the collectivity of standard political jurisdictions (e.g., counties, municipalities, townships) as well as intrastate/provincial entities with a hydrologic or resource-based geographic definition. The latter includes intrastate special districts; watershed councils; conservation authorities; soil and water conservation districts and the like. In most instances, they are membership organizations comprised of and financially supported by communities within their geographic jurisdiction. The emphasis is commonly on information-sharing, coordination, resource conservation and management.

In the United States, an example of an intrastate arrangement is the regional planning commission —generally a multi-county organization focusing on a shared watershed through the cooperative efforts of municipal and county governments, frequently with state financial assistance. These commissions, under the former Section 208 program of the federal Clean Water Act, played a key role in the planning and implementation of nonpoint source pollution control programs. Watershed councils (where they do exist) provide valuable coordinative services for the various jurisdictions within a given river drainage system.

In Canada, a subprovincial resource planning effort of particular note is the system of conservation authorities which extends throughout Ontario. A provincial-municipal partnership, the authorities are local, autonomous organizations with a mandate to "further the conservation, restoration, development and management of natural resources other than gas, oil, coal and minerals." While the principal focus is on water management (erosion and flood control), the authorities are active also in water quality, recreation, and broader conservation/management concerns. Operated with policy, financial and technical assistance from the Ministry of Natural Resources, 37 authorities have jurisdiction in the Great Lakes Basin.

The importance of sub-state/provincial institutions to the Basinwide resource management effort cannot be overstated. Local zoning decisions, shoreline development activities, sewage treatment facilities, erosion control, floodplains and agricultural practices—to name a few—have a tremendous cumulative impact on the use and quality of the Basin resources. Hence, the value of such institutions as the "field level" arm of a broader regional effort must be recognized in institutional analyses.

Nongovernmental institutions

The role of the nongovernmental organization—in both Canada and the United States—is substantial and increasing in stature. Such organizations include citizen groups, academic institutions, labor interests, business associations, and the like. This component of the federal system is under- represented in formal arrangements for Basin governance, and particularly so in regional institutions. Yet the role has been increasing as "new federalism" takes hold. A prime example is in the non-profit sector where activity since 1980 has been unprecedented in scope. Examples include the establishment of The Centre for the Great Lakes, Great Lakes United, the Council of Great Lakes Industries, the Great Lakes Maritime Forum, and the International Great Lakes Coalition, to name a few. The role of such organizations in the management process varies widely, but generally includes education, information sharing, advocacy, coordination, and issue analysis.

In recent years, many such organizations have become influential participants in the policy/management process. The "maturation" of the environmental movement provides one explanation. Nongovernmental involvement in resource management issues has become increasingly sophisticated. Antagonistic approaches and public demonstrations have largely given way to well-informed and politically astute advocacy activities, coupled with cooperative ventures with government and less confrontational means of dispute resolution.

A growing appreciation of the Great Lakes-St. Lawrence system as an economic as well as environ-

mental asset has also strengthened the non-governmental role—particularly that of the business/industrial community. A growing portion of that community is recognizing its vested interest in management and protection of the Lakes for sustainable development. This recognition has lead to active involvement in water resource policy and management matters.

Also, the continuing redefinition of federal and state/provincial roles in Great Lakes management has broadened opportunities for non-governmental influence. Both countries are experiencing policy shifts and budgetary adjustments which have increased responsibilities of state, provincial and local governments and constrained financial resources and program activity. Nongovernmental organizations have assumed some of the vacated functions and, over time, have been increasingly relied upon by government jurisdictions. Such organizations number in the hundreds if one were to include all those at the regional or intra-state/provincial level with a Great Lakes-St. Lawrence focus.

Trends in water policy and their implications

In the binational Great Lakes Basin, water policy is not a finite process where issues emerge, are sequentially addressed and permanently resolved. The Great Lakes management arena is simply too dynamic and too complex. Issues do not disappear, but their characteristics change constantly. Progress is more typically measured in years than months, but it does occur. From the environmental/resource management standpoint, for example, the last two decades have brought dramatic improvements in point source pollution control; a revitalized sport fishery; improved coastal zone management practices; and a better understanding of the sources and impacts of toxic contamination, to name a few. From the political/governmental standpoint, the last two decades have witnessed unprecedented binational cooperation, the development and maturation of multi-jurisdictional institutional arrangements and, in general terms, a greater recognition of the economic and environmental importance of the resource.

Water policy professionals throughout the Great Lakes Basin can be justifiably proud of their

collective contributions over the years. A well established institutional and policy framework is in place and, despite its limitations, has demonstrated an ability to manage the resource for environmental, economic and quality of life benefits. Past accomplishments, however, can pale in comparison to the challenge ahead. Presented below is a sampling of leading trends in water policy and their implications for the future management of the resource. The trends themselves speak to the economy/environment linkages in the region, and confirm the fact that solutions to emerging problems and opportunities will demand multi-jurisdictional and multi-disciplinary approaches.

1) "Creative financing" will be the rule, rather than the exception, in water resource management programs at all levels of government. The "new federalism" philosophy espoused by the present and previous U.S. administrations is no longer new; it has been institutionalized and accepted (reluctantly in some cases) as standard operating procedure. At the Basin level, an historic reliance upon federal funds for water programs and projects has been replaced by a "partnership theme" that includes an array of options. Federal/state; interstate; state/provincial; and public/private sector financing options will increasingly be the norm in an era of fiscal austerity where "cost-share" and "user pay" philosophies will prevail.

Implications of this trend have already affected water policy in the Great Lakes-St. Lawrence system. For example, cost-share provisions in the federal Water Resources Development Act of 1986 have effectively halted progress on a second large navigation lock at Sault Ste. Marie, Michigan. A prohibitive non-federal contribution requirement has few prospects of being met and the Congress has exhibited little interest in a variance from cost share provisions. As a second example, federal funding for basic research, monitoring and enforcement programs for Great Lakes environmental protection has declined 11 percent in real dollars between fiscal years 1981 and 1990, prompting the Great Lakes states to take a new look at funding options. [35]

Also, the "creative financing" challenge will be encountered in dramatic fashion with impending implementation of Remedial Action Plans (RAPs) for the Basin's 42 designated Areas of Concern. As high profile "experiments" in multi-jurisdictional cooperation, the success of the RAPs will be determined in large part by creative, non-traditional funding sources.

2) The Great Lakes states will increasingly embrace and act on their "stewardship responsibility" for the resource. Historically, the Great Lakes states have deferred to the federal government on matters of water policy, an indication of their reliance upon federal programs and funding assistance. The "new federalism" philosophy has changed this practice. States that once looked to Washington, D.C. for a hand-out are now looking for a hand—a new paradigm emphasizing state-federal partnerships. This philosophy is reflected in the Great Lakes Charter, which proclaims that the states and provinces "have a mutual legal and political obligation to take primary responsibility for protecting the lakes...".[36] It is also reflected in the recent creation of a $100 million Great Lakes Protection Fund, capitalized entirely by the Great Lakes states under gubernatorial leadership. The future is likely to bring other major interstate policy and program initiatives that further assert and act on a philosophy of state primacy and self-determination in the use, management and protection of water and related land resources.

3) Pollution control efforts, by necessity, will continue to shift from the "technological fix" to practices that affect individual and organization behaviors. Point source pollution control was the success story of the last two decades. A $10 billion expenditure for construction and upgrading of municipal sewage treatment plants, coupled with detergent phosphate bans and "end of the pipe" technology, brought dramatic improvements in the control of conventional pollutants. In comparative terms, however, the job was not prohibitively difficult; adequate finances and suitable technology were available, and the point sources were readily identified.

Attention is shifting to non-point pollutant sources which now contribute the majority of conventional and toxic pollutants to the environment through atmospheric transport, urban and rural land runoff, groundwater and landfill pollution, and related pathways. Control costs can be prohibitive, pollutant sources and impacts are difficult to ascertain, and the "technological fix" is simply not an option. Behavior modification —anathema to private enterprise whether it be a major industry or family farm—is fast becoming the inescapable solution to ongoing environmental problems. Conservation tillage procedures, industrial "pollution prevention" strategies and waste reduction processes will increasingly become accepted and, in some cases, mandatory components of business activity.

With few exceptions (e.g., Soil Conservation Service, state/provincial Departments of Natural Resources) government agencies have little experience in extension/public outreach activities designed to modify behavior at either the individual or corporate level. By necessity, this will change dramatically in coming years.

4) Government agencies will be held increasingly accountable for their actions. Lines of accountability associated with government activity are typically well defined within political jurisdictions, but tend to fade at the regional level. In the Great Lakes Basin, regional organizations generally lack "hard" management (i.e., enforcement, regulatory) authority, relying instead on advisory and persuasive powers to effect change. State, provincial and federal governments are, in most cases, not compelled to subscribe to the declarations and recommendations of regional organizations. Furthermore, such organizations are little known among the general population and, as a consequence, accountability for their actions is compromised.

In the years ahead, multi-jurisdictional cooperation throughout the Great Lakes-St. Lawrence system will no longer be a marriage of convenience; it will be a marriage of necessity. Lines of accountability will be strengthened in all directions as regional organizations assume increasing stature and profile in the universe of regional economic development, environmental quality and economic development issues. They will be increasingly accountable to their membership, whether it be comprised of state, provincial and/or federal governments. In turn, political jurisdictions will be compelled to do more than simply acknowledge the recommendations of regional organizations; they will be expected to embrace and act upon them as well. Finally, the trend toward an active and informed citizenry will continue, and regional organizations will experience unprecedented levels of public interest and expectation.

5) Private sector interests will abandon their peripheral role in water policy, organizing for action and becoming central players. The business community has historically operated on the periphery of the water policy arena. Until recently it was largely a reluctant—even unwilling—participant whose involvement was typically issue-specific and reactive in nature. It entered the arena primarily to defend its interests, explain its actions or position itself for future growth.

This characterization has changed dramatically in recent years and will continue to do so. The "stewardship" philosophy now being embraced by water-dependent business and industry is indicative. Evidence of such is found in the formation of the Canadian Roundtables on Economy and Environment, the new Council of Great Lakes Industries, a growing assortment of corporate environmental councils and coalitions, and the assimilation of business and industry leaders into many areas of water policy discussion and debate. The implications are great; an organized and active business community will add a new and vital dimension to all aspects of water resource planning and policy making, including advancement of sustainable development principles. It brings with it as well the potential for heightened debate and conflict where differing views among interest groups are long standing and clearly and irrevocably drawn.

6) The Great Lakes Basin will emerge as both a "test case" and "battleground" for water policy initiatives and issues of national and international significance. The Great Lakes-St. Lawrence system enjoys increasing stature as a global laboratory for scientific inquiry and institutional analysis. From a scientific standpoint, the Basin has stature as the world's greatest freshwater resource: its Lakes are hydrologically diverse; they are the locus of equally diverse and intensive multiple use; they have been

intensively studied and monitored; and an excellent historical data base has been developed.

From an institutional standpoint, the requisite characteristics of a global model are present as well. It is a binational, multi-jurisdictional resource; it has a rather sophisticated management system; it has helped pioneer concepts of sustainable development and ecosystem management; and it has a well-documented history of both crisis-response and proactive planning. In essence, the Great Lakes Basin is a composite—a microcosm—of the array of socio-economic, political and environmental characteristics and issues that one might find in any water-based region—North America or beyond.

The "rust belt" misnomer has long given way to a more appropriate "water belt" label. While other regions of North America have struggled with water shortages and major drought events in the last decade, Great Lakes Basin jurisdictions have rediscovered the plentiful, high quality resource that is as much a magnet for economic development as it is for tourism and recreation. The specter of out-of-basin water diversion, which is tantamount to diverting the region's employment base and economic future, will most assuredly remain with Great Lakes jurisdictions into the future. Issues of contention among and between states will also arise as cooperative regional efforts mature. Uniformity in water quality standards and fish consumption advisories; balancing industrial development and environmental preservation strategies; and reconciling water use and management practices in shared water resources are but a few of the challenges that will face Basin jurisdictions. In many respects, the Great Lakes Basin will be "writing the text" as its ongoing "experiment" in scientific and institutional analysis continues.

7) An aging and increasingly inadequate infrastructure for water supply, treatment and commercial transportation will pose unprecedented challenges to policy leadership. For decades, expansion of the Basin's water supply infrastructure to accommodate a growing population was of the highest priority, with rehabilitation and preventive maintenance of secondary concern. As a result, an aging infrastructure with compromised efficiency is approaching "critical condition"; a problem

exacerbated by increasingly severe fiscal constraints at all levels of government.

The wastewater treatment infrastructure in the Basin is also at a critical juncture. A $10 billion construction and upgrading program (U.S. and Canada) in the Basin since 1970 has yielded an extensive system that now includes over 400 major municipal wastewater treatment plants. Continued maintenance, upgrading and expansion of this infrastructure will be critical, however, in efforts to safeguard past water quality improvements while accommodating emerging demands. Infrastructure needs extend to the Great Lakes-St. Lawrence Seaway as well, where proper maintenance is essential to support waterborne commerce and the entire Great Lakes-St. Lawrence maritime industry. Future years will bring continued demand for adequate operation and maintenance funding without compromising cost-competitiveness. The long-standing call for overall Seaway modernization will continue, as will pressures for a new large lock at Sault Ste. Marie, Michigan.

Costs associated with these various infrastructure needs have not been well documented, but over time might be expected to rival the tremendous costs anticipated for remediation of contaminated Areas of Concern throughout the Basin. Water policy officials will be challenged by the need to reconcile budgetary realities with these major competing needs.

8) Regional economic dependence on water resources will increase, adding new dimensions to the economic base but increasing problems of competing/conflicting uses. Abundant quantities of high quality water, coupled with an efficient waterborne transportation system, were major determinants of community and industrial development patterns during the settlement and early economic growth of Great Lakes Basin jurisdictions. The extent of the economy's water-dependency has ebbed and flowed over the years, but is presently on the rise for a variety of reasons.

Major investments in point source pollution control programs over the last twenty years have improved both the visual appeal and quality of the resource. As a consequence, riparian land has increased dramatically in value and water-based

redevelopment has become a standard in most shoreline communities. Water quality improvements also helped reinvigorate the Great Lakes sport fishery, which is now valued at $3-4 billion per year and supports approximately 80,000 jobs.

On the water quantity side of the equation, the region will continue to retain and attract industry with dependency upon reliable supplies of water for cooling, processing and related purposes. As a factor of production, water has an increasingly prominent role in the decision process for industrial location. Water scarcity and unreliability of supplies in other regions of North America will fuel this trend in coming years.

The finite nature of this seemingly inexhaustible resource will be demonstrated as intensifying multiple use activity will lead to increased competition and conflict regarding access to and use of water resources. Water policy institutions and processes will be confronted with the challenge of translating principles of sustainable development into management strategies.

9) The Great Lakes citizenry will be increasingly well-informed, organized and influential and, as such, in a position to contribute, rather than simply react to public policy decisions. The "top-down" approach that has historically characterized water policy and management at the national and regional levels is literally being turned "upside-down". The long-practiced public participation model, which viewed public input as an inconvenient yet necessary formality in the policy-making process, has given way to a new philosophy. Also gone are the days when the stereotypic "citizen activist" was a dedicated yet poorly informed and marginally effective player in the water policy arena.

The Great Lakes-St. Lawrence citizenry is no longer on the outside looking in; it is becoming a integral part of the policy making process. As a whole, the citizenry is better informed, better organized and more politically astute than in years past. With this new found access and empowerment, the citizenry will be in a position to make substantive contributions to or, conversely, effectively obstruct or delay the water policy process. In future years, the ability of governments to accommodate, encourage and benefit from the citizenry's sense of stewardship will factor heavily into the success of water policy initiatives.

10) Emerging water policy issues will prompt a fundamental departure from established institutional arrangements and management practices. Water policy institutions and officials have long demonstrated an aversion to self-critique and pronounced changes to the status quo. The elaborate "institutional ecosystem" now in place is not the product of a grand design, but of a gradual, unplanned evolution influenced by political priorities, response to crises, inter-organizational dynamics and an unending procession of increasingly complex issues.

Donald Schon once observed that governmental bureaucracies are "memorials to old problems."[37] They are often created to respond to a specific crisis or series of precipitating events, yet ultimately must accommodate myriad problems and issues far removed from their original design capability. Great Lakes-St. Lawrence institutions are cases in point. Many were created decades ago and, while they have demonstrated great flexibility and resiliency, must struggle with new and unanticipated issues.

The current Great Lakes-St. Lawrence governance structure is the object of opinions that literally range from charges of inefficiency and redundancy to praises for their innovation and "global model" characteristics. The last decade has witnessed an unprecedented level of movement toward management innovation and institutional change, but the movement is only beginning. During this decade, many new players in the regional water policy arena have emerged, such as the Council of Great Lakes Governors, the International Great Lakes-St. Lawrence Mayors' Conference, the Association of Great Lakes Counties, Great Lakes United and the Council of Great Lakes Industries, to name a few. As new alliances are formed and the configuration of the water policy process evolves, fundamental changes in the management perspectives of political jurisdictions can be expected, including increased sensitivity to Basin-wide planning and cooperative management efforts. Open and forthright discussion of the efficacy of the current "institutional ecosystem" will emerge as increased attention is given to questions of how we manage as well as questions of what we manage.

NOTES

[1]Great Lakes Basin Commission. 1975. *Great Lakes Basin Framework Study*, Report, Environmental Impact Statement and 25 Appendices. Ann Arbor, MI.

[2]Statistics presented for Lake Superior and other Great Lakes and connecting channels are drawn from: Great Lakes Basin Commission. 1979. *Great Lakes Fact Sheets*. Ann Arbor, MI.

[3]Kelnhofer, Guy J., Jr. 1972. *Preserving the Great Lakes*. Prepared for the National Water Commission Contract No. NWC 72-010. Arlington: National Water Commission.

[4]Dworsky, Leonard B. and G. Francis. 1973. *A Proposal for Improving the Management of the Great Lakes of the United States and Canada*. A Report by the Canada-United States Inter–University Seminar - 1971-72.

[5]Thompson, Stanley R. and R.L. Johnson. 1982. *Grain Transportation on the Great Lakes—St. Lawrence Seaway*. Cooperative Extension Service, Michigan State University. MICH-SG-82-501. East Lansing, MI.

[6]Schenker, Eric, H.M. Mayer and H.C. Brockel. 1976. *The Great Lakes Transportation System*. University of Wisconsin Sea Grant College Program. Technical Report 230.

[7]St. Lawrence Seaway Development Corporation. 1984. "The Seaway", *Seaway Review*. July-August 1984. Harbor House Publishers.

[8]International Joint Commission. 1985. *Great Lakes Diversions and Consumptive Uses*. A Report to the Governments of the United States and Canada under the 1977 Reference.

[9]Great Lakes Commission. 1989. *Great Lakes Regional Water Use Data Base—Annual Report*. Submitted to Water Resources Management Committee, Council of Great Lakes Governors, Chicago IL.

[10]U.S. Congress, Merchant Marine and Fisheries Committee. 1983.

[11]Milliken, William G., Speech to the Twenty Sixth Annual Conference on Great Lakes Research, Oswego, NY. May 25, 1983.

[12]Caldwell, Lynton K. 1982. "U.S. Institutions and The Environment," *Decisions for the Great Lakes*. Hiram, OH: Great Lakes Tomorrow.

[13]Allee, David J., W.W. Andrews and H.R. Cooper. 1975. "Basin Governance," Cornell Agricultural Economics Staff Paper No 75-25. Ithaca: Cornell University.

[14]Donahue, Michael J. 1987. *Institutional Arrangements for Great Lakes Management: Past Practices and Future Alternatives*. Chapter Two: "The Great Lakes Ecosystem-Placing the Physical Resource and Management Framework in Perspective." Michigan Sea Grant College Program, MICHU-SG-87-200T.

[15]Donahue, Michael J. 1987. *Institutional Arrangements for Great Lakes Management: Past Practices and Future Alternatives*. Chapter Three: "The Institutional Setting for Great Lakes Management: Components and Attendant Linkages". Michigan Sea Grant College Program, MICHU-SG-87-200T.

[16]Council of Great Lakes Governors. 1985. *Great Lakes Charter*. Madison, WI.

[17]Council of Great Lakes Governors. 1986. *Great Lakes Toxic Substances Control Agreement*. Chicago, IL.

[18]Carroll, John E. 1984. *Environmental Diplomacy—An Examination and a Perspective of Canadian—U.S. Transboundary Environmental Relations*. The University of Michigan Press, Ann Arbor, MI.

[19]International Joint Commission. 1989. Report of the Great Lakes Water Quality Board. Windsor, Ontario.

[20]Munton, Donald. 1982. "Canadian Laws and Institutions," *Decisions for the Great Lakes*. Hiram, OH: Great Lakes Tomorrow.

[21]Francis, George. 1982. "How Governments Behave, an Overview." *Decisions for the Great Lakes*. Hiram, OH: Great Lakes Tomorrow.

[22]Supra Note 12.

[23]Supra Note 12.

[24]Supra Notes 12 and 21.

[25]Supra Note 20.

[26]Supra Note 20.

[27]MacNeil, J.W. 1970. *Environmental Management*. Study prepared for the Government of Canada. Ottawa, Ontario.

[28]Supra Notes 20 and 21.

[29]Supra Note 1.

[30]Supra Note 12.

[31]National Research Council of the United States and the Royal Society of Canada, Committee to Review the Great Lakes Water Quality Agreement. 1985. *The Great Lakes Water Quality Agreement: An Evolving Instrument for Ecosystem Management*. Washington, D.C. and Ottawa, Ontario.

[32]Environmental Protection Service, Ontario Region, Environment Canada. 1985. *Federal and Provincial Relations Study*. (Unpublished draft).

[33]Canadian Environmental Law Research Foundation. 1986. "An Overview of Canadian Law and Policy Governing Great Lakes Water Quality Management." *Journal of International Law*, Case Western Reserve University, Vol. 18, No. 1.

[34]Supra Note 20.

[35]Northeast-Midwest Institute, et al. 1990. "White paper on Federal Funding for Great Lakes Environmental Programs", Washington, D.C.

[36]Supra Note 16.

[37]Schon, Donald A. 1971. *Beyond the Stable State: Public and Private Learning in a Changing Society*. New York: Random House.

Chapter 7

Energy Issues for the Great Lakes Economy

Athanasios D. Bournakis, Research Economist, Energy Resources Center, University of Illinois at Chicago

James P. Hartnett, Professor of Mechanical Engineering, Director of Energy Resources Center, University of Illinois at Chicago

Energy use patterns by source and sector during the 1970 to 1988 period are reported for the nation and for the eight states comprising the Great Lakes region. These results are related to gross economic output and population. It is shown that considerable energy efficiency improvement has been achieved in energy use per dollar of output and there has been a small improvement in energy use per person. Production and consumption of indigenous energy resources in the nation, the region, and the individual states are outlined. Even though vast coal resources exist in the region, they are mainly high in sulfur content. Thus regional resources are insufficient to meet the region's demand for energy in oil, natural gas, and low sulfur coal. As a consequence, the region imports large quantities of these fuels. The paper concludes by outlining a number of energy policy issues related to the vulnerability of the region to imported oil, the improvement of energy efficiency, the provision of adequate electric capacity, and the major challenge posed by changes in environmental laws.

This paper reviews energy issues in the eight states that comprise the Great Lakes region. The states in the region are: Illinois, Indiana, Michigan, Minnesota, New York, Ohio, Pennsylvania and Wisconsin. The region is characterized by its diversity. It contains the industrial heartland of the country, includes a part of the nation's farm belt and possesses almost 30 percent of the nation's coal reserves. The Ohio and Mississippi rivers flow through the region providing access to the Gulf of Mexico and the bordering Great Lakes provide access to the Atlantic Ocean through the St. Lawrence Seaway. The size and heterogeneous nature of the region provide political strength but also make it difficult to achieve unanimity on many policy issues.

In terms of land area, the region represents only 11.8 percent, or 427,358 square miles, of the United States [9]. In 1970, the population of the region was 36.5 percent of the U.S. total. By 1988, although growing in absolute terms, the regional population had dropped as a fraction of the U.S. population to 31.1 percent.

The paper begins with a review of the national energy consumption and the gross national product for the 1970 to 1988 period, then goes on to present the same information for the region. The nation and the region are compared on the basis of per capita energy consumption and energy consumption per dollar of real output. Since there is considerable interest in the generating of electricity, the national and the regional per capita energy input to produce electricity is discussed.

The paper then analyzes the patterns of energy use and economic activity in each state of the region and compares these to the region as a whole and to the United States for the years 1970, 1975, 1980, 1985 and 1988. Special attention is given to the distribution of energy use among the end-use sectors and to the relative changes in fuel use patterns. The region's energy resource base is outlined briefly and shifts in energy production within the region are analyzed. These results suggest some important policy issues which may have an impact on the future of the region.

National energy use and economic activity

The population of the country grew 20.9 percent, from 203.3 million to 245.8 million, during the period between 1970 to 1988 [9]. In contrast with the steady population growth, the national energy consumption and the gross national product (in 1982 dollars) have experienced rather dramatic ups and downs over the 19 year period as shown in Figure 1 [9, 19]. From 1970 to 1973 the nation's energy consumption grew 12.1 percent, or at an average annual rate of 3.9 percent, and was accompanied by a comparable 13.6 percent increase in GNP, or a 4.3 percent annual growth. In October of 1973 the Arab oil embargo occurred, followed by a large jump in OPEC oil prices, which in turn caused substantial price increases for many end-users. This is reflected on Figure 2 [18, 20, 24] which gives the ratio of real (deflated in 1982 dollars using the consumer price index) prices relative to the 1970 price (i.e., this removes the influence of inflation and price differences among alternate fuel types; a value greater than 1.00 means that the inflation adjusted price has increased during the period under review). It can been seen that the price of distillate fuel rose precipitously by 52.8 percent from 1973 to 1974 and remained stable until 1978. Motor gasoline prices (in real term) were less affected, rising only by 25.4 percent compared to 1973. Real

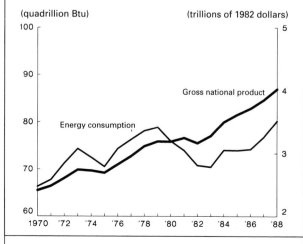

FIGURE 1

Total United States energy consumption and gross national product

(quadrillion Btu)   (trillions of 1982 dollars)

Gross national product

Energy consumption

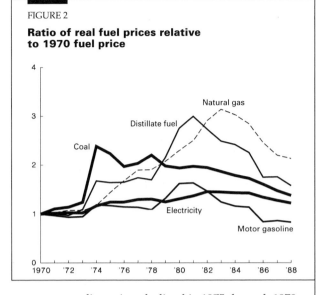

FIGURE 2

Ratio of real fuel prices relative to 1970 fuel price

motor gasoline prices declined in 1975 through 1978. Coal prices rose by 92 percent in 1974 and declined by a rate of 8.3 percent annually until 1976. Following smaller price increases in 1977 and 1978, coal prices were eased the following years. During the 1980s coal prices exhibit a downward trend. Electricity prices exhibit a small but steady increase following the oil embargo, during 1974 to 1978. Prices increased at an average annual rate of 5 percent compared to 1973. Natural gas prices increased 9.5 percent in 1974 compared to 1973. Prices continued to rise at an annual rate of 11.5 percent until 1983.

The increase in OPEC oil prices negatively influenced the balance of trade. The annual outflow of U.S. dollars increased from approximately 7.6 billion dollars in 1973 to 24.3 billion dollars in 1974 to pay for the imported petroleum and petroleum products. Crude and partly refined petroleum cost rose from 4.6 billion dollars in 1973 to 16.5 billion dollars in 1974 [9]. Net imports of crude oil and petroleum products imports were 40.3 percent of our total crude oil and petroleum products consumed in 1974, and was equivalent to 18.6 percent of the total energy requirements during that year.

The increased fuel prices and the increased outward flow of U.S. dollars resulted in a downturn

in the energy consumption, at an annual rate of 2.5 percent, while real GNP declined at an annual rate of 0.9 percent during the 1974 to 1975 period. The economy recovered during 1976 to 1978, while the real prices of petroleum products remained relatively constant although there was some increase in the real price of natural gas.[1] During this period both the energy consumption and the gross national product increased and the country appeared to be on the road to recovery.

The economic recovery period was interrupted by the Iranian revolution in early 1979, which caused a rapid increase in distillate fuel prices that continued until 1981 (Figure 2). Distillate fuel prices increased at an annual rate of 20.8 percent in the 1979 to 1981 period. Natural gas prices also increased significantly, at an annual rate of 10.4 percent, during the 1979 to 1983 period as compared to 1978. Electricity prices decreased in 1979 but rose during the 1980 to 1982 period, declining afterwards. Motor gasoline prices increased in 1979 to 1981 at an annual rate of 14.4 percent and declined afterwards. Coal prices were not significantly affected by the oil supply interruption. This can be attributed to the limited opportunity for substituting coal for crude oil in electrical generation and the large coal reserves of the country.

Again, as in 1973, energy price increases contributed to a decrease in national energy consumption and a slowdown in the gross national product. However, it should be noted that the decrease in national energy consumption from 1979 to 1982, while in part due to the economic slowdown, also reflect some improvement in energy efficiency, as shown by an increasing GNP in 1981. This second point will be discussed later. Events such as the oil embargo of 1973 and the oil supply interruption due to the Iranian revolution in 1979 bring out the continuing vulnerability of our economy to events beyond our borders and beyond our direct control.

Regional energy use and economic activity

The population of the Great Lakes region grew from 74.11 million in 1970 to 76.34 million in 1988 [9], an increase of approximately 3 percent, equivalent to an annual growth rate of 0.16 percent. In contrast, the U.S. population increased by 20.9 per-

cent, a 1.06 percent annual growth rate, during the same period. The U.S. population growth rate was approximately seven times the population growth rate of the Great Lakes region. All the states in the region have population growth rates well below the national growth rate. The two smallest, in population terms, and less industrialized states—Minnesota with a population increase of 13.2 percent and Wisconsin with 9.9 percent—have the higher population growth during the 1970 to 1988 period. Indiana with 6.9 percent, Illinois with 4.5 percent, Michigan with 4 percent, Ohio with 1.9 percent, and Pennsylvania with 1.7 percent show small population growth over the 18 year period. New York, the most populous state, shows a population decline. These figures reflect the population shift to the sunbelt states.

The economic activity in the Great Lakes region, as measured by the gross regional product[2] (in 1982 dollars) of the region is given on Figure 3

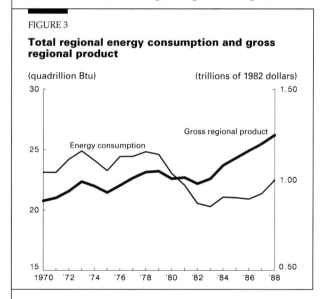

FIGURE 3

Total regional energy consumption and gross regional product

[10, 19]. The Great Lakes region shows the same general trends as the nation (Figure 1) up to 1979. This is not surprising given the fact that the region contributes more than 30 percent to the national gross domestic product and is subject generally to the same economic disturbances. Since 1970 the

FIGURE 4

Gross domestic and regional product per capita and energy use per capita

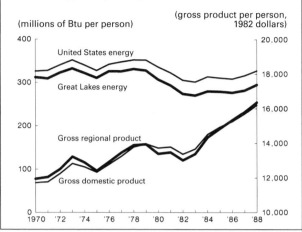

(millions of Btu per person) (gross product per person, 1982 dollars)

gross regional product (in 1982 dollars) has increased from $885.8 billion in 1970 to $1,249.3 billion in 1988, a 41 percent increase, equivalent to an average rate of 1.9 percent per year in real growth. During the same period the United States gross domestic product increased by 66.3 percent, or at an average rate of 2.9 percent per year, from $2,399 billion in 1970 to $3,989 billion in 1988. Thus, the region's real economic output grew at an average rate which was 61.8 percent of the growth rate of the nation's gross domestic product.

The region's total annual energy consumption, also shown in Figure 3, generally reveals the same peaks and valleys shown in Figure 1 for the nation. A more meaningful comparison of the regional and national economies is shown in Figure 4, which gives the regional and national economic output (1982 dollars) in the U.S. and Great Lakes and the corresponding energy consumption on a per capita basis. The gross domestic product per capita of the region is within 3 percent of the per capita gross domestic product of the nation. From 1970 to 1978 the output per capita for the region is higher than the output per capita for the nation. In 1979, following the Iranian revolution, the national economic output per capita slightly exceeded the regional economic output per capita. This trend

continued until 1986, when the regional economic output per capita surpassed the national output per capita. This could be attributed to the recovery of the industrial sector and the tax reform that reduced considerably the tax burden of larger industries.

The economic output per capita reveals clearly the effect of the oil shocks to the economy. Both the regional and the national output per capita declined following the 1973 and 1979 oil supply interruptions. During 1974 and 1975, after the 1973 oil embargo, the economy declined (in terms of output per capita) by an average annual rate of 3.0 percent for the region and 1.9 percent for the nation. Following the 1979 Iranian revolution, the regional economy declined until 1982 by an average annual rate of 2.2 percent while the national economy declined by 1.4 percent annually.

The regional economy grew at an average annual rate of 3.9 percent and the national economy grew at a rate of 3.3 percent during 1983 to 1988. This is indicative of the greater sensitivity to energy

FIGURE 5

Energy use per real output
(thousands of Btu per dollar of output, 1982 dollars)

disruptions of the regional economy compared to the national economy. For the entire period under review, the regional economy, in terms of output per capita, grew at an average annual rate of 1.76 percent while the national economy grew at a rate of 1.81 percent per year.

Figure 4 reveals that the eight state region consumes less energy per capita than the nation. Between 1970 and 1988, the regional energy use per capita decreased by approximately 5.6 percent while the national energy use per capita in 1988 is equal to the energy use per capita during 1970.

Another meaningful measure of energy performance is the energy use per real dollar of economic output, which is shown in Figure 5 [10, 19] for the United States and the region. The national figure decreased from 27.8 to 20.1 thousand Btu per dollar of real output (in 1982 dollars), a decrease of approximately 27.6 percent over the period, reflecting a decrease in the use of energy. The regional figure, although showing the same trends, is approximately 5 to 11 percent lower than the national figure. This may be the result of energy-efficiency improvement in the energy intensive industries of the region. Over the 1970 to 1988 period, the regional energy use per dollar of real output dropped from 26.1 to 18 thousand Btu per dollar of real output, a decrease of 31 percent. The downward trend of the energy use per dollar of output leveled off during the 1986 to 1988 period. The nation and the region have the potential for additional improvements in the efficient use of energy (i.e., to a continuing decrease in the energy use per real dollar of output). However, it should be noted that the relatively inexpensive methods of improving energy efficiency through modified operating procedures and minor capital improvements will soon run out. Continued efficiency increases in the use of energy will then depend on much larger capital investments.

A more detailed look at the regional energy consumption flows is given on Figure 6 [19]. Although the data are shown for 1988, the overall picture has not changed substantially over the period of the study. In particular, there is little shift in the percentage figures given in the parentheses shown on the chart. The dominant role of petroleum (36.7 percent) is evident in this flow chart, with coal (30.1 percent) and natural gas (22.8 percent) in second and third place as fuels for regional energy needs. Nuclear fuel and renewable resources (including hydroelectric power) provide approximately 10.4 percent of the total

FIGURE 6

Energy flows in the Great Lakes region, 1988
(trillion Btu)

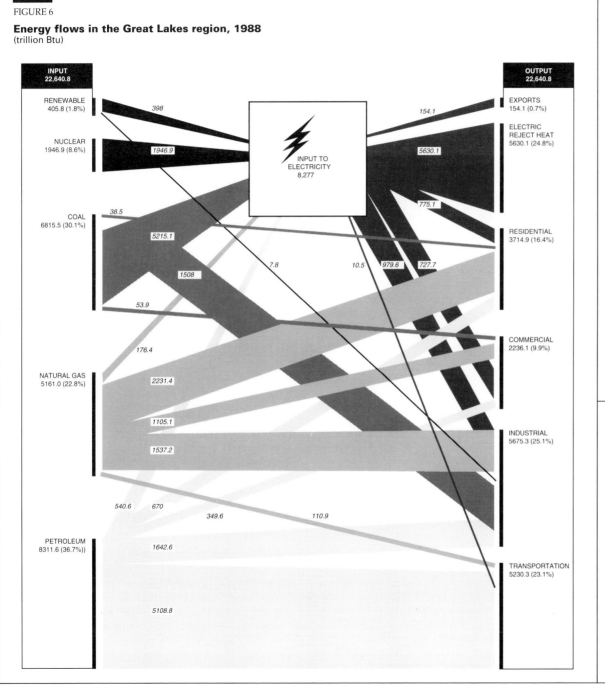

INPUT
22,640.8

OUTPUT
22,640.8

RENEWABLE
405.8 (1.8%)

398

NUCLEAR
1946.9 (8.6%)

1946.9

COAL
6815.5 (30.1%)

38.5

5215.1

1508

53.9

176.4

2231.4

NATURAL GAS
5161.0 (22.8%)

1105.1

1537.2

540.6   670

349.6   110.9

PETROLEUM
8311.6 (36.7%))

1642.6

5108.8

INPUT TO
ELECTRICITY
8,277

7.8   10.5   979.6   727.7

775.1

154.1

5630.1

EXPORTS
154.1 (0.7%)

ELECTRIC
REJECT HEAT
5630.1 (24.8%)

RESIDENTIAL
3714.9 (16.4%)

COMMERCIAL
2236.1 (9.9%)

INDUSTRIAL
5675.3 (25.1%)

TRANSPORTATION
5230.3 (23.1%)

regional energy, with more than 80 percent of this being nuclear.

In the end-use sectors, it can be seen that the transportation sector uses almost a quarter of the total energy consumed in the region, fueled predominantly by petroleum (97.7 percent). This emphasizes the need to improve the energy efficiency in the transportation sector (or to find alternative fuel for transportation) if there is to be a substantial decrease in the use of petroleum. The industrial sector, with 25.1 percent of the region's total energy consumption, is the largest consumer of energy, with petroleum (28.9 percent), natural gas (27.1 percent), coal (26.6 percent), and electricity (17.3 percent) supplying its basic fuel needs. The commercial and residential sectors together use approximately the same amount of energy as the industrial sector, but are more dependent on natural gas which supplies 49.4 percent of the commercial and 60.1 percent of the residential sector energy requirements. The remaining commercial requirements are primarily electricity (32.5 percent), oil (15.6 percent) and coal (2.4 percent). The remaining residential requirements are primarily electricity (20.9 percent), oil (18 percent) and coal (1 percent).

Reject heat associated with the generation of electricity constitutes almost one-fourth of the

FIGURE 7

Per capita energy input to electrical generation
(millions of Btu per person)

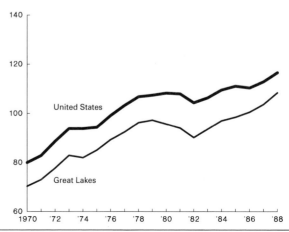

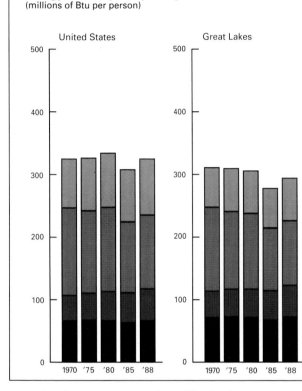

FIGURE 8

Energy consumption per capita
(millions of Btu per person)

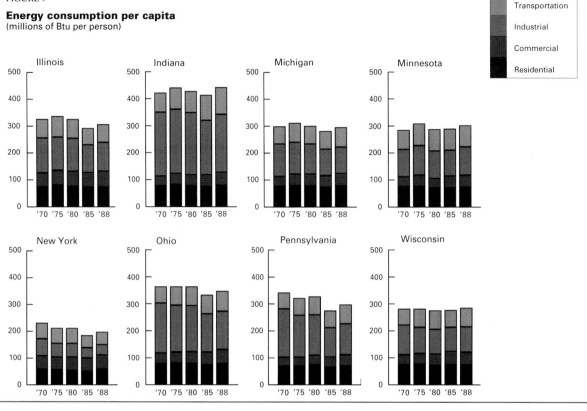

FIGURE 9

Energy consumption per capita
(millions of Btu per person)

regional energy consumption. This is a large amount of energy, but it is generally low temperature energy. It is possible to put this energy to productive use, but it is usually expensive to do so. Current design and development projects in district heating and cogeneration are evaluating the economic feasibility of these options.

The flow diagram demonstrates clearly that electrical generation is a conversion process, taking input fuel, which is primarily coal (63 percent) and nuclear (23.5 percent) and relatively less oil (6.5 percent), natural gas (2.1) and renewable energy sources (4.8 percent), and converting this to useful electricity and reject heat. Since the fuel input to electricity constitutes some 36.6 percent of the total energy consumed in the region, the electrical sector is of special interest.

Figure 7 [7, 19] shows the per capita fuel energy input to the electrical sector for the United States and the region for the 1970 to 1988 period. The per capita fuel input to the electrical sector for the region is approximately 10 percent lower than the per capita fuel input of the nation. The average annual growth rate of the per capita fuel input to electrical generation is approximately 1.8 percent for the region and 1.5 percent for the nation during the 1973 to 1988 period. This is in sharp contrast to the pre-1973 growth which had been on the order of 5.6 percent per year for the region and 5.5 percent for the nation. Estimating the future electrical needs of the country is an important regional and national problem since it requires over ten years to design and construct an electrical plant. If the needs are underestimated, the nation will not have sufficient

electricity to support our industrial and commercial sector. If the needs are overestimated, electrical power plants will be lying idle, leading to higher prices for electricity which in turn will negatively influence the competitive position of U.S. products on the world markets.

State energy use and economic activity

State level energy consumption per capita, 1970-1988

The end-use energy consumption statistics on a per capita basis are shown on Figures 8 and 9 [9, 19], for the nation, the region and each of the eight states. From Figure 8, which shows the United States and the Great Lakes region for selected years from 1970 to 1988, it can be observed that, relative to the country as a whole, the region used more energy per capita in the residential sector, somewhat less

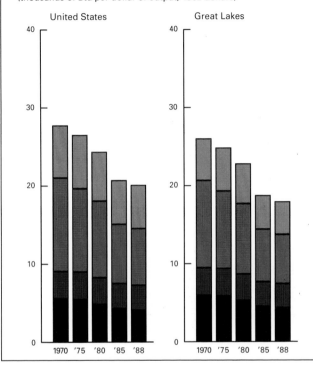

FIGURE 10

Energy consumption per dollar of GSP by end-use sector
(thousands of Btu per dollar of output, 1982 dollars)

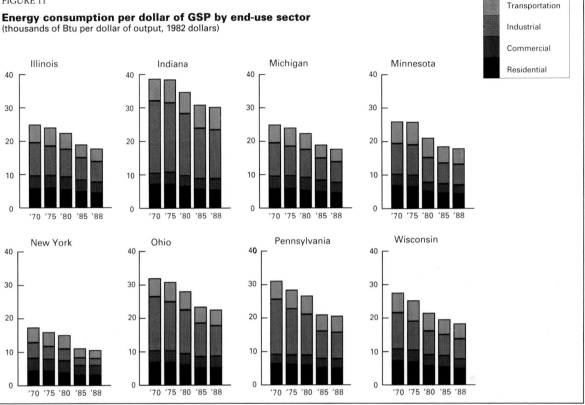

FIGURE 11

Energy consumption per dollar of GSP by end-use sector
(thousands of Btu per dollar of output, 1982 dollars)

Transportation
Industrial
Commercial
Residential

energy in the commercial, and significantly less energy in the industrial and transportation sectors during the 1980s. The higher residential energy consumption can be explained by noting that the weather of the Midwest is colder on the average than that of the overall nation. The region includes the industrial heartland of the United States, involving such energy intensive industries as steel, automobiles and petrochemicals that have undergone large energy efficiency improvements. This may account for the fact that the regional industrial energy consumption is lower than the national average. In addition, the transportation sector uses approximately 20 percent less energy per capita. This is probably the result of the industrialization of the region, with large concentration of population in cities.

Figure 8 highlights the fact that the per capita energy consumption for the United States, while varying during the 1970 to 1988 period, was at the same level in 1988 as in 1970. However, the region's energy consumption per capita decreased by more than 5 percent over the same period, mostly due to energy efficiency improvements in the industrial and transportation sectors.

Figure 9 shows the large variations that occur from state to state in the per capita energy consumption in each of the end-use sectors and in the overall figure. For example, in 1988 the energy consumption per capita ranged from a low of 200 million Btu for New York to a high of 446 million Btu for Indiana, compared with a regional average of 295 million Btu and a national average of 326 million Btu. The unusually high value for Indiana reflects the presence of the steel industry in that state.

New York, surprisingly, is the smallest consumer of energy in the region with a value of 200 million Btu per capita in 1988. This may be due to the large concentration of population in the New York City, and the large public transportation system that results in lower average travel distances and more use of mass-transit than other states.

A few general observations can be made for each end-use sector. For the residential sector, New York has the lowest energy requirements while Indiana has the highest—the obvious result of high population concentration in New York and more energy awareness. The per capita requirements of the commercial sector are lowest in Pennsylvania and highest in Illinois followed by New York. Indiana has the highest per capita energy consumption in the industrial sector while New York has the lowest. In the transportation sector, again

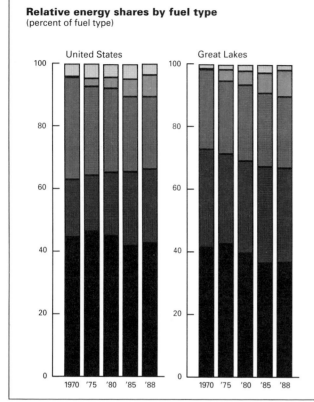

FIGURE 12

Relative energy shares by fuel type
(percent of fuel type)

United States / Great Lakes

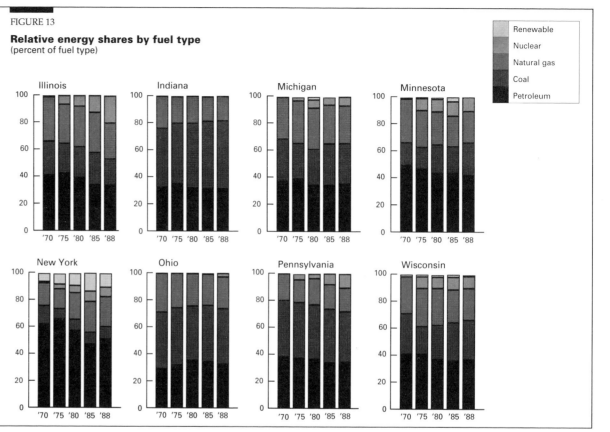

FIGURE 13

Relative energy shares by fuel type
(percent of fuel type)

Illinois / Indiana / Michigan / Minnesota / New York / Ohio / Pennsylvania / Wisconsin

Legend: Renewable, Nuclear, Natural gas, Coal, Petroleum

New York has the lowest energy consumption per person requirements, while Indiana consumes the largest amount of energy per capita. It is possible to make many more comparisons on a state by state basis, but in the interest of space this will be left to the reader.

Energy consumption per dollar of gross state product, 1970-1988

Figures 10 and 11 [10, 19] show the energy consumption per real dollar output of goods and services for the nation, the region, and each state in the region. Figure 10 presents, in bar chart form, the same basic information shown on Figure 5, but gives more detail on the contribution of each end-use sector. Overall, the energy consumption per real dollar output for the Great Lakes region was lower by 10.4 percent compared to the nation in

1988. With the exception of the residential sector, all other sectors of the regional economy showed lower energy consumption per real dollar of output than the national economy.

Figure 11 presents the state by state performance. The national and regional trend of decreasing energy required to produce a real dollar of output is also displayed by every state of the region, with improvements ranging from a low of 22 percent in Illinois to a high of 39 percent in New York during the 1970 to 1988 period.

The actual magnitude of the energy consumption per dollar of gross state product within the individuals states in 1988 ranged from a low of 10.7 thousand Btu for New York to a high of 30.4 thousands of Btu for Indiana (probably reflecting the steel industry). Illinois, Michigan, Minnesota, New

York and Wisconsin were below the national average in energy consumed per real dollar of gross state product (GSP). All of the other states show values higher than the average national values. Illinois and New York were the only states below the regional average in energy consumed per real output.

A few general observations can be made for the energy consumption per gross state product for each end-use sector in 1988. In the residential sector, New York has the lowest energy requirement while Minnesota has the highest. The energy requirements of the commercial sector are lowest in Minnesota and the highest in Ohio. Indiana has the highest energy consumption per output in the industrial and transportation sectors, while New York has the lowest.

FIGURE 14

Net electrical energy use per person, input to electricity
(millions of Btu per person)

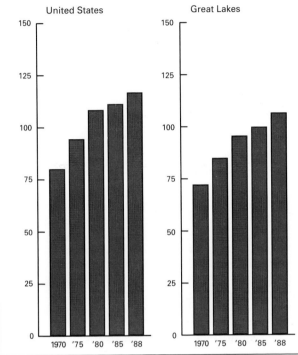

FIGURE 15

Net electrical energy use per person, input to electricity
(millions of Btu per person)

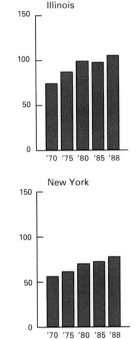

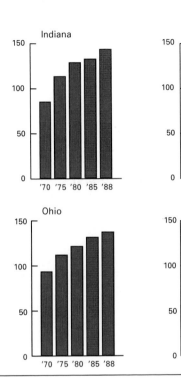

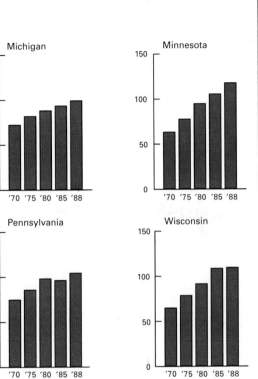

State fuel use patterns, 1970-1988

The energy problem is clearly the result of our over-dependency on imported oil. Accordingly, it is of interest to review the fuel use patterns in the region to determine if there are significant shifts away from oil, particularly in the direction of increasing use of coal, a major national and regional fuel resource. Figure 12 [19][3] brings out the fact that both the nation and the region slightly reduced their reliance on oil during the period, with the nation being somewhat more dependent on oil than the region. Although the petroleum share decreased from approximately 44.5 percent in 1970 to 41.8 percent in 1985, since that time the petroleum share has increased to 42.6 percent in 1988. There is not any clear indication that the nation has turned the corner to its petroleum dependency. The region also

experienced the same trends in the use of petroleum over this same period, with a decrease in the oil dependency from 41.4 percent to 36.4 percent between 1970 and 1985, increasing to 36.7 percent in 1988.

The region is generally more dependent on coal than the nation, although coal's share dropped regionally from 31.3 percent in 1970 to 30.1 percent in 1988. Nationally, coal carried approximately 18.4 percent of the country's energy requirements in 1970, increasing to 23.6 percent in 1988.

The regional share of the energy carried by natural gas was slightly lower from 25.5 percent in 1970 to 22.8 percent in 1988, while the national share of gas use declined from 32.7 percent in 1970 to 23.1 percent in 1988. The reduced role of natural gas may reflect the effects of less expensive western coal and the increased role of nuclear power. Deregula-

tion that was supposed to improve gas availability did not increase the share of gas use at the national or regional level.

Nuclear power carried a greater share of the energy burden at the regional and national level in 1988 as compared to 1970. At the national level, nuclear power accounted for 7.1 percent of the energy requirements of the country in 1988, compared to less than 0.4 percent in 1970. The region's share of nuclear power was 8.6 percent in 1988 compared to less than 0.4 percent in 1970. The national and regional share of renewable resources, which includes hydroelectric power, did not show any significant change over the period.

Within the region, the states most dependent on petroleum were New York with a 50.8 percent share of its energy consumption and Minnesota with 41.6

percent share in 1988 (Figure 13 [19]). Indiana, with 31.3 percent, was the least dependent on petroleum. Indiana, at 50.5 percent, is the largest user of coal on a percentage basis, while New York with a 9.2 percent coal share of its energy consumption is the lowest user. Michigan, with a natural gas share of 27.8 percent, and Illinois, with a 26.7 percent share, are the most dependent on natural gas. Pennsylvania with 17.7 percent and Indiana with 18.1 percent share are the less dependent in natural gas among the eight states. Illinois has the largest nuclear program that serves 20.2 percent of its energy needs, while Indiana does not have any nuclear power generating capacity. New York has the most renewable resources that provide 10.8 percent of its energy needs.

State level electrical use, 1970-1988

Figures 14 and 15 [9, 19] present the per capita energy input to the electrical sector on a national, regional and state by state basis. The figures are corrected for exports and imports of electricity and reflect the net energy input used for electricity consumed within the state. Of interest is the increasing pattern of electricity use per person over the period. While both national and regional energy use per capita remained stable or declined over the years, electricity use shows a steady increase. In 1988, national electricity use per capita increased by 45.8 percent compared to 1970 or at an average annual rate of 2.1 percent. Regional electricity use per capita increased by 47.4 percent, or at an average annual rate of 2.2 percent.

On the state level, electrical consumption per person ranges from a high of 143.4 and 137.6 million Btu for Indiana and Ohio respectively, reflecting the steel industry in Indiana and the fuel enrichment plant in Portsmouth, Ohio, to a low of 78.0 million Btu for New York. It is of interest to note that Ohio, as a consequence of the Portsmouth facility, is the largest importer of electricity in the region, with net imports of 227.2 trillion Btu in 1988, while Pennsylvania exported 304.2 trillion Btu during the same year.

Regional energy resources and production

Regional reserves, production and consumption of natural gas for 1988 are presented on

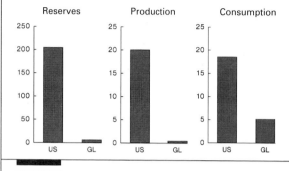

FIGURE 16

Natural gas reserves, production, and consumption, 1988
(quadrillion Btu)

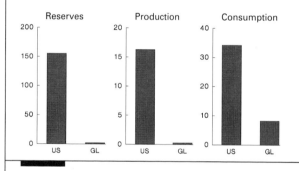

FIGURE 17

Petroleum reserves, production, and consumption, 1988
(quadrillion Btu)

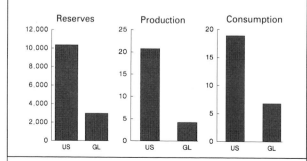

FIGURE 18

Coal reserves, production, and consumption, 1988
(quadrillion Btu)

Figure 16 [12, 19, 22]. The region possesses approximately 2.7 percent of the national gas reserves and produces 2.4 percent of the nation's natural gas. Total reserves for the region amount to 4,996 billion cubic feet of gas, mostly in Pennsylvania (41.5 percent), Michigan (26.5 percent), Ohio (24.6 percent), New York (7 percent) and Illinois (0.3 percent). Natural gas liquid reserves for the region amount to approximately 100 million barrels, almost all of them located in Michigan. The region consumes 27.8 percent of the nation's natural gas consumption. The 1988 regional production of natural gas and natural gas liquids was approximately 9.5 percent of the regional consumption of this fuel. It can be concluded that while the production of natural gas may be of importance to a few states in the region, it is clear that the region will continue to be a heavy importer of natural gas.

The region's petroleum reserves, production and consumption for 1988 are presented on Figure 17 [12, 19, 22]. The regional petroleum picture is not markedly differently from that of natural gas. Petroleum reserves amount to 393 million barrels, equivalent to 1.5 percent of the nation's reserves. Most of the petroleum reserves are located in Illinois (36.4 percent), Michigan (33.6 percent), Ohio (16.3 percent), Pennsylvania (6.9 percent), and Indiana (5.6 percent). The region produced approximately 57.8 million barrels of oil during 1988, approximately 2.1 percent of the nation's oil production. Illinois, Michigan, and Ohio, accounted for 88 percent of the region's petroleum production. The 1988 regional petroleum production was approximately 4 percent of the regional consumption of this fuel. The region's demonstrated petroleum reserves are sufficient to meet the consumption needs of the region for less than 4 months.

Figure 18 [12, 13, 14, 16, 19] displays the regional reserves, production and consumption of coal in the region. Demonstrated coal reserves amount to 137 billion short tons, which constitutes 28.9 percent of the national coal tonnage. The region's reserves lie in the Interior coal region (Illinois, Indiana) and in the Appalachian coal region (Pennsylvania and Ohio). Illinois with 78.5 billion short tons has the largest demonstrated reserves, followed by Pennsylvania with 29.5 billion short tons, Ohio with 18.6 billion short tons, and Indiana with 10.3 billion short tons. In 1988, the region produced 194.5 million short tons, equivalent to 20.5 percent of the national production. Coal consumption was 295.4 million short tons, or 33.4 percent of the national coal consumption. The coal consumption is higher than the regional production by more than 100 million short tons. This is the result of increasing imports of low sulfur coal (mostly western coal) to the region. As a consequence, the region's share of the nation's coal production dropped from 38 percent to 20.5 percent between 1970 and 1988. Regional coal production increases came only from Indiana, the only state among the major coal producers to register an increase in coal consumption.

Figure 19 [16, 17, 21, 23] shows coal production in the nation, the region and the three coal producing regions of the country (Appalachian, Interior, and Western). National coal production grew by almost 55 percent from 1970 to 1988, while the regional coal production fell by 16.5 percent during the same period. Appalachian coal production rose by only 4.1 percent, while Interior coal production rose by 32.5 percent over the same period. Western coal registered the greatest increase rising by 776 percent. The large increase in the production of

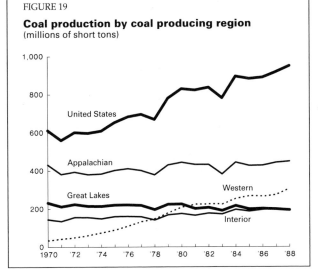

FIGURE 19

Coal production by coal producing region
(millions of short tons)

western coal is the result of the need for cleaner coal for electrical power generation.

Changing trends in coal use, 1970-1988

The Great Lakes states' coal consumption was relatively constant, exhibiting a decline of 2.9 percent, during the period from 1970 to 1988 (Figure 20) [16, 17, 19, 21, 23]. At the national level, coal consumption grew by 69 percent during the same period. However, this growth in coal use is not being shared by all coal producing states. This was brought out in Figure 19 which shows coal production by the three major coal producing regions of the country and the region. It is clear that the increases in coal use have been supplied primarily by the western region, while the Great Lakes region showed a decrease in coal production. This pattern is the result of the environmental constraints that have been placed on the burning of high sulfur coal, such as the coal of the Illinois basin. Western coal and eastern Appalachian coals, with a low sulfur content, have captured an increasing share of the market.

Table 1 shows the magnitude of western coal imports to the states in the Great Lakes region. Illinois, with the largest bituminous coal deposits in the nation, imported 26.2 percent of its coal requirements from the West. Indiana, the second largest coal consumer in the Great Lakes region, imported 9.2 percent of its coal requirements from the West. Western coal was used in both Illinois and Indiana exclusively by electric utilities. Ohio and Pennsylvania did not use any western coal, neither did they import any significant amount of coal from Illinois and Indiana. However, both states used a significant amount of Eastern Appalachian coal. Michigan imported only 29.2 percent of its coal requirements from the West and less than 1 percent from Illinois and Indiana which produce high sulfur coal. Most of the coal consumed in Michigan came from the Appalachian region. Minnesota and Wisconsin, with no coal production, imported 96.5 percent and 61 percent western coal respectively. New York, due to its distance from western coal, imports coal almost exclusively from the Appalachian region. This pattern, while bringing prosperity to Western and Eastern states, creates economic concerns in the

coal mining regions of Illinois, Indiana, Ohio, and Pennsylvania. The future of the coal industry in these Great Lakes states is critically dependent on a number of factors including: (1) the outcome of the Clean Air Legislation; (2) the outcome of the global warming debate; (3) the future growth of electric utilities; (4) the public attitude toward nuclear power; and (5) the development of overseas markets.

The current environmental laws, last amended in 1977, require that all new facilities using coal, regardless of sulfur content, must install sulfur dioxide removal systems (i.e., scrubbers). This, of course, was a major political concession intended to improve the economic position of the high-sulfur coal industry, thereby keeping one of our major energy resources a

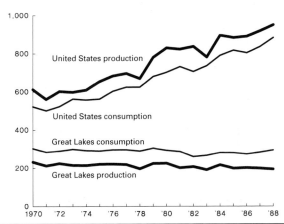

FIGURE 20

Coal production and consumption in the United States and the Great Lakes region
(millions of short tons)

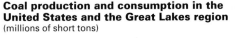

key link in our regional efforts to replace imported oil with indigenous coal. However, a major environmental challenge to coal is the Clean Air Act legislation currently pending in the U.S. Congress. Canada and legislators from the northeastern United States have long contended that sulfur emissions from coal-burning electric power plants are responsible for the acidification of lakes and streams in their regions. Consequently, the U.S. Congress is currently discussing the passing of legislation aimed at resolving this problem. A Clean Air Bill will most likely be approved in early 1991. The intense debate now emerging from the House-Senate Conference Committee which is reconciling differences between versions passed by the respective chambers and the President's proposal is evidence of the statute's complexity. Observers of this process have made it clear that the major impacts of this legislation will be felt most strongly in coal producing regions of the Great Lakes region.

The Clean Air Act Amendments [1, 5, 6, 7, 8], are aimed at strengthening the Clean Air Act, which was last revised in 1977, and target toxic air pollution and urban smog (i.e. ozone production) as well as acid rain. The acid rain statutes require utilities to reduce sulfur dioxide (SO_2) emissions to an approximate level of 2.5 lbs/million Btu by 1995. Phase II further reduces emission levels to 1.2 lbs/million Btu by the year 2000. Units using "clean coal technology" will be granted an extension in Phase II for repowering technologies. The legislation also focuses on nitrogen oxide (NO_x) emissions which, in general, will require utilities to cut NO_x emissions by approximately 2 million tons from projected levels by the year 2000.

The air toxics section of the bill puts forth a "set schedule", calling for reductions in public health risk from emissions of 191 toxic chemicals by 75 percent to 90 percent. According to the White House, the regulations will be set on the basis of "Maximum Achievable Control Technology", a concept which requires existing sources of air toxic chemicals to achieve the same emissions standards as those achieved by the best performing plants now operating. New sources would be subject to even tougher standards.

The urban smog section of the bill requires approximately 3 percent per year reduction in mobile sources of pollution for urban areas until a predetermined attainment goal has been reached by the year 2000. A few cities (four or nine, depending on the Bill), have been singled as having especially serious problems in smog-forming emissions and will probably be given more time (2005 to 2010) to reach attainment. These cities include Los Angeles, Houston, New York and Chicago. This part of the Clean Air Act Amendments would establish programs for the use of vehicles operated on clean-

burning alternative fuels including methanol, ethanol, natural gas, electricity, propane, reformulated gasoline or any other comparable low emission fuel. In the nine major urban areas (Chicago is one) where the greatest ozone concentrations exist, the Administration plan calls for the phase-in of clean-fuel vehicles at the rate of 500,000 vehicles in 1995, 750,000 in 1996, and one million vehicles each year from 1997 through 2004. If any of the nine cities can reach attainment through other measures, they may "opt-out" of the clean fuel vehicle and alternative fuels program.

Assuming that the coal industry can adjust to the Clean Air Act Amendments, there is another environmental issue on the horizon which could

TABLE 1

Imports of western coal, 1988

State	Western coal (000s short tons)	% of imports to consumption
Illinois	8,653	26.2
Indiana	5,232	9.2
Michigan	10,294	29.2
Minnesota	16,686	96.5
New York	210	1.6
Ohio	1	0.0
Pennsylvania	0	0.0
Wisconsin	12,226	61.0
Great Lakes region	53,302	18.0

SOURCE: U.S. Department of Energy, Energy Information Administration, *Coal Distribution;* and U.S. Department of Energy, Energy Information Administration, *State Energy Data Report, Consumption Estimates 1960-1988.*

have a devastating effect. This is the controversial issue of global warming. Most scientists now concede that the increasing concentration in the earth's atmosphere of so-called "greenhouse gases", including carbon dioxide (CO_2), will lead to increases in the global temperature. However there is considerable debate about the rate of change of the earth's temperature and even more debate about national and international policies needed to respond to the problem. Some countries are proposing to establish a tax on CO_2 emissions to reduce the amount of this gas added to the global

environment. This directly affects the use of coal. Indeed, for coal to have a long term future it must either be demonstrated that the global temperature effects of CO_2 are minimal or alternatively a technical solution to the problem of global warming must be found.

Even if these complex environmental problems are overcome, the future of the coal industry in the region will still largely be dependent on the national growth rate of electricity. This is because the major use of coal (76.5 percent) is for the production of electricity, with 22.1 percent being used in industry and the remaining for commercial and residential use. The only domestic sector with possibility for expansion of coal use is the industrial sector. As mentioned earlier, the growth rate of the electrical sector (on a energy use per capita basis) is over 2 percent per year during the past 18 years, but this has been accomplished with relatively little increase in installed capacity. This reflects the industry's concern about the changing environmental laws placed on coal-fired plants coupled with the changing safety constraints placed on nuclear power facilities. The accidents at Three Mile Island and Chernobyl exacerbated the already difficult problem of public support for the nuclear option. The electric utility industry today is at a crossroads as it urgently needs new capacity to meet the growing demands. As a transition, it is highly likely that natural gas will be the fuel of choice for new electrical capacity during the 1990s. The longer term options are new generations of nuclear plants with improved safety features and coal-fired plants using clean coal technology. How this plays out will depend on many complex factors including economics, public acceptability, national environmental laws and other public policy decisions. Clearly the coal industry has a major stake in the outcome.

In the meantime, there is little doubt that the Great Lakes region will experience the most severe economic impacts from enactment of the Clean Air Act legislation. This is principally because the region maintains the greatest number of high sulfur coal burning power plants. For example, the House Energy Committee [7] has issued a list of 111 power plants currently in operation which will be immediately affected by the legislation. Indiana and Ohio are tied for the largest number of plants on the list at 15 apiece. In Ohio these fifteen facilities represent a total of 41 operating units. Indiana's fifteen plants total up to 37 individual units. Given that both states have an active high sulfur coal industry, it is not likely that they will consider switching to low sulfur coal, but will rather rely on expensive high technology solutions such as stack gas scrubbers. The economic costs of such solutions to the industrial rate payers relying on those utilities for service will be considerable. Initial estimates predict a "rate-shock" in the first year of the program for some Great Lakes utilities to be as high as 15 percent (then declining). Switching to a low sulfur coal could reduce this impact but this option may not be politically possible in some states because such a switch could put thousands of coal mine workers out of work. Essentially, without cost-sharing mechanisms, ten states will currently bear 80-90 percent of the cost to achieve a mandated 10 million ton SO_2 reduction. Those states include Illinois, Indiana, Michigan, Pennsylvania, Ohio, and Wisconsin from the Great Lakes region. Within these states the coal-burning utilities will bear the brunt of the costs.

In light of the above uncertainties many of the regional states are looking to foreign markets for future coal production. The success of this approach, of course, will depend on many factors including the development of rail and barge access to Gulf and East Coast ports; the development of port facilities; the competitive position of regional coals relative to coal from other countries such as Poland, South Africa, and Australia; and the compatibility of the region's coal with the environmental laws of the prospective foreign customer.

All in all it is clear that those states possessing large deposits of low sulfur coal will fare well in the immediate future, while the future of the high-sulfur coal industry is more in question and subject to a number of factors which are still being resolved.

The regional energy future—some policy issues

This paper has reviewed the national and regional trends in population, economic activity, and energy consumption over the 1970 to 1988 period. It is clear that the regional population

growth is not keeping up with that of the nation, and this is true in every state in the region.

One of the challenges to the region is to reverse the population shift to the sunbelt, since this trend will have negative impacts on the economic vitality of the region. This is already evident in the differential growth rate of the nation's gross national and gross domestic product rising at an average annual rate of 2.9 percent and the gross regional product growing at an average annual rate of only 1.9 percent. Furthermore, this out-migration will decrease the region's political presence in the Congress of the United States, just at the time when it needs to have a strong voice in influencing national policy.

The energy statistics reveal that the region, like the rest of the nation, is making real improvements in energy efficiency as demonstrated by the decreasing amount of energy needed to produce a real dollar output of goods and services. If this trend is to continue, regional industry will need to make large financial investments to replace their older, less efficient installations. Such changes are necessary not only from an energy point of view but also to improve the productivity of regional industry. Unless such steps are taken, the goods produced in the states of the region will not be able to compete with those coming from Japan, Germany, Korea, Taiwan, and other countries or states that have moved to modernize their industrial base, or from developing countries with lower labor costs such as Brazil and Mexico.

There is evidence that the nation and the region started to replace imported oil with indigenous coal. However, the growth in coal use is not being shared by all coal-producing states. Rather, it has been concentrated in the states producing low sulfur coal, primarily the West and the Eastern Appalachian region. With the imminent passage of the Clean Air Act, the constraints on the sulfur emissions from coal burning plants will place the region's coal industry in greater jeopardy. In fact, this is perhaps the most important policy issue facing this industry today.

A review of the regional energy resources bring out the fact that its largest resource is relatively high sulfur coal which has had difficulty in the past remaining competitive with low sulfur western coals.

Furthermore, the region has only limited gas and petroleum supplies. As a consequence, the region imports the overwhelming share of the oil and gas consumed in the eight states, as well as increasing amounts of western coal.

The energy statistics in the late 1980s indicate that the nation and the region are becoming more dependent on imported oil. As a result, the country is still vulnerable to another oil embargo. Constant vigilance, coupled with contingency planning, is essential if the impacts felt in 1973 and 1979 are not to be repeated. Regional policy makers should keep this item in the forefront of their policy agenda.

A number of other issues facing regional policy makers are associated with the electric power industry. It is critical that the region have adequate electric capacity to support a strong industrial and commercial base. The establishment by public utility commissions of a rate structure that allows such a growth is essential. At the same time a review of procedure to ensure that the industry does not add unnecessary capacity is needed. This entire process will be aided if a mechanism is established to accelerate siting decisions so that the lead time from the decision to build to the date of start-up is brought down to five to six years, thereby reducing the uncertainty in establishing future capacity and aiding in estimating future needs.

It is not possible to talk about the electrical industry and the related siting problems without bringing up the question of the future of nuclear power. Certainly since Three Mile Island and the subsequent Chernobyl nuclear accident, the nuclear industry has been placed on public trial. Siting decisions are even more carefully scrutinized by the public and the added safety requirements have modified the economic position of nuclear power. An especially sensitive issue related to nuclear power is that of waste disposal, both high-level and low-level radioactive wastes. If the nuclear option is to go forward, agreement must be reached on processes and procedures that will ensure that the advantages of nuclear power and the burdens of waste disposal are shared in an equitable manner, while protecting the health and the safety of the public. At this point in history it would be extremely risky to abandon the nuclear option which now constitutes as much as

23.5 percent of the input to electrical generation in the region. The challenge confronting policy makers is to keep the nuclear option and the nuclear industry viable during the decade of the nineties.

Turning from electric power to the natural gas industry, as pointed out earlier, natural gas prices have increased at a rate considerably higher than inflation, even outpacing petroleum price increases. However, the price of natural gas is still priced far below petroleum fuels on a Btu basis. It is reasonable to expect that as natural gas starts replacing petroleum for electricity generation, the increased demand for natural gas supply would cause the price of natural gas to move toward a price approximately equivalent to the price of heating oil on a Btu basis. Thus natural gas would be priced at a level reflecting its relative energy value and decisions related to the use of natural gas would be made on a more rational economic basis. One outcome of this would be improved efficiency in the use of natural gas, a socially desirable objective, but this will also increase the energy cost in the Great Lakes region especially in the residential and commercial sectors that are heavily dependent on natural gas.

There are many energy policy questions relating to such topics as alternative energy systems, solar and biomass (a major resource of the region); the future of regional transportation systems, including mass transportation, the railroads and the waterways; land-use planning and natural resources; automobile fuel economy standards; and priorities in energy research and development, to name a few. Their omission from this paper does not suggest that they may not be as important as the issues discussed here. Rather, limitations of space necessitated that choices be made. It was the judgment of the authors that the highlighted topics—the regional out-migration, the revitalizing of regional industry, the Clean Air Act issues, and the future of the electric power industry—occupy high places on the agenda of the states in the region over the next decades.

NOTES

[1] Natural gas prices while showing increases in real terms were still below the prices of petroleum products and electricity when compared on a Btu basis. For example, the price of natural gas in 1980 in current dollars per million Btu was $2.86 compared to $13.95 for electricity, $9.84 for motor gasoline, and $6.70 for distillate fuel. The price of coal was $1.47 per million Btu [20].

[2] Gross domestic product and gross state product for 1987 and 1988 is estimated using the growth rate of state personal income [2, 4, 11].

[3] Figures do not include interstate flow of electricity.

REFERENCES

[1] Congressional Research Service, The Library of Congress, "Acid Rain: Issues in the 101st Congress". *CRS Issue Briefs*, Order Code IB87045, Updated September 1, 1989.

[2] *Economic Report of the President* (February 1990).

[3] Hartnett J.P, and Galen P.S., "Energy Use and Economic Trends in the Midwest", *The Midwest Economy Issues and Policy*, University of Illinois, 1982.

[4] Illinois Department of Commerce and Community Affairs. *Illinois Bi-Monthly Economic Data Summary*, December, 1989 - January, 1990.

[5] The Bureau of National Affairs, Inc., *Environment Reporter*, "Clean Coal Legislation: Comparison of Provisions", July 27, 1990.

[6] *The Energy Report,* "Clean Air Act Revisions". Pasha Publications, June 4, 1990.

[7] *The Energy Report*, "West Dominates in Use of Scrubbers; Eastern U.S. Lags, EEI Study Says". Pasha Publications April 30, 1990.

[8] The White House, *The Clean Air Act Amendment of 1989: Highlights*, Washington.

[9] U.S. Department of Commerce, Bureau of the Census, *Statistical Abstract of the United States*, 1978, 1981, 1986, 1988, 1990.

[10] U.S. Department of Commerce, Bureau of Economic Analysis, *Gross State Product, Annual Estimates, 1963-86*, (computer tape, diskette, BEA/REA 88-401 or 88-402/88-410).

[11] U.S. Department of Commerce, Bureau of Economic Analysis, *Survey of Current Business*, July 1990.

[12] U.S Department of Energy, Energy Information Administration, *Annual Energy Review*. DOE/EIA-0084(84).

[13] U.S. Department of Energy, *Coal Data: A Reference*, July 1980.

[14] U.S. Department of Energy, *Demonstrated Reserve Base of Coal in the United States on January 1, 1980*, May 1982.

[15] U.S. Department of Energy, Energy Information Administration, *Coal Distribution*. January-December 1988, DOE/EIA-0125(88/4Q).

[16] U.S. Department of Energy, Energy Information Administration, *Coal Production 1988*. DOE/EIA(88).

[17] U.S Department of Energy, Energy Information Administration, *Energy Data Report: Bituminous and Subbituminous Coal and Lignite Distribution, Calendar Year 1979*. DOE/EIA-0125(79/4Q).

[18] U.S Department of Energy, Energy Information Administration, *Monthly Energy Review*. DOE/EIA-0035(82-89).

[19] U.S Department of Energy, Energy Information Administration, *State Energy Data Report, Consumption Estimates 1960-1988*. DOE/EIA-0214(88).

[20] U.S Department of Energy, *Energy Information Administration, State Energy Price and Expenditure Report*. DOE/EIA-0376(1970-1982, 1987).

[21] U.S Department of Energy, Energy Information Administration, *Quarterly Coal Report*. DOE/EIA-0121(85/4Q).

[22] U.S Department of Energy, Energy Information Administration, *U.S. Crude Oil, Natural Gas, and Natural Gas Liquids Reserves*, 1988 Annual Report, DOE/EIA-0216(88).

[23] U.S. Department of the Interior, Bureau of Mines *Minerals Yearbook*, (1970, 1971, 1972, 1973, 1974, 1975, 1976).

[24] U.S. Department of Labor, *Monthly Labor Review*, Bureau of Labor Statistics, 1970, 1989.

Chapter 8

The Great Lakes Region Transportation System

STEPHEN J. THORP, PROGRAM MANAGER, TRANSPORTATION AND ECONOMIC DEVELOPMENT, GREAT LAKES COMMISSION

ALBERT G. BALLERT, DIRECTOR OF RESEARCH EMERITUS, GREAT LAKES COMMISSION

The Great Lakes region transportation system is characterized by a well-developed multiple mode infrastructure and strong intermodal connections. Low-cost water shipment coupled with abundant natural resources provided a base for population settlement and large-scale industrial and agricultural development. An extensive rail, road and pipeline grid was laid out and eventually a high-capacity air transportation network was built.

Among the principal freight modes, a competitive environment has evolved. The region's relatively high freight generation level is, in part, attributable to the system's transport efficiencies. Particular modal patterns are evident in commodity/passenger movement and route structure.

Economic deregulation of the rail, air and motor carrier industries during the 1980s has improved transport operations and profits but has caused some service dislocations. Investment in transport infrastructure has become a major concern at all government levels and for the private sector. Modal and regional equity issues, as well as user fees, are becoming increasingly important.

Transportation was a pivotal factor in the development of the Great Lakes region. The combination of an in-place water transport infrastructure and a strong natural resource base promoted population settlement, agricultural development and a manufacturing economy. With an extensive inland river system and the Great Lakes, the region's early advantage was the foundation for a more elaborate transport network involving all of the major modes. Water transportation in the region, because of its historic role and present importance, will be emphasized in the following discussion. Pipeline transportation, although a significant tonnage mode in the region, will not be addressed.

Today, the region's strong multi-modal transportation system compares favorably with that of any other place on earth. Much of modern transportation technology was either invented or first implemented on an efficient scale in the region. Six of the eight Great Lakes states are among the top thirteen in total freight tonnage. The region has a dense, well developed road and rail network. Twenty-five region airports account for more than 25 percent of all U.S. air travelers. The 145 U.S. and Canadian ports/terminals on the Great Lakes-St. Lawrence River system move more than 200 million tons of commodities per year and hundreds of river terminals contribute as much as 200 million tons of waterborne commerce on an annual basis. These impressive facts illustrate the intensive development of the region's commodity and passenger transportation system as well as the historical growth of a multiple mode infrastructure.

The development of a new national transportation policy is underway. In emphasizing the critical role of transportation in the economy, the U.S. Secretary of Transportation stated in 1990, "No industry in the nation is more important to U.S. economic growth and international competitiveness than transportation." Although the goal of the national transportation policy is articulated as a "decisionmaking framework for government, industry and the public", detailed plans and policies will be part of the process.

The implications of future federal transportation policies will, no doubt, be significant for the Great Lakes region. Key regional issues for the 1990s include: maintenance of competitive balance among the modes; adequate infrastructure investment at all government levels; review of deregulation effects particularly for passenger transportation; introduction of new transportation technology and related energy conservation and land use planning. The region's transportation system operates in a dynamic environment. Its infrastructure allows goods and people to move among areas of economic importance matching demand with supply. Circumstances change and new transportation arrangements come into play. Public policy with respect to transportation activity has also undergone changes responding to historical and political developments. However, the vital connection between a strong transportation system and a prosperous economy remains unchanged.

Freight and passenger transportation: The early days

As a trade route among native peoples and a corridor of discovery and commerce for the Europeans, the Great Lakes-St. Lawrence River system and tributaries were an established transport system long before the United States and Canada became nations. Military conflict between the colonial powers and shifting alliances with tribal groups interfered, at times, with the free flow of commerce. Beginning in 1763, a British embargo on private navigation on the Great Lakes lasted for twenty-two years. The British relinquished complete control of the region in 1813 after losing the Battle of Lake Erie.

In the early 1800s, increased trading activities took place along the shores of Lakes Erie and Ontario where sailing vessels transported commodities such as grain, salt and some passengers. The limited extent of transportation was largely due to the lack of harbor development, difficulty in passage between the Great Lakes and small area population. The lure of the Trans-Appalachian West resulted in the building of the National Road which connected the Eastern Seaboard at Baltimore with the Ohio River at Wheeling, West Virginia. Through-traffic was limited by high transport costs and as a result, the Ohio River gradually become a regional trunk line for Midwest products. It is estimated that three-quarters of the export flow downstream originated in Ohio country. Between 1820 and 1840, westward expansion accelerated and significant economic development took place in the Great Lakes region. A canal/river navigation system was built and expanded during this time.

The Erie Canal opened in 1825 creating a water transportation route from New York City at the mouth of the Hudson River to Buffalo on Lake Erie. The first Welland Canal, connecting Lake Ontario with Lake Erie and bypassing Niagara Falls, was completed a year earlier. In 1835, the Ohio Canal was completed from the Ohio River to Cleveland on Lake Erie, spanning the state of Ohio. The influx of settlers and the development of the farm economy promoted the growth of such Lake Erie cities as Sandusky, Buffalo and Cleveland and the river cities of Pittsburgh and Cincinnati. Grain harvested in Ohio and Indiana could be economically transported by canal and connecting waterway to eastern cities. Buffalo became a major trade center during this time recording the receipt of more than one million bushels of grain in 1836 and surpassed New Orleans, its main grain port rival, two years later.

Travel and transport by steamship was first introduced to the Great Lakes above Niagara Falls in 1818 when the Walk on the Water traveled from Buffalo to Detroit. Steam and sail vessels operated together for many years. In one year, 1838, Cleveland counted 1,095 sailing ships and 1,318 steamship arrivals. In the 1840s, a new era of passenger transportation began with the introduction of larger steamships on the Great Lakes. Some steamers were capable of trans-ocean voyages utilizing an improved St. Lawrence River navigation system for access to the Atlantic Ocean. Minimum draft, paddlewheel steamboats gradually replaced keelboats and flatboats over the 981-mile course of the Ohio River, whose connection with the Mississippi provided a long water link to New Orleans and the Gulf of Mexico.

As waves of immigrants poured over the Great Lakes route, the shore became a magnet for urban and industrial growth. Packet steamers combined freight and passengers to become the principal mode for long distance movement. The packet steamers or night boats usually operated overnight

between two principal ports during a navigation season of eight to twelve months. These vessels plied the waters of the Great Lakes for over a hundred years. The early wood-hulled steamers carried a few hundred passengers including some in make-shift space on the freight decks. As the vessels grew in size with iron construction and more advanced coal-fired propulsion systems, their appearance and function resembled that of "floating hotels" with accommodations for all kinds of travelers. River boats also increased in size and comfort and provided scheduled service. After the mid-1800s, settlement and commerce followed the Upper Mississippi River as far as the Minnesota-Wisconsin border area. For many years, the principal downbound cargo was rafts of timber to riverside saw mills. During the river steamboat era, channel obstructions and widely fluctuating water levels combined to create difficulties for river traffic. Snag removal and construction of wing dams to enhance channel flows were constant activities. Dredging in port areas on the Great Lakes was also required.

From 1840 to 1860 total railroad mileage increased from 2,818 to 31,246 with much of the expansion occurring west of the Appalachians in the core Great Lakes region. During the 1850s, railroads began to connect major cities in the region which resulted in a slow-down in the shipbuilding and Lakes/river transportation industries. For a period of transition, new vessels were built smaller and carried fewer passengers and less cargo as a way of reducing operating costs. The railroad network that laced the area was at times a competitor and partner to the Lakes passenger trade. For particular city pairs, the rail link siphoned business from the boat lines. In some instances, the water route provided the only connection, but usually the comfortable and convenient vessel service was designed to complement rail as in the case of transcontinental or other "bridging" hauls. For example, a subsidiary of the Pennsylvania Railroad, the Anchor Line, inaugurated 14-day round-trip service in 1871 between Buffalo and Duluth with intermediate calls at Erie, Cleveland, Detroit, Port Huron, Mackinac Island, Sault Ste. Marie and Houghton. Other similar operations were run by

the Great Northern Railroad (Northern Steamship Co.) and the Canadian Pacific Railroad. Another aspect of the railroad connection was the establishment of cross-lake ferries at various locations that hauled railcars and later, motor vehicles and their passengers.

River transport

Major federal navigation improvement projects, combined with more powerful towboats, heralded a rebirth of river transportation in the 1930s following decades of stagnant growth, relentless competition from the railroads and World War I demand that strained both rail and river capacity. A series of locks and dams (29 on the Upper Mississippi and 21 on the Ohio) along with other facilities on significant tributaries including the Illinois River, created "slackwater pools" and a systemwide 9-foot navigation draft. Commodity tonnage increased substantially during the 1930s and 1940s because of greater capacity, relatively low cost and war-connected demand. Tonnage on the Ohio increased from 22.5 million tons in 1930 to 38 million tons in 1942 where coal, oil and fuels were the tonnage mainstays. From 1946 to 1953, approximately 2,500 industrial plants located along the Ohio River and shipping tonnage increased to 62 million tons. In 1954, a modernization program was begun to replace obsolete locks on the Ohio River. As a result, the river has remained a specialized transport artery for its industrialized hinterland. Upper Mississippi River trade was anchored by Minneapolis/St. Paul and St. Louis, two commercial centers without a strong heavy industry base. Channel improvements, a growing agriculture export market and the building of coal-fueled power plants along the river helped propel shipments on the Upper Mississippi from 2.4 million tons in 1939 to 84.2 million tons in 1985.

River transportation has established itself as a key component of the Great Lakes region's transportation system. Commodity movement by water in 1985 was more than one billion short tons or 18.6 percent of total U.S. intercity freight. Inland waterways (not including the Great Lakes) accounted for 606.4 million tons of the total. The Upper Mississippi and Ohio River system and tributaries which serve the Great Lakes region are high volume transport routes for relatively low value, bulk shipments. Coal, petroleum/chemicals, sand/gravel and grain are the principal commodities moved on the system. Where it is an option, fuel-efficient barge transport at 500 ton-miles per gallon has a substantial advantage over other modes in the longhaul movement of bulk commodities. Intermodal operations are commonplace. River navigation has its problems though, such as delay and disruption during times of low water which occurred a few times in the midwest over the past decade. Environmental regulation regarding channel maintenance and barge fleeting operations has also affected the industry.

Commodity flow data for three states illustrate the important role barge transport has in the region. Total barge shipments from Minnesota in 1987 amounted to 20.6 million tons with grain and mill product loadings predominant. An estimated overall economic impact of more than $300 million and nearly 6,000 jobs is attributable to the river transportation industry in the state. In recent years, Ohio's 125 Ohio River terminals have handled around 53 million tons with coal accounting for two-thirds of the total. In 1987, river shipments in Illinois were nearly 96 million tons with half of the tonnage moving through 87 terminals on the Illinois River. Farm products represented 25 percent of all river tonnage in Illinois and coal was 30 percent.

Great Lakes–St. Lawrence River System

Great Lakes transportation was the foundation on which the U.S. and Canadian regional and national manufacturing economies were built. Navigation system improvements ranging from channel and lock construction to innovative vessel designs and loading-unloading equipment resulted in increased cargo capacity and lower transportation costs. This immense deep draft transportation system stretches 2,340 miles from the Atlantic Ocean at the Gulf of St. Lawrence to the center of North America at the twin ports of Duluth-Superior (Figure 1). The 600-foot elevation difference between the Atlantic and Lake Superior required a lock and channel system for through transportation. Navigation locks were built more than 200 years ago

FIGURE 1

Great Lakes–St. Lawrence River system

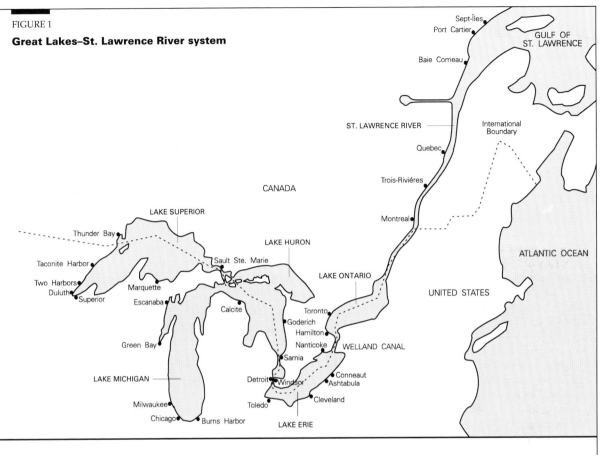

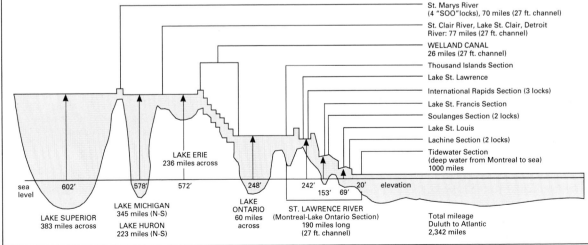

on the St. Lawrence River. Since then, new river locks have been built and rebuilt at 30- to 40-year intervals.

The first ship canal and lock facility on the St. Marys River, which connects Lake Superior with Lake Huron, was completed by the state of Michigan in 1855 at Sault Ste. Marie. Subsequent lock improvements and the transfer of ownership to the federal government in 1881 set the stage for substantial commodity movement and particular flow patterns: Midwest grain to eastern lake ports; Lake Superior area iron ore to Chicago, Detroit, Cleveland and Pennsylvania steel mills; backhaul coal cargoes and timber and lumber through many ports. Tonnage just through the Soo Locks has amounted to 7.7 billion tons to-date. The flow of bulk commodities throughout the Great Lakes system was directly tied to the large-scale industrial development taking place in the Great Lakes Basin.

The most extensive Great Lakes-St. Lawrence River navigation system improvement was the building of the modern Seaway. In 1954, after decades of debate, the Wiley-Dondero Seaway Act was signed into law. Construction of five new Canadian locks and two U.S. locks along with the world's largest joint hydropower facility took five years. Canadian costs were $336.5 million and U.S. costs amounted to $133.8 million, excluding the deepening of Great Lakes connecting channels and harbor entrances. From 1959 through 1989, Seaway (Montreal-Lake Ontario) tonnage has amounted to nearly 1.3 billion metric tons with an estimated value of $200 billion (Figure 2). With a few exceptions, annual tonnage increased until the peak year of 1977, when over 57 million metric tons were reported. While there have been year-to-year fluctuations, the 37 million tons in 1989 are representative of the general decline in average Seaway tonnage. High-value general cargoes have declined from their tonnage peak in the early 1970s. Seaway tolls, strong competition from rail carriers, increased use of container shipping and use of large vessels in trans-ocean shipping (only a third of the world's fleet can transit the Seaway locks), a limited navigation season due to winter ice, along with inadequate regional promotion all combined to depress the general cargo situation.

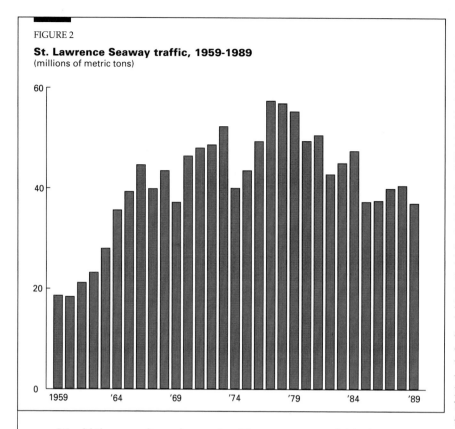

FIGURE 2

St. Lawrence Seaway traffic, 1959-1989
(millions of metric tons)

Would the area often referenced as "the heartland of North America" exist without the Great Lakes-St. Lawrence waterway system? Certainly the present network of transportation routes and urban centers in the region would have far different distribution patterns and economic roles. And the movement to markets for such prominent natural resources of the region and its tributary area as iron ore, coal and limestone would be void of the physical dictates as well as the benefits provided by the inland seas. It is within a unique framework that we view the Great Lakes region's infrastructure of transportation routes and their commodity flows.

The connecting basins of the Great Lakes system constitute the world's largest inland water body, having a total surface area of some 95,000 square miles and bordering U.S./Canadian mainland shorelines of more than 6,800 miles. The

longest navigation routes through the lakes system extend from the eastern end of Lake Ontario to Duluth-Superior and Chicago-Gary, distances of 1,155 and 1,065 miles, respectively. Eastward from Lake Ontario to Montreal is the 190-mile Seaway section of the St. Lawrence River. Channel controlling depths of 27 feet here are similar to the standard for the waterways connecting the Great Lakes and for most of their major harbors. Along with vessel draft limits of 26 feet through the Seaway and the 26-mile Welland Canal which links Lakes Ontario and Erie are the dimensions of 15 locks along these waterways which limit vessel sizes to a maximum length of 730 feet and a beam of 75.5 feet. Limitations imposed by structures of this size were overcome for upper lakes commerce in 1969 when the Poe Lock at Sault Ste. Marie, Michigan was placed in service to accommodate ships of up to 1,100 feet in length and a beam of 105 feet.

Most of the vessels engaged in the interlakes, Seaway and overseas trade are structured for the movement of dry bulk cargoes. The U.S. lakes fleet presently numbers about 65 vessels which are predominantly self-unloaders (dry bulk carriers equipped with conveyor belt/boom systems for the rapid discharge of cargoes). Canadian-registered vessels engaged in the Lakes-Seaway trade in 1990 totaled about 105.

During the period 1972-1983, the U.S. lakes fleet was markedly altered by the construction of 30 vessels and the lengthening of 10 others. This development was prompted by the increased vessel-size availability provided by the new Poe Lock, and, importantly, by the passage of the Merchant Marine

Act of 1970 which, for the first time, permitted Great Lakes shipping firms to establish tax-deferred construction reserve funds and set up a ship mortgage insurance program for use in the building of new vessels and in major reconstruction projects. This period of high shipbuilding activity marked a new era in Great Lakes transportation as it brought a notable change in vessel design by adopting the ocean-going ship arrangement of an all-aft superstructure. This consolidation of ship operations and use of a cylindrical-shaped bow have been key factors in maximizing cargo space.

For the present U.S. fleet, the most notable feature has been the construction of 13 ships in the 1,000-foot class. Their total single-trip carrying capacity of some 778,000 gross tons represents about 42 percent of the tonnage capability of the entire U.S. fleet. During the period when these supercarriers were built, the dimensions of seven other new vessels and all ten of those jumboized made them limited to the Poe Lock. In addition, these thirty ships—close to half of the U.S. fleet and about 70 percent of its single-trip carrying capacity—are limited in their range of operations to the four Great Lakes west of the Welland Canal.

The Canadian laker fleet, unlike its U.S. counterpart, has a dual role which includes the transporting of cargoes to and from eastern Canada via the Seaway as well as engaging in interlake and cross-lake commerce. With bulk carrier service largely dependent on operations through the Seaway and Welland Canal locks, overall vessel lengths are limited to 730 feet. This size, however, was a great stimulus to Canadian shipbuilding since the pre-Seaway St. Lawrence canal system had limited vessels to a 259-foot maximum length. Upgrading and expanding the fleet's cargo-carrying capacity supported new shipbuilding projects until the mid-1980s when major shipbuilding subsidies were terminated. From 1972, when the modern round of U.S. laker production began, additions to the Canadian fleet included 32 bulk carriers and 6 tankers. Six of the bulkers were designed to permit extension of operations into the coastal and ocean trade. Presently, three are in the Lakes-overseas trade and the other three operate exclusively outside the Lakes. In 1983, as U.S. laker construc-

tion ended, the fleet totaled about 117 ships and the Canadian roster included 144 vessels. The reduction in these fleets to their present size has been achieved by extensive sales and scrapping programs.

Useful indicators of the commodity structure of Great Lakes cargo traffic are contained in government reports issued annually for checkpoints along the Lakes-Seaway navigation route; the Soo Locks; at

TABLE 1

Iron ore, coal and grain traffic at three Great Lakes-Seaway checkpoints, 1989
(in thousands of short tons)

	Soo locks	% of total	Welland Canal	% of total	St. Lawrence Seaway	% of total
Iron ore	46,827	55	8,040	18	12,330	30
Coal	17,165	20	6,968	16	856	2
Grain	11,783	14	13,035	30	12,442	30
Total	75,775	89	28,043	64	25,628	62
All traffic	84,989	100	43,993	100	40,863	100

the Welland Canal and for passages through the Seaway section of the upper St. Lawrence River (Table 1).

The overall commodity leaders in the transport of Great Lakes cargoes are iron ore, coal and grain. Their relative positions, however, show marked variances in different sectors of the Lakes-Seaway route as indicated in the accompanying tabulations of 1989 waterway tonnages for the checkpoints noted above. Some features and factors relating to these commodity flows are discussed in the following sections.

Iron ore shipments through the Soo Locks are derived from Minnesota and Michigan mines, producers of about 98 percent of the nation's annual output, which move to markets primarily via the Lakes from six ports (an iron ore terminal at Silver Bay, Minnesota, recently resumed shipments following several years of inactivity); Seaway ore tonnage is entirely westbound from four eastern Canadian ports, three of them handling domestic ores from inland mining areas and from Quebec City, a transshipment port for overseas ore, principally from Brazil; the Welland traffic is largely a westbound continuation of that portion of the Seaway ore

tonnage that does not go to the Hamilton, Ontario, steel mills (Table 2).

Coal, the most widely distributed commodity in the Lakes-Seaway trade, had annual shipments of about 40 million short tons in 1988 and 1989. Cargoes are loaded at six U.S. and one Canadian terminal and move to about 60 Great Lakes and St. Lawrence River ports and several overseas destinations. Much of this traffic moves between ports located within the central lower lakes area, but the prominent position of coal in the Soo Locks traffic includes a record 14.3 million tons of low-sulfur fuel railed more than 1,000 miles from western U.S. and Canadian mines to western Lake Superior transshipment terminals. Welland Canal coal traffic is principally a movement from U.S. Lake Erie terminals to Lake Ontario utility plants and industries. Normally, well under a million tons continues on down the St. Lawrence to industries and to Sept-Iles Bay, Que. where cargoes are transferred directly to ocean-going colliers.

Grain is the principal international (overseas) trade commodity in the commerce of the Lakes and Seaway and, hence, moves predominantly eastward to transshipment ports on the lower St. Lawrence River or directly overseas on ocean carriers. The volume of grain exports is subject to wide year-to-year fluctuations due to changing world economic, political and weather conditions. Canadian shipments in 1989 were at a 20-year low and sharply reduced the relative position of grain in the total Lakes-Seaway trade for that year. Perhaps more representative of the present status of grain in the Lakes-Seaway trade is its average for the prior five years (1984-88) when the volume of 19-20 million short tons accounted for about 43 percent of the Seaway traffic.

An additional major tonnage commodity in the Lakes trade is limestone. In 1988, U.S. and Canadian shipments totaled approximately 35 million tons compared to an average of about 21 million for the 1981-85 period. Being abundant and widely available in the Great Lakes region makes this bulky, low-unit value rock very sensitive to transportation cost. Shoreline locations for both the production and consumption of limestone and gypsum by a major segment of its users have been

TABLE 2

Ranking Great Lakes ports in cargo tonnage, 1988
(in short tons of 2,000 lbs.)

U.S. ports	Total	Loaded	Unloaded	Leading commodities[a]		
Duluth-Superior, MN/WI	38,822	36,215	2,607	20,601 (Ore)	10,090 (Co)	4,978 (Gr)
Chicago, Illinois Total	20,173	3,971	16,202			
Lakes	6,878	1,101	5,777	*1,693* (Ore)	*1,182* (St)	*1,072* (Li)
Illinois Waterway	13,295	2,870	10,425	*3,968* (Co)	1,140 (Pet)	
Lorain, OH	16,960	6,209	10,751	*10,310* (Ore)	6,021 (Li)	
Indiana Harbor, IN	16,622	2,139	14,483	*12,374* (Ore)	*1,470* (Li)	1,064 (Pet)
Detroit, MI[b]	15,170	1,247	13,923	*6,244* (Ore)	*3,062* (Li)	*1,402* (Co)
Toledo, OH	14,593	9,324	5,269	7,756 (Co)	*4,060* (Ore)	1,000 (Gr)
Cleveland, OH	14,551	810	13,741	*8,867* (Ore)	*2,640* (Li)	*528* (Ce)
Marquette, MI	12,163	8,977	3,186	8,914 (Ore)	*1,722* (Co)	*1,462* (Li)
Two Harbors, MN	12,116	12,098	18	12,098 (Ore)		
Ashtabula, OH	10,335	6,252	4,083	5,991 (Co)	*3,070* (Ore)	
Conneaut, OH	10,220	7,570	2,650	7,481 (Co)	*2,162* (Ore)	
Calcite, MI	10,205	9,685	520	9,560 (Li)	*488* (Li)	
Gary, IN	8,634	624	8,010	*7,457* (Ore)	*391* (Li)	
Stoneport, MI	8,337	8,304	33	8,304 (Li)		
Taconite Harbor, MN	8,267	8,250	17	8,250 (Ore)		
St. Clair, MI	8,212	0	8,212	*8,149* (Co)		
Escanaba, MI	7,873	7,514	359	7,514 (Ore)		
Burns Harbor, IN	7,468	626	6,842	*5,553* (Ore)	*513* (Li)	
Ontario ports						
Thunder Bay	19,082	18,357	725	11,236 (Gr)	3,683 (Co)	1,501 (Po)
Hamilton	14,256	1,127	13,129	*6,824* (Ore)	*4,131* (Co)	
Nanticoke	10,692	455	10,237	*8,121* (Co)	*2,044* (Ore)	
Sarnia	7,112	2,986	4,126	*2,794* (Co)	1,558 (Pet)	760 (Ch)
Sault Ste. Marie	6,498	847	5,651	*2,396* (Ore)	*1,999* (Co)	
Windsor	4,597	2,140	2,457	1,805 (Sa)	*1,171* (Li)	
Clarkson	3,349	487	2,862	*2,458* (Li)	322 (Ce)	
Colbourne	2,458	2,458	0	2,458 (Li)		
Goderich	2,426	2,141	285	1,961 (Sa)		
Toronto	1,794	1119	1,675	*804* (Ce)		

NOTES:

[a]Cargo tonnage unloaded (receipts and imports) in italics for commodities listed.

Ce-Cement	Gr-Grain	Pet-Petroleum	St-Steel
Ch-Chemicals	Li-Limestone	Po-Potash	
Co-Coal	Ore-Iron Ore	Sa-Salt	

[b]Includes Detroit River from Detroit to Trenton and Rouge River terminals.

self-unloading lakers to storage docks and facilities throughout the Great Lakes with their major uses being, respectively, for road de-icing, highway and building construction and in fertilizer product.

The 145 ports/terminals of the Great Lakes-St. Lawrence system range from small, one-or-two-commodity terminal operations to large facilities handling bulk, palletized, containerized and heavy-lift cargo. With their warehouses, sophisticated cargo transfer equipment and intermodal connections, port operations are a vital part of the shipping scene as well as the larger economic picture. For example, an analysis by the port of Duluth-Superior indicated that 3,141 jobs and a $171 million total economic impact were generated by the handling of 34.6 million metric tons in 1987. A recent University of Toledo study showed that Toledo port-related activities resulted in 5,000 jobs and a $100 million payroll in a five-county surrounding area. Certain commodities such as steel make a major economic contribution by themselves. In Cleveland, for example, the 743,000 tons of import and export steel in 1989 represented most of the port's total general cargo tonnage. Steel industry officials estimate that these steel shipments resulted in a $56 million local economy impact.

Great Lakes-St. Lawrence Seaway transportation has had a remarkable past. The waterway's geographic position inducing the low-cost movement of raw materials to industrial centers and its access to the ocean assured its success. Questions about commodity flows and government policy have cast some uncertainty over the system's future. Many past forecasts of commodity shipment levels have been inaccurate. The world grain market is continually adjusting to quirks in supply and demand. North American steel production and related raw material movement have been affected by unfair steel trade in the past (dumping of import steel) and this situation may recur. U.S. coal flows to Ontario are likely to be reduced substantially because of a planned increase in nuclear power and government preference for Canadian-source coal. On the other hand, intermodal transshipment operations such as the low sulfur coal movement from Wyoming and Montana by rail to Superior and then by vessel to lower lake utilities are likely to

key factors in the development and maintenance of a large, but limited limestone market served by the lake shipping industry. From mines adjacent to or near company-owned harbors, special grades of the

carbonate rock are transported in self-unloaders directly to such large-volume users as the steel, cement and chemical industries. Salt, cement and potash are other dry bulk cargoes transported by

increase especially in response to new power plant emission regulations.

Great Lakes maritime interests have expressed concern about particular government policies that have raised costs and may create serious difficulties in the future. The imposition of Seaway tolls was a regional inequity—no other deep draft navigation segment incurred a similar cost. Since 1987, U.S. toll amounts have been rebated but substantial Canadian tolls remain. Particular rail rates during the 1960s and 1970s were challenged as discriminatory but Interstate Commerce Commission review did not produce relief. Mandated pilotage throughout much of the Great Lakes St. Lawrence system costs two to three times as much as that for tidewater areas. Stiff U.S. flag shipping requirements for government generated cargo like Food for Peace shipments have disadvantaged Great Lakes ports because they lack U.S. ocean vessel service. The rapidly diminishing U.S. flag ocean fleet is concentrating its services at high volume, general cargo ports. A deep-draft navigation cost recovery policy instituted with the Water Resources Development Act of 1986 has complicated Great Lakes commercial navigation. Although the ad valorem tax (4 cents per $100 of cargo value—more than twelve cents with 1990 Budget law) did not discriminate against the region's low value, bulk commodities, a substantial non-federal cost share requirement for new construction projects such as a much-needed $268 million lock at Sault Ste. Marie has stalled modernization efforts. The United States is investigating Coast Guard user fees for such services as icebreaking, aids to navigation and ship inspection which will add to commercial navigation's total burden. In Canada, a navigation services charge is under consideration to reduce the federal "subsidy" for the marine mode. These problems present a challenge to system users. Regional and modal equity issues will continue to be in the forefront as government policy makers address transportation needs for the nation.

The road report

Public road and street mileage for the eight Great Lakes states is more than 923,000 miles or nearly 24 percent of the national total. The Great Lakes region has a relatively dense road network compared with the nation as a whole. Most of this road mileage is concentrated in rural areas (723,000) and reflects the influence of the township and range land survey system as well as the historical development of farm-to-market access. At 52.5 million, total motor vehicle registrations in the region for 1988 represented 28.5 percent of the U.S. total. Per capita auto ownership was .57, the same as the national rate with four states above (Minnesota, Wisconsin, Michigan and Ohio) and four below. As for highway gasoline use, the states accounted for only 27.7 percent of total consumption which suggests less intensive vehicle use compared with other areas of the country.

Personal motor vehicles (autos, light trucks, vans and motorcycles) dominate passenger transportation in the United States. In 1988, the 141 million automobiles accounted for 80 percent of the 3.5 trillion passenger miles traveled and $400 billion in auto-related expenditures. The ubiquitous automobile has been called the cornerstone of industrial development and for the Great Lakes region, its status is particularly important from a manufacturing standpoint. The region is the birthplace of automobile assembly and much of the basic vehicle technology. Auto, truck and bus assembly in the Great Lakes states represents about three-fifths of U.S. production. Proximity to markets and suppliers is a key location factor but overall business costs remain a negative. This automobile connection with the region is vulnerable to volatile consumer spending patterns induced by downturns in the national economy and a longer-term threat to the fuel supply. Increasing dependence on imported oil is likely to result in supply disruption down the road and the attendant economic dislocation. In response, the major American auto companies have stepped up battery research in recent years searching for that elusive combination of power output, less weight and recharging potential. Another fuel problem solution the region has a large stake in is the manufacture and use of gasohol (gasoline blended with ethanol or methanol). In 1988, six region states accounted for 3.7 billion gallons of gasohol sold or 45 percent of the national total. Two states, Illinois and Indiana, reported that gasohol represented more than 24 percent of total highway-use gasoline.

The construction and maintenance of the regional and national road system is an immense task not only dollar-wise but for manpower deployment and materials requirements. Seventy-three percent of all government expenditures for transportation infrastructure are spent on the road system. Highway expenditures have been increasing in recent years due, in part, to the growing size of the system, deferred maintenance and increases in state fuel taxes. Since 1988, eighteen states have raised fuel taxes that generally provide a dedicated revenue stream. The funding picture for the highway mode is somewhat complex. For example, Minnesota spends, on average, about $400 million per year on trunk highway construction and another $130 million on maintenance for the 12,000 mile system, which represents about 9 percent of the total road mileage in the state (129,650 miles). Federal money covers about two-thirds of the construction outlays. State road user fees including the fuel tax, registration fees and 30 percent of vehicle sales taxes make up a Highway User Tax Distribution Fund which is apportioned among state, county and municipal road funds. Other sources of funds including general revenues and bonding are used particularly at the local level. In 1988, total disbursements from Great Lakes states highway-user revenues amounted to $4.8 billion, nearly 32 percent of the U.S. total. Federal apportionments are also significant. For example, in FY 90, the amount for the region was nearly $400 million for non-interstate programs. For the region's nearly 10,500 miles of interstate highways (23 percent of U.S. total) the FY 91 formula apportionments represent 15.7 percent ($822.7 million) of the national total.

The region's road and bridge system has a continuing need for repair including replacement where required. It is estimated that one-third of the region's bridges are deficient (Figure 3). In Wisconsin and Indiana the percentage is 40 percent. Freeze-thaw cycles wreak havoc on road and bridge structures. Damage to vehicles and weight restrictions particularly for rural farm areas add up to significant costs for the transportation system. In

FIGURE 3

Great Lakes states' bridges in need of repair

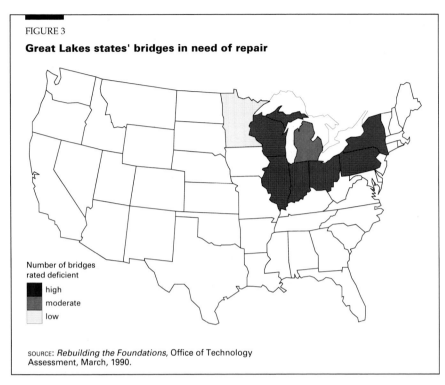

Number of bridges
rated deficient

■ high
▨ moderate
☐ low

SOURCE: *Rebuilding the Foundations*, Office of Technology
Assessment, March, 1990.

one state, Ohio, more than $10 billion is needed over the next decade to remedy road/bridge problems and add capacity. Although these road system problems are serious, the region compares favorably when total system conditions are considered. According to the Federal Highway Administration at the beginning of 1989, only 520 miles of the region's interstate system were rated as having poor pavement condition. This is 13.7 percent of the national total. For other principal arterial routes, the region accounts for only 15 percent. The road system's importance pervades all aspects of the region's economy and its physical integrity can only be maintained if the necessary financial resources are available.

Motor carrier and rail freight transportation

Rail and motor carrier operations together account for two-thirds of intercity freight tonnage in the U.S. From 1980 to 1988, mode share for rail and truck ton-miles combined in the U.S. increased from

59.7 to 62.2 percent. Substantial changes have occurred in the operating environments for both rail and motor carriers particularly since 1980 when both were substantially deregulated. These two modes are heavily represented in the Great Lakes region because of the freight tonnage that is generated and the historical development of the nation's transportation infrastructure. However, their relative importance is somewhat less compared with more insular states and regions where ocean and inland water transportation is less developed or not available.

Railroading is not what it was—it is better in some respects and worse in others. The Great Lakes area was the core region in the development of U.S. rail operations. The region's freight generation potential has remained strong. When total freight tons (including pipeline commodities) are compared for all states, the Great Lakes states rank relatively high: IL-4; OH-5; PA-6; NY-8; MI-11; IN-13; WI-20; and MN-23. Total major railroad (Class 1) tonnage has undergone slight growth during the 1980s after decades of decline due to inroads from other modes. Ton-miles have been increasing though, indicating a trend toward longer hauls. Interstate Commerce Commission carload data for the 1980-85 period indicate how the Great Lakes area fared vis a vis the nation and particularly during the recession years. For the Great Lakes states (not including New York and Pennsylvania) the region's share of carloadings was about a quarter of the U.S. total with a slight percentage improvement in share over five years. Total U.S. carloadings declined 13.4 percent whereas region carloadings were down 12.4 percent. As for commodity mix in the Great Lakes area, motor

vehicle and equipment rail shipments have been increasing but food product shipments have been losing ground to trucks. The heavy taconite (iron ore) shipments in Northern Minnesota and Michigan have given these two states a more than 90 percent share of total U.S. metallic ore rail shipments. With respect to grain/farm product shipments, the Great Lakes area has more than 30 percent of the total.

In 1988 commercial trucks hauled 2.45 billion tons with revenues of $240 billion. The number of major motor carrier operations based in the Great Lakes states is about 12,000 which represents about 30 percent of the major regulated carriers in the country. Intercity trucking has a general advantage over rail up to the 500-mile range. Timely delivery to points all over the road network assures the motor carriers a service advantage. However, intermodal operations with rail have been growing steadily. The percentage of trailer/container loadings for rail reached 25.5 percent of total carloadings in 1988, up from 14.1 percent in 1978.

Over the past decade, the most important development affecting the region's surface transportation industry has been economic deregulation through the Staggers Rail Act of 1980 and the 1980 Motor Carrier Act. Significant transport inefficiencies caused by federal rate and entry/exit regulation for both modes gave impetus to regulatory reform. It has been estimated that the annual cost to society of rail and motor carrier regulation was $4 to $5 billion. For the railroads, relaxed exit rules permitted substantial abandonment of unprofitable track. More than 43,372 miles of track were shed by the major Class I carriers from 1979 to 1988 although some of this track has been sold to local and regional carriers. In the eight Great Lakes states, Class I mileage has declined from 43,829 in 1984 to 33,595 miles in 1988 (26.3 percent of national total). New volume and contract rate authority under Staggers has given the railroads much greater pricing flexibility and permitted quicker response time. Now, more than half of all rail traffic is shipped under contract rates. In the less-than-truckload sector, regulatory reform promoted network efficiency by reducing circuitry of routes and promoting backhaul opportunities. The industry has also seen tremendous growth in nonunion high density, corridor operations that take advantage of maximum vehicle use. Problems for the over-the-road trucking sector include the hodgepodge of state vehicle weight and safety laws and growing public concern about safe truck operation. Relatively low fuel economy for tractor-trailer units and escalating fuel prices have also created problems for the industry.

Commercial aviation

Commercial aviation is a fundamentally important part of U.S. passenger transportation and the national economy. According to an industry trade group, Partnership For Improved Air Travel, commercial aviation-related activity employed 7.8 million people in 1989 who earned $165 billion. For the Great Lakes states, the Partnership projected the industry's impact excluding aircraft manufacturing at $125 billion, almost 26 percent of the national total. The number of related jobs was 1.77 million. In terms of total civil aviation manufacturing employment (including general aviation), the Great Lakes states had 126,394 positions in 1989. Over the past twenty years, the air transportation mode has been steadily increasing its share of the U.S. intercity passenger market. In 1989, the 484 million passenger enplanements represented nearly a fifth of all intercity travelers. Although the number of passengers has more than doubled since 1979, much of this increase is due to connecting flight activity. Air travel has reached such high levels that airport capacity is strained in major urban markets and needed improvements will cost billions and take years to complete.

By all standards, the airplane is the safest and fastest way to move long distances. Business travel predominates as the purpose of commercial aircraft trips. As a result, airplane travel can serve as a barometer of economic conditions. During recessions and cyclic downturns, there is a noticeable drop-off in air travel. The Great Lakes region is home to nearly half of the "Fortune 500" company headquarters and these nodes of the regional and national business community generate a significant share of business-related air travel. The airplane is so important to business that availability and

frequency of scheduled air service can be a major factor in business location decisions. It is also a factor in planning conventions and business meetings. For vacation travel, the airplane's importance has increased particularly with the development of major North American resort areas. The burgeoning airport car rental service, even though it is wedded to the business traveler, has made the air option more attractive to those vacation fliers who need a vehicle to complete their journey. Also, discount air fares are available when a trip is coupled with a Saturday stayover thus creating combined business/vacation trips and increasing hotel occupancy rates during weekends. Several region cities are gateways for overseas air operations and Canadian connections are available at the major hubs. The 13 million passengers traveling between the U.S. and Canada annually represent each country's largest international aviation market. U.S. and Canada "open skies" negotiations are intended to reduce carrier and service restrictions for the cross-border travel and may eventually induce more air travel. U.S. Travel and Tourism Administration survey data indicate that a business/convention trip purpose is given by around 60 percent of foreign air travelers. Gateway status for certain airports in the region and their metropolitan areas is seen as a prestige factor and very important in establishing international travel opportunities even though such service is available at other U.S. airports.

Airline deregulation has become a principal issue for the airline industry, the traveling public and government policy makers. In 1978, the Airline Deregulation Act was signed into law and the old industry ground rules were left behind. Carrier market entry and exit were no longer the purview of the Civil Aeronautics Board and fare regulation was dispensed with. Market forces were in control. Upstart operations, small town route abandonment, carrier mergers and bankruptcies, fare wars and unprecedented passenger growth were some of the consequences of the deregulated environment. One dramatic result of deregulation is the consolidation of the industry into a few major carriers. In 1989, 90 percent of revenue passenger miles were provided by only 8 airlines whereas in 1984 there were 38

large carriers. Feeder and regional operations in the U.S. have also declined—the number is now more than 150. A major study of the air deregulation situation was completed in 1990 by the U.S. Department of Transportation. The study concluded that deregulation has overall lowered fares and increased service. In 1988, more than 55 percent of air travel was between city pairs served by three or more airlines compared with only 28 percent ten years earlier. Air fares, adjusted for inflation, have declined by 26 percent since 1981. The "hub and spoke" feeder system that evolved has proved to be an efficient means to collect passengers and redistribute them, but hub airport congestion has increased, resulting in delays and potential air traffic hazards. In some markets, a single carrier has become dominant and the reduced competition has pushed fares upward on many routes. The U.S. DOT study indicated that four of the eight "higher fare" metro areas are in the Great Lakes region—Minneapolis/St. Paul, Cincinnati, Dayton and Pittsburgh. For example, in the Minneapolis/St. Paul market, Northwest Airlines has a 78 percent share and in Pittsburgh, USAir handles 85 percent of all passengers.

For the Great Lakes region with high levels of air travel, airport capacity has become a major issue. In 1989 passenger activity at the busiest airport in each of the eight Great Lakes states totaled 165.7 million enplanements and deplanements. Chicago's O'Hare International with 59,130,007 passengers in 1989 ranked first in the world. O'Hare is also a major air cargo center with a 958,430 metric tons recorded in 1989. Toronto's main airport is the busiest in Canada with 18.35 million passengers (1987). At O'Hare and other major airports in the region, an increasing number of noise problems and an inadequate number of gates are focusing attention on airport expansion projects and even the need for new airports. The major regional airports are vital elements of the national airport system—12 are in the top 50 in terms of enplanements. A third major airport is proposed for the Chicago metro area. In Detroit, a proposed $630 million expansion of City Airport may create 8,000 new permanent jobs but would destroy 3,600 occupied homes. Across town, Detroit Metro Airport has proposed a

$1 billion expansion including new terminals and runways.

These high-dollar airport projects have not only raised land use and noise concerns in localities, but system financing issues are also part of the debate. Past federal funding has come from the dedicated federal Airport and Airway Trust Fund supported by user fees including a ticket tax. Proponents of more federal support decry the several billion dollar surplus in the Trust Fund which is retained as a budget maneuver. The 1990 Federal Budget legislation addressed airport financing by raising the passenger ticket tax from 8 to 10 percent as well as the air cargo tax. The legislation also provided new authority for local airport fees to boost resources for improvement projects but tied this initiative to a new national airport/aircraft noise policy to be implemented during the 1990s.

Rail passenger transportation

Railroad passenger transportation was nothing but a ghost of its past in 1970 when the National Railroad Passenger Corporation (Amtrak) was created to revitalize intercity rail travel. In FY 88, Amtrak carried a record 21.5 million passengers or around one percent of total mode share. A decade earlier, mode share was .76 percent representing only 4,094,000 person-trips. In contrast to the air mode, only one-fifth of Amtrak's riders are traveling on business. This fact demonstrates the train's role in vacation/pleasure travel and much of the organization's promotion is aimed at this market.

Amtrak operates more than 24,000 route miles with more than 20,000 employees. About half of its patronage comes from the Amtrak-owned 800-mile Northeast corridor, the highest density and highest speed rail route in the U.S. There is a relatively dense network of Amtrak lines in the Great Lakes states compared to other regions. Rail patronage on some Great Lakes-Midwest routes is substantial, but none of these routes are near break-even revenue/cost levels based on current ridership. Total region station activity (arrivals and departures) for FY 89 was more than 16 million or about three-quarters of all U.S. rail passengers (Table 3). The total for the single busiest stations in each of the Great Lakes

states was 11.4 million indicating a concentration factor for Amtrak travel generation.

The federal subsidy each year for Amtrak is relished by budget cutters but Congressional resistance to federal assistance elimination has kept Amtrak rolling. Amtrak reported a record income of $1.3 billion in FY 89 and reliance on federal money is gradually diminishing. The federal subsidy in FY 89 was $585 including $80 million for capital spending. This figure has declined from

---

TABLE 3

Amtrak rail passengers in the Great Lakes states, fiscal year 1989

States and total Amtrak passengers		Busiest Amtrak stations and station totals	
Illinois	2,657,613	Chicago	2,023,399
Indiana	199,175	Indianapolis	55,590
Michigan	576,983	Ann Arbor	87,747
Minnesota	128,855	Minneapolis/St. Paul	96,639
New York	7,994,202	New York City (Penn Station)	5,372,940
Ohio	182,286	Toledo	68,095
Pennsylvania	4,246,510	Philadelphia (30th & Market St. Station)	3,448,632
Wisconsin	285,662	Milwaukee	231,837
GL states	16,271,286		
U.S.	21,363,151		

SOURCE: National Railroad Passenger Corporation.

NOTE: Rail passenger data represents total station activity (arrivals and departures).

---

nearly $900 million at the beginning of the 1980s. Amtrak officials predicted in 1990 that the system will cover its operating costs by the year 2000, something no major passenger railroad in the world can presently claim.

Many people argue that Amtrak fills an important niche in the intercity passenger market and should not be summarily shunted to a siding to allow the "Budget Express" to pass. For those people who can conveniently use Amtrak, the loss of rail service or a substantial increase in ticket prices may force reliance on alternative means of

transportation. However, intercity bus service has declined and the private auto or the airlines may be out of reach for those with slim pocketbooks. In Canada, government action to reduce the deficit will affect future rail passenger service. In a plan announced in 1989, government-run Via Rail may cut up to half of its 400 trains a week by 1993. Much of the remaining service would be concentrated in the Windsor-Quebec City corridor which accounts for two-thirds of nationwide traffic. The role of transcontinental and rural train service in Canadian history has been so strong in terms of linking together far-flung areas and building a national identity that the cutbacks have generated fierce debate.

Future passenger train service in the Great Lakes area may entail several high-speed routes. Amtrak, for much of its regional network, uses right-of-way of an owner railroad and as track conditions in major corridors are improved, passenger service also benefits. Six Great Lakes states are members of the Interstate High Speed Rail Compact, a coordinative organization. The Compact has identified a series of incremental improvements to the existing passenger system as a first step toward more comprehensive system upgrading. Three route initiatives that have been identified are Chicago-Philadelphia, Chicago-St. Louis and Chicago-Indianapolis. In Canada, a Quebec-Ontario study is also considering a high-speed rail route that would include a segment linking the two provincial capitals (Toronto and Quebec City) and extending to Windsor and Ottawa. The 280-mile Detroit-Chicago route offers a glimpse of the near-term. For three daily trips between the nation's sixth and third largest metro areas, maximum train speed is 80 mph with 40 percent of the route stuck at 70 mph or less. More than $60 million has been spent recently on improving track and signals and another $10 million for new or renovated stations. A multi-year rail passenger improvement project, Michigan Mainline 90, involving Amtrak, Conrail and the Michigan Department of Transportation will upgrade infrastructure and equipment to raise operating speeds to 90-125 mph, as well as promote expanded ridership and improved service. Train operations beyond 125 mph throughout much of the regional intercity network will require substantial changes in route alignment and corridor segregation for safety purposes.

New technology such as magnetic levitation (Maglev) has been discussed for several short, high ridership potential areas in the region and particular intercity routes. Maglev has been proposed for initial development as an airport-city connector. Orlando may be the first, but a serious proposal is being studied for Pittsburgh. In fact, Pennsylvania interests are urging consideration of using old steel mills to build equipment and guideway for the country. Maglev capital costs have been estimated at $5 to $15 million per-mile which compares favorably with interstate highway costs. The two modes may come together in more ways than for comparative purposes—the interstate highways are also likely to be used for Maglev rights-of-way.

The motorcoach industry and transit

In the Great Lakes region, thousands of buses travel routes that make up metropolitan transit systems, school routes and the intercity network. The motorcoach industry has been waging a difficult battle for the journey-to-work and intercity mode share but its connection to group tour travel/ tourism is becoming more important. In 1970, the 1,000 U.S. intercity bus companies owned 22,000 buses, employed 49,500 and carried 400,000,000 revenue passengers over 1.2 billion bus miles. By 1987, a larger number of companies operated 3,600 fewer buses with 10,500 fewer employees. This smaller fleet carried 333 million passengers and traveled 914 million bus miles. The number of major intercity bus companies (Class 1 carriers— with gross annual revenues of $5 million or more) has declined from 143 in 1960 to around 50 today. One-fifth of these companies (Greyhound Lines, Inc. and nine regional carriers) carried 12.4 million passengers in 1987 and accounted for about 85 percent of total Class 1 carrier revenues. The Greyhound strike, related bankruptcy and reduced service in 1990 resulted in a 36 percent decline in operating revenues and 28 percent fewer passengers for the 10 largest companies during the first six months of 1990 compared with the same period in 1989.

According to the Census Bureau's last National Travel Survey, the Great Lakes states accounted for about one-third of U.S. person-trips by bus in 1977 (at least 200 miles round-trip). Of these 5.02 million trips, 92 percent were intrastate in nature. The average round-trip by bus was 590 miles and such trips were 2.7 percent of total person-trips. Intercity bus travel received a boost in the 1970s from the gasoline shortfall and fuel and auto price increases. Overtime, the influence of these trends has decreased. The bus still has a role in intercity travel, but with passage of the Bus Regulatory Reform Act of 1982, many areas no longer have scheduled service. The legislation permitted widespread route abandonment. An Interstate Commerce Commission study found that 3,750 communities (mostly rural) lost all intercity service from 1982 to 1986. On the other hand, around 10,000 places still had such service as the 1990s began. Long distance bus travel has been declining in recent years. The Greyhound situation has reinforced this trend and caused particular problems for the Great Lakes states because of the company's well-developed regional route structure.

Many intercity motorcoach companies operate charters and tours—an important tourism market segment. Tour and charter travel in the U.S. is estimated to be a $10 billion industry with a 10 percent annual growth rate. Lower cost and greater convenience are principal reasons for the growing popularity of group travel. Trip/tour itineraries are packaged to take advantage of a group's purchasing power. Such group travel was initially dominated by the motorcoach alone but intermodal arrangements with rail, cruise or air transportation are also popular now. In surveys conducted by the U.S. Travel and Tourism Administration, about 20 percent of overseas visitors to the U.S. use intercity bus services during their stay compared to only a third as many for train. According to the National Tour Association (NTA), the primary group travel industry organization in North America, group tours and charters involved about 1.2 million bus trips, 47.1 million passengers and 83.8 million total passenger days in 1987. The Great Lakes states accounted for nearly 211,000 trips and a $1.4 billion economic impact. NTA reports that a typical

busload of 40 people will spend over $3,000 for each travel day including lodging and meals.

Another major component of passenger transportation is transit. There are 438 mass transit systems in operation in the U.S. Most of the systems are not self-supporting from fare revenue and require a government subsidy. Urban and rural transit agencies received $2.2 billion from the General Fund in 1988 and about $1 billion plus from the Highway Trust Fund. A little over one cent of the current federal gas tax is dedicated to transit funding and transit operations are exempt from the federal diesel fuel tax. For FY 90, federal transit apportionments to urban areas with a population of 200,000 or more were $1.2 billion. Bus systems are the chief beneficiaries but rail operations also qualify. However, most transit funding comes from the fare box and local jurisdictions. In Minnesota, only 28 percent of annual operating costs are met with state or federal money. Rural areas, as in the case with intercity bus service, have not fared as well in transit funding even though the need is great. With 38 percent of the nation's population, rural areas contribute 41 percent of federal gasoline taxes but only get back 4 percent in transit aid. The rural poor are even more disadvantaged because more than half do not have a car. Increasing traffic congestion, related pollution and significant land use conflict in urban areas and particularly major cities in the region will require more attention to public transit. Some cities have relatively high levels of transit use but most do not. One good example is Minneapolis where approximately 40 percent of the downtown workforce commutes using public transit and another 20 percent engage in car and van pooling. Ride-share programs, special high-occupancy vehicle lanes and special toll roads along with traditional bus service development will be the likely "package" approach to the future people moving problem in the region's cities.

Conclusion

The Great Lakes region's transportation system has a well-developed infrastructure and strong intermodal connections. An abundant supply of natural resources coupled with low-cost water shipment provided a base for population settlement and large-scale industrial and agricultural development. An extensive rail, road and pipeline grid was laid out and eventually a high-capacity air transportation network was built. Among the principal freight modes, a competitive environment has evolved. The region's relatively high freight generation level is, in part, attributable to the system's transport efficiencies. Particular modal patterns are also evident in commodity movement and route structure. Economic deregulation of the rail, air and motor carrier industries during the 1980s has improved transport operations and profits but caused some dislocations particularly in service areas. Investment in transport infrastructure has become a major issue especially since the federal contribution has declined almost 20 percent since 1980. The future is full of user fees for all modes where public revenue support has been a factor. Modal and regional equity concerns will be center stage as the finance/investment issue plays itself out.

Chapter 9

Agriculture and the Great Lakes Region

GARY L. BENJAMIN, ECONOMIC ADVISER AND VICE PRESIDENT, FEDERAL RESERVE BANK OF CHICAGO

Most observers are optimistic that continued gains in world population and standards of living will translate into expanding markets for Great Lakes agriculture, especially if the GATT negotiations for reducing trade-distorting subsidies are successful. However, the trend toward fewer but larger farms will likely continue as farmers strive for economic efficiency in an increasingly competitive world market.

The Great Lakes encompasses a significant portion of the nation's vast farm sector. Similarly, the farm sector is a major part of the overall economy of the nation and of the nine-state Great Lakes region.[1] The region's farmers generated more than $45 billion in gross sales of farm commodities in 1989, nearly 30 percent of all farm commodity sales nationwide. A large share of the gross sales are recycled through the nonfarm economy as a result of farmers purchases of manufactured inputs, labor, and services and their tax payments to various governmental units. Moreover, the economic value added by the many firms and industries that process and distribute the raw farm commodities into finished products for consumers worldwide is a significant multiple of the farm value of the raw commodities. Reflecting the latter, it is estimated that only about 30 percent of all consumer expenditures on domestically-produced foods goes to farmers.

The production unit

Estimates for 1990 show that the region contained nearly 170 million acres of farmland, accounting for a sixth of all land in farms nationwide and well over half of the total land area in the region. Reflecting the region's favorable topography, soils, climate, and rainfall, the most distinguishing feature of its farmland is the high proportion that can be used to grow crops. Cropland accounts for 81 percent of the region's land in farms, more than double the 39 percent share for all other areas of the United States. Only 4 percent of the region's farmland (versus 50 percent elsewhere) is in permanent pasture or rangeland. Woodlands account for 10 percent of the region's land in farm, marginally above the 8 percent share elsewhere. The remaining 5 percent encompasses homesteads, ponds, roads, wasteland, etc.

The region's farmland is distributed among nearly 654,000 farms,[2] 30 percent of all farms nationwide (Table 1). Farms vary widely in size, both within the region and elsewhere. In general, however, farms in the Great Lakes are smaller than those in other areas. In terms of acreage, the average farm in the Great Lakes encompasses about 260 acres, less than half the average for farms

elsewhere. But interregional comparisons of farm size in terms of acreage can be misleading because of differences in land quality. Reflecting its much larger share of high quality cropland, farm commodity sales per acre in the Great Lakes region in 1989 was nearly double that for all other areas. Hence, commodity sales per farm in the Great Lakes was less than a tenth below the average elsewhere. The distribution of farms and farmland by gross sales of farm commodities provides evidence of the variation in farm size. Only a fifth of the farms in the Great Lakes typically achieve $100,000 or more in annual sales of farm commodities. These "commercial farms", with an average of 670 acres each, account for more than half of all land in farms in the region. At the other extreme, 36 percent of the region's farms generate commodity sales of less than $10,000 annually. Most of these units, which average less than 70 acres in size, are part-time or hobby-farms. In between these extremes lies a mix of commercial and part-time farms that average 225 acres in size and have annual sales of $10,000 to $99,000. Some 43 percent of the region's farms and 38 percent of its land in farms fall within this latter category.

Whether distributed by acreage or annual commodity sales, there is no single point of delineation that clearly distinguishes commercial farms from part-time or hobby farms. Yet in terms of numbers, most farms are probably too small to be economically viable; i.e. able to generate annual net earnings that provide an acceptable standard of living for the farm operator. This has been true for decades as technological advances in farm machinery, management, and genetics have expanded the production capacity of individual farms and farmers. The productivity gains which have accompanied these technological advances in agriculture have been truly remarkable in terms of the improved diets that were afforded a growing world population. The productivity gains were also remarkable in terms of the land and labor resources that were released from employment in basic food production to other economic uses which have broadly enhanced our standard of living. But this remarkable success story has been accompanied by declining real returns per unit of agricultural

TABLE 1

Farms, land in farms, and commodity sales per farm and per acre[a]

		Land in farms		Farms with sales of		Land in farms with sales of		Average sales[b]	
	Number of farms	Total	Average per farm	less than $10,000	$100,000 or more	less than $10,000	$100,000 or more	Per farm	Per acre
	(000s)	(mil acres)	(acres)	(% of farms)		(% of farmland)		($)	
Illinois	83	28.5	343	23	26	3	67	86,500	260
Indiana	68	16.3	240	40	18	8	53	65,500	280
Iowa	104	33.5	322	19	28	4	56	96,200	300
Michigan	54	10.8	200	52	15	14	56	58,200	300
Minnesota	89	30.0	337	36	21	9	52	79,200	240
New York	38	8.4	218	45	22	19	49	75,200	350
Ohio	84	15.7	187	51	12	16	43	47,500	260
Pennsylvania	53	8.1	153	47	15	22	35	67,600	440
Wisconsin	80	17.6	220	33	21	14	43	71,600	330
Great Lakes	654	168.9	258	36	20	9	53	73,400	290
Other states	1,490	818.8	550	53	12	10	49	80,500	150
United States	2,143	987.7	461	48	15	10	50	78,300	170

SOURCE: U.S. Department of Agriculture.

[a]Figures shown for farm numbers and land in farms are based on 1990 data. Figures shown for average sales per farm and per acre are based on 1989 data.

[b]Combines cash receipts from farm commodity marketings and direct government payments to farmers. Sales per farm are rounded to the nearest $100. Sales per acre are rounded to the nearest $10.

output, a continuing consolidation of farms into fewer—but larger—units, and the economic demise of many rural towns and communities as employment and vocational opportunities shifted to more urban areas.

That so many small, economically unviable farms continue to exist is due to several factors. The long history of federal government farm income and price support programs has helped small farmers to hang on longer. The typically older age of farmers and the limited job mobility training in rural areas could also be a factor. Other, and probably more relevant factors include the long history of real (inflation-adjusted) gains in farmland values and the "good-life" that many people in and outside of agriculture associate with farming and rural living in general. These latter factors encourage small farmers to supplement their limited farm earnings with off-farm work while maintaining their ties to agriculture and the rural community.

As suggested above, the average size of farms has increased over time as the decline in the number of farms has far outstripped the decline in the amount of land in farms. Farm numbers nationwide declined 12 percent over the past ten years while the amount of farmland declined 5 percent. In the Great Lakes, the decline in farm numbers was higher than elsewhere (16 percent versus 10 percent) while the decline in the amount of land in farms was slightly lower (3 percent). Compared to earlier decades, the rate of decline in farm numbers nationwide during the 1980s was about comparable to that of the 1970s and less than half the rate of decline experienced during the 1950s and the 1960s. The rate of decline in the amount of land in farms has been stable since the mid 1950s.

Characteristics of farm operators and their organization

Farmers that own all the land they operate represent the most common form of land tenancy

among farmers in the Great Lakes and elsewhere. But the incidence of rented or leased farmland is still rather substantial. The 1987 Census of Agriculture shows that 54 percent of the farmers in the Great Lakes region own all the farmland that they operate (Table 2). But these full-owner farms tend to be much smaller than the average in terms of acreage, accounting for only 30 percent of the region's land in farms. At the other end of the tenancy spectrum, some 13 percent of the region's farmers, accounting for 14 percent of its land in farms, are strictly tenant farmers. The remaining one-third of the region's farmers operate farms that combined both owned and rented land. These part-owner farms tend to be much larger than average in size, accounting for 56 percent of the region's land in farms. The rented acreage accounts for more than half (54 percent) of the land in these part-owner farms. The acreage that is operated by tenant farmers plus the rented portion of the land operated by part owners accounts for 44 percent of the region's land in farms, slightly more than the 41 percent share applicable for all other areas of the United States.

Among individual states of the region, the proportion of farmers who own all the land they operate is considerably lower in Illinois and Iowa (about 45 percent) than it is in most other region states (about 60 percent). The proportion of part-owner farmers ranges from 29 percent in Ohio and Pennsylvania to less than 37 percent in Illinois. The proportion of tenant farmers varies from 6 percent in Michigan and New York to about 20 percent Illinois and Iowa. The combined share of farmland that is rented by part-owner and tenant farmers ranges from a fourth in New York and Wisconsin to 60 percent in Illinois.

Rising farmland values are often considered a sign of strength for farmers and agriculture in general. For farmers who own their own land, this is undoubtedly true. Yet with over 40 percent of the farmland rented or leased by farmers, it is clear that non-operating landlords (including a large contingent of retired farmers) capture a sizable chunk of any rise in land values. Moreover, since land rents parallel changes in value, rising land values quickly translate into higher production costs for farmers who cash rent their land. For those who use share-rental arrangements, a common practice in many areas, the impact of rising land values on production costs is somewhat diluted.

Some 86 percent of the farms in the Great Lakes region, accounting for 78 percent of all farmland in the region, are organized as the sole proprietorship of the farm operator or his/her family. Another 10 percent of the region's farms, accounting for 15 percent of its land in farms, are organized as a partnership. Less than 3 percent of the region's farms are organized as family-owned corporations, the bulk of which have fewer than 10 shareholders. These family-held farm corporations operate a little over 6 percent of the region's land in farms. All other forms of organization (including nonfamily-held corporations, cooperatives, estates or trusts, and institutional) account for less than 1 percent of the farms and farmland in the region. The distribution of farms by type of organization in the Great Lakes is virtually identical to that found among all other regions. The distribution of land in farms differs somewhat, with the Great Lakes region having a larger share operated by sole proprietorship farms and a smaller share operated by both family-held corporations and by all other non-partnership forms of organization.

Farm operators tend to be advanced in age and have lengthy ties to their present farms (Table 3). The average age of farm operators in all states of the region, at the time of the 1987 Census, closely approximated 50 years. Nearly a fifth (18 percent) of the operators were at, or above, the "normal" retirement age of 65. The proportion under the age of 35 was nearly comparable (17 percent). The average length of time that farm operators had been affiliated with their present farm was 20 years.

The commonality of part-time farming, although less prevalent in the Great Lakes than elsewhere, was vividly apparent in the most recent Census. For instance, 38 percent of the farmers in the Great Lakes region regarded their principal occupation to be something other than farming.

TABLE 3

Selected characteristics of farm operators

	Average age	Years on present farm	With another principal occupation	Farmers who worked off-farm[a] 1 day or more	100 to 199 days	200 days or more
	(years)			(% of farmers)		
Illinois	50	20	36	53	9	32
Indiana	50	20	48	62	9	43
Iowa	49	20	28	47	7	26
Michigan	51	20	49	60	9	43
Minnesota	48	19	31	49	9	27
New York	51	20	39	49	9	32
Ohio	51	20	50	62	9	44
Pennsylvania	51	20	42	55	10	36
Wisconsin	50	20	29	43	7	27
Great Lakes	50	20	38	53	8	34
Other states	53	18	49	59	9	39
United States	52	19	45	57	9	38

SOURCE: 1987 Census of Agriculture.

[a]The percentages shown for off-farm work are based on the number of responding farmers. About 6 percent of the operators, both nationwide and in the Great Lakes region, did not respond to the Census question on off-farm work.

TABLE 2

Distribution of farms and land in farms by the land tenancy of the farm operator

	Percent of farmers by their land tenancy			Percent of land in farms by operator's land tenancy			Percent of farm-land rented or leased[a]
	Full owner	Part owner	Tenant farmers	Full owner	Part owner	Tenant farmers	
Illinois	44	37	19	19	60	20	60
Indiana	58	31	11	28	60	12	49
Iowa	46	33	21	25	55	20	52
Michigan	61	33	6	34	61	5	35
Minnesota	53	34	12	32	56	12	40
New York	61	33	6	40	55	5	24
Ohio	60	29	11	34	55	12	44
Pennsylvania	61	29	10	42	49	9	31
Wisconsin	58	33	9	41	51	7	26
Great Lakes	54	33	13	30	56	14	44
Other states	62	28	11	34	53	13	41
United States	59	29	12	33	54	13	42

SOURCE: 1987 Census of Agriculture.

[a]Combines the farmland operated by tenant farmers and the rented acreage operated by part-owner farmers.

Similarly, over half (53 percent) of the region's farmers worked one or more days in off-farm jobs during the Census year. A large majority (64 percent) of those with off-farm jobs worked 200 days or more in those jobs.[3] Overall, farmers who worked in off-farm jobs for 100 days or more accounted for 42 percent of all the region's farmers (versus nearly 49 percent elsewhere). Among individual states of the region, the proportion of farmers who worked off the farm for 100 days or more ranged from about a third in Iowa and Wisconsin to about 52 percent in Indiana, Michigan, and Ohio.[4]

The large segment of farmers who work off the farm, whether of necessity or choice, warrants some elaboration. The dedication and work ethics of farm families in their off-farm jobs have long been highly regarded attributes. It is important that these attributes continue to be complemented in the future with quality education in rural areas. In addition, it is worth noting that off-farm earnings tend to be more stable than farm earnings and that off-farm earnings typically account for well over half of the annual earnings of farm operator families. These aspects

TABLE 4

Great Lakes farm commodity sales and government payments, 1989

	Billions of dollars	Percent of region's total	U. S.
Livestock/poultry and product sales	24.9	50.8	30
Milk and dairy products	10.0	20.4	52
Cattle and calves	6.2	12.7	17
Hogs	5.9	12.0	62
Eggs	1.1	2.3	29
Turkeys	.7	1.5	33
Broilers and chicken	.4	0.8	4
Other	.6	1.2	18
Crop and related product sales	20.3	41.4	27
Corn	7.0	14.3	63
Hay and other feed crops	1.0	2.0	17
Soybeans	6.6	13.3	61
Vegetables	1.6	3.2	14
Wheat	1.3	2.6	18
Greenhouse/ nursery products	1.3	2.6	18
Fruits and nuts	.7	1.3	7
Other	.9	1.9	7
Government payments	3.8	7.8	35
Total	49.0	100.0	29

SOURCE: U.S. Department of Agriculture.

are often overlooked in discussions on the well-being of farmers.

The region's share of U.S. agriculture

By most measures, the Great Lakes region accounts for about 30 percent of U.S. agriculture. From a balance sheet perspective (which combines the farm-related assets and debts of both farm operators and non-operating owners of farmland) the Great Lakes accounted for 29 percent of the nation's nearly $800 billion in farm sector assets as of the end of 1989, and nearly 31 percent of its $130 billion in outstanding farm sector debt.[5] From an income perspective, farmers in the Great Lakes received nearly $49 billion in cash receipts from farm commodity sales and direct government farm program payments in 1989, 29 percent of the nationwide total of $170 billion.[6] By major compo-

nents, the region's share was 27 percent of all receipts from crop sales, 30 percent of all receipts from livestock, poultry and milk sales, and 35 percent of direct government payments (Tables 4 and 5). The vast bulk of government payments go to crop farmers.

Cash receipts from farm commodity sales in Great Lakes states surpassed $45 billion in 1989. As is typically the case, nearly 80 percent of the region's receipts were generated by five commodities; milk ($10.0 billion), corn ($7.0 billion), soybeans ($6.6 billion), cattle and calves ($6.2 billion), and hogs ($5.9 billion). With the exception of cattle and calves, the Great Lakes region accounts for a dominate share of the nation's total production of these commodities. Last year the region accounted for 69 percent of the nation's corn harvest; 63 percent of its soybean production, 63 percent of all hogs and pigs on U.S. farms, and 51 percent of the nation's milk production. The region's receipts from cattle and calf marketings represented a sixth of the nationwide total and, as usual, contained a proportionately large share from the sale of dairy cattle as opposed to beef-type cattle. With respect to the latter type, the region usually accounts for about a fifth of all cattle in feedlots being raised to produce high quality beef.

Although dominated by five commodities, agriculture in the Great Lakes region is fairly diversified. Receipts from other major field crops in 1989 included wheat ($1.3 billion) and hay ($700 million). With nearly a one-third share of the nation's egg and turkey market, the region's poultry producers generated $2.4 billion in receipts last year. Farm sales of all fruits and vegetable in the Great Lakes exceeded $2.2 billion last year, while receipts from greenhouse and nursery product sales (one of the fastest growing farm markets in recent years) approximated $1.3 billion.

The diversity of Great Lakes agriculture is further evident in the dominate position it holds in a number of small (in scope) but still important "niche" markets. For instance, Wisconsin typically ranks a close second to Massachusetts in cranberry production and is the leading state in sales of mink pelts. Strongly anchored by Pennsylvania, the Great Lakes region accounts for half of the nation's annual

farm sales of mushrooms. Michigan accounts for three-fourths of the nation's tart cherry production and 60 to 70 percent of the navy bean production. Minnesota, with an individual share of 20 percent, is the largest producer of sugarbeets.

The fortunes of the farm sector

Agriculture, both within the Great Lakes and elsewhere, has always been a very cyclical industry. The balance between shortage and surplus in the available supply of most farm commodities is delicate and can be easily tipped in either direction as a result of numerous, and largely unpredictable influences on production and consumption. In general, however, the cycles over the past two decades have been among the most profound of the last century. The 1970s were highlighted by an extraordinarily strong growth in world demand for grains and oilseeds. Several factors contributed to the strong growth, including the resumption of trade with the USSR and China, the recycling of the oil wealth generated by the initial energy crises, and a falling value of the U.S. dollar relative to other major currencies. As a result of the strong growth in world demand, the value of U.S agricultural exports rose from $8.0 billion in fiscal 1971 to a still

FIGURE 1

U.S. agricultural exports, 1960-1990
(billions of dollars)

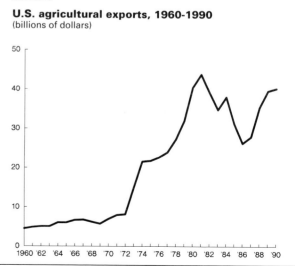

TABLE 5

Farm commodity sales and government payments for Great Lakes states, 1989
(millions of dollars)

	Livestock sales	Crop sales	Government payments	Total	Top five commodities and share of total commodity sales[a]
Illinois	2,252	4,458	726	7,436	Corn (30%), Soybeans, Hogs, Cattle, Wheat; (89%)
Indiana	1,817	2,502	334	4,652	Corn (26%), Soybeans, Hogs, Cattle, Dairy; (77%)
Iowa	5,209	3,911	981	10,100	Hogs (27%), Cattle, Corn, Soybeans, Dairy; (95%)
Michigan	1,313	1,627	262	3,202	Dairy (24%), Vegetables, Cattle, Corn, Greenhouse; (61%)
Minnesota	3,716	2,809	600	7,125	Dairy (20%), Cattle, Soybeans, Hogs, Corn; (76%)
New York	1,946	911	76	2,933	Dairy (54%), Vegetables, Greenhouse, Cattle, Fruit; (87%)
Ohio	1,698	2,114	274	4,086	Soybeans (19%), Dairy, Corn, Cattle, Hogs; (71%)
Pennsylvania	2,595	986	68	3,650	Dairy (38%), Cattle, Greenhouse, Eggs, Mushrooms; (68%)
Wisconsin	4,337	941	522	5,800	Dairy (60%), Cattle, Vegetables, Hogs, Corn; (89%)
Great Lakes	24,883	20,259	3,843	48,985	Dairy (22%), Corn, Soybeans, Cattle, Hogs; (79%)

SOURCE: U.S. Department of Agriculture.

[a]Commodities are listed in rank order of sales. Share of total commodity sales (not including government payments) are shown in parenthesis for both the top-ranked commodity and for the top five commodities in farm sales. The rankings are based on individual commodities, except for vegetables, greenhouse products, and fruit which are broad categories of several commodities.

standing peak of nearly $44 billion in fiscal 1981 (Figure 1). The export gain reflected both higher commodity prices and a larger tonnage of shipments, particularly (to the benefit of Great Lakes farmers) for grains and soybeans. Although high grain prices contributed to some losses for livestock producers, the export boom propelled real (inflation-adjusted) farm sector earnings to highs unprecedented since the war years of the 1940s and early 1950s. Moreover, the combination of strong world markets and high earnings, coupled with a surge in debt-financing, created a speculative boom in farm capital expenditures and in bidding on farmland. Reflecting the latter, per acre farmland values soared 4-fold nationwide during the 10 years leading up to the 1981 peak (Figure 2). The Great Lakes recorded a 4.6 fold rise in farmland values as all states of the region except Michigan and New York registered gains equal to, or larger than, the nationwide increase.

The "fortunes" of U.S. and Great Lakes agriculture in the 1970s abruptly turned into misfortunes in the early 1980s. World trade for agricultural commodities levelled off and even declined for awhile. For a variety of reasons, U.S. agricultural exports retreated 40 percent between

fiscal 1981 and the trough in 1986. U.S. agriculture was again faced with price-depressing surpluses that, under government farm income and price support programs, resulted in a sizable cut in crop acreage.[7] The combination of shrinking exports and heavy drought losses in 1980 and 1983 led to a severe squeeze on farm earnings during the first half of the 1980s. The depressed exports and earnings broke the speculative bubble in farmland values, triggering declines unparalleled since the era that ended with the Great Depression. These developments culminated in extensive bankruptcies among farmers and heavy loan losses and failures among farm lenders in the mid-1980s.

Fortunately, the last four years have brought marked improvement for farmers. The recovery was triggered by major legislation in late 1985 that permitted U.S. farm commodities to be more competitive in world markets and led to a temporary surge in federal government outlays for farm income and price support programs. The ensuing recovery in exports (to $40 billion in fiscal 1990) has bolstered farm sector earnings in recent years. The farm sector balance sheet has been strengthened by a partial recovery in land values since the end of 1986 and the combination of marked pay-downs

and write-offs on farm debt over the last seven years. As a result, farmers nationwide embark on the 1990s with a much stronger financial footing than was true in the mid 1980s and with a more mature economic perspective than was the case during the speculative boom of the 1970s.

What lies ahead for Great Lakes agriculture

A number of recent and emerging developments will influence the fortunes of U.S. and Great Lakes agriculture in the years ahead. The recent five-year compromise for reducing federal budget deficits foreshadows a significant downscaling in

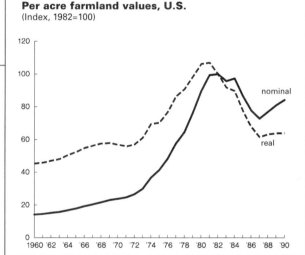

FIGURE 2

Per acre farmland values, U.S.
(Index, 1982=100)

the government safety net for farm earnings. It is difficult to project how significant the downscaling will be in terms of farm earnings and federal government outlays for farm income and price support programs.[8] Yet it is clear that farm support programs will be restructured beginning in 1991 and that the restructuring could present new risks, challenges, and opportunities for all farmers. Producers of supported commodities will be most directly affected. But because of the increased flexibilities that the new programs will offer for planting non-program crops, the effects could spread to other farmers.

As implemented by the Budget Reconciliation Act of 1990, most of the savings in federal government outlays for farm income and price support programs over the next five years will arise from a 15 percent cut in the amount of acreage in program crops (major grains and cotton) that will be eligible for certain direct government payments. In the Great Lakes, this change will mostly trim benefits for corn farmers. Additional savings will arise from the imposition of new fees to be assessed, directly or indirectly, on producers of most other supported commodities. In the Great Lakes, these new fees will especially hit dairy farmers and soybean producers. Because of their dominance in corn, milk, and soybean production, Great Lakes farmers may be somewhat more vulnerable than others to the shrinkage in the government safety net for agriculture.

The implications for agriculture from the downscaling of the federal safety net are difficult to assess. In the first year or two, farm earnings may be pulled somewhat lower than would otherwise have been the case. But because farmers will have more flexibility to plant alternative crops, some of the cuts in program crop benefits may be partially offset. What happens in the long-run will depend primarily on the fundamental strength in agricultural commodity markets, here and abroad. If markets shrink and/or production outstrips consumption, U.S. agriculture will be more vulnerable to the cyclical downturns that typically accompany a return to surplus production. Alternatively, if agricultural markets remain comparatively strong, the shrinkage in the safety net may go relatively unnoticed.

The still uncertain outcome of the latest round of multi-lateral trade negotiations among member countries of the General Agreement on Trade and Tariffs (GATT) could be a significant factor in determining the strength of agricultural markets in the years ahead.[9] The negotiations started in 1986 and were scheduled to end in December 1990. The negotiations focused on a number of trade issues, but those for agriculture were the most pivotal and the most contentious. The U.S. and many other agricultural exporting countries insisted upon a substantial phase-down of all agricultural trade-distorting subsidies among the 107 member-countries of the GATT. In contrast, countries of the European Community (EC) and, to a lesser extent, Japan and South Korea insisted on only a limited phase-down. The negotiations on all issues under discussion "collapsed" in December when participants failed to reach a compromise on agricultural trade reforms. But subsequent calls for extending the negotiations, coupled with signs the EC may be more willing to reduce its trade-distorting agricultural subsidies still offer some hope for an eventual compromise.

U.S. and Great Lakes farmers have a lot at stake in the outcome of the GATT negotiations. Failure to compromise on agricultural trade could confine future growth in world markets for many U.S. agricultural commodities. Some observers believe it could also lead to an escalation in costly trade wars and/or export subsidies. Alternatively, successful compromise on the agricultural trade issue, depending on the extent of the phase-down in subsidies, could lead to stronger market growth for those agricultural commodities in which the U.S. enjoys a comparative economic advantage in production and distribution. Presumably, this would be particularly true for meat, most grains (especially feed grains) and, to a lesser extent, soybeans; commodities particularly prevalent in the Great Lakes. In contrast, a significant phase-out of trade distorting subsidies might have some negative implications for dairy farmers.

Numerous other issues that have surfaced recently will continue to influence the fortunes of U.S. and Great Lakes farmers in the future. These include the growing focus on the environment, animal welfare, and the multitude of issues surrounding the dietary value of food and the safety and quality of food and water. Farmers are as concerned about most of these issues as consumers. But farmers are much more vulnerable to the cost of environmental clean-up and/or the market impacts of changes in consumption patterns that might be triggered by dietary concerns, food safety concerns, and/or concerns about how farm animals are raised and processed. Technological advances in testing for residues (or contaminates) will continue to outstrip our scientific knowledge of safe levels of residue and, in some cases, our knowledge of the sources of the residue. Recent experience with grapes and apples are vivid reminders of the enormous disruptions that occur with unwarranted reactions to detected (or publicized) levels of residue. Regardless, the whole food industry, from producer to food scientist and processor, will have to be increasingly diligent about the need to produce foods that meet the range in consumer standards of acceptable quantity and wholesomeness in a manner that is relatively benign to the environment. Achieving this goal will lead to more structured controls on farmers and their production practices.

U.S. agriculture will undoubtedly continue to experience economic and/or weather-related cyclical swings in the future. In terms of a prevailing trend, it is difficult (and probably foolish) to project how those swings will play out in the 1990s. Analysts were surprised at the boom and bust cycles that emerged in the 1970s and the 1980s, respectively, and have become humbled in their projections for the decade ahead. But on balance, most observers are optimistic that continued gains in world population and standards of living will translate into expanding markets for agriculture commodities. U.S. and Great Lakes agriculture will likely fare well in such an environment. However, the past trend of consolidating farms into fewer, but larger units will likely continue as U.S. farmers strive for economic efficiency in production in an increasingly competitive world market.

While the future looks promising, the commodity mix of Great Lakes agriculture may pose some challenges. A sizable portion of the region's agriculture is devoted to commodities that have witnessed little, or no market growth in recent years. Much of the region's livestock-related production is concentrated in red meats, milk, and eggs. For various reasons, these commodities are constrained almost exclusively to the domestic market. (On balance, the U.S. is a net importer of small amounts of red meats while net exports of eggs and dairy products represent only a nominal share of production). In addition to being constrained by the comparatively slow population growth of the domestic market, dietary concerns about fat and cholesterol have limited the market growth for these protein-rich commodities for the past several years.

Per capita domestic consumption of all meats has risen about one-half percent annually over the past two decades. But dramatic gains in poultry and fish have captured all the growth in domestic meat consumption. Great Lakes turkey farmers have benefitted from this growth. But Great Lakes agriculture has only a token stake in the much larger broiler market and virtually no stake in the modest, but rapidly developing market for "fish farming." And unfortunately for the preponderance of hog and cattle farmers in the Great Lakes and elsewhere, per capita consumption of beef has declined about a fourth since the mid 1970s while per capita pork consumption has, at best, been stable when compared over the past several cycles in production. The long-term decline in per capita egg consumption has continued, dropping nearly a fourth over the past two decades. The milk equivalent of domestic per capita consumption of all dairy products (milkfat basis) has been flat for a number of years as consumers' increasing preference for cheese and low-fat milk and dairy products has been offset by shifts away from butter and whole milk.

Cattle, hogs, milk, and eggs accounted for over half of the cash receipts from farm commodity sales in Great Lakes states in 1989. Elsewhere, those same commodities accounted for 40 percent of cash receipts. If the stable to declining per capita consumption pattern in domestic markets continues, Great Lakes agriculture might shrink somewhat relative to the agricultural production plant nationwide. Producers of red meats, milk, and eggs have a strong interest in the ongoing efforts to make these commodities more compatible with consumers' dietary preferences. Red meat producers in particular also have an interest in U.S. efforts to encourage foreign countries to relax their restrictions on meat imports so that the high-quality beef and pork produced here could find growing markets elsewhere in the world. Many analysts believe that quotas and other import restraints, although easing recently in Japan, still unnecessarily restrain potential U.S. meat exports.

The potential for growth markets for Great Lakes corn and soybean farmers would appear to be more promising than for livestock producers. The potential for growth in domestic markets for corn and soybeans will hinge largely on population growth and the outcome of efforts to expand U.S. meat exports. Expanding world markets for U.S. meat would translate into increased domestic demand for corn, soybeans, and other crops used as livestock feed. The demand for corn could also be enhanced if the environmental issues and/or the energy situation should evolve into increased domestic use of ethanol.

Export demand for U.S. corn and soybeans would also be expected to grow as long as world trade patterns are not unduly encumbered by restrictions abroad. Export shipments typically account for 25 to 30 percent of the annual disappearance (consumption) of U.S. corn. Similarly, export shipments of soybeans and soybean meal typically account for 50 to 55 percent of the annual disappearance of U.S. soybeans. In recent years U.S. exports of these commodities have faced increased competitive pressures from abroad. In the European Economic Community (EC), the combination of high internal price supports and large export subsidies have shifted that market from a net importer of feed grains to a net exporter in recent years. In addition, oilseed production has risen substantially in recent years in the EC and in the major exporting countries of Brazil and Argentina. But in the absence of major trade restraints, the combination of highly productive soils and the unsurpassed export-transportation infrastructure in this country suggest that the United States should remain a very competitive supplier of grains and oilseeds to world markets. The success of the current GATT negotiations in achieving a substantial phase-down of agricultural trade distorting subsidies and barriers among member countries would be a major factor in helping to assure the competitive position of U.S. and Great Lakes agriculture in world markets.

NOTES

[1]This study defines the Great Lakes region as encompassing the states of Illinois, Indiana, Iowa, Michigan, Minnesota, New York, Ohio, Pennsylvania, and Wisconsin.

[2]A farm is defined as any establishment from which $1,000 or more of agricultural products were, or would normally be, sold during the year.

[3]The Census data do not distinguish by hours worked in off-farm jobs. Aside from this, 200 days or more spent in off-farm jobs would approach full-time equivalency. Depending on vacation, holidays, and other excused absences, most "full-time" jobs would consume 220 to 235 days a year.

[4]The role of farmers in nonfarm labor markets is further amplified if one were to consider the off-farm work of spouses and other members of farm operator families.

[5]The balance sheet figures cited exclude the household-related assets and debt of farm operator families.

[6]From 1960 through 1987, the region's share of annual cash receipts from farm commodity marketings and government payments held in the narrow range of 30.5 to 33.9 percent. The slightly smaller share the last two years partially reflects the heavy drought losses that hit the region in 1988. Other factors include the region's smaller share of milk production and its modest stake in the rapidly growing broiler receipts.

[7]After dropping to virtually zero during most years from 1974 through 1981, the amount of U.S. cropland idled from production under government farm programs surged to levels that ranged between 60 and 78 million acres during five of the past eight years. At the peak (in both 1983 and 1988) the amount of cropland idled by these programs was equivalent to nearly a fifth of all cropland.

[8]For comparison purposes, the estimates associated with the Budget Reconciliation Act suggest that federal government outlays for farm income and price support programs will total about $41 billion over the next five fiscal years; down from the original base-line projection of about $55 billion. Actual outlays for such programs totaled $79 billion over the last five years.

[9]In this regard, it is noteworthy that the five-year cuts in farm income and price support programs outlined in the recent Budget Reconciliation Act are contingent upon reaching agreement on agricultural trade reforms in the current GATT negotiations. Without agreement, many of the cuts could be restored by 1992.

Chapter 10

Forest Resource Trends and Issues

Larry Leefers, Associate Professor, Department of Forestry, Michigan State University

Non-Fuel Mineral Resources

Henry P. Whaley, Former Senior Vice President, Cleveland-Cliffs Inc.

Forests cover 55 percent of the Great Lakes region's land area (below Hudson Bay). These diverse forests provide raw material for wood products industries, essential habitat for plant and animal species, and desired locations for recreation and tourism activities. In both countries, owners manage their forests for a variety of purposes. In the Great Lakes states, there has been a 2.5 percent increase in timberland area since 1952. Timber volume has attracted a number of wood processing facilities and recreation activities in forested environments have increased. Forest resource issues (e.g., forest decline, timber availability, forest-related employment, etc.) will influence future management directions for the region's forests.

Four non-fuel minerals comprise the lion's share in the Great Lakes states: crushed stone, sand and gravel, iron ore, and portland cement. Except iron ore, three of these products are mined in close proportion to the economic size of the region. In contrast, the region's iron ore deposits account for an estimated 98 percent of the nation's production value of this mineral.

Forests provide the foundation for many activities in the Great Lakes region. They supply timber for the wood products industries, habitat for plant and animal species, and settings for recreation and tourism. In addition, they help stabilize soils, cleanse air, and circulate water. Forests cover vast areas of the Great Lakes region (Tables 1 and 2). Overall, fifty-four percent of the area below Hudson Bay is covered by forests. These forests vary in composition, ownership, and productivity.

Wood products industries make significant contributions to the economic welfare of the region, particularly in Ontario and in states with large areas of forests. Industries create a variety of products. Primary forest products include sawlogs, poles, pulpwood and fuelwood. These primary products form the first link between the forests and the wood products we desire. Most primary products undergo processing to create secondary forest products such as lumber, particleboard, furniture, woodpulp and paper. Sustaining these industries through stewardship of forest resources is a common goal across the region.

Contemporary issues will greatly influence our utilization of forest resources in the twenty-first century. Issues range from concerns about the effects of acid precipitation to the underutilization of the region's timber resources.

Forest area

In the United States, approximately 38 percent of the region's land area is forested (Waddell et al., 1989). Timberland, which is producing or is capable of producing industrial wood, comprises most of the forest land. Timberlands have not been withdrawn from timber utilization by statute or administrative decision (e.g., harvesting is not permitted in federally designated wilderness areas). Area and percent of forest and timberlands varies considerably by state with Illinois having the least acreage in timberlands and Michigan having the most (Table 1). In total, about 19 percent of the nation's timberland is located in the Great Lakes region.

TABLE 1

Area of land, forest land, and timberland in the Great Lakes region by state, 1987

State	Total land area	Total forest land	Total timberland	Forest	Timberland
	(000s of acres)			(% of land)	
Illinois	35,531	4,265	4,030	12.0	11.3
Indiana	22,895	4,439	4,296	19.4	18.8
Michigan	36,362	18,220	17,364	50.1	47.8
Minnesota	50,640	16,583	13,572	32.7	26.8
New York	30,273	18,775	15,798	62.0	52.2
Ohio	26,211	7,309	7,141	27.9	27.2
Pennsylvania	28,601	16,997	16,186	59.4	56.6
Wisconsin	34,740	15,319	14,726	44.1	42.4
Total	265,253	101,907	93,113	38.4	35.1

Of Ontario's 263.7 million acres, approximately 131.1 million acres of land were inventoried and reported in a recent study (Ontario Ministry of Natural Resources, 1986). These lands are roughly those south of Hudson Bay. Most of this area is covered by productive forests which are capable of growing commercial timber (Table 2).

TABLE 2

Total and productive forest land in Ontario's inventoried area, 1986

Total inventory land	Total forest land	Productive forest	Forest	Productive forest
(000s of acres)			(% of land)	
131,069	113,849	98,585	86.9	75.2

Ownership

Two broad classes of timberland ownership are used in the United States: public and private. Public lands include federal, Indian, state, county and municipal categories. Private lands include forest industry, farmer and other private categories. Private lands comprise 74 percent of the region's

TABLE 3

Area of timberland by ownership in the Great Lakes region by state, 1987

State	Timberland	Public lands	Private lands	Timberland	Public lands	Private lands
	(000s of acres)			(% of US)		
Illinois	4,030	389	3,641	0.8	0.3	1.0
Indiana	4,296	535	3,761	0.9	0.4	1.1
Michigan	17,364	6,310	11,054	3.6	4.6	3.2
Minnesota	13,572	7,279	6,293	2.8	5.3	1.8
New York	15,798	1,215	14,583	3.3	0.9	4.2
Ohio	7,141	423	6,718	1.5	0.3	1.9
Pennsylvania	16,186	3,545	12,641	3.3	2.6	3.6
Wisconsin	14,726	4,522	10,204	3.0	3.3	2.9
Total	93,113	24,218	68,895	19.3	17.8	19.9

TABLE 4

Areas of inventory land, forest land, and productive forest in Ontario by ownership, 1986
(thousands of acres)

Ownership	Total inventory area	Total forest land	Productive forest		
			Protection	Production reserve	Production
Crown	95,923	95,400	4,736	5,299	73,042
Patent	32,106	16,162	587	624	13,353
Federal	3,040	2,286	97	66	783
Total	131,069	113,848	5,420	5,989	87,178

timberlands (Table 3). The upper Great Lakes states (i.e., Michigan, Minnesota and Wisconsin) have the greatest acreages in public lands.

In Ontario, three broad classes of ownership are used: crown lands, patent lands and federal lands. Crown (i.e., provincial government) lands include recreation reserves and provincial parks as well as the larger acreage general crown lands. Patented lands include all lands with some form of private ownership. The greatest percentage of patented lands is in southern Ontario where the population is concentrated. Indian reserves and other federally owned lands are aggregated to form the final class, federal lands. These lands represent the smallest ownership class in Ontario.

Ontario's productive forests are classified as protection forests, production forest reserves and production forests (Table 4). Protection forests are managed primarily for soil, water and landscape purposes. Production forests are managed primar-

ily for growing timber for industry, and production forest preserves may have logging or other management obstacles that preclude them from being classified as production forests. Most of Ontario's productive forests are in the production classification.

The objectives of these owners differ. Public ownership entails a focus on societal goals which includes sustaining forests for future generations, providing employment opportunities and maintaining a setting for recreational activities. Private, non-industrial owners have different goals for owning forested land, including use for recreation, personal residence and investment purposes. Harvesting of timber is often not an individual's primary reason for ownership. Industrial owners, however, are concerned with adequacy of supply for their manufacturing facilities. Thus, the many

TABLE 5

Area of timberland in the Great Lakes states
(thousands of acres)

State	Year					1952-1987 change
	1952	1962	1972	1977	1987	
Illinois	3,830	4,034	4,033	4,033	4,030	200
Indiana	4,015	3,930	3,840	3,815	4,296	281
Michigan	19,121	19,121	18,800	18,199	17,364	-1,757
Minnesota	16,580	15,412	14,495	13,395	13,572	-3,008
New York	11,952	13,417	14,281	15,405	15,798	3,846
Ohio	5,450	6,041	6,422	6,916	7,141	1,691
Pennsylvania	14,574	16,279	16,115	15,924	16,186	1,612
Wisconsin	15,349	14,693	14,537	14,478	14,726	-623
Total	90,871	92,927	92,523	92,165	93,113	2,242

FIGURE 1

Great Lakes states timberland area and volume trends,1952-1987
(thousands of acres, billions of cubic feet)

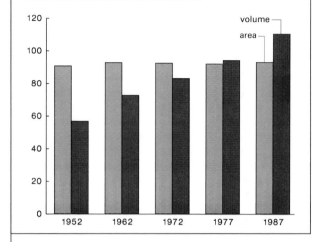

types of owners across the region lead to diverse uses of our forests.

Forest resource trends

Timberland area and volume increased in the Great Lakes states during the 1952 to 1987 period (Figure 1 and Tables 5 and 6). Total area increased a modest 2.5 percent, but net volume (i.e., tree volume less volume lost to rot, poor form, or roughness) of growing stock increased a dramatic 94 percent during that period. This is due primarily to faster growth associated with timber stands that were fairly young in the early 1950s. As these stands mature, their growth will slow. Thus, timber volumes are currently much greater than they have been in recent times. This has provided an impetus for expansion in forest products industries.

The upper Great Lakes states' timberland acreage declined during the 1952 to 1987 period. The decline is concentrated mostly in the farmer and other private categories. This is due largely to increased urbanization that occurred over the last three decades. However, there has been a reduction in federal timberlands as well. This can be attributed in part to wilderness designations and administrative withdrawals of timberlands. Nonetheless, timber volumes for both hardwoods and softwoods have increased in all states. Volumetrically, the largest increase has been for hardwood types such as aspen, red oak, white oak, hard maple, and soft maple. Hardwood volumes almost doubled. Softwood volumes, for types such as white and red pine, jack pine, spruce and fir, and eastern hemlock, have more than doubled over the same period.

Comparable trend data are not available for Ontario. However, gross timber volumes on pro-

duction forests are significant (Table 7). These volumes are not directly comparable to those presented for the United States because volume from the stump and top is included along with defective and decayed wood. The net volumes reported for the United States generally include only the portion of the tree from 1 foot above the ground to the point where the tree is 4 inches in diameter outside the bark.

Forest resource issues

Specific forest resource issues differ by country and by sub-region. However, several issues transcend national boundaries, notably concerns about acid precipitation, forest decline, the role of timber in industrial development, timber availability, public and private land management, and funding levels for forest resource management agencies. In Ontario, where forest products industries are significant, concerns include providing adequate regeneration of harvested lands to insure the sustainability of the resource base, creating employment opportunities, and earning money through exports of forest products. In the United States, issues include concerns for biological diversity, old growth, use of chemical versus natural controls for pests, forest fragmentation, and the "urban/wildland interface".

In Ontario and the United States, acid precipitation has been a major forestry-related issue for several years. The effects of acid precipitation on forests is still not well understood, and its effects

vary across the region. Legislation aimed at reducing industrial emissions is an important step in a long-term strategy for improving air quality. Also, research is being pursued on the magnitude of the effects on productivity and decline of some forests. Other issues relate to long-term productivity too. For example, in both countries, timber is viewed as an important resource that must be sustained for industrial development. Various government and industry policies and programs focus on the need to insure the renewability of timber resources. These policies and programs focus on the adequacy of timber supply for meeting current and projected needs and on the role public and private lands will play in satisfying these needs. While regional timber volume has increased, there are local situations where volumes are decreasing. In addition, there is concern that funding for public forestry agencies may be difficult to sustain in the future as some agencies, particularly those in the United States, expand their non-timber emphases relative to timber production. Potentially, this could lead to a reduction in public harvest levels (and related revenues and costs) which may be replaced by harvests on private lands. Recent public forest planning efforts in the United States have galvanized interest in maintaining biological diversity in the Great Lakes region's forested ecosystems. This

TABLE 7

Volumes of gross growing stock on production forests by ownership and species group in Ontario, 1986
(millions of cubic feet)

Ownership	Species group	Production forest
Crown	Hardwoods	50,111
	Softwoods	106,771
Patent	Hardwoods	16,071
	Softwoods	7,746
Federal	Hardwoods	879
	Softwoods	657
Total	Hardwoods	67,061
	Softwoods	115,175

TABLE 6

Net volume of growing stock on timberland in the Great Lakes region by state
(millions of cubic feet)

State	Species group	1952	1962	1972	1977	1987	1952-1987 change
Illinois	Hardwoods	2,387	3,387	3,813	4,185	4,717	2,330
	Softwoods	17	25	54	81	118	101
Indiana	Hardwoods	2,876	3,366	3,470	3,671	5,015	2,139
	Softwoods	27	52	68	88	201	174
Michigan	Hardwoods	7,610	10,668	12,184	13,103	14,414	6,804
	Softwoods	2,370	3,624	4,250	5,201	6,558	4,188
Minnesota	Hardwoods	4,253	6,060	7,210	7,978	9,645	5,392
	Softwoods	2,698	3,384	3,416	3,477	4,086	1,388
New York	Hardwoods	7,775	8,605	9,226	9,732	15,154	7,379
	Softwoods	2,748	3,037	3,292	3,524	4,935	2,187
Ohio	Hardwoods	3,153	3,762	4,109	6,121	7,227	4,074
	Softwoods	96	109	125	274	326	230
Pennsylvania	Hardwoods	11,716	15,602	18,671	21,625	19,983	8,267
	Softwoods	1,229	1,436	1,601	1,778	1,765	536
Wisconsin	Hardwoods	6,412	7,731	9,077	10,117	12,300	5,888
	Softwoods	1,549	2,112	2,662	3,340	4,112	2,563
Total	Hardwoods	46,182	59,181	67,760	76,532	88,455	42,273
	Softwoods	10,734	13,779	15,468	17,763	22,101	11,367
	All timber	56,916	72,960	83,228	94,295	110,556	53,640

involves, in part, the creation and expansion of areas dedicated to old-growth timber. The eventual effects of managing forests for their ecological attributes may have significant impacts on the availability of economical timber supplies from public lands. On the other hand, it may enhance their value for recreation and tourism.

Growing environmental concerns have led to pressure to reduce reliance on chemical controls for pests such as the gypsy moth. Continued trends away from chemical controls and towards natural and mechanical pest control (referred to as integrated pest management) will increase the financial costs for managing forests. These trends are not likely to abate due to the growing number of people living in rural, forested areas.

Migration of people from urban centers to rural areas creates an "urban/wildland interface". That is, more people are in forested areas and often have high expectations for protection from pests, fire and other natural agents associated with forests. These expectations tax the ability of public agencies to protect new rural residents. The extent of harvesting and traditional harvest methods such as clearcutting will be debated more stridently as rural populations increase. Forest fragmentation and subdivision of larger tracts of forest land are outcomes of increased rural populations, too. Fragmentation will affect our ability to maintain ecosystems and to supply timber products.

Finally, administrative actions or legislation that specifies acceptable and unacceptable forest practices on public and/or private lands may evolve. These forest practices policies may greatly influence the quality and nature of the Great Lakes region's forests in the next century. If adopted, they will likely restrict the supply of timber. Environmental advocates and industrial development proponents have a great stake in the outcome of this issue.

Summary

Forests in the Great Lakes region provide an important resource for industrial development and for the well-being of the general population. The resources have grown considerably in volume over the past 35 years. As our regional population continues to increase, additional demands will be placed on these resources. Contemporary issues reflect expanding and new demands on our forests that along with environmental factors may influence future productivity. Resolution of these issues will bring about new management direction for both public and private forests.

REFERENCES

Ontario Ministry of Natural Resources, 1986. *The forest resources of Ontario 1986*. Forest Resources Group. Ontario, Canada: Queen's Printer for Ontario.

Waddell, K.L., D.D. Oswald, and D.S. Powell. 1989. *Forest statistics of the United States, 1987*. USDA-Forest Service Resource Bulletin PNW-RB-168. Washington, D.C.: U.S. Government Printing Office.

Non-Fuel Mineral Resources

HENRY P. WHALEY

In 1989, the eight states of the Great Lakes region produced non-fuel minerals totaling an estimated $6.7 billion in value. This represents over 21 percent of the national total value on a land area comprising only 11.8 percent of the nation's total.

The mineral resources of the Great Lakes have a long history. Before the Europeans came to North America, the Indians were engaged in mining in what are now the Great Lake states. Many evidences can be found of their mining activities, as with the native copper deposits of Michigan.

Before the American Revolution, the early Europeans were mining lead and iron ore in what is now New York, Pennsylvania, and Wisconsin. Mining of the native copper and silver in the upper peninsula of Michigan began in 1845. Iron ore, found first in Michigan and later in Minnesota,

TABLE 1

Major non-fuel mineral products by tonnage and by value, 1989
(millions)

	Tonnage			Value		
	US	GL	Share	US	GL	Share
Iron ore	56	55	98%	$1,720	$1,137[a]	66%
Sand and gravel	950	250	27%	3,500	945	27%
Portland cement	74	17	23%	3,575	842	24%
Crushed stone	1,250	350	28%	5,750	1,678	29%

SOURCE: U.S. Bureau of Mines.

[a]The value of iron ore in the Great Lakes region is considerably higher than the $1,137 million reported by the Bureau of Mines. Because of proprietary data, Michigan does not report its iron ore value. Including an estimated value for Michigan, the Great Lakes' value would rise to $1,635 million, a 98 percent share.

quickly became the dominant non-fuel mineral in the region and remains so today. On the Canadian side of the Great Lakes, rich and abundant mining resources provided the incentive for much of the development of the northern portion of Ontario.

TABLE 2

Value of non-fuel mineral production by state, 1989
(millions of dollars)

	Value	Rank	Per capita Value	Per capita Rank
Illinois	$644	17	$51	40
Indiana	437	24	73	32
Michigan	1,586	4	172	13
Minnesota	1,283	7	294	8
New York	746	15	39	44
Ohio	787	14	68	35
Pennsylvania	1,041	12	87	28
Wisconsin	202	37	42	42

SOURCE: U.S. Bureau of Mines.

Four non-fuel minerals comprise the lion's share in the eight Great Lakes states: crushed stone, sand and gravel, iron ore and portland cement (Table 1). With the exclusion of iron ore, three of these products are mined in close proportion to the economic size of the region. Indeed, these products are widely dispersed across the nation's landscape and are accordingly produced locally where possible to meet construction and building needs.

In contrast, the region's iron ore deposits account for an estimated 98 percent of the nation's production value of the mineral (Table 1). Minne-

TABLE 3

U.S. iron ore shipments and employment, 1979-89

Year	Gross tons (000s)	Value ($millions)	Total employees (000s)
1979	86,218	2,814	24.9
1980	69,594	2,544	21.0
1981	72,181	2,915	21.8
1982	35,756	1,492	10.4
1983	44,596	1,945	8.4
1984	50,883	2,248	11.0
1985	49,411	2,077	9.2
1986	41,327	1,473	7.0
1987	47,225	1,503	9.1
1988	56,211	1,717	7.2
1989	57,378	1,902	7.7

SOURCE: U.S. Bureau of Mines.

TABLE 4

Non-fuel production, 1989
(millions of dollars)

	Illinois	Indiana	Ohio	Pennsylvania	Michigan	New York	Wisconsin	Minnesota
Total 1989 production	$644	$437	$787	$1,041	$1,586	$746	$202	$1,283
Crushed stone		141	286	509[a]	128		100	34
Iron ore					x	x		1,137[a]
Sand and gravel	164	94	165	88	161	124	74	75
Portland cement	114	111	75	308	233		x	
Salt			133		x	139		
Lime	x	x	96[a]	80	32		22	x
Masonry cement	x	25	11	28[a]	24		x	
Dimension stone	x	23[a]	3	10		5	4	13
Clays	1	4	15	6	5	9		x
Gypsum		x			12	x		
Peat	x	1		x	6[a]	x	x	2
Fluorspar	x[a]							
Barite	x							
Lead	x					x		
Zinc	x					x		
Bromine					x			
Copper	x				x			
Gold					x			
Silver	x				x			
Wollastonite						x[a]		
Garnet						x		
Tripoli	x							
Gemstones	x	x	x	x	x	x	x	x
Calcium compounds					x[a]			

SOURCE: *State Mineral Summaries 1990*, Bureau of Mines

NOTE: Most of the estimates are based on nine months data. "x" denotes other minerals produced in unknown/undisclosed amounts. (Preliminary 1989 data.)

[a]Largest producer in nation.

sota and Michigan produce iron ore mineral in abundance, and its high value is reflected in the relatively high mineral value per capita in these states (Table 2).

Iron ore is the most important metallic mineral on the United States side of the Great Lakes and was mined on a large scale during the recent past in New York, Pennsylvania, Wisconsin, Michigan and Minnesota. Michigan and Minnesota are the only two states where it is still currently being mined.

As iron ore mining changed from direct shipment ore to those ores which are pelletized, the number of mines reduced drastically. And during

the severe curtailment of mining in the early 1980s (Table 3), all of the seven pellet plants in Ontario were closed, along with those in Wisconsin, Pennsylvania, and New York. In Minnesota one plant was permanently shutdown, and two were permantly shut down in Michigan. Also, single mines in each of the two states were placed on hold position.

The one on hold in Minnesota, Reserve Mining Co., is reopening under a new owner and name. Thus there are just 10 taconite plants in the Great Lakes area, eight in Minnesota and two in Michigan. In Ontario, one of the last remaining underground iron ore mines is still operating, but its future viability is doubtful.

The region's taconite mines are world class operations which undertake large capital spending on equipment and computers. Their operating costs have been brought down as much as 30 percent since 1980, and are competitive against any pellet produced in the world.

The total economic impact of the iron ore industry on its host regions cannot be measured by its value and number of employees alone. For one, iron ore uses the water of the Great Lakes for its transportation. Of the 173 million tons of all cargo shipped on the Lakes in 1989, 66.7 million tons were iron ore, and 35 million tons were stone related to the iron ore and steel industry. Great Lakes iron ore has been the driving force behind the region's heavy concentration in the steel industry. Certainly, without the iron ore reserves of the Great Lakes, the U.S. steel industry would be hard pressed for raw material and its present location uneconomical.

Except for iron ore in the few aforementioned areas, mining of metallic minerals, which helped to develop many areas in the region, are no longer a major influence (Table 4). In addition to exhaustion of low cost deposits, a growing appreciation of environmental purity has discouraged development of remaining deposits. Ironically, Wisconsin has no metallic mining, yet it holds some of the greatest undeveloped mineral resources left in the Great Lakes states. Plans are being developed for mining copper, zinc, and lead in Wisconsin—if permits and taxes can be resolved.

The industrial minerals, especially sand and gravel and crushed stone, are greatly tied to the construction activities in close proximity to the deposits. These industrial minerals are essential for a state to economically provide the necessary infrastructure needed in the modern world.

While not as great in monetary value, there are many products that are produced in the Great Lakes that are extremely important to the United States. These include abrasive, bromine, calcium chloride, copper, fluorite, gold, peat, salt, silver, talc, wollastonite and zinc.

Chapter 11

An Analysis of Midwestern Research and Development Spending

RANDEL A. PILO, LEAD ECONOMIST, DIVISION OF RESEARCH AND PLANNING, WISCONSIN DEPARTMENT OF DEVELOPMENT

DAVID D. WEISS, ASSOCIATE ECONOMIST, FEDERAL RESERVE BANK OF CHICAGO

Research and development activity is paramount in improving an economy's overall competitiveness in both domestic and international markets. Improved competitiveness derives from higher productivity levels, reduced production costs, increased long-term profitability, and the new and higher quality products which are the end results of successful R&D efforts.

A strong regional presence in R&D activity can provide a wealth of well-paying jobs and derivative income. Moreover, spin-off businesses as well as technology adoption are both more likely to occur near the source of innovation than at a distance. For these reasons the location of R&D is an important issue.

Although the midwest does not receive much federal support for industrial R&D, it has a higher rate of spending from internal financing. University/college R&D lags the nation, once again because of lack of federal support. And for federal government performed R&D, the region also lags the nation. Despite this handicap, both the midwest and the nation are about the same in terms of intensiveness of total R&D spending. This strength chiefly derives from the region's ability to generate financing for R&D despite the dearth of federal funding.

Successful commercialization of the outputs of research and development programs yield significant benefits. New technology and designs mean increased production efficiency and the saving of scarce resources. New products can improve not only our economic standard of living, e.g. new computers, but also our quality of life, e.g. new pollution containment technology. Successful research and development (R&D) programs can also be an end in and of themselves. As an export producing sector, the sale of knowledge and education to other regions directly increases a region's earnings and income. For firms, R&D programs are important not only for their original output, but for their ability to monitor the current state of technology. As researchers read the R&D literature and talk to other scientists and engineers they become aware of new technologies and how they may be incorporated into their firm.

The importance and relevance of R&D has been strikingly demonstrated by both recent political events and recent academic economic research. For example, in July 1990, the United States government indicated, in an agreement with Japan to ease current trade tensions, that the U.S. would work to balance its federal budget and increase the amount of funding for research and development. This negotiated agreement was part of the Structural Impediments Initiative which was initiated in response to the passage and implementation of the 1988 U.S. Trade Act. In a summer 1990 survey of leading economists conducted by the National Association of Business Economists, the two policy actions deemed most important and effective in improving U.S. competitiveness were improving K-12 education and expanding research and development efforts. In February 1990, the Economic Report of the President called for "substantially increasing funding for basic research essential to America's future."[1] The Council on Competitiveness, a non-profit research group, has constructed what it calls the "pyramid of competitiveness."[2] Basically, a nation's or region's standard of living is the result of successful marketplace trading which, in order to be successful, requires advances in productivity brought about through investment in such things as capital equipment or research and development.

In drawing from academic research, a near consensus opinion appears to be that, "R&D contribute[s] positively to productivity growth; basic research appears to be more important as a productivity determinant than other types of R&D; and privately financed R&D expenditures are more effective at the firm level than federally financed ones."[3] More specifically, "Government funded R&D and industry R&D together have contributed between 30 and 70 percent of multi-factor productivity growth."[4] Multi-factor productivity refers to the productivity growth arising from all factors in production such as labor, capital, management, and materials working simultaneously.

The region's R&D trends

Levels and intensiveness of R&D

The most recent data that documents the extent of research and development spending at both the national and regional level is compiled by the National Science Foundation. The regional economy is defined here to include the states of Illinois, Indiana, Iowa, Michigan, Minnesota, Ohio, and Wisconsin. The following table contains a summary of R&D spending for the nation and the midwest.

TABLE 1

Research and development spending and estimates of gross state product, 1987
(millions of dollars)

Category	US	Midwest	Midwest as percent of US
R & D			
Industrial	$94,282	$21,014	22.3
Federal government	13,413	1,283	9.6
University	16,284	2,558	15.7
Miscellaneous	3,883	190	4.9
Total	127,862	25,046	19.6
GSP	$4,480,933	$876,916	19.6

NOTE: GSP estimates are the result of using the U.S. Department of Commerce's last official estimate at the state level for 1986 and then adjusting such value by the 1987 rate of change in U.S. GNP. This was necessary to allow use of the latest NSF data for 1987; otherwise, 1985 would have been the latest year for comparison.

In 1987, the United States spent a total of $127.9 billion on research and development in all its forms (Table 1). This includes R&D performed by the federal government at its own labs and installations, R&D performed at universities and colleges, and R&D performed by the private industrial sector. The federal government performed $13.4 billion itself, the academic community performed $16.3 billion, and the industrial sector performed $94.3 billion.

In the region, a total of $25.0 billion was spent on all forms of research and development. The midwest accounted for about 19.6 percent of all R&D performed in the U.S. in 1987. This share of total R&D accounted for by the midwest matches the respective share of total U.S. gross state product (GSP) in the midwest region, 19.6 percent.

All R&D categories do not fare equally well in the region. The federal government performed $1.3 billion or about 9.6 percent of its own R&D in the

FIGURE 1

United States gross national product spent for research and development
(percent)

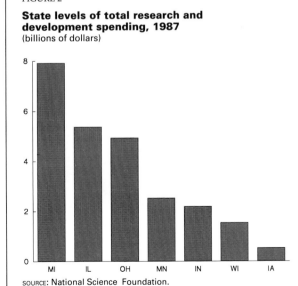

SOURCE: National Science Foundation.

midwest, significantly below the midwest's share of the national economy. With respect to the university/college community, the midwest accounted for about $2.6 billion or 15.7 percent of all academic R&D performed in the nation; this is only slightly below the region's share of the national economy.

TABLE 2

Total and nondefense R&D share of gross national product, 1987
(percent)

	Total R&D	Nondefense
Midwest	2.9	NA
United States	2.8	2.0
Japan	2.8	2.8
West Germany	2.8	2.6
France	2.3	1.8
United Kingdom	2.3	1.7

SOURCE: National Science Foundation.
NOTE: NA refers to data unavailable.

As for the industrial sector, there was $21.0 billion performed in the midwest; this was about 22.3 percent of all industrial R&D in the country and a slightly larger percentage than the midwest's share of the U.S. economy. But because private industry performance in the United States dominates the government and academic sectors, the region's overall R&D share of nation holds its own.

A general measure of R&D intensiveness is the ratio of total R&D spending to the overall size of the economy. Weighting a region's R&D in relation to its output allows comparison of the extent that the region's economy is jointly produced along with R&D. By this measure, both the midwest and the nation have about the same level of R&D intensiveness.

The total R&D share of U.S. GNP is now at historically high levels (Figure 1). During the late 1960s and early 1970s, the share declined from about 2.8 percent to about 2.2 percent. This reduction in U.S. R&D intensiveness has been cited by some economists as contributing to the slowing of U.S. productivity and standard of living growth in the late 1970s and early 1980s. During the 1980s, however, the total R&D share of GNP rebounded to earlier levels and once again lies in the 2.8 percent range. Eventually, many expect this recovery to translate into improved productivity performance in the future.

International comparisons of midwestern and national total R&D

In terms of the percent of GNP spent on total research and development, the United States and the midwest compare favorably to their chief economic competitors (Table 2). In 1987 the United States had the same economy-wide intensiveness as Germany and Japan, 2.8 percent, while the midwest stood about the same or slightly higher.

In contrast to many nations, the United States commits a much larger proportion of its total R&D to defense related activities. The differing R&D emphasis is no small concern because recent research has indicated that because much of defense R&D is directed towards development of specific military systems, its effect on overall economic productivity is lower than either basic research or industrial R&D. This is not to say that defense research and development has no commercial spin-offs, but that researchers generally believe that the expected economic benefits of non-defense R&D, including basic research, are higher than those generated by defense-directed research and development. While the United States spent only 2 percent of its GNP on nondefense R&D in 1987,

FIGURE 2

State levels of total research and development spending, 1987
(billions of dollars)

SOURCE: National Science Foundation.

TABLE 3

Top ten states compared to the midwest in terms of total research and development spending as a share of gross state product, 1987

Rank	State	Percent
1	New Mexico	9.5
2	Delaware	7.7
3	Massachusetts	6.3
4	Maryland	5.6
5	**Michigan**	**4.9**
6	California	4.5
7	Washington	4.2
8	New Jersey	4.1
9	Utah	4.0
10	Alabama	4.0
14	**Minnesota**	**3.1**
	Midwest	**2.9**
	National average	2.8
	West Germany	2.8
	Japan	2.8
19	**Ohio**	**2.6**
21	**Indiana**	**2.4**
22	**Illinois**	**2.4**
27	**Wisconsin**	**1.9**
33	**Iowa**	**1.1**

SOURCE: National Science Foundation and Bureau of Economic Analysis.

West Germany and Japan had levels of 2.6 and 2.8 percent. The current state of affairs appears even worse when one looks at the long-term trends. While the U.S. share has remained fairly constant since 1970, Japan has increased its share of GNP spent on nondefense R&D from 1.9 to 2.8 percent, and this is with a more rapidly growing economy. West Germany shows a similar pattern moving from a nondefense R&D expenditure level of 2.0 to 2.6 percent.

R&D trends for individual states

Total R&D levels and intensiveness

When looking at the individual states, it quickly becomes apparent that it is not a homogeneous region. Individual states within the region vary widely in R&D spending. Within the region, Michigan is by far the leader in absolute amounts of total research and development at $7.92 billion

(Figure 2). States in the region with the lowest absolute levels of total R&D include Wisconsin at $1.55 billion and Iowa at $0.54 billion.

A more meaningful way to compare the states is to consider the share of their respective economies dedicated to total R&D.[5] Such a normalization produces a measure of R&D intensiveness that takes into account the fact that larger economies are more likely to have larger absolute amounts of total R&D.

Overall R&D intensity in the midwest compares closely with the United States and its major economic competitors, but individual states vary widely (Table 3). Michigan leads the region with an intensity of 4.9 percent while Wisconsin and Iowa lag with intensities of 1.9 and 1.1 percent.

Figure 3 below represents those states with less than 2 percent of gross state product in total R&D. Among states in the region, Iowa and Wisconsin are among the least intensive states in the nation with respect to total R&D. In general, those areas of the

FIGURE 3

States with less than 2 percent of gross state product in total research and development spending, 1987

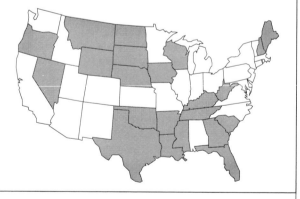

country with low total R&D intensities are widely found in the Southeast and Great Plains.

To understand why states exhibit such a high variance in R&D intensities we can decompose research and development into its components in one of several ways. One method is to divide R&D

into three major components describing the specificity of the R&D activity; basic research, applied research, and development, which, in turn, accounted for 14, 23, and 63 percent of R&D expenditures in 1990. The difference between these three is that basic research takes place before an invention and need have been identified. Applied research takes place when no invention exists but a need has been spotted and leads to an invention. The development stage takes place after the invention has been made and turns it into a commercially viable product. R&D can also be broken down by either source funder of R&D or by the final performers or both. Four groups: industry, federal government, universities and colleges, and miscellaneous (i.e. essentially other nonprofit institutions) are commonly identified as source or funder. The distinction between performers and funder is important. The gains they achieve through the research are quite different. The funder not only obtains the results but also guides the direction of research. The performers, on the other hand, are developing the practical skills necessary to work with the new knowledge.

Industrial R&D

Most R&D is performed by the industrial sector and, of this share, development accounts for three quarters. Figure 4 contains regional levels of industrial research and development spending for 1987. Like the preceding section, Michigan once again leads the region in absolute amounts of industrial R&D at $7.42 billion. Both Wisconsin and Iowa have the lowest levels, $1.2 and $0.3 billion respectively.

The midwest is slightly more intensive in industrial R&D than the U.S., spending 2.4 percent of its output on R&D versus 2.1 percent for the nation (Table 4). However, the seven states are widely dispersed across the national rankings. Michigan leads the way among midwest states, ranking second nationally by spending 4.5 percent of its output on industrial R&D. Iowa ranks lowest at 33rd in the nation, spending only 0.7 percent. Why this great disparity within the midwest states? Insofar as 91 percent of industrial R&D expenditures, representing two thirds of all R&D, is performed by the manufacturing sector, we hypothe-

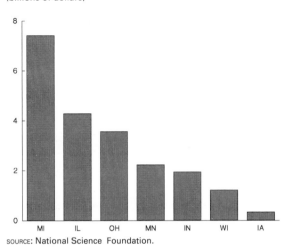

FIGURE 4

Regional levels of industrial research and development spending, 1987
(billions of dollars)

SOURCE: National Science Foundation.

TABLE 4

Top ten states compared to the midwest in terms of industrial research and development spending as a share of gross state product, 1987

Rank	State	Percent
1	Delaware	7.3
2	**Michigan**	**4.5**
3	Massachusetts	4.4
4	New Mexico	3.9
5	New Jersey	3.7
6	Washington	3.7
7	Idaho	3.5
8	California	3.4
9	Utah	3.2
10	Connecticut	2.9
11	**Minnesota**	**2.8**
	Midwest	**2.4**
16	**Indiana**	**2.1**
	National average	2.1
19	**Illinois**	**1.9**
20	**Ohio**	**1.9**
25	**Wisconsin**	**1.5**
33	**Iowa**	**0.7**

SOURCE: National Science Foundation and Bureau of Economic Analysis.

size that these rankings are related to a state's manufacturing share of total output, and therefore it might be better to compare industrial R&D performance in manufacturing to manufacturing output. In doing so we find Michigan still leading, spending 13 percent of its manufacturing output on R&D. However, Iowa spends over 3 percent on industrial R&D, representing an intensity level that is 24 percent of Michigan's versus 15 percent when not accounting for a state's manufacturing propensity. The midwest falls below the United States with an intensity of 8.3 per dollar of manufacturing output versus 9.1 percent.

Decomposing further, a state's specific mix of manufacturing industries might influence these rankings. For example, the aircraft industry is highly R&D intensive. One would expect that those states in which the aircraft industry accounts for high levels of their output would have higher R&D intensity levels than states concentrated in lower R&D intensive industries such as textiles. Ideally, to test this reasoning, we would take each state's R&D intensity by industry and weight these intensities by some factor such as the industry's share of national output. If the weighted sum of each state yields an overall intensity level that is closer to the national level, we would be able to conclude that part of the difference is due to industry mix. However, state level data on R&D spending by industry is unavailable. As an alternative test, the *national* R&D intensities by industry are weighted by each state's industry share of output. If the sum of these intensities is lower (higher) than the actual state level then on average, the industries in the state are spending more (less) on R&D per dollar of output than industry in the nation.

Before adjustment, the United States ratio of manufacturing R&D to GSP measures 9 percent and the midwest 8.3 percent (See Appendix for numeric detail). After making the mix adjustment the midwest jumps to 10.7 percent. This tells us that on average midwest industries are performing research and development less intensively than the same industries at the national level. In accounting for this, it has been pointed out elsewhere that while nationally the industry sector finances less than 70 percent of its R&D, midwest companies finance 90

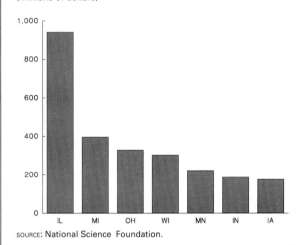

FIGURE 5

Regional levels of academic research and development spending, 1987
(millions of dollars)

SOURCE: National Science Foundation.

percent of their own R&D.[6] By performing the same experiment on corporate financed manufacturing R&D *only*, contrasting results appear. The nation displays an intensity of 6.1 percent while the midwest has an intensity of 7.2 percent. If the national intensities are applied to the midwest states the intensity drops to 6.7 percent which suggests that, in general, midwest corporations finance more R&D per dollar of output than their counterparts across the country.

University/college R&D

Although universities and colleges perform only 12.7 percent of overall R&D in dollars, they account for over half of all basic research.[7] Universities' R&D stimulates private industry growth and productivity in two important ways. First, their basic research provides the stepping stone for many commercial technological innovations. For example, the initial use of nuclear magnetic resonance was for an application in theoretical physics. Once Varian Associates commercialized the technology, its use quickly spread into chemistry and biology labs, leading to its widespread use in medicine for diagnostic scanning. Second, university graduate students perform much of the university's research.

The hiring of these students by firms provides a quick method for transferring state of the art knowledge from the university into firms and commercial products.

TABLE 5

Top ten states compared to the midwest in terms of academic research and development spending as a share of gross state product, 1987

Rank	State	Percent
1	New Mexico	3.82
2	Massachusetts	0.87
3	Maryland	0.87
4	California	0.64
5	Utah	0.47
6	**Illinois**	**0.42**
7	Rhode Island	0.41
8	**Iowa**	**0.38**
9	Colorado	0.38
10	**Wisconsin**	**0.37**
	National average	0.36
	Midwest	**0.29**
22	**Minnesota**	**0.27**
28	**Michigan**	**0.24**
31	**Indiana**	**0.21**
40	**Ohio**	**0.17**

SOURCE: National Science Foundation and Bureau of Economic Analysis.

Among states in the region, Illinois performs the largest amount of university/college R&D at $942 million (Figure 5). States with the lowest absolute levels of academic R&D are Indiana ($188 million) and Iowa ($177 million). Although the midwest region contains some high ranking states in terms of academic R&D intensity, the region as a whole has a below average R&D intensity (Table 5). Much of this difference can be accounted for by the lack of federal funding which finances about two thirds of academic research. If we adjust each state's expenditures on academic research to focus on non-federally funded research, the midwest shoots ahead of the nation with an R&D intensity of 0.19 percent versus 0.11 percent for the nation.[8]

In viewing those states with a larger ratio of university/college R&D to total gross state product than the national average, two areas in the U.S.

stand out for their relative intensiveness: the upper midwest and the southwest (Figure 6).

Federal government R&D

The federal government maintains a key role as both a funder and a performer of R&D. As a funder the government pays for 43 percent of overall R&D in the U.S., but only 16 percent of the R&D in the midwest. As a performer, the federal government accounts for about 10 percent of R&D while in the midwest it accounts for only about 5 percent.

Figure 7 contains regional levels of 1987 U.S. government research and development spending performed at its own labs and institutions. Among states in the region, by far the largest absolute amount of federal government R&D is performed in Ohio at $991 million. The state of Ohio has nearly 10 times the amount of federal government performed R&D than the second highest state in the region (Michigan at $87 million). The remaining midwestern states have quite low levels of U.S. government performed R&D with spending ranging from $20 million in Iowa to $73 million in Illinois.

It terms of federally performed R&D intensity, the region again fares poorly. Indiana, Michigan, Iowa, Illinois, Minnesota, and Wisconsin all have low relative intensities of federal government R&D spending in their respective economies. National rankings for these states range from 46th for Wis-

FIGURE 6

States with larger proportion of gross state product in university/college research and development than the national average, 1987

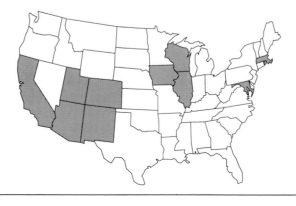

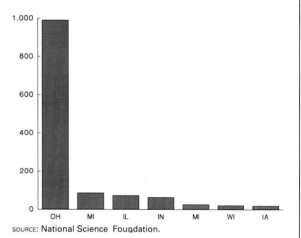

FIGURE 7

Regional levels of United States government research and development spending, 1987
(millions of dollars)

SOURCE: National Science Foundation.

consin to 32nd for Indiana (Table 6). The only exception, and a notable one again, is Ohio. Ohio ranked 6th nationally at 0.53 percent of gross state product. Examination of a map with the lowest intensities of R&D performed by the federal government visually displays the relatively low intensiveness in the region (Figure 8).

Caveats

The above analysis documents the extent of the R&D base in the midwest region. In considering the above analysis, remember that while some states in the midwest do in fact have relatively low intensities or absolute amounts of various kinds of R&D expenditures, this conclusion should not be seen as necessarily alarming. This chapter has examined solely the levels and intensiveness of R&D. A subsidiary issue and an important one is the actual adoption and spread of those products and technologies that result from R&D. The main point here is that while a state may not have large expenditures and/or intensiveness in R&D, this does not necessarily imply that businesses in the respective state are necessarily becoming less competitive. Those businesses could still remain quite competitive if they are successfully adopting those new products and technologies invented elsewhere. Also, as Nathan Rosenberg explains, much of the economic gains made through technological improvement

---

TABLE 6

Top ten states compared to the midwest in terms of federal research and development spending as a share of gross state product, 1987

Rank	State	Percent
1	Maryland	3.07
2	New Mexico	1.67
3	Rhode Island	1.48
4	Alabama	0.99
5	Virginia	0.79
6	**Ohio**	**0.53**
7	Massachusetts	0.47
8	Utah	0.39
9	Florida	0.38
10	Mississippi	0.37
	National average	0.30
	Midwest	**0.15**
32	**Indiana**	**0.07**
36	**Michigan**	**0.05**
41	**Iowa**	**0.03**
43	**Illinois**	**0.03**
44	**Minnesota**	**0.03**
46	**Wisconsin**	**0.03**

SOURCE: National Science Foundation and Bureau of Economic Analysis.

---

come not from the new technology but rather through the learning process associated with its use.[9]

When the efficiency gains of new technologies are studied, it is often found that there is some initial efficiency gain. However, when the same technology is examined later, it usually turns out to be significantly more efficient. This is due to learning. This learning can be broken down into two types, learning by doing and learning by using. Learning by doing is knowledge gained in the production of the new technology that allows for more efficient production, such as an aircraft manufacturer producing an airplane. Learning by using is knowledge gained by using the new technology. This knowledge can be incorporated in two manners, embodied and disembodied. Embodied improvements

might come from the user of a new airplane going back and telling the manufacturer that by changing a certain component, performance would be much improved. The knowledge then becomes embodied in the airplane. Disembodied improvements would be those incorporated into the use of the new technology such as better maintenance methods. So although the performance of research is important to regions, the consistent adoption of new technology and its use also play an important role in gaining economic efficiencies. Therefore, one question for later research would be to examine the relationship between the cost of capital and technological change. The theory is that lower costs of capital increase both capital expenditures and the pace of technological change. If the capital stock turns over more quickly new technology will be incorporated sooner allowing time for improvements through learning and economic gains.[10]

Nevertheless, the point about the ability to adopt new technology does not diminish the importance of R&D activity actually taking place in the region. For a competitive economy, R&D is necessary and it has to be performed somewhere. Spin-off business as well as technology adoption are both more likely to occur nearer the source of innovation than at a distance. For these reasons the location of regional R&D is an important issue.

Summary

Research and development activity is paramount to any industrial economy. There are substantial benefits to research and development spending, namely improving an economy's overall competitiveness both in domestic and international markets. Improved competitiveness derives from higher productivity levels, reduced production costs, increased long-term profitability, and the development of new and higher quality products and technologies which are the end results of successful R&D efforts.

Although the midwest does not receive much federal support for industrial R&D, it has a higher rate of spending from internal financing. University/college performed R&D lags the nation, once again because of lack of federal support. And for federal government performed R&D, the region also

---

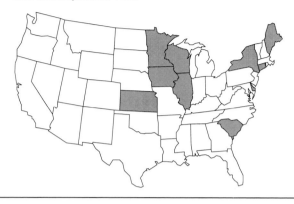

FIGURE 8

Ten states with the lowest proportion of gross state product in federal research and development, 1987

---

lags the nation. Despite this handicap, both the midwest and the nation are about the same in terms of intensiveness of total research and development spending. This strength chiefly derives from the large relative size of the manufacturing sector in the midwest and from the region's ability to generate financing for the R&D despite the dearth of federal funding.

In terms of the percent of GNP spent on total research and development, the United States and the midwest compare favorably to their chief economic competitors. As of 1987, the United States maintains the same economy-wide intensiveness as Germany and Japan, 2.8 percent, while the midwest is marginally better at 2.9 percent. The United State's increasing propensity to maintain this equality by hikes in defense-oriented R&D continues to worry proponents of U.S. industrial competitiveness. Despite the lesser defense orientation of midwest industry, the concern is no less.

NOTES

[1]See *Economic Report of the President 1990*, Council of Economic Advisers, U.S. Government Printing Office, Washington, D.C., February 1990, page 117.

[2]See *Competitiveness Index 1990*, Council of Competitiveness, Washington, D.C., 1990, page 1.

[3]See Zvi Griliches, "Productivity, R&D, and Basic Research at the Firm Level in the 1970," *American Economic Review*, American Economic Association, Nashville, Volume 76, Number 1, March 1986, page 151.

[4]See Martin Neil Bailey, "Productivity and Innovation: Regional Issues," *REI Review*, Center for Regional Economic Issues, Case Western Reserve University, Cleveland, Fall 1989, page 8.

[5]R&D spending does not necessarily comprise regional product arising from R&D activities. For example, R&D spending may also reflect purchases of test tubes from outside the region.

[6]See Bill Testa and David Weiss, "The Midwest looks to R&D for a payoff", *Chicago Fed Letter*, Federal Reserve Bank of Chicago, June 1990, Number 34.

[7]These figures include R&D performed at those federally funded research and development centers that are administrd by colleges and universities. See below:

Region	Academic R&D ($000s)	Federally financed ($000s)	Academic R&D per $ GSP	Non-federally financed academic R&D per $ GSP
U.S.	16,284,000	11,543,472	0.36¢	0.11¢
Midwest	2,558,000	1,627,073	0.29	0.19

[8]This statistic was calculated by subtracting federally funded academic R&D from academic R&D and dividing by GSP.

[9]See Nathan Rosenberg, "Learning by Using," *Inside the Black Box*, Cambridge University Press, New York: 1986, pp. 120-141.

[10]*Ibid.*

REFERENCES

Bailey, Martin Neil, "Productivity and Innovation: Regional Issues," *REI Review*, Center for Regional Economic Issues, Case Western Reserve University, Cleveland, Fall 1989.

Council of Economic Advisers, *Economic Report of the President 1990*, U.S. Government Printing Office, Washington, D.C., February 1990

Council on Competitiveness, *Competitiveness Index 1990*, Washington, D.C., Copyright 1990.

Grilliches, Zvi, "Productivity, R&D, and Basic Research at the Firm Level in the 1970s," *American Economic Review*, American Economic Association, Nashville, Volume 76, Number 1, March 1986.

Grilliches, Zvi, "Productivity Puzzles and R&D: Another Nonexplanation," *Journal of Economic Perspectives*, American Economic Association, Nashville, Volume 2, Number 4, Fall 1988.

Lerner, Urban C., and Alan Murray, "Strained Alliance: Will the U.S. Find the Resolve to Meet Japanese Challenge?," *Wall Street Journal*, New York, July 2, 1990.

Maddison, Angus, "Growth and Slowdown in Advanced Capitalist Economies: Techniques of Qualitative Assessment," *Journal of Economic Literature*, American Economic Association, Nashville, Volume XXV, Number 2, June 1987.

National Association of Business Economists, *Policy Survey*, NABE, Cleveland, July 1990.

National Science Foundation, *Geographic Patterns: R&D in the United States*, Washington, D.C., NSF 89-317, July 1989.

National Science Foundation, *National Patterns of R&D Resources: 1990*, Washington, D.C., NSF 90-316, May 1990.

APPENDIX 1

Research and development spending, 1987
(millions of dollars)

Category	US	Midwest	IL	IN	IA	MI	MN	OH	WI
Total	127,862	25,046	5,369	2,197	540	7,922	2,533	4,936	1,549
Industrial	94,282	21,014	4,284	1,944	343	7,415	2,242	3,569	1,217
Federal Government	13,413	1,283	73	64	20	87	26	991	22
University	16,284	2,558	942	188	177	397	222	329	303
Miscellaneous	3,883	190	70	1	0	23	42	47	7

SOURCE: National Science Foundation.

APPENDIX 2

Manufacturing research and development, 1987
(millions of dollars)

Corporate and federally funded R&D

Region	R&D	Hypothetical R&D	Ratio R&D to GSP	Ratio R&D to GSP
Iowa	309.8	844.0	3.12	8.49
Illinois	3,875.3	3,764.7	8.44	8.20
Indiana	1,781.4	2,963.7	6.53	10.86
Michigan	6,819.7	8,275.4	13.10	15.90
Minnesota	2,028.3	1,271.8	11.90	7.46
Ohio	3,270.6	5,668.5	5.83	10.10
Wisconsin	1,111.9	1,883.5	4.58	8.21
U.S.	87,562.0	87,559.0	9.06	9.06
7 States	19,197.0	24,672.0	8.30	10.67

Corporate funded R&D

Region	R&D	Hypothetical R&D	Ratio R&D to GSP	Ratio R&D to GSP
Iowa	247.9	667.3	2.49	6.71
Illinois	3,023.9	2,856.1	6.58	6.22
Indiana	1,457.5	1,891.3	5.34	6.93
Michigan	6,711.9	4,174.5	12.90	8.02
Minnesota	1,622.7	1,029.0	9.52	6.04
Ohio	2,571.5	3,593.8	4.58	1.40
Wisconsin	1,078.6	1,348.6	4.70	5.88
U.S.	58,990.0	58,990.0	6.10	6.10
7 States	16,714.0	15,560.0	7.23	6.73

National Science Foundation, *National Patterns of Science and Technology Resources: 1987*, Washington, D.C., NSF 88-305, January 1988.

National Science Foundation, *Research and Development in Industry: 1987*, Washington, D.C., NSF 89-323, January 1988.

National Science Board, *Science and Engineering Indicators - 1989*, Washington, D.C., NSB 89-1, December 1989.

Rosenberg, Nathan, *Inside the Black Box*, Cambridge University press, 1982

Schacht, Wendy, "Trade, Technology, and Competitiveness," Congressional Research Service/Library of Congress, Washington, D.C., May 9, 1990.

Schlesinger, Jacob, "U.S., Japan, Set Economic Pact to Ease Tension," *Wall Street Journal*, New York, June 29, 1990.

Testa, William A., and David D. Weiss, "The Midwest Looks to R&D for a Payoff," *Chicago Fed Letter*, Federal Reserve Bank of Chicago, Number 34 Essays on Issues, June 1990.

Chapter 12

Travel, Tourism and Outdoor Recreation in the Great Lakes Region

STEPHEN J. THORP, PROGRAM MANAGER, TRANSPORTATION AND ECONOMIC DEVELOPMENT, GREAT LAKES COMMISSION

STEPHEN L. J SMITH, PROFESSOR OF RECREATION AND LEISURE STUDIES, UNIVERSITY OF WATERLOO, ONTARIO

Travel, tourism and outdoor recreation in the binational Great Lakes region are important economic sectors. The "pursuit of happiness" by residents and visitors alike has led to the establishment of a wide range of attractions, facilities and services—ranging from wilderness areas to highly developed urban facilities. Communities, states, and provinces working independently as well as cooperatively have undertaken many conservation measures, promotional campaigns, policy and project initiatives, and data collection efforts. Despite occasional economic slowdowns, travel, tourism, and outdoor recreation continue to show a generally healthy pattern of growth. Properly managed, such growth contributes not just to the regional economy, but also to the total quality of human life.

Travel and tourism, by most accounts, is growing. Seasonal and longer-term cycles reflect sensitivity to general economic conditions and current events. Overall though, national and state/provincial economies have responded to increasing expenditures in this principal sector with a proportionate growth in related employment. New sector businesses are continually established. Changing products and marketing strategies reflect the dynamics of this growth industry. Vacation and business trips are so commonplace among residents that the itinerant lifestyle has become a fact of modern life.

Outdoor recreation generates travel activity and it often is part of the tourism experience. Recreation is one of the reasons for becoming a tourist. However, tourism, as an activity, is not easily defined.

One definitional point is that all tourists are travelers but not all travelers are tourists. For example, business/convention travel is not generally categorized as tourism. Tourism does include all vacation/pleasure travel and incorporates a kind of travel that is typically more discretionary. Going beyond the requirement of discretionary travel, "tourism" usually entails a distance-traveled or distance-plus-time-spent as additional requirements. Some definitions also include the specification that a night or 24 hours be spent in the place visited. This leads to a designation of a traveler who does not spend a night as an "excursionist." Further qualifications on who is and who isn't a tourist turn on the question of whether there is an economic impact for the area visited.

Travel flows and trip characteristics

The U.S. Travel Data Center, a private nonprofit center for travel and tourism research, estimated a total of 664.3 million trips of at least 200 roundtrip miles were taken by Americans in 1989. These trips entailed a total of 1.26 billion person-trips. The person-trip as a measurement unit is one person traveling at least 100 miles one-way and returning. The overall trend for total trips and person-trips has been upward but the early 1980s recession and gasoline shortage periods in the early 1970s reduced travel significantly at the time. Around two-thirds of the person-trips are classified as vacation trips with half of them occurring over a weekend—a

trend that is increasing along with the number of two-worker households.

For the Great Lakes region and individual states, specific and comprehensive travel data have been hard to come by since the discontinuance of the U.S. Census Bureau's comprehensive National Travel Survey (NTS), last conducted in 1977. However, the U.S. Travel Data Center's survey and travel activity projection methodology does make reasonable estimates of interregional travel. For example, in 1987 the East North Central census region, which includes Illinois, Indiana, Michigan, Ohio and Wisconsin, originated 110.8 million person-trips out of the region but received only 52.2 million, thus a 58.6 million net outflow. This region benefits from a large amount of internal travel. Of the millions of person-trips in 1987 with a final destination in the East North Central region, 64 percent of them originated in the same five states. This percentage of intraregional travel is the third highest of the nine regions. The 1977 National Travel Survey data also do not indicate specific interstate movements but present detail on state-origin interstate travel and to-or-through state movements originating in designated travel regions. For the 469 million person-nights spent by Great Lakes state travelers in 1977 (traveling at least 200 round-trip miles) 420 million were spent in the region or 90 percent. Ohio was the leading Great Lakes region state in generating out-of-state vacation and weekend person-nights. Geographic position is the major explanation for the one-two ranking of Pennsylvania and Indiana in person-trips and nights originating from nearby states but traveling "to and through." Major east-west highways in these states point to their connector and gateway status for interstate auto travel.

Travel-related impacts and employment

Regional travel and tourism activity generates billions of dollars in expenditures and makes a substantial contribution to tax revenue at all government levels. According to the U.S. Travel Data Center's Travel Economic Impact Model, nearly $69 billion dollars of travel-related expenditures were attributed to the eight Great Lakes states in 1987. This figure was 25 percent of the U.S. total and had increased from $56 billion in 1984. Seven states are ranked in the top half of travel-related expenditures and five are in the top ten (New York, Pennsylvania, Illinois, Ohio and Michigan). Ontario and Quebec received approximately $13.1 billion (CDN) in tourism receipts. This is 54 percent of the Canadian total of $24.2 billion. These figures represent a growth of 28 percent over 1986 receipts. In 1988, tourism accounted for 3.6 percent of the Gross Provincial Product in Ontario, and 2.9 percent in Quebec. With respect to total travel-generated tax revenue, the eight states received $2.9 billion with local governments receiving another one billion dollars. Federal tax revenue derived from travel activity in the region totaled $5.2 billion—28 percent of the national amount. Differences among states at the local level reflect more than varying levels of travel activity. Lodging industry presence and different tax treatment from city to city and among sub-state areas are major factors.

A wide range of economic enterprises and activities can be identified as providing services to tourists in the Great Lakes region. These cover both private and public establishments and facilities and include such functions as transportation, lodging, food, amusements, recreation, retail trade and the provision of information services. The common denominator for these important sectors is that they serve in some fashion the traveler/tourist. While they form the necessary infrastructure to meet tourism demands for services, except for the amusement/cultural/recreational sector, they are not prime generators of travel demand and tourism. Many of the defined industries in these sectors do not exclusively or principally serve the traveler and tourist. For example, many restaurants (which, in terms of employment comprises the largest tourism sector component) depend almost exclusively on "local trade." Alternatively, fast food restaurants on or near major highways may be highly dependent upon "family travelers".

As measured by employment growth over the 1978 to 1985 period, the travel and tourism industry in the Great Lakes states performed substantially better than aggregate indicators, such as total non-agricultural employment and total non-manufacturing employment. In the region on a state-by-state

basis, travel and tourism employment growth for six of the eight states was close to the regional average of 15.8 percent. Only Michigan was significantly below at 10.9 percent and Minnesota higher, at over 21 percent. The relatively strong growth in the travel and tourism sector for all the Great Lakes states is in sharp contrast to the slow growth for total non-farm payroll employment exhibited for all the states, except New York and Minnesota. Substantial declines in the manufacturing sector and the adverse effects of the farm crisis in the Midwest were the underlying factors in affecting the economies of the six other states.

While travel and tourism industry employment grew in the region and constituent states, as a general sector in 1985 it represented less than 10 percent of total non-farm payroll employment in all the states except Minnesota (11 percent). Nevertheless, tens of thousands are employed in very specific tourism related areas. For example, there were 52,717 travel agency and tour operator employees in the Great Lakes states representing more than 7,400 business establishments in 1987. Illinois and New York accounted for 57 percent of the region total. New York City and Chicago are tremendous travel generating places—for all purposes. 1988 tourism employment represented approximately 5.0 percent of all civilian jobs in Ontario and 3.1 percent in Quebec. Nationally, tourism accounts for about 3.5 percent of the Canadian labor force, up from 2.8 percent in 1971 (for a growth rate of 25 percent over that period).

It would appear that given continued growth in travel and tourism demand in the Great Lakes region, new businesses and jobs will be needed in significant numbers to service this demand. The travel and tourism industry does, however, have some employment characteristics that are not overly positive. For example, a sizable number of jobs are relatively low-skilled/low-wage ones compared to manufacturing and other sectors. Restaurants, hotels and other service industries in particular resort areas and communities cannot attract enough workers because of a diminishing labor pool caused by overall demographics and low wages. The labor shortage may eventually result in higher wages. Many positions are also seasonal as well as part-

time. The trend to larger enterprises in some travel and tourism businesses also raises capital financing problems for small firms and individuals seeking entry or survival in the field.

International and overseas travel

The United States is a major player in world tourism. In 1988 nearly 41.2 million U.S. travelers visited another country and stayed for at least one night. Foreign visitors to the U.S. numbered 34.2 million or more than 8 percent of world international tourist arrivals. These figures show impressive gains from 1986 when 37.6 million U.S. residents became international travelers and 25.4 million people visited the United States. In 1988, Canada registered 15.6 million overnight person trips by international visitors—Quebec and Ontario received 61 percent of the total. The world travel situation represents a dynamic mix of variables even though the reasons for travel have not changed much in recent years. Fluctuating foreign exchange rates, terrorism activities, airline safety issues and national economic conditions have all played a role in spurring or dampening travel demand. The large number of travelers entails a substantial amount of economic activity including the direct expenditure of billions of dollars. Data from the U.S. Bureau of Economic Analysis indicate that U.S. international travelers spent $32.1 billion in other countries during 1988 irrespective of destination transportation costs. As for inbound visitors, travel receipts amounted to $29.2 billion with $7.9 billion added for transportation. For Canada, $5.2 billion (CDN) was spent by foreign visitors in 1988. Nearly two-thirds of the 1988 U.S.-connected international travel is focused on Canada and Mexico.

For the example year 1987 the eight Great Lakes states had 11,156,000 foreign visitors or 38 percent of the national total. New York had over half of the regional total and nearly a fifth of the national figure with 5.8 million. New York City was the country's leading port of entry with 28 percent of all overseas air travelers but New York state's large share of international travelers also included 2.3 million arriving from Canada. The next leading Great Lakes states in attracting foreign travelers were Michigan, Illinois and Pennsylvania, with 10.5,

9.1 and 9 percent of the region total respectively. Toronto is Canada's leading port of entry, with 42 percent of all international air travelers (7.7 million in 1986) entering through Pearson International Airport. Montreal's Dorval and Mirabel Airports, together, are the second most frequent port of entry, contributing 22 percent of international arrivals. Overseas arrivals in 1987 were a category where the Great Lakes states stood out. Fifty-one percent of 10.5 million such U.S. arrivals landed at area airports. New York, Illinois, and Pennsylvania, were the leading destination states. Japan, West Germany and the United Kingdom are the principal overseas sources of foreign travelers to the region. The Great Lakes states' relative share of overseas arrivals has declined since 1987.

In-flight surveys of visitors from overseas by the U.S. Travel and Tourism Administration have produced interesting profile information. As a percent of all such travelers, a purpose of the trip in 1987 was: vacation (48); business/convention (45); visit friends and relatives (36); and study/other (5). Shopping is a major activity for many foreign visitors accounting for about 25 percent of total visitor expenditures in the U.S. A third of all 1987 visitors came during the summer and more than half of these travelers used a travel agent to book transportation and lodging. Nearly half came alone and a third were in a family group. The average number of nights spent in the U.S. was 21.9. While in the States, fifty percent of the visitors used domestic airlines.

Canadian travel and the Great Lakes states

Minnesota, Michigan and New York share a land/water boundary with Canada and for Ohio and Pennsylvania, the Province of Ontario is just across Lake Erie. The eight Great Lakes states have much more in common with Canada than geography. The economic linkages are substantial. The transboundary region is the industrial heartland of North America and accounts for more than a third of the two countrys' combined population. The U.S. and Canada are each other's largest trading partners and over half of Canada's trade with the United States is with the Great Lakes states. The U.S.-

Canada connection in travel and tourism is a significant part of the regional economy.

With Canada and the United States generating the largest number of travelers to each other's country, tourism and travel parallel the trade picture. In recent years Canada has accounted for about a third of U.S. international travel. Canada hosted 13.3 million U.S. visitors in 1988, a slight increase from 1987. Growth in the U.S. outbound market to Canada, and particularly for Ontario, has slowed recently. The number of Canadian visitors to the U.S. was similar in 1988 at 13.8 million and represented 40 percent of foreign travel to the United States. Canadian visits increased 11 percent in 1989 to 15,365,900 accounting for more than 50 percent of all foreign arrivals. Although Canadians generated more than 133 million person-trips in 1988 involving one or more nights, the great majority of these trips were intraprovincial (only 16.5 million person-trips to other countries were taken). Ontarians and Quebecois were more likely to stay in their home province—83 and 82 percent respectively, compared to the national average of 78 percent. This pattern is likely due to the large geographic area of each province and the wealth of tourism and recreation opportunities in each.

The Great Lakes states have benefited significantly from Canadian travel. Statistics Canada data indicate that nearly half of the visitors to the United States reported a "presence" in the region during 1989. Canadian travel to the Great Lakes states is dominated by day-only stays and pass-through travel. Total Canadian person-nights in the U.S. in 1989 were 114.7 million but the Great Lakes states accounted for only 17.3 million or 15 percent of the national figure (Table 1). Five states had more than one million person-nights with New York (7.8 million) and Michigan (3.2 million) leading the way. All region states showed significant improvement in such visits from 1988 except for Indiana which declined 6.7 percent. As a whole, the region gained 3,687,400 person-nights since 1987. Ontario, the most populous province (9.5 million-1989) and centrally positioned to the Great Lakes area, generates the largest number of visitors to each of the states accounting for 75 percent of all visits. Quebec is second with less than 7 percent.

In 1989 Canadian visitors spent $4.38 billion in the U.S. exclusive of transboundary transportation costs. Canadian spending is generally more than for any other country except for Japan. U.S. travelers' spending in Canada was $3.2 billion in 1988—a 10 percent increase from the previous year reflecting a general upward trend during the decade. Total spending in the Great Lakes states in 1989 was more than $765 million or 17.4 percent of the national total. New York is far ahead followed by Michigan with Ohio, Pennsylvania, Illinois and Minnesota clustered together at the next level. All states showed a significant increase in expenditures from the previous year. In two years, the Great Lakes states have gained $264 million in Canadian expenditures and have also improved their percentage share of the U.S. total.

TABLE 1

Canadian travel to the Great Lakes states, 1989
(thousands)

	Person-visits	Person-nights	Total spending
Illinois	261.6	933.2	$54,743.9
Indiana	128.0	337.3	12,082.1
Michigan	1,333.3	3,216.2	126,084.0
Minnesota	456.4	1,182.6	54,749.2
New York	3,079.4	7,766.5	378,609.3
Ohio	722.2	1,864.4	60,127.4
Pennsylvania	656.1	1,497.0	58,830.0
Wisconsin	198.0	471.1	20,092.7
Great Lakes region	6,835.0	17,268.3	$765,318.6
United States	15,365.9	114,691.9	$4,386,411.8

SOURCE: United States Department of Commerce, United States Travel and Tourism Administration.

The exchange of visitors between Canada and the region reveals certain patterns of travel. Because of proximity, autos are the mode of preference for 60 to 70 percent of the travelers. With the Great Lakes, connecting waterways and the St. Lawrence River dominating the region's international border, there are only 13 major border crossings that can handle vehicle traffic. A primary purpose for cross border trips is categorized as "pleasure". Fifty-five percent of Canadian visits to the region in 1989 were so described. Residents of the region and Canada also have family and friends across the border and visits with this connection are more numerous than for other states. Even with the difference in exchange rates, US consumer prices and sales taxes, as well as the variety of products, have made US shopping attractive to Canadians, and, it is becoming an important travel purpose with respect to short trips. The bridges in the Buffalo-Niagara Falls area and at Detroit have become particularly congested with truck, commuter and shopping traffic. Business travel, although growing, is still far down the list in generating total visits. Cross border travel in the region is highest in the July through September period. The region receives half of its Canadian visitors during this time. First and fourth quarter Canadian trips to the U.S. reflect the pull of "sun spots" and warmer weather locales away from the northern tier states. This pattern is also evident in U.S. travel. Even though Canadian tourist travel during end periods of the calendar is not the Great Lakes region's strong suit, the general affinity on the part of Canadians for winter recreation gives the Great Lakes states an opportunity to attract more winter travel from its northern neighbor. When Canadians vacation outside their country during the warmer months, the Great Lakes states benefit, although a significant amount of this benefit is derived from pass-through travel expenditures.

Promotion at the state level

States have an important role in tourism development and promotion. A principal goal is to maximize the economic return from the industry. The adage, "you must spend money to make money" is no less true for the travel and tourism industry. Much of the supply side of infrastructure is privately owned and operated (e.g., commercial aircraft, hotels and entertainment places). Public control is focused on park systems, parts of the transportation system such as ferries, airports and roadways and convention and miscellaneous facilities. In some cases state and local units of government are assisting (subsidizing) new tourism-related development in a variety of ways including preferential tax treatment, land acquisition and preparation and road access. A significant

level of state assistance comes in the form of promotion. Business promotion activities are usually centered in Departments of Commerce or Economic Development, and that is where state tourism offices or agencies are usually based. According to the U.S. Travel Data Center, the FY 1988-89 Great Lakes states' tourism budgets totaled more than $82.5 million of the fifty-state total ($320 million). The region figure has increased $13.5 million from FY1986-87 but the region's share of the U.S. total declined by nearly 4 percent.

Each of the states has developed a full complement of specific promotional materials. Some states have detailed calendars of events or "travel planners". Seasonal activity brochures are available. For example, New York has one titled "Skiing and Winter Adventures" and Minnesota puts out a "Guide to Cross Country Ski Trails". The advertising outlays cover all media. Market research with a focus on target groups is of special interest to the state tourism/travel offices. An important aspect of state tourism promotion programs is evaluation. State legislatures and their appropriations committees seek ways to measure the effectiveness of a promotion effort in order to justify funding/expenditure levels. Surveys and trend/market share analysis are the principal means by which state agencies attempt to measure performance but some difficulties persist in obtaining reliable data.

The Great Lakes Council of State Travel Directors has begun to explore areas of potential cooperation in the regional promotion realm. Several studies and surveys have revealed that the Great Lakes area lacked a strong regional tourism image, particularly among residents of other states and countries. The states are working together on international promotion activities but strong competitive positions limit mutual promotion opportunities with respect to the domestic market. The Great Lakes have become a focus for new efforts at the state and region level. State travel directors are recognizing this shared water resource and the opportunity for coordination/cooperation in attracting visitors to the coastal zone. Michigan adopted a "Celebrate the Great Lakes" promotion program and theme which guided some of the state's and community-based tourism promotion

during the late 1980s. Two regional Great Lakes promotion initiatives were begun in 1990. The Great Lakes Circle Tour, established under the leadership of the eight-state Great Lakes Commission, ties existing scenic roadways and individual lake tours into a region-wide 6,500 mile/10,500 km designated system. Ontario and Quebec are also participating in the initiative. The Council of Great Lakes Governors (along with Ontario) has launched the Great Lakes International Tourism Marketing Campaign. This three-year program has an overseas promotion emphasis. A Great Lakes travel planner is proposed with an initial distribution to British tour operators and travel agents.

International travel marketing has become an important avenue of cooperation among the Great Lakes states. And the U.S. Travel and Tourism Administration (USTTA) has become a partner with states throughout the country in providing international tourism data and facilitating cooperative marketing programs. These marketing efforts include: trade advertising, travel and trade shows, seminars, travel agent and journalist familiarization tours and travel missions to other countries. A "Great Lakes States USA" marketing committee with representation from the six western-most Great Lakes states was formed in 1984 to strengthen international marketing efforts of individual states by combining staff and financial resources. This organization is also the principal vehicle through which USTTA's marketing assistance programs are implemented.

Data development—United States and Canada

The availability, quality and analysis of tourism and travel data are perennial concerns to researchers, planners and policy analysts. These issues arise from the inherent fragmentation of the tourism industry. This fragmentation directly contributes to the complex structure and geographic diversity of the industry. Such diversity and complexity, in turn, gives rise to inconsistent statistical measures and definitions. Inconsistent and sometimes questionable statistical information contribute to the lack of political credibility for the industry. The lack of political credibility at the state/provincial and federal levels limits the ability of the industry to command greater public resources for improved data collection.

In 1985, a U.S. survey identified twenty-six federal agencies with dozens of programs involving tourism and travel data collection and analysis, e.g., National Park Service—Facility Descriptions and Visitation Statistics; Federal Highway Administration—National Personal Transportation Survey; Bureau of Labor Statistics—Employment and Earnings; and U.S. Travel and Tourism Administration—In-Flight Survey of International Air Travelers. Also, the government collects trade data for 10,000 categories of goods but little attention has been paid to the service sector where much of the tourism economy is based. The granddaddy of all statistical gathering agencies is the Bureau of the Census in the Department of Commerce. This agency's economic census conducted every five years provides a wealth of specialized industry data pertinent to tourism such as number of guestrooms in hotels and motels and gallons of gasoline sold by service stations.

Statistical reliability of some national data sources is suspect for various reasons including insufficient sample size and excessive reliance on secondary data. Information voids also characterize part of the U.S. government's effort in this area. Federal Budget difficulties and a policy of encouraging private sector initiatives partly explain the problems with comprehensiveness. Even the leading private data collector, the U.S. Travel Data Center, cannot justify increased sampling or data development without responsive support from data subscribers. The Travel Data Center's main survey activity is comprised of monthly telephone interviews of 1,500 adults. Data on trip and traveler characteristics along with travel intentions have been published quarterly and annually since 1979. Reliable state-specific interstate data are not available from the survey because of the small sample size. The non-profit organization's Travel Economic Impact Model developed in 1976 estimates travel industry expenditures and is widely respected.

The current lack of suitable U.S. tourism and travel data has been exacerbated by the discontinuation of the National Travel Survey (NTS). This population-based survey had been conducted as part of the economic censuses in 1963, 1967 and 1972 at the state and substate levels. In 1977, additional funding from the U.S. Travel Service (now the U.S. Travel and Tourism Administration) and the Department of Transportation was obtained to enlarge the sample so as to produce more reliable state estimates. The sample size was increased to more than 20,000 households and methodology was changed from mail distribution to in-home interviews. These survey improvements produced very good results and the survey is widely recognized as the most comprehensive and accurate U.S. travel data acquisition effort ever conducted. Budget support was not forthcoming in 1982 and loss of the NTS has hurt those public and private sector organizations which need baseline statistics for domestic marketing and policy development. Advocacy of a new National Travel Survey with a few methodology changes draws widespread support ranging from the International Association of Travel Research and Marketing Professionals and the Travel Industry Association of America to the National Council of State Travel Directors and the National Governors' Association. Funding remains a major problem but proposals for non-federal cost sharing may resurrect the survey.

In an attempt to improve the usefulness of existing data sources and to make recommendations for the collection and dissemination of new data, the federal and provincial governments of Canada, in cooperation with industry, established a Task Force on Tourism Data that operated from 1985 to 1987. Many of the Task Force's recommendations have not yet been implemented. One problem is the projected cost of the recommendations at more than $5 million. Another issue relates to lack of consensus among particular government agencies. Nonetheless, some modest improvements have been made in data collection and dissemination. In particular, Statistics Canada has refined several surveys as well as revamped several publications devoted to tourism statistics. The Task Force's efforts led directly to the creation of the Canadian Tourism Research Institute. Work is also progressing on the development of a satellite account for tourism. A tourism satellite account would allow the extraction of data related to the flow of money through tourism-related businesses from the general system of national accounts. This development would provide valuable, precise and credible economic information regarding trends in the national tourism industry and, further, would provide an integrated framework for the collection and organization of other tourism data, especially that related to supply-side issues. The satellite account would ensure that tourism economic statistics were collected, verified and reported in a manner consistent with statistics collected for all other industries and industry sectors.

The Task Force's work also resulted in refinements in the two main sources of national tourism statistics related to tourism demand: the Canadian Travel Survey (CTS) and the International Travel Survey (ITS). The CTS is conducted biennially as a supplement to Statistics Canada's quarterly Labour Force Survey. The CTS is based on a minimum of 10,300 respondents in each quarter of the study year. Individual provinces can negotiate (and pay for) a larger sample of their own residents. CTS results are generally disaggregatable to the provincial level and to the 25 Census Metropolitan Areas. The CTS provides information on socio-economic characteristics of travelers and basic trip characteristics (e.g., origin, destination, purpose, duration, activities, accommodation, expenditures) for overnight trips as well as same-day trips of at least 50 miles (80 km) one-way.

The ITS is a continuous survey of international travel into and out of Canada. It is based on a "stint sampling scheme". A "stint" is a selected period of several days during which questionnaires are distributed to every eligible travel party coming to Canada through designated ports of entry. Four different forms of the questionnaire are used to accommodate four different populations of international travelers: 1) U.S. visitors entering Canada; 2) residents of other countries entering Canada; 3) Canadian residents returning from trips of at least 24 hours outside Canada; and 4) Canadian residents returning to Canada within 24 hours of departure. Surveys of travelers between Canada and the U.S. are conducted under a cooperative agreement. Each country surveys its own residents and exchanges data with the other country on a regular basis. The questionnaires for all but same-day travelers provide information on origin and destination, purpose of travel, mode of transportation, duration, and expenditures. Data for same-day travelers is limited to mode of travel, re-entry port, purpose of trip, party size, expenditures, and previous trips within the last seven days.

State/provincial and local governments as well as the private and non-profit sectors are involved in tourism and travel data collection and analysis. Traveler and facility-specific surveys are common. Administrative data sources, such as gate receipts, room reservations and credit card charges, are used by both government and business, but for the outside researcher, confidentiality requirements may limit access. Contract work by university researchers and consulting firms accounts for a growing share of research expenditures. Demographic and travel activity information is very important for efficient marketing of travel industry products and services. Theme periodicals and even newspapers are interested in this information not only to improve circulation but enhance advertising revenue. For example, travel and tourism are key national advertising classifications for the *Chicago Tribune*. The paper's Quarterly Market Study entails a telephone survey of 1,750 Chicago-area adults and is one of the most carefully controlled proprietary research studies in the newspaper industry. One interesting result of this study shows that about one-fifth of the 4 million plus vacationing adults in the study area take an annual driving vacation in nearby states.

An innovative process through which periodic collection and reporting of specific travel/tourism data is known as travel monitoring. Travel monitors with a balance of primary and secondary data, a good representation of sectors and timely reporting of data have given both the private and public sectors a better handle on activity levels and trends. One of the best travel monitors, Michigan Travel Activity, was developed by the Michigan Travel Bureau in 1982 and transferred with funding assistance to the Travel, Tourism and Recreation Resource Center at Michigan State University. Michigan data includes: state park overnight stays,

highway traffic volume, air passenger traffic and overnight stays, hotel/motel sales and use tax collections. Multi-state travel monitors have also been proposed with university participation a key element.

Outdoor recreation and the Great Lakes region

For residents of the Great Lakes region and visitors to the area, outdoor recreation is more than a quality-of-life issue. It is a way of life. Outdoor recreation is a major leisure-time pursuit for many North Americans. Although such recreation usually relates to the natural environment, leisure activity out-of-doors, irrespective of place, can also be categorized as outdoor recreation. Outdoor recreation activities are incredibly diverse. A walk in a park and cross-country skiing may take an individual over the same route. A houseboat and ice-fishing shanty may occupy the same spot at different times during the year. And in the air, the hot-air balloonist or hang glider can look down on the kite flyer.

Outdoor recreation is both a public and private sector concern. The linkage or interface between the two can be competitive or complementary. For example, the private sector provides lodging for publicly administered historic sites whereas both sectors may "compete" for campers or skiers. Recreation in the out-of-doors raises many public policy issues particularly as they pertain to funding levels and program development at the community level. On the public level, adequate funding is tied to agreement on funding sources. The perennial question centers on user fees versus public revenues or what combination of the two is appropriate and acceptable. As the individual sees it, outdoor recreation opportunity presents a plethora of options to be balanced with personal goals and lifestyle preferences. This web of public/private connections describes modern society and in it outdoor recreation has an important role to play.

National and state/provincial parks

Many natural and cultural assets of the region are preserved and managed through separate state/provincial and national park systems. These places are an integral element of the outdoor recreation

infrastructure. The U.S. Department of Interior's National Park Service (NPS) has jurisdiction over 1.26 million acres in the Great Lakes states or only 5 percent of its national total. These areas include twelve categories (with 1989 national total in parentheses): 2 national parks (50); 4 national lakeshores (4);1 national seashore (10); 17 national historic sites (68); 5 national historical parks (29); 5 national monuments (79); 1 national battlefield (11); 1 national military park (10); 4 (scenic) rivers (9); and 4 national scenic trails (9). Although the states' representation of large acreage national parks and national recreation areas is relatively small, the number of other NPS facilities and the region's population have produced a 10 percent region share of total system recreation visits. It should be noted that the Great Lakes states are within a day's drive of more than half the U.S. population and this geographic factor enhances the potential demand for recreation visits.

Environment Canada oversees five national parks in Ontario and three in Quebec, out of a national total of 34 parks. Although the eight parks in the two provinces represent 24 percent of the total number of parks in Canada, their combined area of 3106 square km in Ontario and Quebec is only 2 percent of total national park area. These parks, though relatively small, experience reasonably high use levels due to their proximity to major urban areas. Ontario's national parks experienced 600,000 visits in FY 1989-90 or 4.7 percent of the total; Quebec's national parks generated 640,000 or 5.0 percent of the total.

The Great Lakes states have more than 625 state parks. New York, the fifth largest state in the region and most populous, has the greatest number at 147 followed by Michigan and Pennsylvania. New York created the first such park in the country in 1885 at Niagara Falls and the first unified state park system in 1924. For 1987, more than a quarter of a billion visits were recorded in the eight states. This number is more than a third of the national total. Ontario has the largest absolute area of any province reserved in provincial parks. The Ontario provincial park system represents 41 percent of the nation's total provincial park area even though the province accounts for only 11 percent of the area of

Canada. Since both Quebec and Ontario played pivotal roles in the emergence of the Canadian nation, these provinces tend to have proportionately more historic sites than national parks. Ontario's historic sites account for 19 percent of the national total, while Quebec accounts for 25 percent. The Canadian Travel Survey provides an aggregate measure of attendance at all national, provincial, and regional parks and historic sites, regardless of location. Of the estimated 6.9 million person-trips made to such sites in 1989 by all Canadians, Ontario residents generated 2.2 million (33 percent) and Quebec residents 0.75 million (11 percent). Both these rates are less than what one would expect given each province's share of the Canadian population: 36 percent for Ontario and 26 percent for Quebec.

A principal public policy issue pertaining to state park systems is the need for adequate funding for maintenance, upgrading and adequate staffing. For example, Michigan state park staffing levels have declined by a fourth over the past decade. Michigan voters addressed these issues in 1988 by voting in favor of a $140 million bond measure. The money is to be evenly divided between state and local parks. Another major issue concerns the Great Lakes Coastal zone with its high scenic and environ-

mental value. Park system planners in acknowledging the threat of development and the need for public access have created 110 state parks that border on the Great Lakes. The popularity of coastal parkland is evident in Michigan where the coastal parks have accounted for 50 percent of total system attendance over the last 25 years. Other important issues concern the need to provide for park recreational programming and facility development/use management in and near large urban areas and certain places with high visit potential. In Minnesota where state park visits have increased from 6 to 9 million since 1986, 10 of the state's 64 parks are subject to continual overcrowding. One example of program planning that has received high marks in the region is Indiana's Natural Resources Cultural Arts Program. The state parks in the Hoosier State entertain visitors throughout the summer with theatrical and dance performances, storytelling and a variety of music.

Hunting

The U.S. Fish and Wildlife Service (FWS) reports that the number of hunting licenses issued by the 50 states peaked in 1982 at 16.7 million and the trend is now downward. For the Great Lakes states, the number of hunters, as indicated by a FWS

national survey conducted every five years, decreased from 5.8 million in 1980 to 5.4 million in 1985. Ontario had 500,000 hunters for the FY 1986-87 period and a total $471 million (CDN) economic impact within the Province. In Quebec 600,000 hunters generated a $244 million impact. Hunting may not be what it used to be—it's better in some cases and worse in others. Demographic changes are overtaking the activity. Older hunters are retiring and many urban young people are not attracted to the sport. The decline in hunting habitat coupled with more interest in wildlife appreciation indicates future hunting may never be the same.

However, hunting remains a major avocational pursuit and accounts for a substantial economic impact. Days of hunting projected for the Great Lakes states in 1985 were 99.3 million or about 30 percent of the national total. Pennsylvania is the leading hunting state with 21 percent of the region's hunters. The Great Lakes states appeal mostly to resident hunters. For example, in 1986, 99 percent of the hunters in Minnesota were Minnesotans and nearly as high percentages held for New York, Michigan, Pennsylvania and Wisconsin. One area of particular interest to outstate innkeepers, restauranteurs and auto service people is the amount of money spent by hunters—total expenditures were estimated at $2.6 billion compared with more than $10 billion in the U.S. (Table 2).

Hunting is a species-specific activity and therefore across-the-board generalizations do not adequately describe the variability regarding particular game, habitat conditions and wildlife management practices. Ducks and deer are good examples. Region duck hunting suffered greatly in the fall of 1988 after summer drought and heat wiped out the prairie potholes in the Canadian plains and played havoc with duck brooding elsewhere. On the other hand, deer harvests in the northern Great Lakes states are at record levels and the number of deer hunters is not far behind. In Wisconsin, 680,000 hunters participated in the 1988 nine-day firearms season. Michigan claims more than 700,000 deer hunters. Bowhunting is also becoming more popular particularly in Minnesota, Wisconsin and Michigan. This phenomenon has been explained by some sportsmen as a need for

TABLE 2

Hunting, fishing and recreational boats in the Great Lakes states
(thousands)

	Total hunters and related expenditures, 1985		Total anglers and related expenditures, 1985		Total Great Lakes anglers and days of fishing, 1985		Total registered boats and US rank, 1988	
Illinois	406	$297,878	1,625	$895,450	339	2,568	326	(9)
Indiana	361	168,140	1,360	575,949	102	734	214	(18)
Michigan	943	440,311	2,444	1,403,429	1,300	15,430	788	(1)
Minnesota	545	216,158	1,793	778,268	86	705	693	(3)
New York	791	280,479	2,312	1,056,818	492	8,420	385	(7)
Ohio	515	210,979	2,083	1,015,924	918	13,242	375	(8)
Pennsylvania	1,148	714,211	1,626	1,032,668	155	1,793	266	(12)
Wisconsin	723	303,415	1,827	640,800	495	3,260	480	(6)
Great Lakes region	5,432	$2,631,571	15,070	$7,399,306	3,766	46,417	3,527	
United States	16,684	$10,059,386	46,357	$28,145,527			10,362	

SOURCE: U.S. Department of the Interior, Fish and Wildlife Service, *National Survey of Fishing, Hunting and Wildlife-Associated Recreation* (1985); and National Marine Manufacturers Association, *Boating 1989.*

NOTE: Total anglers, hunters and Great Lakes days of fishing are indicated by state where activity took place. Total expenditure data are indicated for hunters' and anglers' state of residence. Anglers and hunters are 16 years old and older.

more hunting challenge in response to the growth in deer populations. Increased logging in the deer range throughout the northern part of the Great Lakes region is creating prime deer habitat. Even farm areas in the southern part of the range have experienced an increase in deer. One forest management/deer habitat issue that generates controversy is the old growth forest versus traditional timber harvest policies. Ecologists are arguing for retention of more continuous acreage of post-mature forest to create greater environmental diversity. Unfortunately, this type of habitat does not support large deer populations.

Other game species have benefited from habitat preservation and game resource management practices by the states. For example, in Michigan an elk herd has been established. Wild turkeys have been planted in most of the states to re-establish populations long gone. Even bear seasons are flourishing in some states. In Wisconsin, 1,110 bears were killed in 1988. All hunting is not confined to "wild" lands and a growing number of hunters are taking their business to private clubs and preserves. These places can make the "hunting experience" convenient and more-often-than-not successful. Indication of success comes from Minnesota where licensed hunt clubs have increased from 18 in 1978 to 100 in 1988.

Fishing

The Great Lakes region is a year-round angler's paradise. Where else would one find the national Fresh Water Fishing Hall of Fame but in Hayward, Wisconsin? According to the FWS's 1985 comprehensive survey, the region's eight states accounted for nearly one of three anglers 16 years or older in the country (15.0/46.4million) and twenty-nine percent of fishing days (283.9/976.5 million). In the region, the number of anglers increased about 9 percent from 1980 and the number of fishing days increased slightly more. Michigan was number one in number of anglers and four states each registered more than a billion dollars in related angling expenditures (Table 2). In Ontario nearly 2.2 million adults were active anglers in 1985 accounting for 34.4 million fishing days. Quebec's 800,000 licensed anglers were responsible for 15.3 million fishing

days in 1988. Three reasons principally explain this strong presence of fishing activity: large population, government fish management programs and a natural resource base (the states have over 16 million acres of inland lakes and reservoirs, 183,804 miles of fishing streams and 65,000 square miles of Great Lakes water). Ontario's 227,000 lakes comprise 17 percent of provincial area.

Fishing is most common in the state of residence but that does not diminish the importance of non-resident activity. Nearly a quarter of all anglers fish at some time in other states than where they live. For Ontario, non-resident anglers accounted for 28 percent of all fishing days. Non-resident fishing activity is an important generator of "extra" tourism/recreation dollars for a state and participating communities. The U.S. Fish and Wildlife Service reported for 1986 that four Great Lakes states were among the top 10 states fished by non-resident license holders with Wisconsin and Michigan one-two. Total fishing expenditures by both residents and others amount to surprisingly big bucks. For the eight states, a total expenditure level of $7.39 billion was identified in the 1985 federal survey with $1.56 billion attributed to Great Lakes fishing. The statewide totals show that Michigan at $1.4 billion is the clear region leader but that New York, Ohio and Pennsylvania are over the billion dollar level. Total fishing trip-related expenditures for the states was over $3 billion. In Ontario nearly a billion dollars was spent by anglers in 1985.

The Great Lakes sport fishery is a major part of the regional fishing picture. For 1985, the federal government projected 3,766,000 Great Lakes anglers. This figure compares with 3,016,000 in 1980, a 25 percent increase. The increase in fishing activity is reflected in recreational boat sales, tackle expenditures and overnight stays near prime fishing areas. The survey indicated that Great Lakes fishing days increased from 40.5 to 46.4 million or a 14.5 percent gain. Great Lakes trip expenditures included $265 million for food, $65 million for lodging, $202 million for transportation and $143 million for equipment expenditures. Great Lakes angler expenses for licenses, stamps, tags and permits totaled $26,740,000.

Great Lakes fishing has had its ups and downs. At first, the pristine Great Lakes supported large, stable populations of fish including lake trout, lake herring and lake whitefish. Fishing, whether by native people or settlers and their commercial enterprises, was fabulous. But when large scale lumbering and shoreland development interfered with water conditions in tributaries and coastal marshes, spawning success declined. By 1885, 10,000 commercial fishermen began to take their toll. Increasing water pollution also had an adverse impact on fish populations. The U.S. Great Lakes commercial fish harvest reached its peak in 1899 at 119 million pounds. The invasion of the parasitic sea lamprey on top of all the other problems ruined the commercial fishery and set the stage for a vigorous counterattack on the lamprey and development of the sport fishery. The Great Lakes states, the FWS and the binational Great Lakes Fishery Commission have all played a major role in fishery rehabilitation. Effective lamprey control using lampricides provided the opportunity for successful hatchery/planting programs. Stocking has made a major contribution with the release of huge numbers of trout and salmon particularly for Lake Michigan. More than 75 million chinook and 100 million coho salmon have been released since the late 1960s. For Lake Michigan alone, more than 50 million trout have been stocked giving it the title of "world's largest lake trout fishery".

These actions along with stocking and commercial fishery controls resulted in the creation of a huge sport fishery with its associated charter/recreational boat industry and economic impact. The U.S. charter fishing industry in the Great Lakes has grown from 500 boats-for-hire in 1975 to around 3,000 entailing more than $35 million in charter revenues. Lake Erie illustrates the changes in Great Lakes sport fishing. The Lake Erie fishable walleye population rebounded from an all-time low in 1969 to the 20 to 40 million range during the 1980s. After the basin states and Ontario implemented in the early 1970s a commercial fishing ban (due to mercury contamination) and a walleye quota management system in 1976, Lake Erie charter fishing operations in Ohio responded to the improved fishing by increasing from just 25 in 1975 to more than 700 by 1986.

A new problem on the scene is the zebra mussel, a small bivalve mollusc. This non-indigenous species was probably introduced in the mid-1980s and has colonized Lake Erie and is spreading to the other Great Lakes. The mussel will impact sport fish populations (particularly walleye) in three ways: rapid buildup on hard surfaces including rocky shoals can interfere with walleye spawning; efficient filtration (one liter per day per mussel) will reduce plankton and possibly disrupt the food chain; and decaying mussel beds can result in oxygen depletion. Control strategies are currently a major research issue.

Recreational boating

The Great Lakes region is the setting for tens of thousands of lakes and hundreds of miles of navigable rivers. Several major "lake districts" have large numbers of second-homes and are magnets for seasonal waves of vacationers. With more than 100,000 square miles of navigable water and a resident U.S. and Canadian population of more than 40 million, the Great Lakes Basin anchors an important and growing marine recreation industry. According to state registration data, the number of recreational boats in the Great Lakes states was approximately 3,527,000 in 1988. This figure represents more than a third of all registered watercraft in the country (Table 2). An exact figure representing boat numbers by jurisdiction is not available because some state data contain inactive or expired registrations and not all categories of water craft require registration.

With respect to Great Lakes recreational boat activity, no comprehensive, system-wide data is available. A Michigan State University/Department of Park and Recreation Resources study based on a statewide survey of 10,089 Michigan registrants indicated for 1986 that 245,000 boats were used on the Great Lakes or 41 percent of the total active fleet. However, for exclusive Great Lakes boat use, the figure for Michigan was 104,000 or 17.4 percent. The best indicator of Great Lakes boating activity is the usage measure of "boat days". For 1986, the Michigan study estimated 28 percent of all boat

days in the state were spent on the Great Lakes. Earlier studies for Michigan have indicated a similar percentage. The Michigan studies also demonstrated the remarkable growth of Great Lakes boat days in recent years: 1974 to 1980—63 percent and 1980 to 1986—41 percent. On the basis of boat registrations for counties proximate (adjacent and next-adjacent) to the Great Lakes and a 75 percent estimate of Great Lakes usage for those boats and 50,000 boats from other locations, approximately 700,000 U.S. recreational boats are used on the Great Lakes each year. This figure is about 20 percent of total region-wide boat registrations.

The recreational boating industry in the Great Lakes is represented by boat manufacturers and retailers, marina operators, marine business suppliers and the hundreds of thousands of recreational boaters/anglers. Retail boat/trailer, outboard motor, and marine accessories sales for the Great Lakes states amounted to more than $3 billion in 1988 or more than a third of national spending. Trip-related expenditures by recreational boaters approximately double the direct spending impact. According to the U.S. Bureau of Labor Statistics, the eight Great Lakes states account for about 6,000 private sector, marina-related jobs and 10,000 boat dealer and supplier jobs. Annual boat shows play an important part in industry promotion and local economic impact. The Detroit Boat and Fishing Show has doubled its attendance since 1981 and sales volume has grown much more rapidly. In 1988, the Detroit show generated $61.5 million in sales. The Cleveland Mid-America Boat Show held every January is the nation's largest.

Marina development particularly on the Great Lakes and area rivers has been expanding to keep pace with recreational boat usage. Studies of waterfront development and marina use trends in the Great Lakes by the Laventhol and Horwath accounting firm show that the high level of economic activity in these sectors should continue through the early 1990s. For example, the area around southern Lake Michigan (Kenosha, Wisconsin to Muskegon, Michigan) will generate 850 new shoreside dwelling units and 1,000 boat slips at marinas and residential developments each year. A study by Ohio Sea Grant based on a survey of Lake

Erie marinas in 1986 profiled the "typical" marina. Such a facility had been in operation for 18 years, grossed $894,000 in annual sales, (boat sales, repair charges, dockage and launch fees, etc.), and employed 5.5 people on a full time annual basis and a similar level of full time equivalent employment during the average 6.6 month season. The mean annual payroll for the marinas was nearly $100,000. Increased household income and maturation of the early baby-boomers along with continued loan interest deductibility for second homes and boats with galleys and heads are the principal reasons for sector prosperity. However, renewed Congressional scrutiny of tax "loopholes" and new "luxury" taxes along with a smaller baby-boom bulge may roil future waters. Also, increasing marina congestion for transient boaters and new restrictions on shore home building and marina construction could dampen Great Lakes boating trends.

Another regional boating activity is related to the growing passenger vessel sector on the Great Lakes and St. Lawrence River. At present, several million people take these excursions and ferry trips during the navigation season. Overnight cruise passengers visiting Canadian ports on the St. Lawrence River reached a modern-day record of 35,000 in 1987. Passenger capacity for the approximately 150 regularly scheduled U.S. and Canadian operations is nearly 60,000. Now, passenger movement by vessel mode is substantially less than what it was when immigrants boarded boats for westward destinations and millions of travelers embarked on trips during the famed 'Resort Era' in the early twentieth century. In the wake of this current interest, feasibility studies and marketing surveys have been completed indicating substantial demand for multi-day cruise service for the Great Lakes/St. Lawrence System. There is budding state/provincial interest in encouraging re-establishment of overnight service on the Great Lakes.

Outdoor recreation: Participants and spectators

Outdoor recreation can be an individual or group activity. These activities can be both participative or passive (spectator). Interest in all facets of outdoor recreation appears to be increasing. Attendance at events, sales of sporting equipment and level of individual involvement indicate the positive growth trends and changes in societal attitudes about leisure-time pursuits. The President's Commission on Americans Outdoors (1987) acknowledged that contrary to earlier expectations, the amount of time Americans devote to leisure is decreasing—a loss of eight hours per week since the 1970s. However, the amount of leisure time spent on recreation activities has not changed thereby indicating its increasing priority status. A Commission sponsored survey indicated that many Americans see outdoor recreation as an enjoyable way to maintain a healthier lifestyle. The President's Commission also reported that recreation is big business with a total of $262 billion of related expenditures in 1984—$100 billion of which was categorized as outdoor recreation.

Although the automobile may be the most important vehicle involved in outdoor recreation, the bicycle should be considered *the* outdoor recreation vehicle. Bicycles outnumber cars in the world two-to-one, but in the U.S., cars have a 37 million edge. Nevertheless, in recent years more bicycles have been sold in the U.S. than cars. Most U.S. bicycle manufacturers are based in the Great Lakes Region—mainly in Illinois and Ohio. The U.S. industry is experiencing serious competition from overseas—imports now capture more than 50 percent of the market compared with only 20 percent in the late 1970s. Estimated "bicycle days" for the region add up to more than 1 billion on a yearly basis.

The thousands of miles of trails in the region are as diverse as the terrain they traverse. There is a trail for practically everyone whether they are cross-country skiers, bicyclists or hikers. Of the principal trail types (not including snowmobile trails), the eight states have more than 60,000 miles. Quebec and Ontario account for an additional 25,000 miles. Most states in the region have special trail development programs. Cooperation with the private sector is a fundamental component of these programs. Trails advisory groups have been established in several states to make policy recommendations and assist in public information/promotion efforts. Route planning over the last decade has turned certain imaginative concepts into reality. For

example, abandoned rail lines are prime trail candidates. The Rails to Trails Conservancy indicates with rail deregulation, related branchline abandonment represents a million-acre trail potential. Already, more than 3,200 miles of rail right-of-way in 35 states have been converted to trails. The Great Lakes states have 1,724 miles of trails developed from abandoned rail lines or 54 percent of the national total. Wisconsin with 503 miles is number one nationally. Ontario is also developing trails from rail routes no longer in use.

Another significant outdoor recreation activity that entails substantial infrastructure development is golf. In the Great Lakes states golf was played in 1989 at 4,659 golf courses. The ratio of public to private facilities is 2 to 1. The region total is about 34 percent of the national figure indicating a strong demand for the sport. Golfing is also attractive north of the border where the number of courses in Ontario (524) and Quebec (193) represent 46 percent of Canada's total. According to National Golf Foundation data, the region's states accounted for nearly 8.5 million golfers in 1988. With an average expenditure of $551 per golfer in 1988, the total impact in the Great Lakes states is certainly something to swing at. The Great Lakes golf season is shorter than in the South and Pacific Coast states, but this "handicap" is offset by summer climate conditions more conducive to golf play. When the southern links wilt under heat and humidity, the northern continental air masses, along with the moderating influence of the Great Lakes, combine to produce better "golf weather".

Another activity category in which the Great Lakes region has a decided advantage is winter sports. Much of the region usually receives sufficient snowfall and cold to sustain interest in outdoor winter recreation. "Lake effect" snowfalls in the Great Lakes coastal areas have put some places in the record book. Favorite activities of residents include ice skating, ice fishing, sledding, skiing and snowmobiling. The economic impact of winter recreation is substantial. When winters are warm or have low snowfall, newspapers are filled with stories on retail sales impacts. Downhill ski areas in recent good years have produced revenues of $2.75 billion nationwide and the 191 downhill ski

areas in the Great Lakes states represent more than a third of the U.S. total and receive their share of the receipts. More than half of all alpine ski areas in Canada are in Ontario and Quebec. However, the industry is growing at only 1 percent annually, a far cry from boom periods during the past two decades. Skier visits as measured by lift ticket purchases are around 50 to 54 million nationally but the number of skiers does not appear to be expanding and, in fact, demographics point to more trouble ahead. The simple fact is that as people get older they are less likely to ski and the U.S. population is getting older with fewer children. On top of this, operator costs have skyrocketed with liability insurance and marketing costs leading the way. The region also attracts worldwide attention as thousands of crosscountry skiers from the U.S. and around the world meet each year in northern Wisconsin to participate in the American Birkebeiner crosscountry ski race. Snowmobiling also accounts for large expenditures—$1.3 billion annually. In 1987, the Great Lakes states had 742,868 registered snowmobiles or 70 percent of the national total. Michigan, Minnesota, Wisconsin, and Illinois are among the top five in the country. More than 72,000 miles of snowmobile trails have been established in the eight states and two Canadian provinces. A Wisconsin survey showed that there were nearly two snowmobiles per snowmobiling household and each such household averaged 25 snowmobiling occasions.

Organized sports, whether at the amateur or professional level, are a major component of outdoor recreation. Participation in school and community-sponsored athletic programs is at high levels. As an example, Ann Arbor, Michigan's recreation department organizes 460 adult softball teams each season and 150 youth baseball/softball teams. The city also cosponsors with Peterborough, Ontario, the "Arborough Games" where around 750 people cross the international border each year to engage in planned play. Even states have recognized the importance of organized sports competition and have developed special competitions. The "state games" concept was pioneered by New York in 1978. The Empire State Games attract approximately 100,000 athletes each year and is America's largest, annual amateur event. Wisconsin held its first Badger State Winter Games in 1989, one of only four states that organize such seasonal activity. Ontario has a province wide summer and winter games program.

Spectator sports complement participation activity in the "outdoor" recreation field. Professional and collegiate level sports can be a big part of a local economy. Restaurant and other retail services usually benefit from the auto/pedestrian flow to and from stadiums and arenas. These impacts are noticeable whether the sports facility is located in a rural town or downtown in a major city. For example, proprietors in college towns do a land office business on football days. The Great Lakes states account for about one-fourth of all senior college football attendance (four-year schools) and the 27 NCAA Division 1-A schools in the eight states had over 5.8 million paid football spectators in 1989. On the professional side of the field, a major-league baseball stadium can generate incredible attendance. For example, the thirteen major league teams based in the Great Lakes states and two Canadian provinces counted more than 27 million fans in 1989 or 50 percent of total attendance. Racing events are also big generators of revenue. Thoroughbred Racing Association data indicate that the 17 tracks in the Great Lakes states had nearly 14.5 million attendance in 1989. The largest of all races, the New York City Marathon claims more than one million spectators, but the Indianapolis 500 attracts between 350,000 and 400,000 spectators making it the number one paid attendance, single day sporting event in the world. Auto race tracks predominate in rural areas and have a significant economic impact on individual locales.

Private-sector employment and business establishment data for the outdoor recreation/activity sectors show clearly their role in the national as well as regional economy. It is recognized that all business establishments categorized as such can not accurately be said to be connected to the outdoors but many of them are. Retail sports (Standard Industrial Classification Code 5941) as an example, includes sporting goods and bicycle stores. Bureau of Labor Statistics data which covers almost all workers who are paid salaries indicate that in 1987 there were 5,792 retail sports business estab-

lishments in the Great Lakes states, compared with 19,828 nationally. These stores had a total employment of 38,328. For amusement and recreation services (SIC 799) which covers a large spectrum of commercial operations including, of course, indoor activity, the employment numbers are even more impressive. 154,364 people were working in this sector in the Great Lakes Region at 11,742 establishments. For the U.S. more than 580,000 livelihoods were tied to amusement and recreation services.

Conclusion

The economic importance of travel, tourism and outdoor recreation for the Great Lakes states and provinces is now widely recognized. These sectors demonstrate that a healthy environment and a good economy are interdependent. With appropriate levels of investment in tourism and outdoor recreation, the private and public sectors gain with increased employment, profit and tax revenue. Given the decline in many of the region's traditional goods production industries and the growth potential for tourism and travel, the Great Lakes states and provinces have an opportunity to strengthen and diversify the region's economic base as well as enhance the travel/leisure experience of residents and non residents. The Great Lakes, as the primary natural resource and geographic feature common to the eight states, should be considered a basis for the development of cooperative, interstate policy pertaining to travel, tourism and outdoor recreation in the region.

Development Policy and Outlook

Chapter 13

Joint Initiatives in the States and Provinces

Timothy McNulty, Executive Director, Council of Great Lakes Governors

Entering the 1990s, a strong case can be made that the level of cooperation within the Great Lakes states exceeds that of any other region in the United States. Moreover, a claim can also be made that the region provides a model for transborder cooperation. A wide range of cooperative ventures among states and provinces and cities emerged amidst discussion and implementation of the Free Trade Agreement. These ventures range from trade and tourism activities to rural development, training, and infrastructure initiatives.

Introduction

A quiet revolution took place throughout the Great Lakes basin in the 1980s. The decade witnessed a dramatic surge in the volume and nature of cooperative ventures between and among the states and provinces.

The revolutionary nature of these developments partly stems from the fact that in the 1970s the region had been the site of one of the most bitter interstate economic development conflicts—that being interstate "smokestack chasing" as characterized, for example, by the protracted bidding war between Ohio and Pennsylvania for the now closed Volkswagen assembly facility.[1]

While competition for plant locations still exists between the states and provinces, a nexus of cooperative economic development efforts has emerged around trade, tourism, technology and natural resources development, and workforce issues. These cooperative initiatives provide a foundation for the continued transformation of the regional economic policy making environment.

This chapter reviews the emergence of cooperative ventures. The analysis will unfold in three sections. The first section assesses the factors contributing to increased cooperation. This assessment examines the institutional, strategic, personal leadership, and economic elements that appear to have contributed to the growth of cooperative action.

The second section reviews actual examples of cooperative ventures. The review does not attempt to provide an exhaustive summary of those ventures. Given their diverse nature, the universe of collaborative projects is unknown. Rather, the review highlights the variety of forms joint initiatives have taken—broad regional projects, bi-state and bi-province efforts, and ventures aimed at specific industries or single program areas.

The concluding discussion focuses on possibilities for the continued evolution of joint initiatives in the region: What are the key lessons, what is the potential impact of these projects, how are they likely to evolve?

The emergence of a framework for cooperation

The dynamics of regional cooperation are not well understood. Attempts to explain the nature of regionalism have often centered on cultural factors, partisanship or conflicts with external authorities over shared resources.[2] Managing these shared resources has provided the historical foundation for regional cooperation in the Great Lakes' region (see: Donahue, Chapter 3).

In tracing the path of the Great Lakes region from the VW conflict to the substantive transborder cooperation of the late 1980s, the following analysis asserts that a complex web of elements has created the foundation for collective action. These elements include: institutional structures for analyzing issues in a regional context and for designing and implementing joint projects; a convergence of economic strategies among the ten Great Lakes jurisdictions; and overall international economic trends that are dramatically recasting the role of regions and the environment for regional cooperation. Together, these elements have provided a clear definition of the ends, an apparatus to deliver the means, and the personal leadership to ultimately guide joint initiatives in the Great Lakes region. In essence, these elements have provided the framework for the collaboration.

The emergence of institutional structures for regional cooperation

The case has been made that the revival of New England from its 1950s depression began not with a rise in any particular industry or indicator, but with the emergence of a broad set of institutions studying its problems as a region, advocating regional action, and providing turf where governments and economic interests in the region could meet. Such a regional institutional network is essential. While regional action must stem from the will and prerogatives of sovereign jurisdictions, the ultimate survival of joint initiatives may depend on the capacity for those initiatives to exist external to any single jurisdiction. The metamorphosis from common interests among separate jurisdictions to collective projects seems to depend upon institutional settings for "incubating" project ideas, designing implementation strategies, and carrying out a joint agenda.

A number of such institutions have emerged in the Great Lakes region in the last decade, providing a broad capacity for cultivating, supporting and implementing joint projects.

The analysts

The region contains a number of institutions which conduct research and analysis of "Great Lakes" issues. The Federal Reserve Bank of Chicago has provided pictures of the region as an economic whole—most notably through the production of the 1984 *Great Lakes Economy* book. Major studies on the alternative paths for the Great Lakes economy were undertaken by Ameritrust and The Long Term Credit Bank of Japan, along with regular trend analysis by First National Bank of Chicago.

The creation of the Center for the Great Lakes in 1984 provided the region with a permanent institution to undertake research and analysis on a range of more focused policy questions. The Center's first major effort sought to outline in detail the economic significance of the lakes. In addition, the Ameritech Corporation was instrumental in creating regional economic policy analysis centers at the University of Illinois, Indiana University, and Case Western Reserve University. Each of these centers have undertaken research of policy problems and trends in a regional context.

Together, these institutions provide an essential foundation for the germination of joint initiatives. They provide a capacity for defining common problems, recognizing common stakes, and forging alternatives for collective action.

Vehicles for action

The Great Lakes region also contains a number of institutional mechanisms for the states and provinces to undertake collective action. Most notable among these are The Great Lakes Commission and The Council of Great Lakes Governors. The Commission brings together a broad base of state actors. The Council serves the governors alone. The distinction provides a basis for the organizations to pursue different types of collective agendas.

In addition to the Commission and the Council, the Great Lakes-St. Lawrence Conference of Mayors and the Council of Great Lakes Counties provide forums for dialogue, and program and policy exchange among local leaders in the region. Institutions for program specific regional action

have also emerged, bringing together state and provincial officials in a specific policy area. The Lakes States Forestry Alliance is one example of a vehicle for implementing joint initiatives in single issues areas.

Formed in the late 1970s, the Northeast-Midwest Institute was created (by the Northeast-Midwest Congressional and Senate Coalitions) to provide a source of research and analysis of issues facing the northern industrial states. The Institute's numerous studies tend to focus on public policy approaches to reshaping the region's economy.

Finally, by the end of the 1980s, efforts were underway to form a Council of Great Lakes Industries. The Council would provide a forum for private sector interaction and collective action in the states and provinces. While each of the vehicles for joint action cited above engage the private sector in specific programs, private industry currently has no mechanism for setting its own regional agenda.

The catalysts

Finally, the environment for collaborative ventures has been aided by the presence of institutions supporting the development of regional agendas. The Joyce, Ameritech, Gund, Kellogg, and Mott foundations have provided both financial support for developing cooperative ventures and played a critical role in creating dialogue among state and provincial officials and the policy community.

The evolution of common economic strategies

A second major enabling condition for joint initiatives has been the degree of convergence among state and provincial economic development strategies. By the mid-1980s, the core economic strategies of the states and provinces shared similar principles and premises. The strategies converge around the notion that states and provinces must invest in the creation of new economic capacities: technology transfer, export development, education, work training, and workplace organization. These strategies reflect a marked departure from the dominance of smokestack chasing in the 1970s.

The implicit premise of capacity building strategies is that the future of state and provincial economies depends upon the creation of an infrastructure for innovation and adaptability. The cornerstone of the state and provincial programs

has been science and technology initiatives. As Figure 1 reveals, most of these programs are less than 10 years old, and they share a common focus of fostering public/private partnerships to improve the technological base of existing businesses and provide a catalyst to the formation of new enterprises . Moreover, as they have evolved, most of these programs have invested in the common economic base of the region—advanced manufacturing.

The convergence of economic strategies around policies and programs for new business formation and retention creates a context for collective action. In contrast to business recruitment strategies, programs concerned with technology, export, tourism, and training clearly lend themselves more readily to exchange and cooperation. Moreover, the development of these programs has created a cadre of state agency officials who share common tasks, orientations and program settings. Interaction and greater comfort with the concept of cooperation has been an outgrowth of program staffs proceeding along a common learning curve together.

Finally, and most importantly, it is essential to recognize that this strategic convergence is a by-product of the personal leadership of the governors and premiers. These programs and strategies reflect their vision of the future of the states and provinces and they have given personal encouragement and support to cooperative ventures.

The emergence of the global economy

The final factor contributing to the creation of a framework for joint initiatives has been the clear recognition that economic competition is international in nature. Regional economic cooperation is more viable and essential in an international context. In the context of a domestic economy, cooperation among jurisdictions is largely framed by disputes over federal policy questions or natural resource issues and is, therefore, inherently limited.

An international focus fosters a framework for cooperation along broader and often common concerns. This contextual difference stems from the fact that international competition expresses itself regionally. International competition is essentially sectional in nature and, with sectors continuing to remain regionally clustered, competitiveness strategies lend themselves to a regional focus.[3] In

FIGURE 1

State technology programs

Illinois

Illinois operates 13 Technology Commercialization Centers. The Centers receive $3-4 million a year to aid business, inventors, and entrepreneurs with new venture creation, commercializing and marketing new technology, product testing, and developing prototypes.

The state provides an additional $18.6 million through a Technology Challenge Grant Program, which supports the advancement and development of pre-competitive or enabling technologies. A Technology Venture Investment Program provides up to $500,000 in equity or debt financing to technology-driven businesses commercializing new or advanced technologies.

Indiana

The Indiana Corporation for Science and Technology is a public/private partnership that identifies and develops technology-intensive products, processes and services. CST has recruited more than 500 volunteer scientific and technological experts in the university and industrial communities who counsel and assist small business growth and stability.

Each year CST distributes $10 million in grants for research aimed at commercializing and marketing new products. CST also funds a Manufacturing Technology Service and the Indiana Microelectronics Center, which help small companies achieve competitiveness through the use of modern manufacturing processes and products.

Michigan

Using private resources to build a more effective business financing infrastructure is the philosophy behind the Michigan Strategic Fund(MSF). MSF has established nine industry-university consortia that are meeting grounds for technical leaders, small technology vendors and customers who work together to define the projects that will keep Michigan's economy competitive. MSF established the Industrial Technology Institute, the Michigan Biotechnology Institute, the Metropolitan Center for High Technology, and NSFNET, a computer system connecting the National Science Foundation's supercomputer centers.

Minnesota

The cornerstone of Minnesota's technology initiatives is the Greater Minnesota Corporation(GMC), a non-profit agency funded by proceeds from the state lottery. GMC promotes applied research, technology transfer, and product development, concentrating on enhancing the economy outside of the Minneapolis/St. Paul metropolitan area. GMC programs include the Agricultural Utilization Research Institute, the Natural Resources Research Institute, technology research grants, regional manufacturing technology centers, and regional seed capital funds.

The state funds a variety of other programs, including Minnesota Project Outreach which provides on-site computer access to expertise at the University of Minnesota. Nationally-recognized research centers include the Minnesota Supercomputer Institute, the Center for Interfacial Engineering, the Institute for Advanced Studies in Biological Process Technology, and the Microelectronic and Information Sciences Center.

New York

The New York Science and Technology Foundation, a public corporation, operates a range of financial and technical assistance programs. Among them is the Corporation for Innovation Development Program, which provides vital start-up capital to new technology-based ventures; the Centers for Advanced Technology, which facilitate the transfer of technology from New York's top research universities into commercially viable products; and the Regional Technology Development Organization Program, which develops support networks in management, finance, and resource planning.

New York provides grants to universities, colleges and non-profit laboratories to conduct research having distinct potential for industrial application. The Education and Research Network (NYSERnet) accelerates the rate of technology transfer through a unique high-speed data communications network linking the Cornell University supercomputer with New York's leading research institutions, laboratories and industrial firms.

Ohio

Private investments of more than $149 million have more than matched Ohio's $104.2 million investment since 1983 in eight Edison Technology Centers. The centers, which focus on specific applied research, are one of three components in the state's internationally-recognized Thomas Edison Program.

The Edison Seed Development Fund offers matching grants of up to $300,000 for business and university research partnerships that will turn innovative ideas into commercial successes. Seven Edison Incubators help young companies by providing low-cost space, office services, and technical and business consulting to ease their transition to the open market.

Pennsylvania

Named for Pennsylvania's foremost inventor, the Ben Franklin Partnership(BFP) fund supports a wide range of initiatives to spur new advanced-technology companies, to improve the competitive stance of small, technology-oriented firms, and to develop a technologically skilled workforce.

BFP administers a Challenge Grant Program for Technological Innovation. Four state technology centers track fundable projects that promote research and development between private companies and universities, technology transfer, entrepreneurial development, education and training, and regional or statewide technology development initiatives.

BFP also administers a Technology Business Incubator Program, which makes grants and loans up to $650,000 to business incubators in economically distressed areas, and a Research Seed Grant Program, which awards up to $35,000 to help individuals or small companies develop and market new technology.

Wisconsin

Wisconsin allocates more than $7 million a year to the Wisconsin Development Fund—Small Projects Program, which operates under the Department of Development, Division of Research and Planning. The money supports technology development, customized labor training, applied research, technology-based incubator programs, and a Small Business Innovation Research (SBIR) program, which supplements participants in the federal SBIR up to $40,000 a year.

The Technology Development Fund provides matching grants and loans of up to $250,000 to a consortia of business and higher education institutions to support research and development of significant technology for Wisconsin business growth, retooling, or diversification. DOD also administers an Applied Research Program and a Technology Incubator Program.

A Manufacturing Assessment Service Center will begin work this year to help firms identify ways to improve productivity and quality.

addition, international trade continues to play an increasingly central role in defining the economic vitality of the national economy. The major trade developments of recent years, the Free Trade Agreement (FTA), the 1992 unification of European markets, and the prospects for a North American trade zone all hold distinct policy consequences and imperatives for regions.

Joint initiatives of the 1980s

This Great Lakes framework of cooperation has played a role in the flowering of many joint initiatives. For example, major studies of the regional economy, the management of task forces creating an environment for the states and provinces to interact, and forums and conferences on regional problems are all evident in the activities of the 1980s. The projects below highlight the broad range and diversity of collaborative initiatives. The mix includes state and provincial cooperation to address specific sectors, to manage shared resources, and to respond to national and international policy developments. The projects have experienced disparate histories. Some evolve into ongoing efforts, others are short-lived.

The Midwest Technology Development Institute: Creating synergy among state technology programs

One of the first efforts to shape a common agenda for the economic transformation of the Great Lakes region was the formation of the Midwest Technology Development Institute (MTDI) in 1984. MTDI was spearheaded by Control Data founder William C. Norris, and sought to create a vehicle for states, universities and industries to collectively invest in technologies which would provide a foundation for a revitalized economy.

Norris specifically sought to model MTDI after Japan's Ministry of International Trade and Industry (MITI). The intent was to use MTDI as a mechanism for setting a consensus agenda for technology development, creating consortia among industries and universities, leveraging federal and foreign investment, and ultimately speeding the introduction of new technologies into the marketplace.[4] While MTDI involved twelve midwestern states, it was the Great Lakes states of Illinois, Indiana, Minnesota, Michigan and Ohio that provided the

driving force. In its initial stages, MTDI concentrated on creating consortia to enhance the dissemination and adoption of low input agriculture technologies, which ultimately led to the formation of a center at the University of Illinois at Champaign for alternative agriculture.

MTDI was largely disbanded by 1989, but not before it had made important contributions to the evolution of regional cooperation. First, MTDI helped foster dialogue among the state technology programs (most were less than a year old at the time). This dialogue set the stage for a wide range of collaboration actions among individual states and also for more focused regional efforts later in the decade. Second, while the formation of consortia proved difficult to manage on a multi-state basis, MTDI succeeded in clearly establishing a sense of a common regional stake in key technologies and industries. Finally, MTDI's commitment to focus its initial energies on environmentally sound technologies provides an important model for linking economic and environmental objectives.

Lake States Alliance: Collective action to manage and promote a common resource

The Lake States Forestry Alliance (LSA) was created in 1987 by the governors of Wisconsin, Minnesota and Michigan. The impetus for the Alliance stemmed from a 1984 conference and report by the Conservation Foundation. The report stressed that joint action was critical both to improve management of forests in three states and to increase regional and national awareness of the forests' economic significance.[5]

In its initial years LSA has worked to balance its management and development agendas. The Alliance has developed mechanisms for the states to collectively recruit forest product firms and produced a multi-language catalogue of products and services in the region. LSA officials have also sought federal support for a forest products trade center. The center would be housed at universities in the three states and assist small forest product firms to develop export strategies.

Paralleling these development initiatives has been LSA's efforts to devise a common inventory of forest resources, improve coordination among state forestry programs, and shape a more responsive

federal forest management agenda. Toward this end, the LSA played a key role in securing passage of provisions in the 1990 Farm Bill to increase funding for the development of professional management plans to better guide commercial timber harvesting.

Great Lakes Machine Tool Commission: Fostering recognition of a common stake in Great Lakes industries

The Great Lakes Machine Tool Commission was one of the first economic initiatives of the Governors following the formation of the Council of Great Lakes Governors in 1983. The intent of the Commission was to bring together industry, government, labor, and academic leaders to focus on the competitive health of a sector common to each of the Great Lakes states.

The Commission was divided into work groups focusing on technology, training, trade, finance, and tax issues. The Commission report set forth common federal policy positions and outlined innovative proposals for technology consortia and the creation of financial pools to fund modernization.[6]

The work of the Commission played a role in coalescing industry support for the creation of a National Center for the Manufacturing Sciences. The Center, located in Ann Arbor, is a federal-industry partnership for developing machine tool technologies.

In retrospect, potential follow-up on many Commission actions was not fulfilled. At that time state programs, which could have provided a vehicle for action on technology and training recommendations, were either in formative stages or not yet in place. Hence, while the Commission experience demonstrated that the region could successfully recognize economic interdependence, it also underscored the need for an infrastructure to support follow-up on regional initiatives.

The Great Lakes Circle Tour: Building intergovernmental cooperation around the tourism potential of the Great Lakes

The Great Lakes Circle Tour spearheaded by the Great Lakes Commission represents a significant effort to build state and provincial cooperation by cultivating a rapidly emerging regional industry—tourism. By the end of the 1980s revenue and employment gains in tourism had made the sector the second or third largest industry in virtually every state and province.

The Commission's goal was to create a state and provincial cooperative venture to develop and promote the 6,500 mile scenic road system connecting the Great Lakes and the St. Lawrence River. In doing so, the Commission created a task force bringing together state and provincial tourism and transportation staff. The Task Force assisted in identifying common signage for the tour, created a common promotional piece and fostered dialogue on the tourism potential among communities along the route. By mid-1990 several new sections of the tour had been opened.

The Circle Tour represents a critical contribution to the evolution of collaborative activity. The Tour project both linked states and provinces and fostered cooperation across development and infrastructure departments and interests. In addition, the Circle Tour project provided a link between state and provincial cooperation, and local communities. The high degree of coordination required to develop the Tour infrastructure provides a prototype for linking state and provincial local community strategies for the purposes of integrating tourism and promotion into an economic development framework.

The Midwest Manufacturing Network Project

In general, collaboration among the states, and among the states and provinces, has been project focused, i.e. aimed at enabling agencies to perform a common function cooperatively. In contrast, the Midwest Manufacturing Network Project (MMNP), seeks to foster collaboration around the incubation and development of strategies themselves.

Funded by the Joyce Foundation, the MMNP brings together the states of Illinois, Indiana, Michigan and Ohio. The goal of the project is to encourage interaction among the states in the development of programs to stimulate and assist the growth of manufacturing networks. These networks are organized clusters of competing firms collaborating in analysis, research, production, marketing or distribution activities.

More specifically, the project explores the applicability of the "Italian Model" to the region.

The model focuses on the economic evolution of the Emilia-Romagna region of Italy. As with the Great Lakes, Emilia-Romagna experienced a dramatic shakeout in its large scale manufacturing base during the 1960s. It has since returned to economic vitality through the emergence of highly diverse small manufacturers. These small firms have remained competitive through complex cooperative networks which facilitate exchange and provide a cost-effective means for high quality, high value added production.

The states have developed network programs under the direction of C. Richard Hatch, a leading proponent and implementor of the network model. The exchange of ideas has led to challenge grant programs in three of the states to encourage network development. Efforts are currently underway to develop cross-state training of network "brokers" and to undertake a joint project to assist a multi-state network.

Great Lakes: Great Future—The Governors Economic Development Agreement

The governors of the Great Lakes states established a broad based collective agenda in signing a regional economic development agreement in 1988. The Agreement was an outgrowth of the work of a 60 member commission drawing on business, labor, and academic leaders and state, federal, and local officials.

The report accompanying the Agreement, *Great Lakes Great Future: Growth Through Cooperation*, identified three basic factors as central to the future of the regional economy: maximizing skills and opportunities for individuals; fostering a climate conducive to innovation; and strengthening the international orientation of the region. The Agreement set forth a set of initiatives in each of the areas. Implementation of the Agreement has centered in the following areas.

GREAT LAKES CANADIAN TRADE LIAISON: In 1990 the states opened the first joint trade office in Toronto. The office focuses on export and joint venture development in six targeted sectors.

NORTH AMERICA'S FRESH COAST CAMPAIGN: Launched in 1989, the Campaign links the states and the Province of Ontario in an effort to attract international visitors. The Campaign has initially

targeted the United Kingdom. By the end of 1990 the campaign had developed three new promotional pieces, introduced 20 new tour packages to bring U.K. visitors to the region, and begun a London based marketing effort aimed at educating the British travel industry.

GREAT LAKES RESEARCH NETWORK: Since 1989 the states have collectively identified and supported a common agenda for federal research funding. Through the Network, the governors collectively adopt an agenda of regional research projects aimed at key commercial technologies. The overall goal of the Network is to foster innovation by increasing federal investment in technologies critical to Great Lakes industries. In its first two years, the Network assisted in attracting $100 million in federal funds for projects ranging from plant biotechnology to superconductivity.

INTERNATIONAL TRADE POLICY: Under the auspices of the Agreement, the governors conducted a joint trade policy mission to Canada at the outset of the FTA and created a process for annual dialogue with the premiers of Quebec and Ontario. The first governors-premiers roundtable focused on the common challenges and opportunities facing the region as a result of the 1992 unification of European markets.

GREAT LAKES STRATEGY BOARD: In the fall of 1990 the governors convened the Great Lakes Strategy Board. The Board consists of representatives of business, labor, and government in each of the states. The mission of the Board is to develop policy positions and projects for consideration by the governors which build upon partnerships among management, labor, and government, to improve the competitiveness of the region.

The Agreement aspires to identify and implement a broad based agenda for the region's governors. The key challenges are to create a synergy among these diverse initiatives and also to stimulate the region's capacity to adapt to changing conditions and opportunities.

Binational ventures: Bringing the FTA to life

The enactment of the Canadian-U.S. Free Trade Agreement acted as a catalyst to the emergence of a wide range of binational cooperative initiatives. Formal agreements outlining a common agenda for cultivating greater economic interaction were developed between Ontario and Michigan, Quebec and New York, and Minnesota and Manitoba. These agreements set in motion activities ranging from joint trade and tourism missions in Europe to initiatives aimed at improving infrastructure and transportation systems.

A similar wave of activities unfolded at the local level. Efforts are underway to form a binational coalition of chambers of commerce. Sister city arrangements have been developed to stimulate trade and tourism and improve air travel service. An especially promising focus of these ventures has been to establish dialogue on common economic problems—ranging from rural development to labor force retraining.

The long term value of these initiatives will depend on their ability to instill a sense of shared economic destiny. As the emergence of regional trade blocs continues, the vitality of the states and provinces will be increasingly linked. Consequently, the capacity to evolve modernization, training, and technology programs for the industrial Great Lakes as a whole will be the major economic policy challenge of the 1990s.

Conclusion: Looking ahead to the 1990s

The emergence of collaborative activity within the Great Lakes region during the 1980s has clearly been dramatic. The ventures outlined in the preceding section include a diverse set of jurisdictions and agencies, and they focus on a broad array of issues.

Several conclusions warrant emphasis. First, collaboration has taken many forms and paths. Regional ventures flow not from any over-arching structure, but rather are as decentralized and pluralistic as government in the two nations. This diversity facilitates flexibility, experimentation, and a wide range of activity. It places a premium, however, on creating interaction and partnerships across initiatives. Efforts are underway to link the Circle Tour and the Fresh Coast Campaign. If collaborative efforts are to ever reach the scale and scope needed to effect both the economic and policy making landscapes, interaction and synergy will be essential.

Second, an unstated but common factor in each of the initiatives outlined has been the instrumental role of personal leadership of governors, premiers, agency heads and key private sector leaders. The 1980s were years of collaboration in part because it was a decade dominated by regional leaders. It will be essential to nurture a new generation of regional leaders.

Third, while industry and labor have played roles in several of the initiatives covered in this chapter, the private sector as a whole has not been sufficiently engaged in regional action. Mechanisms for integrating a broader array of actors and interests in regional initiatives will be critical.

Finally, it must be stressed that the success of cooperative ventures among states and provinces depends upon the vitality of the overall environment which nurtures and supports collaboration, i.e. the analysts, vehicles for action, and supporters. Much of the impetus for joint action in the 1980s stemmed from studies and conferences that the region's institutions undertook focusing on common regional, economic, and environmental problems. The evolution of cooperative action may depend upon how well these institutions contribute to assessing the region's changing conditions and imperatives as the touchstone for further collaboration in the 1990s.

In looking to the 1990s the key question to be addressed is whether the initiatives summarized above prove to be merely isolated episodes, or the beginning of an ongoing transformation of governance. The revolution of cooperation begun in the 1980s has demonstrated that this region can recognize and act on its common interests. As a result, entering the 1990s the economic position of the region is distinctly different.

The Great Lakes states have evolved from being the "rust belt" to the "export machine", with some analysts holding that manufacturing exports from the region were the last safeguard against a prolonged national recession. At the same time, the region's industrial revival has put the region's economic and environmental challenges on a collision course. The imperatives for economic modernization and competitiveness continue to face those industries that will also be called upon to meet

increasingly stiff environmental regulations. Regional action holds the greatest promise for forging a sustainable economic agenda. The challenge of the 1990s will be for the region to build upon the foundation set in the 1980s to shape a vision of common future.

NOTES

[1]See Robert Goodman, *The Last Entrepreneurs: America's Regional Wars For Jobs and Dollars*, South End Press, Boston, 1979, pp. 2-9.

[2]For a review of the broad theories of regionalism, see Ann Markusan, *Regions, The Economics and Politics of Territory*, Rowman and Littlefield, New Jersey, 1987.

[3]For a more precise linkage between geographically based industries and the dynamics of international competition, see Michael Porter, "The Competitive Advantage of Nations", *Harvard Business Review*, March-April 1990, pp. 73-93.

[4]See *Introduction to the Midwest Technology Development Institute*, (pamphlet), MTDI, St. Paul, Minnesota, 1986.

[5]See William Shands and David H. Dawson, *Policies for the Lakes States Forests*, The Conservation Foundation, 1984.

[6]See *Final Report of the Great Lakes Machine Tool Commission*, Council of Great Lakes Governors, Madison, Wisconsin, 1984.

Chapter 14

Toward Sustainable Development in the Great Lakes and St. Lawrence River Basin

DANIEL K. RAY, HEAD OF RESEARCH,
THE CENTRE FOR THE GREAT LAKES

MADHU KAPUR MALHOTRA, PARTNER,
KAPUR AND MARTIN ASSOCIATES

CHRISTOPHER A. BAINES, DIRECTOR (TORONTO OFFICE),
THE CENTRE FOR THE GREAT LAKES

The resources, labour, population and wealth of the Great Lakes-St. Lawrence region have not protected the basin from the forces restructuring its economy. The region's economy has lagged behind due to maturing traditional manufacturing industries and incomplete application of technology. Increasingly competitive world markets, high energy prices, scarcity of some resources, and shifts in population have also affected demand for the region's goods and services.

The region's businesses and governments have new economic strategies to respond to these changes. These include the areas of high value added products, services, growth of mid-sized and small business concerns, increased use of skilled labour, and export markets. The priorities of sustainable development are just beginning to be considered in these programs. Also beginning to emerge are natural resource and environmental policies that complement high value added economic activities.

The Great Lakes-St. Lawrence region should prepare and adopt economic development policies that are sustainable. By sustainable development, we mean development that meets the needs of the present without compromising the ability of future generations to meet their own needs, and that respects the limits imposed by the ability of the Great Lakes-St. Lawrence River ecosystem to absorb the effects of human activities.[1]

This study was developed by examining the economic development strategies of the provinces and states in the Great Lakes-St. Lawrence basin.[2] Each strategic plan was analyzed for the focus of future policy-making decisions. The areas of focus in each of the provinces and states will influence the economic activity and environmental conditions in the Great Lakes-St. Lawrence basin.

In April, 1990, The Centre convened a panel of Great Lakes-St. Lawrence River stakeholders to review this analysis of the region's economic development strategies. The panel was asked to identify ways in which the economic strategies being pursued by the region's governments could affect the Great Lakes-St. Lawrence River environment. Panelists were also asked to identify policies the region could use to sustain these economic developments by better managing its natural resources, while anticipating and preventing adverse effects. The Centre has supplemented the panel's findings with its own research into policies recommended to anticipate and prevent adverse impacts of the region's economic development strategies.

This report summarizes The Centre's findings. It includes three main sections:

■ Development of the Region's Economy (summarizing the development of the Great Lakes-St. Lawrence region and its effects on the Lakes).

■ Strategies for the Future (summarizing the programmes of provincial and state governments to respond to the region's changing economy).

■ Towards Sustainable Development (outlining policies recommended to integrate consideration of environmental and economic objectives and anti - cipate adverse effects on the region's ecosystem).

Other parts of The Centre's study are examining the environmental strategies of business sectors and firms that are leading the region's economic transformation. They will assess how those sectors and firms interact with the environment, particularly their use of water, energy, natural resources, and toxic substances, and the strategies they are developing to integrate the consideration of environmental and economic factors. Results of these ongoing studies will be presented in future reports by The Centre.

Development of the region's economy

The Great Lakes-St. Lawrence River[3] economy was founded on abundant natural resources.[4] Its lakes and rivers contributed to an efficient and low cost water transportation system, and assisted in the generation of electric power. The presence of resources such as iron ore, coal, other minerals and timber fostered the region's early industries.

The advantages offered by the region's natural resources and its central location led to the development of a network of specialized, mutually supportive industries, making the region a centre for the manufacture and distribution of agricultural and industrial products. For example, 72 percent of Canadian and 45 percent of U.S. steel production occurs in the region,[5] as does 95 percent of Canadian truck and car production and about 40 percent of the U.S. auto production.[6] Other key manufacturing sectors include food processing, forest products (such as pulp and paper, lumber and furniture), chemicals, rubber and plastics, electrical and non-electrical machinery (such as farm equipment, aircraft, telecommunications equipment and machine tools) and fabricated metals. The development of these industries was enhanced by the region's quality education institutions, which helped produce a highly skilled labour force.

This vibrant economy made the region a centre of wealth and population.[7] Seventy-two percent of the largest Canadian corporations and 46 percent of the largest U.S. corporations[8] are headquartered within the basin, and it is a home to 42.5 million people.[9]

The region's prosperity did not buffer the Great Lakes-St. Lawrence ecosystem from the serious damage that accompanied economic growth. Forests, prairies, wetlands, and other natural communities were severely reduced by logging, farming, and urban development. The Lakes, St. Lawrence River and their tributaries were polluted with nutrients and toxic chemicals discharged from cities, factories and farms. Pollution, overfishing, and the invasion of new species through the region's navigation system reduced or eliminated many kinds of fish. Some species of wildlife were also harmed, and the health of people exposed to toxic contamination was threatened.[10]

The concentration of resources, population, and wealth around the Great Lakes-St. Lawrence River was also unable to protect the region from the powerful forces restructuring its economy. In the past decade, the region's economy lagged as a result of maturing traditional manufacturing industries, changing demand, foreign competition, and rising energy prices. A variety of factors contributed to these effects:

■ The region's firms were often unprepared to deal with the transformation of manufacturing, distribution and marketing that resulted from the application of technology and automation. This application has been unbalanced, leaving many of the basin's firms at a disadvantage in comparison with those elsewhere. Innovative information technologies, such as computers and telecommunications, have since increased the productivity of individual firms and improved the performance of entire networks of suppliers, manufacturers, distributors and sellers.[11]

■ World markets became more competitive due to the recovery of European and Asian industries, the development of manufacturing capacities in previously undeveloped countries, and the decline in world shipping prices. At the same time, unfavorable currency exchange rates[12] and the inability of Great Lakes ports and the St. Lawrence Seaway to accommodate large, highly efficient ships[13] decreased the region's ability to compete for international markets.

■ The population base of the region shifted. Population grew in some metropolitan areas such as Ontario's Golden Horseshoe, metropolitan Chicago, and Indianapolis. Toronto's population, for example, increased 21.2 percent from 1976 to 1988,

twice the Canadian average.[14] These metropolitan areas offered a high quality of life, including cultural and environmental amenities, that helped to attract and maintain a skilled labour force. Small businesses and the service sector were able to prosper in these cities due to the concentration of the population.[15]

Population growth slowed in many other parts of the region, and in some areas population has actually declined. For example,[16] Quebec's population grew at a rate of less than 1 percent annually, while the populations of Michigan, Pennsylvania and Ohio declined between 1980 and 1985.[17] Those who left were often the most skilled and productive workers.[18]

The maturation of the "baby boom" generation and the large numbers of women and minorities entering the workforce also influenced the region's economy increasing the demand for a diversity of goods and services.[19] Facilitating the entry of these new participants into the work force has required major investments in education and other training, and the restructuring of jobs and the work place with services such as day care.

■ Some key resources of the region have been depleted, driving up the cost of raw materials. For example, reserves of high grade iron ores in the iron ranges of Minnesota have been largely used up. The lower grade ores that remain must now be processed before they are shipped, thus increasing costs to steel producers. The development of new materials and the improved efficiency with which many industries use resources have also reduced demand for some of the region's key products. The reduction in demand for steel due to the increased use of plastics, the advent of mini-mills which recycle steel, and the more efficient use of steel provides an example. As a result, the comparative advantage that the region's abundant resources provide to manufacturers is declining. Rising energy costs have also placed a heavy burden on the region's manufacturers who are more heavily dependent on energy than their European and Japanese competitors.[20]

■ The limits of the environment's ability to absorb waste have eliminated or constrained some activi-

ties, such as tourism, commercial fishing and, in some harbours, navigation. Protecting the environment has imposed new costs on the region's residents and businesses through the introduction of discharge permits, pollution control equipment and cleanup costs. While these pollution control costs are comparable to those of our competitors in western Europe and Japan, concern has been raised because these costs can undermine the firms' abilities to allocate capital to other elements of plant modernization or expansion, and they may place some firms at a competitive disadvantage with businesses in less developed countries.

Strategies for the future

At first, Great Lakes-St. Lawrence River firms and governments reacted to these economic challenges by seeking protection from foreign competition, governmental aid for existing firms, and grants and other "smokestack-chasing" inducements for new industries to locate in the region. Over time, more proactive strategies for anticipating and responding to these changes have evolved. Now, the region's firms and governments are becoming technological innovators, striving to stay one step ahead of competitors springing up across the globe. The region's natural resources and manufacturing sectors have become more efficient, using raw materials and labour more carefully and "raising the technological stakes", improving their manufacturing processes and products to match or exceed those of foreign manufacturers. Their strategy, in the words of one regional economist, has been "to do what we do, smarter and better".[21]

Provincial and state economic development programmes propose further transformations of the region's economy. Many of the policies they propose are intended to assist the region's firms in developing new, higher-value, higher-quality products and services, so as to make the region less vulnerable to low-cost competitors overseas. These policies build on the region's rich legacy of quality education, a tradition of investment in research and development, a mature and highly developed infrastructure and transportation system, and a highly diversified resource base.[22]

These new strategies can be seen in the response of both business and government to the challenges of economic change.

1. HIGH VALUE ADDED PRODUCTS. One response to these economic changes has been to produce higher value added products; especially products requiring precision engineering, testing and maintenance, custom products tailored to buyers' specific needs, and technology-driven products depending on rapidly changing technologies.[23] Examples include precision castings, pharmaceuticals, machine tools employing advanced manufacturing technologies, telecommunications equipment, and specialty papers, metals, chemicals and food products. Other targeted sectors include aerospace equipment, plastics, and biotechnology.[24] Increasingly, these products are replacing the standardized, mass-produced goods that once dominated Great Lakes-St. Lawrence River industries.

In part, these changes in product lines respond to foreign competition, especially from low-wage, newly industrialized countries. For example, precision products are relatively protected from foreign competition because they require technology and levels of worker training available in only a few countries. Manufacturers of custom products seek their edge in finding and supplying highly specialized markets from the Great Lakes-St. Lawrence River region's central location as opposed to an overseas location. Products that depend on rapidly changing technology are also relatively protected against competition from less developed foreign countries and benefit from the region's universities, laboratories, and other research and development centres. The shift to high technology and specialty products is also a response to the possibilities created by computers, telecommunications equipment and the diverse tastes of modern consumers.[25]

Such technologically innovative sectors are becoming critical to the success of the region's economy. They are the focus not only of sectors like transportation equipment, aerospace, telecommunications, instruments and other machinery in which the region's technical skills seem obvious, but also in more traditional, resource-oriented sectors. Specialty food products are growth sectors in parts of the region's farm belt. In the region's forested zones, wood and paper products also display this trend. There are many new manufacturers emphasizing high value added products such as cabinetry and specialty office furniture,[26] commercial printing,[27] the manufacture of windows and doors, and making heavy use of new technologies, like precision forestry tools, optical scanners and lasers.[28]

The region's governments have undertaken a variety of programmes to strengthen and complement this shift to higher value added products by supporting the development and application of new technologies in the region's industries. In 1987, the Great Lakes state governments (excluding New York) provided business incentives for technology development totalling $67.6 million.[29] These incentives take a variety of forms:

■ Centres of Excellence and specialized research facilities to encourage the development of new technologies serving the region's manufacturers have been created or proposed in Quebec, Ontario, Minnesota, Michigan, New York, Ohio, Indiana, Wisconsin and Illinois. They focus research on such priority topics as advanced manufacturing and production technologies, new materials, information and computer sciences, biotechnology, telecommunications, laser and light wave technology and space science. In Ontario, there are six Centres of Excellence which have been granted a total endowment of $200 million over a five year period.[30] Quebec hosts the Institute for Biotechnology Research, constructed at a cost of $61 million.[31]

These facilities build on the region's already strong government and university research facilities, which include fourteen of the top 30 graduate university programmes ranked in the U.S.[32] Several jurisdictions' economic development strategies, particularly Ontario, Indiana, and Wisconsin, stress the importance of focusing government and university research to better serve high value added industries.

■ Clearinghouses and other services to encourage the transfer of new technologies to the region's industries have been developed in Ontario, Minnesota, Illinois, Indiana, Michigan, Ohio, and New York.

■ Tax incentives encouraging investments in research, development and the application of high technology are provided in Ontario[33] and Quebec. For instance, Quebec does not tax federal research and development tax credits and further offers a two year tax holiday on personal income of high calibre researchers.[34] It has also created a $300 million technology fund.[35] Equity investments in technology-based companies are also provided by Illinois,[36] Indiana[37] and New York.[38]

In addition, most of the provinces and states proposed to increase funding for maintenance and improvement of highways and bridges in their infrastructure programmes, recognizing the premium placed on fast, reliable transportation of comparatively high-value products, rather than low-cost transport of bulk materials. In Quebec, infrastructure investments have also included development of deep-draft container-handling port facilities serving transoceanic trade in manufactured goods.

2. SERVICES. Emphasis has also been placed on the service sector which has experienced considerable employment growth. For instance, in Quebec, the service sector accounts for over 70 percent of employment.[39] Between 1975 and 1981, the creation of service jobs equaled the total number of new jobs in the province. In Ontario, the service sector is by far the largest part of the economy and the sector in which the bulk of employment has been created.[40] In Wisconsin, the service sector employs 65 percent of the labour force and created 97 percent of the state's new jobs between 1972 and 1985.[41] Similar trends could be reported for other jurisdictions.

In part, the growth of services reflects the increased importance of service sector workers to the region's manufacturers. While manufacturers produce more with fewer workers, they rely on a growing array of services to enhance their products' distribution and marketing. Producing precision, custom and high technology products, for example, requires the skills of greatly expanded networks of design professionals, information managers, marketing specialists and distributors.[42] Although the region has lost manufacturing jobs such as raw materials processing and product assembly, parts of the region, including Ontario, Illinois, Michigan and Ohio, have large shares of employment in such services as research and development, marketing and distribution which often add the most value to manufactured products.[43] Growth in these service sectors adds to the region's tradeable economy, the portion of the economy exposed to world trade and competition.

Growth in other service sectors, such as tourism, adds new elements to the region's economy. Tourism and recreation are now among the top five industries in every Great Lakes-St. Lawrence River province and state.[44] In part, tourism's growth reflects the increase in leisure time available to the growing retirement-aged population of the region. For example, the retirement-aged population of Toronto is expected to increase by two-thirds between 1981 and 2001.[45] Furthermore, there is a changing trend in the way that people spend leisure time. The "baby boom" generation's interest in recreation, the increased participation of women in the workforce and a slight decline in leisure time available to working people are factors which have contributed to the trend of people taking more frequent but shorter trips. The restoration of the Lakes' fisheries and increased travel by foreign visitors have also led to a growth in the region's tourism and recreation sectors.

Special provincial and state programmes to promote tourism and enhance visitor attractions sustain and complement these trends. Provincial and state tourism marketing efforts are underway throughout the basin. State and local tourism marketing expenditures in Michigan alone totalled $6.1 million in 1987. Regional efforts, such as those organized by the Province of Ontario and Council of Great Lakes Governors[46] and Great Lakes Commission, extend provincial and state efforts. Illinois' programme recommends that new visitor facilities and other tourism investments be focused on the state's Lake Michigan corridor. Similar efforts to improve tourism facilities are underway in New York and Ohio.

3. GROWTH OF MID-SIZED AND SMALL BUSINESSES. Much of the region's growth has been in mid-sized and small organizations rather than large firms. For example, in the U.S. between 1982-1984, employment in small business grew 11.4 percent, while employment growth in sectors dominated by large business was only 5.3 percent.[47] In Wisconsin, between 1969-1976, businesses having 100 or fewer

employees created 77.2 percent of all new jobs in the state, while firms employing 500 or more workers contributed only 14.8 percent of the new jobs.[48] In the period 1977-1981, the same trend occurred. Small business showed a net increase, but large firms actually registered a net reduction in total employment. Similar trends occur throughout the region.

Much of this change results from firms' strategic choices about how to produce the precision, custom and high-technology products that are providing much of the region's growth. Large, rigidly-managed firms have suffered from their inability to move quickly to serve new niche markets or to apply new production technologies.[49] Instead, the economy is increasingly organized into networks of small, highly specialized organizations linked together by information and communication technologies. Where large firms remain, they have often adopted management styles that give subsidiaries greater freedom or operate them as clusters of small "entrepreneurial" units which mimic the flexibility and creativity of small firms.[50]

The regions' provinces and states have developed a variety of programmes to assist the development of mid-sized and small businesses:

■ Equity investments or programmes that encourage investment of private venture capital in mid-sized and small businesses are offered by Ontario, Illinois, Indiana, Michigan, Ohio, and New York. For instance, Ontario fosters entrepreneurial activities by providing loans to start up companies, directing pre-venture equity investments and grant incentives to investors through the Small Business Development Corporation (SBDC). Between 1978 and 1986 this programme attracted an estimated $360 million into Ontario small businesses.[51] The Premier's Council of Ontario has also recommended that the government provide a tax exemption for investments in a special class of early-stage venture capital funds.[52]

■ Information services to assist mid-sized and small businesses in obtaining provincial and state services are offered in every jurisdiction. Ontario provides advice and information to businesses in areas such as exporting and technology licensing.

Ohio's one stop permitting programme offers small business information about the state regulatory programmes.[53]

■ Regulatory flexibility towards mid-sized and small businesses is encouraged by the economic development strategies of Wisconsin, Illinois, and Pennsylvania. One example of this is Illinois' Small Business Assistance Bureau, which reviews state agencies' regulations to assess their impact on small business and to suggest ways to make regulatory processes more flexible.[54]

■ Minority and women-owned firms are eligible for special assistance from some provinces and states. For example, New York's initiatives include efforts to increase minority and women-owned business participation in government purchasing contracts and target small business assistance to minority and women-owned businesses.[55]

The long range success of this shift toward smaller organizations is not yet clear. Recent statistics suggest that the growth of small firms' output has not matched the expansion of their employment and that small firms are less likely to invest in research and development.[56] In response to these concerns, Ontario's development strategies now emphasize mid-sized firms most capable of competing for a share of global markets.[57]

4. INCREASED USE OF SKILLED LABOUR. The region's strategies also recognize that a skilled workforce is a key advantage in a world awash in low-skilled labour. The shift to high value added products and a larger service sector have placed a premium on skilled labour, including workers with both technical and interpersonal skills. The growth of smaller firms has increased the demands for workers able to effectively link small enterprises to create production networks. While automation may replace the "labour" element of tasks, there is an increasing emphasis on imagination, a capacity for learning and an ability to work with other people.[58] Increasingly, ideal employees are those able to adapt to change and unfamiliar work, and learn new trades as a continuous part of their employment experience.

In response to these shifts, Ontario, Quebec and all of the eight states in the Great Lakes-St. Lawrence basin have developed strategic plans for improving education which stress worker training and the development of a skilled work force. Pennsylvania is typical. Its plan stresses the importance of private and public education in order to improve the competitive position and comparative advantages of the state's companies in national and international markets, to realize the full potential of the state workforce, and to assist workers' and communities' adjustment to industrial changes.[59] Overall, seven Great Lakes states (not including New York) invested $67.6 million for labour training in 1987.[60] Typical programmes include:

■ Efforts to improve primary and secondary education, such as Ontario's initiatives to reduce class size in early grades, establish new provincial benchmarks to measure performance of students, and increase use of computer and educational software in early grades.[61] Michigan's programmes emphasize strengthened new teacher certification, financial initiatives to schools which adopt a more rigorous workload and tougher graduation requirements, and increasing state funding for K-12 education.[62]

■ Adult education is another important tool enhancing the region's labour force. An example is Ontario's $50 million increase in its 1988 commitment to the adult educational system. The main objective of the Ontario Training Strategy (OTS) is short-term training in industry. Other training initiatives put forth by the Premier's Council include institutional training, apprenticeship, and specific older worker training programmes. A complementary programme, the Technology Adjustment and Research Programme (TARP), will identify critical skill shortages and changing training requirements in anticipation of the effects of technological change on work and the work place.[63]

■ Labour-management training programmes have been established. For instance, Ohio State University's Center for Labour-Management Cooperation was created to research and evaluate cooperative problem solving arrangements. The State of Ohio's Office of Labour-Management was created to assist business in adopting new management techniques.

5. EXPORT MARKETS. Increasing exports to world markets is seen as a key element in the shift to high value added products. In Ontario and Quebec, the modest size of domestic markets forces producers to seek foreign customers to gain a size sufficient to maintain the research and development costs and management skills they require. In the U.S., overseas exports of manufactured products are seen as a method of offsetting unfavourable balances of trade in other sectors, such as energy, and as a way to recover market shares lost to overseas manufacturers over past decades.

The increased freedom of Canada-U.S. trade is a key element in the growth of the region's exports. One half of the $177 billion-a-year Canada-U.S. trade starts and ends in the Great Lakes-St. Lawrence River provinces and states.[64]

To stimulate exports, the provinces and states have:

■ Opened or maintained trade offices. For example, Quebec maintains trade offices in New York and Chicago, and the Council of Great Lakes Governors has recently opened a joint trade mission in Toronto.

■ Proposed upgrading infrastructure, such as Quebec's container ports and the bridges which link Canada and the US.

■ Provided assistance to firms in marketing exports through trade missions, training, and information services. Export marketing services offered by virtually all the region's provinces and states are particularly targeted at assisting mid-sized businesses, which often lack the personnel to fully explore export opportunities. The State of New York has, through its Strategic Resurgence Fund, created the Export Assistance Programme to assist businesses in their export activities. This programme would give the state an opportunity to sponsor one or more local programmes designed to overcome obstacles faced in developing new export markets.[65]

Toward sustainable development

A commitment to sustainable development is just beginning to emerge in most of these provincial and state economic programmes. Considerations of the plans' effects on the Great Lakes/ St. Lawrence River environment are scarce. Some programmes,

notably those of Ohio and Michigan, include natural resource and environmental protection initiatives within their overall economic development strategies. But none of the provincial or state economic development documents outlines activities that link environmental and economic objectives comprehensively.

Also missing are policies to shift natural resource management towards strategies emphasizing the higher value added products and services promoted for economic development. Instead, the region's natural resource programmes display a mix of strategic orientations often better suited to exploiting low cost resources and standardized production than they are to meeting the needs of high value added manufacturing and services.

The pace at which government policies evolve to integrate environmental and economic objectives and to match public natural resources policies with high value added strategies is particularly critical. First, Canada and each province, through the convening of "round tables" on the environment and the economy, have committed themselves to developing models for sustainable development. Provincial economic development strategies will be a key measure of the depth of this commitment.

In addition, governmental policy is critical because of the public sector's large role in environmental management. Many key resources, such as water and much of the region's forest land and electric power systems, are publicly owned. Private interests impacting on these resources are highly regulated, particularly the withdrawal of water, the discharge of wastes, and the generation and distribution of electric power by private utilities. In these arenas, the public sector management must complement private initiatives if the shift to higher value added products and services is to be accomplished successfully.

Signposts of sustainable development

Sustainable development seems at times a term that means all things to all people. Some view it as development without adverse effect of any kind on the environment. Others see it as sustained development progressing along traditional patterns so long as environmental impacts are not too objectionable. Those who coined the term hoped it would come to signify a new kind of development—development that meets the needs of the present without compromising the ability of future generations to meet their own needs and that respects the limits imposed by the ability of the ecosystem to absorb the effects of human activities.[66] Sustainable development protects the resilience of the ecosystem—its capacity to withstand shocks and maintain its diversity.[67]

Some signposts of sustainable development are:

1. Maintaining the supply of natural resources. Sustainable development uses resources at levels which assure sustained yields and which maintain resources to meet the potential needs of future generations.

2. Maintaining environmental resources. Sustainable development respects ecological limits to the absorption of pollution and waste and the environment's ability to contribute to aesthetic, cultural, and moral aspects of human welfare.

3. Maintaining human populations. The carrying capacity of the land is not exceeded by sustainable development and the habitability of vulnerable sites is protected.

4. Providing equitable access to natural and environmental resources. Sustainable development avoids shifting the costs of economic growth onto the disadvantaged or transferring adverse effects to other countries or future generations. It assures that all groups have equitable access to natural resources.[68]

How can environmental and natural resource policies be integrated with "value added" economic strategies to support development that is sustainable? The sections that follow outline ideas for such policies, drawn from the provinces' and states' economic strategies, from other reports, and from The Centre's April, 1990, workshop.

Resource-based industries

In many areas of the region, resource-based production is leading economic development.[69] The basin abounds in forest and farm land to support this development. Almost 60 percent of the land around the Lakes is covered with forest and woodlands, and farms cover 30 percent. The region is a leader in pulp, paper, and particle board production, with over 170,000 wood products jobs

in just Minnesota, Wisconsin, and Michigan.[70] A quarter of Canada's total farm production, much of Canadian and U.S. dairy, sunflower, and bean production, and half of U.S. corn production occur in the region.[71]

Development of these resources has not been without environmental cost. Wetlands, mature forests, and prairies have been cleared for farming and forestry, and farm pesticides, pulp and paper effluents, and mine wastes contribute to toxic contamination of the Lakes. While the flow of products from farms and forestland continues, there are concerns that the lack of reforestation in some areas of the basin may reduce forestry resources in the future. Excess farm production is depressing some commodity prices and, in some areas, fertilizer runoff contributes to eutrophication of important bays and estuaries.

The forest products sector illustrates the divergence between high value added and standardized, mass production strategies in the region's resource industries. For example, most Canadian pulp and paper manufacturers and the expanding waferboard production in the Great Lakes states produce low-value commodities and standardized products, finding their profitability in low cost, plentiful timber resources, not high value added manufacturing.[72] Pulp and paper manufacturers in Wisconsin demonstrate the alternate, high value added approach. They are producing specialized products, attracting an ever growing number of specialty printers who seek locations close to their paper supplies.[73] Makers of furniture, doors, and windows are other examples of resource industries producing specialty products.

Policies recommended to integrate environmental objectives with the shift to higher value added production in resource industries include:

■ Recycling and improved efficiency. Demand for many resources is declining throughout the region's major markets, as products are redesigned to use fewer materials, substitute composites for basic materials, and increase knowledge content as opposed to material content.[74] Environmental policies encouraging recycling and improved efficiency of resource use are complementing these trends.

The result will be reduced demands on the region's resource base.

These trends, while reducing some impacts on the region's ecosystem, will undermine the competitive edge that some resource industries gain from the basin's abundant, low-cost resources. The effects of these shifts on the region's resource based economies has not been well considered. Nowhere is the challenge greater than in Quebec's pulp and paper industry, the province's second largest manufacturing sector[75] and the supporter of more one-industry towns than any other sector. The province, which depends on the US market for almost three quarters of its newsprint exports,[76] will be challenged by New York's intention to recycle 40 percent of its newsprint by the year 2000, fostering the development of in-state recycled newsprint manufacturers to meet this goal.[77] The province, on the other hand, at present has only one paper mill that recycles newsprint. Quebec has begun to encourage plants that de-ink newsprint[78] and to support other recycling operations. But it is unclear how newsprint mills in rural portions of Quebec and other jurisdictions of the region will successfully compete with producers of recycled paper located closer to the metropolitan areas that will supply their recyclable paper feedstocks. Producers of other raw materials, such as primary steel, face similar challenges as recycling increases and resource use declines.

■ Forest management. Until recently, wood products industries relied largely on the vastness of the basin's forests to secure their raw materials. Only a portion of the timber land harvested has been replanted,[79] and investments in timber management have been low. To maintain the advantages of abundant, low-cost wood supplies, the Great Lakes states' economic strategies are now encouraging greater investments in forest management. In Quebec too, a new forestry law requires that crown lands used for forestry be managed on a sustained yield basis.[80] The vigor with which policies to improve forest management will be implemented is still unclear. For example, while almost 60 percent of the states' forest lands are privately owned,[81] no state regulates private forest practices or requires that professional foresters oversee private forest operations.[82] Equally unclear is whether management of public forest lands will emphasize higher value hardwoods or monocultures of species suited to chipboard and pulp production.

- Forest recreation. Enhancing forest recreation is often suggested as one way to compensate for declining forest products industries. Demand for outdoor recreation, fishing, and hunting is projected to increase 60 percent by the year 2030.[83] Forest management that values environmental amenities as recreational opportunities can complement the shift to higher value added manufacturing, protecting options to develop tourism and recreation[84] to offset declining employment in basic forest products industries.

- Forest resource pricing. Developing improved methods of valuing forest resources has been recommended to better integrate environmental and economic objectives in management of the region's wood supplies. These include reviewing the practice of discounting future benefits and costs in order to factor the needs of future generations into present forest development decisions, and the use of pricing mechanisms that ensure forest management costs are more equitably distributed.[85] Such policies might also favor management of some forest areas for more mature, higher value hardwoods instead of fast growing pulpwoods. The extent to which these practices have been adopted by the provinces and states needs to be reviewed.

- Farm policies. In the farm belt, the states' plans encourage a continued focus on commodity grains and dairy products. They call for continued attention to federal agricultural policies which support farm incomes through subsidies for these products. The economic development strategies of Ohio and Illinois also stress the importance of waterborne transportation facilities which serve primarily low-value commodity producers, further evidence of the region's loyalty to these resource industries.

Alternative agricultural policies focus on increasing the value added to farm products through expanded food processing. This is the approach advocated in the economic development programs of Wisconsin, Pennsylvania, Michigan,

and Quebec. These strategies emphasize the importance of highway transportation.

Electric power

Electric power is one area where access to low-cost raw materials is essential for the continued economic success of the region's emerging industries. While the consumption of steel, cement, paper, many other raw materials, and total energy per dollar of the GNP declined or stopped growing, the use of electric power has continued to increase nearly as fast as the GNP since 1970.[86]

The region is relatively self-sufficient in electric power generation, producing almost all of the power it consumes,[87] and employs a diverse mix of locally available energy sources, including hydropower, nuclear, coal and natural gas. In Ontario and Quebec, hydropower generates 62 percent of the electricity, with 25 percent from nuclear generators and 12 percent from fossil-fueled power plants.

Fossil fueled power plants provide 80 percent of the Great Lakes states' power, and hydropower 5 percent.[88]

The importance of electric power is reflected in provincial and state economic development plans. Much of Quebec's economic development planning has focused on meeting these needs through the development of its hydropower resources. Hydro-Quebec intends to add to its generating capacity through development of the James Bay mega-project in the province's north. The price of Hydro-Quebec's electricity is low compared to the rest of Canada and the U.S, and the province is actively developing electricity-intensive industries, especially aluminum, other electrometalurgy sectors such as alloys and castings, and electrochemistry, including the production of chor-alkalis and hydrogen.[89] The province markets its surplus power in the U.S.[90] The province also funds research and development that encourages the establishment of electricity-using industries.[91]

Ontario hydro also plans to secure new supplies of electricity and expand its generating capacity. Its plans include the purchase of surplus power from Manitoba and, early in the next century, building three new nuclear-powered generators. The utility also promotes energy conservation programmes intended to reduce the growth of

electric power demands by one third over the next 25 years.[92] Other economic policies include creation of new technologies and products through research and development and reduced electric rates for target industries.

State plans also emphasize meeting growing demands for electric power by setting appropriate utility rate structures[93] and developing local coal and natural gas resources.[94]

More efficient use of electric power, on the other hand, is not emphasized strongly in Quebec and the states, receiving only minor attention at best in provincial and state strategies. This influences not only the region's demand for electric power, but also its competitive advantages in overseas markets for manufactured products. The comparative energy inefficiency of the region's products (automobiles and appliances, for example) and production systems makes the basin's products less attractive in international markets and foreign products more attractive here.[95]

In addition, many of the region's preferred new electric power sources—James Bay hydropower, Ontario nuclear generators, Midwest coal-fired plants—may conflict with environmental protection policies. A regional economy based on energy inefficient, electricity-intensive manufacturing sectors may be at risk if environmental considerations prevent construction of these planned generating facilities.

Policies suggested to integrate environmental objectives with the electric power supply policies of the region's economic programmes include:

- Research and development programmes to increase energy efficiency. The Science Council of Canada, noting that many new technologies can enhance energy efficiency through computerized design and the use of less energy intensive materials, has recommended that ministries and departments responsible for industrial competitiveness increase research in energy efficiency.[96]

- Energy pricing. Revised electric power pricing policies have also been suggested as a way to better link environment and economic programmes. Policies that provide power at less than cost or that encourage power-profligate industries may be harmful to overall economic development, diverting capital from industrial modernization or high-value service industries to construct power plants.

Water resources

The competitive advantage of the region's industry is enhanced by one of the basin's most abundant raw materials—the waters of the Great Lakes and the St. Lawrence River. These advantages are especially significant for electric utilities. They are the largest user of Great Lakes-St. Lawrence water, accounting for 97 percent of water withdrawn from the Lakes and River. Access to water is critical not only for the production of hydropower in Ontario, New York and Quebec, but also to cool nuclear and fossil-fuelled generators throughout the basin.

Power generation differs from other sectors where new technologies and environmental controls have improved the efficiency of water use. In power generators, the efficiency of water use has actually declined with advanced technology. For example, nuclear power stations consume more water per kilowatt of production than fossil-fuelled plants. As a result, water consumption in the basin has been projected to increase between 50 percent to 96 percent during the period from 1983 to 2000, largely in response to increasing electric power generation.[97]

The Great Lakes Charter encourages efforts to capitalize on the resource values of the region's water supplies. The Charter is intended to prevent the diversion of the Great Lakes' waters to other regions and encourage more efficient water management within the basin. The Charter is identified as an element of the economic development policies of Illinois, Minnesota, Wisconsin and Ohio. But its implementation has not yet been linked to other provincial and state programmes prodding the region towards a higher value added economy.

Alternative policies have been proposed to complement water resources' contribution to a higher value added economy and to integrate environmental and economic objectives. These include:

■ Manage for water quality. For many sectors, the quality of water available to manufacturing plants is as critical as the volume. The comparative advantage of the Lakes' reliable supplies of clean water is especially dramatic in high-technology applications. Emerging high value added sectors such as electronics, optical equipment, new materials, medicine, and biotechnology require well-characterized, ultra-pure materials and ultra-clean equipment and processes.[98] Increased emphasis on these factors could enhance the value of the region's water management policies in meeting both economic and environmental objectives.

■ Water pricing. Reassessing policies on water pricing has also been recommended as a way to integrate environmental and economic concerns in supply management.[99] Water use fees in the region are typically designed to recover the costs of water-supply infrastructure, and do not reflect supply and demand. Where water conservation practices have been implemented to increase the efficiency of water use, they are typically based on "command and control" procedures, not pricing mechanisms.[100] More market-oriented water pricing policies have been suggested as a way to hold down water withdrawals from the Lakes and River while spurring the increased efficiency of water use which has accompanied the shift to higher value added manufacturing.

Environmental limitations

Another key resource constraining the economy is the environment's limited ability to absorb waste. The region's pollution control and waste management policies attempt to respond to this constraint by controlling the amount of waste discharged into the environment and apportioning it among dischargers. They also emphasize developing the region's waste handling infrastructures, such as wastewater treatment plants, sanitary landfills, and incinerators. These waste management policies, however, have not yet converged with the high value added industrial strategy and the emphasis on mid-sized and small business advanced by the region's economic development plans.

Much of the region's water and air quality policy remains geared toward mass-production manufacturing, emphasizing the application of "best available control technologies" and uniform wastewater treatment standards. For example, the region's hallmark controls on phosphorous and biological pollution have depended on traditional "command and control" pollution abatement strategies and have not embraced the use of such innovations as pollution load "bubbles", transferable pollution offsets, and market incentives for pollution abatement. Several strategic plans include calls for increased regulatory flexibility, especially in dealing with small business, streamlining permit processes [101] and assessment of the impact of regulations on business.[102] Regulatory programs to test potentially hazardous substances before they are manufactured and released to the ecosystem have been swamped by the pace at which new products are being developed.[103]

Other programmes include provisions to facilitate waste disposal, efforts to provide adequate water and wastewater treatment infrastructures, enhance waste incineration and develop additional land disposal capacity.

A variety of new initiatives are reshaping waste disposal practices in the region. While these policies are often advocated to protect the environment, they have yet to be fully integrated into most of the region's economic development strategies. They include:

■ State of the environment reporting. The rapid pace of economic change requires an increased effort to monitor, assess and report potentially-related changes in the environment. These efforts include improved "state of the environment" reporting, waste audits, "cradle-to-grave" monitoring of toxic substances and environmental assessments on projects and technologies.[104] Innovations in information and instrumentation technologies and telecommunications are enhancing the region's state-of-the-environment reporting capability. Further development of these technologies, such as quicker and lower-cost tests of chemicals' toxicity, are needed.

■ Clean technologies. Increasing investment in research and development of clean manufacturing technologies has also been proposed as a way to integrate economic and environmental objectives, particularly in high value added sectors such as industrial machinery and engineering services.[105] The development and application of pollution-prevention technologies create gains in the efficiency of material use and the cost of waste disposal, increasing firms' productivity and competitiveness while reducing environmental impacts. In addition, development of these technologies could spur the competitiveness of the region's water and wastewater treatment equipment firms, a sector whose Canadian market is growing 12 percent annually.[106] New York, Ohio and Illinois offer programmes to assist industries in minimizing the production of hazardous waste. New efforts are needed to share innovative technologies with smaller firms,[107] who may not have in-house research and development capabilities, and to extend pollution prevention training to workers on the shop floor.

■ Market incentives. Market incentives have a largely untapped potential to encourage waste reduction while reducing the cost of traditional command and control technologies in terms of time and inflexibility. The advantages of more market-oriented waste reduction policies may be especially significant for sectors that place a premium on rapidly changing technology or the ability to deliver specialized products on a tight schedule. One favored approach is the use of tradeable emission credits[108] in which firms that reduce their emissions below the permitted level can sell a portion of their remaining allowance to other polluters. Another is the development of "green markets" which identify and promote environmentally benign products.

Quality of life

Portions of the region's resource policies emphasize the Great Lakes' and St. Lawrence River's contributions to tourism, the quality of life and the ability to attract and retain highly paid, well educated workers. Quebec's strategy is one example. It advertises "a quality of life unequaled in North America" as a key asset in its program to attract biotechnology and pharmaceutical manufacturers.[109] State programmes featuring quality of life emphasize waterfront development, acquisition of parks, groundwater protection, and restoration of contaminated landfills. For example, Indiana's plan states that "increasing recreational facilities, improving community appearance and developing

diverse cultural assets can produce significant rewards in attracting high-skilled, high wage earners".[110] Similar efforts are highlighted in Ohio, where economic development plans stress the amenities of waterfront development projects, the state's Lake Erie shoreline and its inland waterways. Investments in tourism and the protection of natural resources also improve these quality of life attributes. The state's programme recognizes that a high level of environmental protection is required to achieve these goals.[111] Policies which protect environmental amenities of the region's forests and waters complement these initiatives.

Contrasting with these are the programmes that call for environmental standards that do not exceed those adopted by the federal government. The report of Wisconsin's Strategic Development Commission is an example of this approach. Wisconsin's Commission acknowledged that the state's high quality of life is an asset in attracting some kinds of development. But it complained bitterly about the state's high standards of environmental protection and the perception that the state's Department of Natural Resources had an inflexible and anti-business approach to environmental protection. The report recommended that Wisconsin lower environmental standards in some key sectors so that they are no higher than the national minimum.[112] These programmes undermine the region's ability to compete with other area's by retaining or restoring a higher quality environment than is found in other areas.

New initiatives to protect shorelines, manage urban development, and reduce congestion are also needed if the quality of life is to be maintained in the region's growing urban areas. People rate low levels or air and water pollution, access to outdoor recreation, and a location near water as important quality of life assets that affect cities' desirability as sites to live.[113] With urban development already occupying 43 percent of the shoreline of Lakes Michigan, Erie, and Ontario,[114] improved efforts to protect natural lakeshores and control urban sprawl will be key in protecting the region's high quality of life.

Regional cooperation

The Great Lakes-St. Lawrence River region's landmark commitments to environmental management include not only the Great Lakes Charter, but also the Canada-US Great Lakes Water Quality Agreement, the Convention on Great Lakes Fisheries, and the Premiers' and Governors' Toxic Substances Control Agreement. These agreements recognize both the environmental and economic objectives related to their purposes. The Toxic Substances Agreement, for example, encourages greater uniformity in waste management standards amongst the region's provinces and states, partly to prevent economic competition on the basis of lowered environmental regulations. New efforts are also underway to expand the participation of citizen groups and businesses in these regional efforts.

The globalization of the economy and the transboundary effects of environmental degradation require that these regional efforts be strengthened. Suggested policies include:

■ Corporate codes of practice. A variety of trade and industry associations, such as the International Chamber of Commerce, have developed codes of practice to guide firms' environmental practices. Conservation organizations have also proffered guidelines for industry, such as the Valdez Principles. These codes often require practices which exceed the minimum standards required by law. Provincial and state economic development agencies could require adherence to such codes as a condition of assistance to targeted sectors and individual firms.

■ Uniform environmental standards. The increasing freedom of trade and the ability of firms to shift production from one jurisdiction to another will require more uniform environmental standards if the region's firms are to compete on a level playing field.[115] These concerns are complemented by the potential for damage to the region from the effects of transboundary pollution. For these reasons, renewed efforts have been recommended to fulfill the Toxic Substances Control Agreements' commitment to more compatible regional waste management standards, and to develop companion agreements on other topics. In addition, these concerns increase the region's stake in the two countries' actions on international environmental issues, such as transboundary air pollution and carbon dioxide emissions.

■ Stakeholder involvement. The increasing diversity of the region's economy and population, coupled with the complexity of the basin's environmental challenges, has increased the need to include persons with a variety of expertise and viewpoints in the policy setting process. Expanded requirements for notice and consultation among stakeholders before new technologies or projects are undertaken is one way to accomplish this. New ways of managing conflict about the environment and economy will also be needed.

Conclusion

This paper set out to examine the economic development strategies adopted by the region's provinces and states to assess how they consider environmental as well as economic objectives, and to anticipate the strategies' impact on the Great Lakes-St. Lawrence River environment. The conclusion is that, in many cases, these strategies' emphasis on higher value added products and services will reduce impacts on the environment, by reducing demands on resources, minimizing waste, and emphasizing services that benefit from a high quality environment. These beneficial impacts are not the result of explicit considerations of how to protect the environment, though, as few of the region's economic development strategies consider their effects on the Great Lakes-St. Lawrence ecosystem.

Assuring that the development advocated by these policies is sustainable will require new efforts in several areas—resource industries, electric power, water management, environmental assessment, toxic substances management, protection of the quality of life, and regional cooperation. In each of these areas, the region already has programmes that can provide the models and pathways upon which efforts to integrate economic and environmental strategies can build.

NOTES

[1]World Commission on the Environment and Development, *Our Common Future* (Oxford: Oxford University Press, 1987) p. 8.

[2]They are: *Competing in a New Global Economy* Ontario Premier's Council (1988); *Investissements Industriels Au Quebec—Les Secteurs Prioritaires: Quebecois Orientations Pour Les Annees90* Quebec Ministere de l'Industrie, du Commerce et de la Technologie (1990); *Five-Year Economic Development Strategy March 1988* Illinois Department of Commerce and Community Affairs (1988); *Technology Research and Development. Transfer and Commercialization in Illinois*, Governor's Commission on Science and Technology (1988); *Looking Forward: The Update of Indiana's Strategic Economic Development Plan*, Indiana Economic Development Council, Inc. (1988); *Looking Back: An Update of Indiana's Strategic Economic Development Plan-Strategies for the Future*, Indiana Economic Development Corporation (1987); *The Michigan Strategy: Building the Future* Michigan Department of Commerce (1988); *Building on Resurgence: Strategic Economic Policy for New York's Future*, Vincent Tese (1987); *Towards a Working Ohio: A Strategic Plan for the Eighties and Beyond—Jobs and Ohio's Economy*, Ohio Cabinet Cluster on Strategic Planning (1986); *Towards A Working Ohio: A Strategic Plan for the Eighties and Beyond—Ohio's Natural and Physical Environment* Cabinet Clusters on Infrastructure, Energy and Water (1985); *Investment in Pennsylvania's Future: The Keystone for Economic Growth* Pennsylvania's Economic Development Partnership (1988); *Report Number One*, Wisconsin Strategic Planning Council (1989); *Governor's Advisory Committee on Business Incentives: Final Report*, Wisconsin Department of Development (1987); *Wisconsin Strategic Development Commission: Final Report*, Wisconsin Strategic Development Commission (1985); *1989 Economic Report to the Governor State of Minnesota*, Minnesota Council of Economic Advisors (1989).

[3]In this text, the term Great Lakes-St. Lawrence basin is used to refer to lands within the watershed of the Lakes and the St. Lawrence River (excluding the Ottawa River) above Quebec City. The term Great Lakes-St. Lawrence region covers a broader area, including the provinces of Quebec and Ontario and the eight Great Lakes states.

[4]Federal Reserve Bank of Chicago and The Great Lakes Commission, *The Great Lakes Economy: A Resource and Industry Profile of the Great Lakes States* (Boyne City: Harbor House Publishers, Inc., October 1985), pps. v-ix.

[5]Ibid.

[6]The Centre for the Great Lakes, Institute of Water Research, Environment Canada, International Joint Commission, Great Lakes Commission and Michigan Sea Grant, *Great Lakes Basin*, Michigan Sea Grant Extension Bulletin E-1865 (1990).

[7]Maclean Hunter, *Financial Post 500* (Toronto, May 1988), pps. 64-92.

[8]Time, *Fortune 500* (New York, April 1988), pps. Dll-D32.

[9]The Centre for the Great Lakes et al.(1990); and The Centre for the Great Lakes, *The St. Lawrence River: Its Economy and Environment* by Sandy Scott, Rene Vezina and Madelyn Webb (Hamilton: W.L. Griffin Printing Limited, 1989), p. 9.

[10]Theodora Colborn, Alex Davidson, Sharon Green, R.A. Hodge, Ian Jackson, and Richard Liroff. 1990. *Great Lakes, Great Legacy?* (Ottawa, Institute for Research on Public Policy, 1990), p. xix - xxix.

[11]U.S. Congress, Office of *Technology Assessment, Technology and the American Transition: Choices for the Future* OTA-TET-283 (Washington, D.C.: U.S. Government Printing Office, May 1988), p. 15.

[12]Wisconsin Department of Development, *Exchange Rates and Interest Rate Effects on Wisconsin Employment: 1972 to 1984* (1985).

[13]The Centre for the Great Lakes, *The St. Lawrence River: Its Economy and Environment* (1989), p. 26.

[14]de Reus, Mary, *Metropolitan Toronto Business and Market Guide 1989* (Toronto, 1989), 153.

[15]U.S. Congress, Office of Technology Assessment, p. 28.

[16]The Financial Post Company Ltd., *Canadian Markets 1988/89: Complete Demographics For Canadian Urban Markets* 63rd ed. (Financial Post Company Ltd, 1989).

[17]Federal Reserve Bank of Chicago and The Great Lakes Commission, p. 17.

[18]Ohio Cabinet Cluster on Strategic Planning, *Toward a Working Ohio: A Strategic Plan for the Eighties and Beyond—Jobs and Ohio's Economy* (April 1986), p. 9.

[19]Indiana Economic Development Council, Inc., *Looking Forward: The Update of Indiana's Strategic Economic Development Plan* (1988), 2:25 (Draft).

[20]U.S. Congress, Office of Technology Assessment, p. 19.

[21]Centre for the Great Lakes, "Recasting the mold", *Great Lakes Reporter* (May/June, 1990), pps. 1-4.

[22]Federal Reserve Bank of Chicago and The Great Lakes Commission, p. vi.

[23]Reich, Robert B., *The Next American Frontier* (1983), pps. 126-133.

[24]Quebec Ministere de l'Industrie, du Commerce et de la Technologie, *Investissements Industriels Au Quebec Les Secteurs Prioritaires Quebecois Orientations Pour Les Annees 90* (May, 1990), p. 13.

[25]U.S. Congress, Office of Technology Assessment, p. 17.

[26]Michigan Department of Commerce, *Forest Products. The Future is in Michigan* (1989).

[27]Tese, Vincent, *Building on Resurgence: Strategic Economic Policy for New York's Future* (April 1987), 9. Wisconsin Strategic Planning Council, *Report Number One* (May 1989), p. 7.

[28]Minnesota Council of Economic Advisors, *1989 Economic Report to the Governor State of Minnesota* (1989), pps. 121-130.

[29]Wisconsin Department of Development, *Governor's Advisory Committee on Business Incentives: Final Report* (September 1987), Appendix A.

[30]Premier's Council, *Competing in a New Global Economy* (Toronto: Queen's Park, 1988), 1:212.

[31]Quebec Ministere de l'Industrie, du Commerce et de la Technologie, p. 23.

[32]The Federal Reserve Bank of Chicago and The Great Lakes Commission, p. vii.

[33]Premier's Council, 1:28.

[34]Premier's Council, 3:56.

[35]Quebec Minstere de l'Insurie, du Commerce et de la Technolgie, p. 11.

[36]Governor's Commission on Science and Technology, *Technology Research and Development. Transfer. and Commercialization in Illinois* (1988), p. 9.

[37]Indiana Economic Development Corporation, *Looking Back: An Update of Indiana's Strategic Economic Development Plan-Strategies for the Future* (1987), 1:18-19(Update).

[38]Tese, pps. 18 and 22.

[39]Ministry of Supply and Service Canada, *Canada-Quebec Economic and Regional Development Agreement* (1985), p. 20.

[40]Premier's Council, 1:187.

[41]Wisconsin Department of Development; Division of Policy Development, *The Economic Development Potential of the Service Industries in Wisconsin* by Dennis Koepke (July 1986), p. vi.

[42]Reich, Robert, *The resurgent liberal* (New York: Times Books, 1989), pps. 98 - 99.

[43]Irailevich, Philip R. and William A. Testa, "The geography of value added," *Economic Perspectives* (1989), XIII:2-11.

[44]The Centre for the Great Lakes, "Tourism on the rise," *The Great Lakes Reporter* (May/June 1989), pps. 1-3.

[45]de Reus, p. 154.

[46]The Centre for the Great Lakes, "Lakes tourism campaign kicks off," *Great Lakes Reporter* (Jan./Feb. 1990), p. 10.

[47]Tese, p. 24.

[48]Wisconsin Strategic Development Commission, *Wisconsin Strategic Development Commission: Final Report* (Madison, August 1985), p. 64.

[49]U.S. Congress, Office of Technology Assessment, p. 27.

[50]Tese, p. 24.

[51]Premier's Council, 1:179.

[52]Ibid., p. 183.

[53]Ohio Cabinet Cluster for strategic Planning, p. 21.

[54]Wisconsin's Strategic Development Commission, pps. 32-34.

[55]Tese, p. 60.

[56]U.S. Congress, Office of Technology Assessment, p. 27.

[57]Premier's Council, 1:51.

[58]U.S. Congress, Office of Technology Assessment, p. 34.

[59]Pennsylvania's Economic Development Partnership, *Investment in Pennsylvania's Future: The Keystone for Economic Growth* (Harrisburg, 1988), pps. 4-5.

[60]Wisconsin Department of Development (1987), Appendix A.

[61]Premier's Council, 1:223.

[62]The Department of Commerce, *The Michigan Strategy: Building the Future* (Lansing: Office of the Governor, 1988), pps. 22-25.

[63]Ibid., pps. 227-228.

[64]"Free Trade: What Does It Mean for the Great Lakes?" *Great Lakes Reporter*, (Jan./Feb. 1988), pps. 1-4.

[65]Ibid., p. 48.

[66]World Commission on the Environment and Development, *Our Common Future* (Oxford, Oxford University Press, 1987) p. 8.

[67]Munn, R. E. *Towards Sustainable Development* Proceedings of a Conference at the University of New South Wales, Australia (1990).

[68]Bartelmus, Peter, *Sustainable Development: A Conceptual Framework* United Nations Department of International Economic and Social Affairs Working Paper No. 13 (1989).

[69]U.S. Congress, Office of Technology Assessment, p. 32.

[70]"A Forestry Renaissance" *Great Lakes Reporter* 5:5 (October/Nov, 1988), pps. 1-3.

[71]Centre for the Great Lakes, et. al.

[72]State of Minnesota, *1989: Economic Report to the Governor* (1989), 121-130; and Premier's Council, 1:96-97.

[73]Wisconsin Strategic Development Commission, pps. 26-27.

[74]Premier's Council, 1:93.

[75]Gamache, Rejean. "The Forests: An Economic Mainstay for Quebec" *Quebec Economique International* (1990) 8(2): pps. 7-9.

[76]Ibid.

[77]"Newsprint Publishers Join State in Developing Plan for Increased Use of Recycled Newsprint," *Opportunity New York*, 4(1):1-13.

[78]"Quebec decides to back new plants", *Pulp and Paper Canada* 91:7 (1990), p. 9.

[79]Bird, Peter M. and David J. Rapport, *State of the Environment: Report for Canada* (Ottawa: Ministry of the Environment, 1986), p. 52.

[80]Legare, Robert. "The New Forestry Plan: Toward Responsible Forest Management" *Quebec Economique International* 8:2 (1990), pps. 16-18.

[81]Centre for the Great Lakes "A Forestry Renaissance", *Great Lakes Reporter* (October/November 1988), pps. 1-3.

[82]Ashenfelter, Barry. 1990. *Forest Practices Legislation: A Four State Comparison.* Sierra Club Midwest Office (Madison, Wisconsin), p. 6.

[83]The Centre for the Great Lakes, "A Forestry Renaissance".

[84]Task Force on Environment and Economy, p. 4.

[85]*Report of the National Task Force on Environment and Economy* (Downsview, Ontario, Canadian Council of Resource and Environment Ministers, September, 1987), p. 4.

[86]U.S. Congress, Office of Technology Assessment, p. 19.

[87]Jeffers, William. U.S. Department of Energy. National Energy Information Center, Personal Communication (May 1988).

[88]Centre for the Great Lakes "Climate Change and the Economy of the Great Lakes-St. Lawrence Basin" *Great Lakes Facts* (1988), p. 4.

[89]Quebec Ministere de l' Industrie, du Commerce at de la Technologie, p. 25.

[90]The Centre for the Great Lakes, "Utilities working to meet power demand", *The Great Lakes Reporter* (March/April 1990), p. 3.

[91]Hydro-Quebec, *Hydro-Quebec Development Plan 1987-1989* (Montreal: Hydro-Quebec, 1987), pps. 31 and 34-35.

[92]The Centre for the Great Lakes, "Utilities working to meet power demand", *The Great Lakes Reporter* (March/April 1990), p. 3.

[93]Illinois Department of Commerce and Community Affairs, *Five-Year Economic Development Strategy March, 1988* (March 1988), p. 20; and Ohio Cabinet Clusters on Infrastructure, Energy and Water, *Towards A Working Ohio: A Strategic Plan for the Eighties and Beyond—Ohio's Natural and Physical Environment* (June 1985), p. 12.

[94]Ohio Cabinet Clusters on Infrastructure, Energy and Water, p. 12; and Indiana's Economic Development, Inc., 2:38.

[95]U.S. Congress, Office of Technology Assessment, p. 19.

[96]Science Council of Canada, *Environmental Peacekeepers: Science. Sustainable Development, and Canada* (Ottawa, November, 1988), p. 15.

[97]International Joint Commission, *Great Lakes Diversion and Consumptive Uses* (1985), p. 82.

[98]The Centre for the Great Lakes, "A Competitive Edge: Great Lakes Water A Plus for Industry," *Great Lakes Reporter* (Jan/Feb 1989) pps. 1-3.

[99]National Task Force on Environment and Economy, p. 4.

[100]The Centre for the Great Lakes, "Reassessing Water: Who Will Get How Much, At What Price?" *The Great Lakes Reporter* (July/August 1989), pps. 1-3.

[101]Illinois Department of Commerce and Community Affairs, 38: and Wisconsin Strategic Development Commission, p. 32.

[102]Illinois Department of Commerce and Community Affairs, 38; and Wisconsin Strategic Development Commission, pps. 31-32.

[103]US General Accounting Office, *Toxic Substances: EPA's Chemical Testing Program Has Made Little Progress* RCED-90-112 (Washington, D.C., April, 1990) 26 pp. and Royal Society of Canada, *The Great Lakes Water Quality Agreement* (National Academy Press, Washington, D.C., 1985) p. 71.

[104]National Task Force on Environment and Economy, p. 4; Science Council of Canada, p. 16.

[105]Task Force on Environment and Economy, p. 4-5; Science Council of Canada, pps. 14-16.

[106]Science Council of Canada, *Water 2020: Sustainable Use for Water in the 21st Century* (Ottawa, 1988) p. 22.

[107]Task force on the Environment and Economy, p. 9.

[108]Task Force on the Environment and Economy, p. 5; The Centre for the Great Lakes "Putting the Market to Work", *The Great Lakes Reporter* (Jan/Feb 1990) pps. 1-5.

[109]Quebec Ministere de l'Industrie, du Commerce et de la Technologie, p. 24.

[110]Indiana Economic Development Council, Inc., 2:46.

[111]Ohio Cabinet Clusters on Infrastructure, Energy and Water, p. 26.

[112]Wisconsin Strategic Development Commission, p. 26.

[113]Eisenberg, Richard and Marguerite T. Smith "The Best Places to Live in America" *Money* (September, 1989) pps. 124-141.

[114]Centre for the Great Lakes "Climate Change and Great Lakes-St. Lawrence River Land Use" *Great Lakes Facts* (1988), 4.

[115]National Task Force on Environment and Economy, p. 6.

Chapter 15

The Great Lakes Economy: A Regional Winner in the 1990s

Diane C. Swonk, Regional Economist, First National Bank of Chicago

After better than a decade of economic decline, the Great Lakes economy is in a position to benefit in the 1990s. Ironically, the region's disproportionate dependence on manufacturing will be its source of strength. In a reversal of the early 1980s, an improvement in the trade situation will boost the demand for capital goods—machine tools and heavy equipment. A lower dollar, coupled with strong growth abroad, has already pushed capital goods exports to record highs. With an expected slowdown in imports, the manufacturers in the Great Lakes area will regain market share. The region's performance relative to rest of the country will also be boosted by cutbacks in the federal budget deficit, and the redistribution of investment from the high-cost coasts to the interior portions of the country.

Summary

The 1980s marked a decade of change for the Great Lakes economy. Two recessions, a rise and fall in the dollar, an oil price collapse, a run up in defense spending, and widespread consolidation in the farm sector all worked to magnify the differences that exist between the region and other parts of the country. The New England states experienced a virtual boom, while the Great Lakes, Southwest, and Plains experienced near depression rates of growth. Indeed, the Southwest moved from the nation's top performing to poorest performing region in the country over the period. The U.S. became a bi-coastal economy, driven by expansion in New England, the Southeast, and the Far West.

Can that type of growth be sustained in the 1990s? New England has already shown signs of weakening. Will this spread to the Great Lakes, or be isolated to the East Coast? The analysis presented in this paper suggests that the 1990s will be another decade of pronounced economic change for the region. In particular, it argues that the factors affecting regional growth in the 1980s will continue to determine regional differences in the 1990s. But a reversal of the dominant trends of the previous decade will establish a new set of regional winners and losers. The Great Lakes will benefit, while New England and the Far West slide in economic performance over the decade ahead:

■ After a slow start in 1990, the real (inflation adjusted) trade balance is expected to narrow by more than $93 billion during the next five years, moving into surplus by 1995. This will breathe new strength into the more trade-sensitive manufacturing areas of the country—the Great Lakes, and parts of the Mideast.

■ Widespread pressure to reduce the federal budget deficit, coupled with the recent developments in Eastern Europe, will force dramatic cuts in defense outlays for military research and high technology weapons production. The crisis in the Middle East will magnify the redistribution of defense outlays away from the "Star Wars" spending of the 1980s to a more traditional build-up in arms. This will adversely affect the more defense oriented areas of the country—New England, the Far West, and the Rocky Mountains.

■ The run up in the relative costs of land and labor in the more expansionary economies of the 1980s —New England and the Far West—will work against growth in those regions of the country, while the less expensive areas of the country—the Southeast, Southwest, and Great Lakes—will grow.

This paper will focus on the Great Lakes economy as defined by the Bureau of Economic Analysis (BEA). The five states of the region are Illinois, Indiana, Michigan, Ohio, and Wisconsin . The paper is organized in two sections. Section I describes the structure of the Great Lakes economy. Section II analyzes the performance of regional income, employment, unemployment, retail sales, and housing starts. These factors are all modeled for the 1980s and an outlook is provided for the 1990s. This section will also detail where the Great Lakes are expected to perform relative to the remaining eight Bureau of Economic Analysis regions.[1]

I. The structure of the Great Lakes economy

This section will discuss the structural differences that exist between the Great Lakes economy and the nation. Attention will also be given to how the Great Lakes differ from other regions in the country. In particular, this section will cover: (a) the industrial structure of the region, including agricultural and defense-related industries, (b) relative costs, and (c) population trends.

Industry structure

Table 1 shows the distribution of employment in the Great Lakes by major industry groups relative to the national average. The employment coefficient measures the distribution of employment in a region relative to the nation as a whole. For a regional industry i, the employment coefficient (EC_i) is defined as the share of employment in industry i (S_i) divided by that industry's share of employment in the nation as a whole (S).

(1) $$EC_i = S_i/S$$

At unity, the employment coefficient shows that the regional distribution of employment in industry i exactly matches the national average. Above unity,

TABLE 1

Index of Great Lakes employment concentration relative to the U.S.

Industry	Employment coefficient
Agricultural services	0.611
Mining	0.542
Construction	0.824
Manufacturing	1.270
Durable goods manufacturing	1.455
Nondurable goods manufacturing	1.005
Transportation and public utilities	0.941
Wholesale trade	0.977
Retail trade	1.021
Financial	0.888
Services	0.943

SOURCE: First National Bank of Chicago, Economic Forecasting Division.

the regional distribution of employment in industry i is greater than the national average.

Like New England, the Great Lakes has a larger share in manufacturing than the national average, especially in the durable goods sector of the economy. The employment coefficient for manufacturing is 1.270–1.455 for durable goods manufacturing and 1.005 for nondurable goods manufacturing. The nonmanufacturing industries, however, are largely underrepresented in the region. The employment coefficients for agricultural services, mining, construction, transportation, financial, and services are all below 1.0. The employment coefficient for retail trade is 1.0.

MANUFACTURING. A two-digit industry breakdown of Great Lakes' employment illustrates the region's concentration of heavy manufacturers. About half of the top 23 ranked industries in Table 2 are in manufacturing—nine durable goods producers and four nondurable goods producers. The top five are durable goods producers—motor vehicles and equipment, primary metal, fabricated metal products, rubber, and non-electrical machinery. The remaining four include: stone, clay, and glass products, electric and electronic equipment, furniture and fixtures, and miscellaneous manufac-

turing. The nondurable goods manufacturers include: paper, chemicals, printing and publishing, and food and kindred products. Combined, these industries account for 18.4 percent of total Great Lakes employment, 1.6 times the national average.

The region's relative distribution of manufacturing employment, however, has shifted over time.

In 1980, manufacturing employment accounted for 29.0 percent of the Great Lakes total. That is 1.25 times the national average for that year. In 1988, the share of manufacturing employment in the region dropped to 23.3 percent of the total. But the relative distribution of manufacturing rose—up from 1.25 to 1.27. Although this move was small, it illustrates

TABLE 2

Great Lakes employment coefficients, 1988

Industry	Ratio	Industry (continued)	Ratio
Motor vehicles and equipment	3.487	Miscellaneous business services	0.902
Primary metal industries	2.227	Miscellaneous repair services	0.898
Fabricated metal products	1.951	Mining and quarrying of non-metallic minerals, excluding fuels	0.896
Rubber and miscellaneous plastic products	1.823		
Machinery, excluding electrical	1.671	Amusement and recreation services	0.892
Paper and paper products	1.321	Furniture and home furnishings stores	0.889
Museums, botanical and zoological gardens	1.207	Instruments and related product	0.872
Printing and publishing	1.160	Special trade contractors	0.869
Stone, clay and glass products	1.150	Holding and other investment companies	0.862
Chemicals and allied products	1.147	Communications	0.850
Non-profit membership organizations	1.142	Local and interurban passenger transit	0.848
Railroad transportation	1.138	Legal services	0.847
Combination real estate, insurance, loans and law offices	1.119	Leather and leather products	0.847
		Forestry	0.820
Insurance carriers	1.102	Security and commodity brokers and services	0.814
Furniture and fixtures	1.094	Pipelines, excluding natural gas	0.802
Trucking and warehousing	1.090	General building contractors	0.792
Medical and other health related services	1.080	Real estate	0.769
Food and kindred products	1.079	Lumber and wood products, excluding furniture	0.755
Miscellaneous retail stores	1.076		
General merchandise stores	1.069	Private household services	0.678
Electric and electronic equipment	1.060	Heavy construction contractors	0.660
Eating and drinking places	1.060	Agricultural services	0.646
Electric, gas and sanitary services	1.020	Hotels and other lodging places	0.622
Petroleum and coal products	1.007	Transportation equipment, excluding motor vehicles	0.598
Personal services	0.998		
Miscellaneous manufacturing	0.991	Motion pictures	0.528
Automotive dealers and service stations	0.989	Metal mining	0.453
Social services	0.974	Water transportation	0.386
Miscellaneous services	0.960	Oil and gas extraction	0.378
Insurance agents, brokers and services	0.957	Apparel and other textile products	0.372
Coal mining	0.949	Building materials and farm equipment	0.354
Food stores	0.935	Textile mill products	0.121
Banking	0.932	Fisheries	0.118
Educational services	0.914	Tobacco manufactures	0.057
Apparel and accessory stores	0.912		
Transportation services	0.903		

SOURCE: First National Bank of Chicago, Economic Forecasting Division.

that the region did not lose manufacturers relative to the national average over the 1980s. Indeed, four of the top five manufacturing industries in Table 2 have either maintained or gained their share of employment relative to the nation over the 1980s. The employment coefficients for primary metals, fabricated metals, and rubber were higher in 1988 than in 1980; remained about the same for motor vehicles and equipment production; and posted a decline for non-electrical machinery production.

NONMANUFACTURING. The distribution of nonmanufacturing industries in the Great Lakes is much less pronounced. The region has an especially high concentration of employment in combination real estate, insurance, loan, and law offices, museums, non-profit membership organizations, railroad transportation, medical and other health services, trucking and warehousing, insurance carriers, general merchandise stores, eating and drinking places, and electric, gas, and sanitary services. Combined, however, these account for 23.5 percent of total area employment, only 1.1 times the national average.

Historically, the region's distribution of non-manufacturing industries was even smaller. In 1980, nonmanufacturing employment accounted for 71 percent of the total, 5.8 percentage points behind the national average. In 1988, nonmanufacturing industries accounted for 76.7 percent of total area employment, 3.6 percentage points behind the national average.

TABLE 4

Great Lakes agriculture

	Average acreage per farm			Average cash receipts per farm ($000s)			Average cash receipts per capita		
	GL	US	Ratio	GL	US	Ratio	GL	US	Ratio
1980	205.4	426	0.482	54.0	57.4	0.941	$579	$620	0.935
1981	206.1	424	0.486	51.4	58.6	0.877	548	623	0.881
1982	209.6	427	0.491	53.6	58.9	0.910	561	611	0.920
1983	212.2	430	0.493	54.0	58.0	0.930	556	589	0.946
1984	216.3	436	0.496	53.1	61.3	0.866	532	605	0.881
1985	221.4	441	0.502	60.2	62.9	0.957	587	604	0.974
1986	225.6	447	0.505	54.5	59.9	0.910	520	559	0.931
1987	231.4	451	0.513	54.1	62.7	0.863	496	570	0.870
1988	231.7	453	0.511	61.9	83.0	0.746	560	734	0.763
1989	234.5	456	0.514	n.a.	n.a.	n.a.	n.a.	n.a.	n.a.

SOURCE: U.S. Department of Agriculture, unpublished data.

NOTE: Ratio is the regional total divided by the national total.

DEFENSE SPENDING. Table 3 shows the distribution of per capita defense outlays for the Great Lakes versus the U.S. In 1988, per capita outlays to the region were $372, 40 percent of the national average. This contrasts per capita outlays to New England of $1279, almost 50 percent above the national average. Between 1980 and 1988, per capita defense outlays increased by $124, less than half the national average. Over the entire period, outlays to the region remained the lowest in the nation.

This lack of defense-related funding shows up in the industrial structure of the Great Lakes. Only one of the top ten defense-related industries has an especially large share of regional employment —engines and turbines manufacturing. Moreover, this actually reflects the region's link to the auto industry rather than support from the federal defense budget.

AGRICULTURE. Agriculture is more important in the Great Lakes than other regions of the country. In 1989, the region had an estimated 380,000 farms —17.5 percent of the U.S. total. The region's share of actual farm acreage, however, was much less —only 9.0 percent of the nation's total. This difference can be seen in Table 4. In 1989, Great Lakes farms were about half the size of the national

average—234.5 acres versus 456 acres—but have been increasing in size relative to the national average since 1980. A loss of more than 72,000 farms—about one third of the U.S. total—contributed to this consolidation.

Regional farm revenues fell short of the national average over the entire period (Table 4). Like New England, the summer drought of 1988 worsened the situation—per farm revenues dipped to their lowest level relative to the nation that year. Per capita farm revenues tell a similar story. For most of the 1980s, per capita revenues were better than 90 percent of the national average. In 1988, however, per capita revenues dipped to less than 80 percent of the national average.

This lower than average revenue performance also contributed to the debt burden Great Lakes' farmers carried over the period. Table 5 shows the distribution of debt in the region relative to the national average. Between 1980 and 1988, farm debt in the region jumped from 14.9 percent to 19.1 percent of total farm assets. This contrasts a shift from 16.8 percent to 18.5 percent nationally (Table 5). Since 1985, however, farm debt as a share of total assets has been shrinking in both the region and the nation.

TABLE 3

Per capita defense outlays

	GL	US average	Ratio
1980	$249	$556	0.448
1981	304	669	0.454
1982	338	757	0.446
1983	342	786	0.435
1984	367	835	0.440
1985	449	905	0.496
1986	446	903	0.494
1987	411	894	0.460
1988	372	859	0.433

SOURCE: Department of Defense, *Prime Contract Awards*.

NOTE: Includes prime contract awards, U.S. outlays only. Ratio is regional outlays divided by national outlays.

The composition of farm revenues in the region has also tended toward the national average. In 1980, regional farm cash receipts were split about 40 percent in livestock and 60 percent in crop production. This compares to a 50/50 split at the national level between livestock and crop receipts. By 1989, the distribution of regional receipts was closer to 50/50, exactly matching the national average (Table 6).

KEY INDUSTRIES. On balance, the Great Lakes maintained a tie to heavy manufacturing over the 1980s. In contrast to New England, however, defense spending did not play a key role in that industrial development. Indeed, the skew of heavy manufacturing in the region is greater than any other region in the country—no other region has a higher share of durable goods producers in their industrial makeup.

Agriculture is also important to the region. Not only does the Great Lakes have a relatively large share of the country's farm land, but the area is also more burdened with farm debt than other parts of the country.

Relative costs

RELATIVE MANUFACTURING WAGES. Table 7 shows the distribution of manufacturing wages across Great Lakes states. The First National Bank of Chicago (FNBC) Relative Manufacturing Wage Index (RMWI) is defined as the average manufacturing wage in a state (AMW_s) divided by the average manufacturing wage in the nation (AMW_{us}).

(2) $$RMWI = AMW_s/AMW_{us}$$

The regional total was compiled from the weighted average of individual state indices. The

TABLE 5

The farm debt-to-asset ratio
(debt as a share of total assets)

	GL	US
1980	14.9	16.8
1981	17.4	18.3
1982	19.1	19.7
1983	19.9	20.5
1984	23.2	22.5
1985	24.6	23.5
1986	24.1	22.9
1987	21.2	20.3
1988	19.1	18.5

SOURCE: U.S. Department Agriculture, unpublished data.

NOTE: Assets are net of non-farm household assets.

TABLE 6

Farm cash receipts in the Great Lakes region
(billions of dollars)

	Livestock	Crop	Total
1980	$10.3	$13.8	$24.1
1981	10.7	12.2	22.9
1982	11.0	12.4	23.4
1983	11.2	11.8	23.1
1984	11.1	11.1	22.2
1985	10.7	13.8	24.5
1986	10.9	10.9	21.7
1987	11.3	9.5	20.8
1988	11.5	12.4	23.9

SOURCE: U.S. Department of Agriculture, *Economic Indicators of the Farm Sector.*

weight for each state was that state's share of regional manufacturing employment.

At unity, the RMWI shows that regional manufacturing wages are exactly the same as national manufacturing wages. Above unity, the RMWI shows that regional manufacturing wages are above the national average. In general, two types of information about a region's wage structure are provided by the RMWI: (1) it shows the *direction* of wage pressures within a region (pushing wages up or down relative to the nation as a whole) over time, and (2) it shows the *level* of wages relative to the nation as a whole at any given point in time. It should be noted, however, that the relative level of wages may be biased by the industrial composition of wages within a particular region. For instance, the auto industry pays the highest wage rates of any manufacturing industry—an average $14.28 per hour in 1989, 36 percent above the average manufacturing wage of $10.46. Regions with a larger share of auto manufacturers will have a larger than average manufacturing wage, while wages across other industries within that region could be significantly lower than the average.

In 1980, manufacturing costs within the Great Lakes were relatively high. Indeed, the average manufacturing wage for the region was 17.6 percent above the national average. In Michigan, wages were 30.7 percent above the national average. This is not surprising, given the region's heavy concen-

tration of auto manufacturing and unionized labor. Between 1980 and 1989, however, the pressure on manufacturing wages within the region was mixed. Although relative manufacturing wages fell across all states during the 1980s, some states were more affected than others. Moreover, most of the relative declines were concentrated in the latter half of the period. Michigan and Indiana were the only states with some upward pressure on wages between 1986 and 1989. On net, even these states saw declines over the decade.

RELATIVE HOME PRICES. Table 8 shows the distribution of relative home prices across Great Lakes states. The First National Bank of Chicago Relative Home Price Index (HPI) is defined as the median price of a home in a state (HP_s) divided by the median price of a home in the nation as a whole (HP_{us}):

(3) $$HPI = HP_s/HP_{us}$$

The regional total is derived from a weighted average of individual state indices. The weight on each state is that state's share of the region's population.

At unity, the HPI shows that median home prices within a state exactly match the national average. Above unity, the HPI shows that median home prices in a state are above the national average. In general, the HPI provides information about both the level and direction of regional land costs over time.

TABLE 7

Relative Manufacturing Wage Index (RMWI)

	1980	1985	1989
Great Lakes	1.176	1.175	1.150
Illinois	1.103	1.088	1.072
Indiana	1.166	1.124	1.111
Michigan	1.307	1.326	1.300
Ohio	1.179	1.194	1.171
Wisconsin	1.105	1.064	1.028

SOURCE: First National Bank Chicago, Economic Forecasting Division.

NOTE: RMWI = AMW_s/AMW_{us}, where AMW_s is the average manufacturing wage in a state and AMW_{us} is the average manufacturing wage in the nation.

TABLE 8

Index of Relative Home Prices (RHPI)ᵃ

	1980	1985	1989
Great Lakes	0.876	0.817	0.865
Illinois	1.019	0.978	1.053
Indiana	0.728	0.633	0.681
Michigan	0.766	0.701	0.676
Ohio	0.871	0.801	0.872
Wisconsin	0.935	0.901	0.966

SOURCE: First National Bank of Chicago, Economic Forecasting Division.

ᵃRHPI = HP_s/HP_{us}, where HP_s is the median price of a home in a state and HP_{us} is the median price of a home in the U.S.

In 1980, home prices in the region were below the national average in all states but one—Illinois. For a time during the 1980s, even Illinois home prices dropped below the national average. Indeed, the region's home prices were trending down relative to the nation as a whole over the period. On net, the median price of a home started the decade 12.4 percent below the national average and ended the decade 13.5 percent below the national average. Even during the latter years of the decade, when falling interest rates were contributing to hefty price increases across most of the nation, prices in the region did not pick up as much. This does not mean that absolute price levels on housing in the region were falling. More simply, the rate of increase on home prices in the region was slower than that for the nation as a whole.

In 1989 there were signs that the relative decline in housing prices in the region was coming to a halt. Relative prices picked up in all five states for the year from 1988. Indeed, relative prices have been on the rise since 1985. Only Michigan experienced a decline in relative prices since that year, which bottomed out in 1987.

Population trends

With 41.9 million people, the Great Lakes account for better than 17 percent of the total U.S. population—only the Mideast and Southeast are larger regions. Between 1980 and 1987, population growth in the region averaged 0.1 percent annually, almost a full percentage point behind the national

average (Table 9). Unlike the U.S., the region was especially hurt during the recession years of 1981 and 1982 when the region's population growth actually declined an average 0.2 percent. Since 1982, however, population has grown, albeit at a moderate pace. In 1987 population growth in the region was 0.4 percent, 0.6 percentage points behind the national average.

Despite a relative pickup in population growth, the region was still losing its population on net to neighboring regions in 1987. Net migration to the Great Lakes registered a loss of 60,477 people that year (Table 10). This marked a slowdown, however, from the migratory losses the region had experienced over the first half of the 1980s. Net migration out of the region averaged 254,746 between 1980 and 1986, almost triple the rate of out-migration of the 1970s. With the net migration to the U.S. positive and increasing over the period, there was clearly a redistribution of population from the Great Lakes to the rest of the country.

Slower than average growth in the 44 to 64 and the 65 and over age groups suggests that some of this shift in the population could be attributed to retirement-induced moves—retirees tend to move to warmer climates (Table 9). The distribution of adults in those age groups, however, has remained fairly close to the national average— 31 percent of the population in the region are over the age 45

TABLE 9

Population by age group in the Great Lakes region

	Levelᵃ	Shareᵃ,ᵇ	Average growth 1980-87
	millions	(%)	
Total	41.9	100.0	0.1
Under age 5	3.1	7.3	0.1
Ages 5-17	8.0	19.2	-1.6
Ages 18-44	17.8	42.6	0.8
Ages 45-64	7.9	18.8	-0.6
Ages 65 and over	5.1	12.2	1.9

SOURCE: U.S. Census Bureau.
ᵃ1987 data.
ᵇFigures do not sum to total due to rounding.

compared with 30.9 percent of the total U.S. population. On the flip side, the Great Lakes has a slightly larger share of 5 to 17 year olds, despite a widespread slowdown in the growth of that group over the 1980s.

II. The FNBC Regional Model: An empirical analysis of the Great Lakes economy

This section describes the methodology behind the FNBC Regional Model. In particular, the model will show the influence exerted by structural differences between the Great Lakes and the nation on the region's economic performance during the 1980s and it will provide insight to the outlook for the 1990s.

Model structure

The FNBC Regional Model is based on a simple premise: Regional economic performance resembles national economic performance only to the extent that the structure of the regional economy resembles the structure of the national economy. The Southwest, for instance, has a disproportionately large distribution of oil producers. When oil prices collapsed in 1986, this structural dependence on oil moved the region from a leading to lagging economic area of the country. Summarizing this framework for regional analysis:

TABLE 10

Net migration of population in the Great Lakes region

1970-79 average	-93,315
1980	-232,254
1981	-262,741
1982	-390,417
1983	-354,691
1984	-193,149
1985	-198,786
1986	-151,183
1987	-60,477

SOURCE: The WEFA Group.

(4) $$E_i=f(E,S_i)$$

where E_i represents the economic performance of region i, E represents national economic performance, and S_i represents the structural factors that differentiate region i from the national average. In particular, S_i represents those economic factors that were especially influential on the economic performance of region i, given that region's industrial structure.

TABLE 11

Sensitivity analysis
(most sensitive to least sensitive)

Employment by industry	Dollar	Oil prices	Business cycles
Durable goods manufacturing	1	1	2
Nondurable goods manufacturing	2	3	4
Transportation	3	6	7
Finance	4	4	9
Services	5	7	8
Farming and agricultural services	6	5	5
Wholesale and retail trade	7	8	6
Government	8	9	10
Construction	9	2	3
Mining	10	10	1

SOURCE: First National Bank of Chicago, Economic Forecasting Division.

NOTE: For more detail, see *On-Going Structural Change: Winners and Losers*, Economic Forecasting Division, The First National Bank of Chicago.

FNBC analysis has identified six structural factors which influenced regional economic performance in the 1980s. These include: the trade situation, oil price shocks, the defense budget, business cycle fluctuations, farm sector volatility, and relative cost shifts. From the structural analysis of the Great Lakes economy, the region is differentiated by its especially high concentration of heavy manufacturers. In addition, the region imports its oil. This has left the region especially sensitive to four of the six factors listed above: the trade situation, oil prices, business cycles, and the relative costs. In contrast to the coastal regions of the country, however, the industry structure of the region was not sensitive to shifts in defense outlays. The region had the smallest concentration of per capita outlays in the country over the 1980s, which isolated it from the positive effects associated with a run up in outlays, and currently is sheltering it from the subsequent cutbacks in defense spending. The region's tie to agriculture during the period was overshadowed by its link to heavy manufacturing.

The remainder of this section will describe: (a) the relationship between these four factors and the Great Lakes economy, (b) the empirical results of that analysis, and (c) the outlook for the region in the 1990s.

TRADE. Shifts in the trade balance were especially influential on growth in the manufacturing sector over the 1980s. In particular, large dollar movements alter the competitiveness of U.S. manufacturers. This sensitivity to changes in the terms of trade is illustrated in Table 11. It shows a list of major industry groupings ranked by the magnitude of their response to changes in the value of the dollar, the price of oil, and the index of industrial production. Durable goods and nondurable goods production were the most sensitive to changes in the value of the dollar. In short, the more industrialized regions of the country are more responsive to shifts in the terms of trade than the less industrialized regions. The Great Lakes has the highest concentration of durable goods manufacturers in the country.

During the early 1980s, the value of the dollar appreciated sharply—up 60 percent between 1980 and 1985. With much of this movement concentrated against the currencies of Europe and Japan, imports of high value added durable goods (capital goods, cars, consumer electronics) surged during those years. Imports of apparel and leather goods also jumped during those years. In particular, our trading partners gained a relative price advantage from the dollar's rise; when the dollar appreciated, import prices fell relative to the price of their domestic counterparts. As a result, both durable goods and some nondurable goods producers lost market share. In turn, those regions with an especially high concentration of durable goods producers deteriorated relative to other areas of the country. Indeed, recessionary levels of performance were reached in the Great Lakes.

Since 1985, however, the value of the dollar has depreciated sharply. Indeed, until 1989, much of the appreciation of the early 1980s was erased (Figure 1). With much of this movement against the currencies of Japan and Europe, this had the effect of reversing the trade imbalances of the early 1980s. Imports of high value added goods fell while exports of these goods were rising. Between 1986

and 1989, the trade deficit improved by $76.9 billion after adjusting for inflation—one-third of that improvement was in capital goods. This benefited those regions with a higher concentration of trade-sensitive industries.

In 1989, the dollar appreciated during the first half of the year. This largely explains the slowdown in trade improvement seen near year-end 1989 and the first half of 1990. Since June of last year, however, the dollar has depreciated and is expected to fall further in 1990. With imports slowing, and the prospects for increased demand abroad for domestic goods growing, the stage is being set for a recovery in the trade situation in 1991, which will culminate in a trade surplus by the mid 1990s.

The FNBC Regional Model accounts for regional sensitivity to trade adjustments by relating regional economic performance to changes in both merchandise exports and imports. Movements in personal income, retail sales, housing starts, employment, and population growth by region are modeled against trade balance shifts in those regions that have an especially high concentration of trade-sensitive producers. That is, we substitute net exports for S_i in (4):

$$(5) \qquad E_i = f(E, NetEx)$$

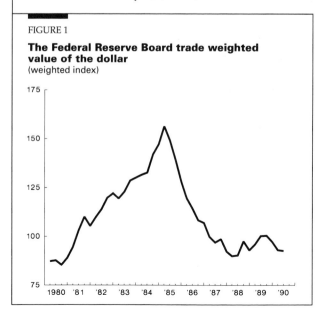

FIGURE 1

The Federal Reserve Board trade weighted value of the dollar
(weighted index)

where NetEx represents changes in the merchandise trade balance. Net exports are the difference between exports and imports of goods and services—a negative net export balance implies a trade deficit.

FIGURE 2

Producer price index of crude petroleum, domestic production
(index, 1982=100)

OIL PRICES. The effect of oil price movements on a region differs whether the region is an oil producer or an oil consumer. Oil producing regions tend to benefit from a rise in oil prices while oil consumers suffer. Indeed, oil consumers boost the profits of oil producers when oil prices rise. This is especially true for the more industrialized oil-consuming regions of the country. Oil is a factor of production. As a result, rising production costs (and falling profit margins) are one consequence of a run-up in oil prices. This industrial sensitivity to oil price shifts is shown in Table 11—durable goods production is the most sensitive of major industry groupings to shifts in the price of oil. Weak profits, in turn, curtail capital spending and reduce investment in oil-consuming areas of the country. Conversely, the profits associated with higher oil prices for oil producers enhance capital spending and investment in the oil-producing areas of the country.

During the first half of the 1980s, oil prices jumped (Figure 2). Initially, this cut into the profits of durable goods producers. Worse, however, weaker profits led to curtailed investment and slower growth among oil-consuming areas of the country. On the flip side, the oil patch, or oil-producing regions of the country made windfall profits during the rapid rise in oil prices. Capital spending and investment in those areas flourished.

In 1986, oil prices collapsed—down 50 percent from January to December. This directly benefitted oil consumers while it hurt oil producers. The dismal performance of the Southwest economy in recent years is evidence of this.

Although oil prices rebounded in the wake of the Kuwaiti invasion by Iraq, the best bet is that they will fall from their current highs and remain relatively low in 1991. A rise in oil production from the OPEC nations is working to offset the losses incurred from a loss in production from Iraq and Kuwait. Oil prices are expected to return to about $22 per barrel, a 1977 price level after adjusting for inflation in 1991. The upfront costs of the oil crisis will be carried by the more industrialized regions of the country, but are expected to quickly dissipate as more oil comes on line.

The FNBC Regional Model accounts for this industrial sensitivity to oil prices shifts by adding oil prices in (5):

$$(6) \qquad E_i = f(E, NetEx, OIL)$$

where OIL represents shifts in the price of oil.

BUSINESS CYCLES. By its nature, manufacturing is more sensitive to business cycle volatility than other sectors of the economy. This means that regions with a larger manufacturing base will be more responsive to business cycle shifts than other areas of the country. Business cycle shifts are defined in the Regional Model by changes in the index of industrial production. Heavy industry, in particular, is sensitive to periods of economic decline. Table 11 illustrates this business cycle sensitivity—mining and durable goods production were the most sensitive of all major industry groupings to changes in the index of industrial production.

During the early 1980s, the economy experienced two recessions, one in 1980, and again in 1981-82. Production in the durable goods sector of the economy lagged economic activity both times (Figure 3). Indeed, heavy producers led the economy into the last two recessions. As a result, the more industrialized regions of the country were especially dragged down by these declines in manufacturing. Indeed, the Great Lakes was characterized by its manufacturing decline in the early 1980s and it is more vulnerable to business cycle risk than other areas of the country.

Since late 1982, however, the economy has enjoyed a recovery. This has eased the pressure of business cycles on the more industrialized regions of the country, such as the Great Lakes. Indeed, with a pick-up in manufacturing sector activity, these regions have recovered from the decline of the early 1980s. Although growth has slowed, our outlook is for no recession through 1991.

The FNBC Regional Model accounts for regional sensitivity to business cycles by adding the index of industrial production to (6):

$$(7) \qquad E_i = f(E, NetEx, OIL, IP)$$

where IP represents changes in the index of industrial production.

ECONOMIC RATIONALIZATION: THE ROLE OF RELATIVE COSTS. Finally, an overwhelming force

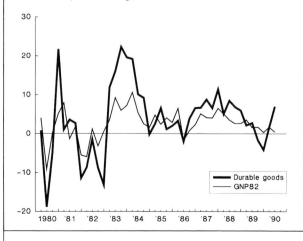

FIGURE 3

Index of durable goods production vs. real GNP growth
(annualized percent change)

FIGURE 4

Great Lakes disposable income growth, actual vs. fitted data
(annualized percent change)

versely, as relative costs are bid up in a region, and the returns to regional investments fall, investors leave the area.

The recent experience of the New England economy is perhaps the most dramatic example of this cycling of regional economies. During the early 1980s, returns to investing in the New England economy were still very high; relative costs were still low. With the rapid expansion of the New England economy over the course of the 1980s, however, relative costs began to rise. Indeed, median home prices in the region were the highest in the country by the end of the decade. It was no longer affordable, let alone profitable, to buy new real estate in the New England area. This repelled investors and contributed to the subsequent decline in home prices in the region in 1989.

Model results

The following sets of charts show the empirical relationship between key economic indicators in the regional economy, their national counterparts, and three of the four structural factors mentioned above: changes in the trade situation, oil prices, and business cycles. Relative costs were not included in the empirical analysis.

HISTORICAL PERFORMANCE. On average, the Great Lakes economy lagged its national counterpart over the balance of the 1980s. Between 1980 and 1989, personal disposable income growth increased 6.7 percent, 1.3 percentage points behind the nation. Employment gains were as dismal—up 0.9 percent on average over the period, 1.2 percentage points behind the nation. The worst of that shortfall, however, occurred between 1980 and 1985. Since 1986, the gap between regional and national performance has narrowed, falling only 0.6 percentage points behind the national average for income growth, and 0.5 percentage points behind the national average for employment growth. The remainder of this section will discuss the empirical reasons behind this lagging economic performance, document its improvement, and provide the groundwork for understanding where the region will be going in the 1990s.

MODEL A: INCOME. During the 1980s, movements in Great Lakes income growth could be largely captured by four factors: trends in national

income growth, the trade situation, oil price shifts, and swings in the business cycle. Beyond national trends, regional income growth tended to contract with the widening trade deficit, the run up in oil prices, and the business cycle recessions. Conversely, regional performance picked up with the reversal of these trends starting in 1985. This relationship between regional income growth, its national counterpart, the trade deficit, oil prices, and business cycles is illustrated by the heavy line in

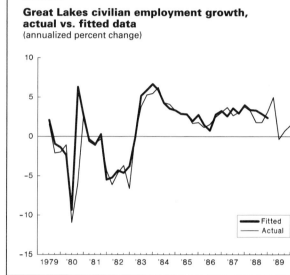

FIGURE 5

Great Lakes civilian employment growth, actual vs. fitted data
(annualized percent change)

Figure 4. Between 1979 and 1988, these factors accounted for more than 97 percent of the actual shifts witnessed in regional income growth.[2]

MODEL B: EMPLOYMENT. Movements in employment growth over the period could be largely captured by three factors: national employment trends, oil price shifts, and changes in the business cycle. In general, employment growth was more volatile than the national average over the 1980s. In the first half of the decade, a run-up in oil prices and a contraction in industrial production hurt regional performance relative to the nation. Moreover, the effects of both a turn in trade and a shift in oil prices tended to linger. By 1986, however, falling oil prices and rising production were contributing to regional

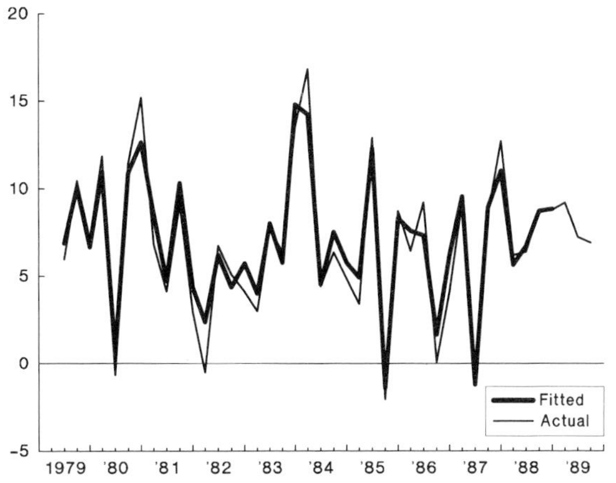

guiding regional economic development can be found in the mechanisms of a market economy. In particular, competition between regions for scarce resources—land, labor, and infrastructure—push regions through long relative economic swings. Periods of relatively rapid economic expansion tend to be followed by periods of relative economic decline. This cycling of regional economies, better termed "economic rationalization", is mentioned here for its influence on regional economic development but it will not be directly included in the empirical analysis that follows.

Economic rationalization can be summed up by the replacement rule: One thing will eventually replace another if it is cheaper and does the job better. In the context of regional growth, this translates into competition for investment—both domestic and foreign. Simply put, investment spills into a region when the costs of land, labor, and infrastructure are low and leaves that region once the costs of those scarce resources reach a level that is higher than can be had in other parts of the country. The key to this process is that investors shift their assets to regions where they believe the returns to their investments are high. Low labor costs, for instance, allow wider profit margins for manufacturers. Con-

employment growth. This relationship between regional employment growth, its national counterpart, oil prices, and business cycles is illustrated by the heavy line in Figure 5. Between 1979 and 1988, these factors helped to explain about 94 percent of the actual shifts in regional employment growth over the period.

MODEL C: UNEMPLOYMENT. The behavior of the Great Lakes unemployment rate over the 1980s could be largely captured by two factors: changes in the national unemployment rate and oil price shifts. In general, rising oil prices contributed to unemployment in the Great Lakes economy during the early 1980s. By 1986, falling oil prices were pushing down the unemployment rate in the region. This relationship between the regional unemployment rate, its national counterpart, and oil prices is illustrated by the heavy line in Figure 6. Between 1979 and 1988, these factors helped to explain 79

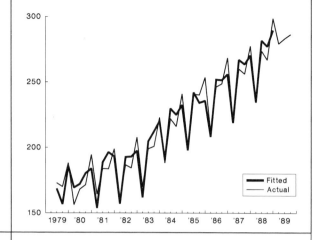

FIGURE 7

Great Lakes retail sales, actual vs. fitted data
(annualized rate, billions of dollars)

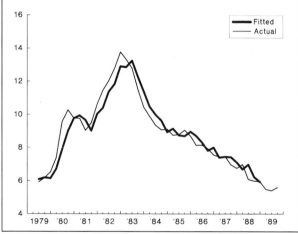

FIGURE 6

Great Lakes unemployment rate, actual vs. fitted
(percent of labor force)

percent of the actual shifts in the regional unemployment rate.

MODEL D: RETAIL SALES. Great Lakes retail sales performance over the 1980s could be largely captured by two factors: trends in national retail spending, and the difference between the regional

and national unemployment rates. The differential unemployment rate is used to proxy shifts in regional consumer confidence—a rise in unemployment shatters consumer confidence in an area economy. During the early 1980s, slow spending growth corresponded to relatively high unemployment rates in the region. By the second half of the decade, however, spending growth picked up with a slide in the regional unemployment rate. This relationship between regional spending, its national counterpart, and the difference between the regional and national unemployment rates is illustrated by the heavy line in Figure 7. Between 1979 and 1988, these factors accounted for 94 percent of the actual shifts witnessed in regional retail sales growth.

MODEL E: HOUSING STARTS. Behavior of the Great Lakes housing market over the 1980s can be largely tracked with two factors: national trends in the housing market, and the difference between regional and national employment growth. In general, regional housing markets tend to move with the national market—mortgage rates are largely set at the national level. But home prices vary across regions. Regions that are experiencing relatively slow growth tend to have lower home prices than regions that are experiencing faster growth. In particular, when employment growth is

strong in one region relative to another, that region's housing market tends to pick up relative to the national average. This relationship between regional housing starts, its national counterpart, and the difference between regional and national employment growth is illustrated by the heavy line in Figure 8. Between 1979 and 1988, these factors helped to explain 57 percent of the actual shifts in the regional home building.

SUMMARY. The FNBC Regional Model has shown that a statistical relationship exists between the performance of the Great Lakes economy and the trade situation, oil prices, and business cycle fluctuations. In particular, it is a deterioration in trade, coupled with rising oil prices and two recessions, that is largely behind the decline in the Great Lakes economy during the early 1980s. Conversely, a reversal of these trends since 1986 helped to boost the performance of the region. In 1989, the rebound in the region continued, albeit at a slower pace.

Another factor contributing to the recovery of the regional economy was its relative cost structure. The burden of relatively high union wages was partially offset during the 1980s by the low costs of land in the region, especially in Michigan where wages were the highest. The lagging economic per-

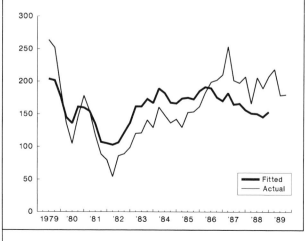

FIGURE 8

Great Lakes housing starts, actual vs. fitted data
(annualized rate, thousands)

formance of the region contributed to the decline in land prices over the first half of the decade, while wages fell at a much slower rate. This added to the pickup in economic activity witnessed since 1986.

Prospects for the 1990s

From the empirical analysis, the prospects for renewed strength in the Great Lakes economy are good. A slowdown in the current expansion, coupled with the temporary jump in energy prices, will moderate regional performance in 1990. With a further deprecia-tion in the dollar, however, and an expected cut in interest rates in late 1990, the stage is being set for stronger regional performance in 1991. Both export growth and increased domestic investment in capital equipment will add fuel to the region's manufacturing indus-tries. Moreover, the region is more sheltered than other parts of the country from cuts in the "high-tech" end of the defense budget while it is well-positioned to benefit from increased investment in more traditional arms outlays for the military efforts in the Middle East.

Another favorable factor contributing to the region's performance in the 1990s is the relative regional decline in land and labor costs. Housing and land prices are especially low in the Great Lakes. Even Illinois, with its concentration of urban pricing in the Chicago area, is only slightly above the national average on median home prices. This will attract continued investment in the region and contribute to the recovery the area has experienced since 1986.

On balance, the Great Lakes economy is expected to outperform the nation as a whole over

TABLE 12

Regional winners and losers in the 1980s versus the 1990s

1980-89	1990-99
Winners	**Winners**
New England	Great Lakes
Far West	Southeast
Southeast	Southwest
Neutral	**Neutral**
Southwest	Far West
Mideast	Mideast
Losers	**Losers**
Rocky Mountain	Plains
Great Lakes	Rocky Mountain
Plains	New England

the course of the decade, despite a slow start in 1990. In contrast to the 1980s, the region will move from the seventh poorest performing of eight BEA regions to the top. Conversely, New England will lose in the 1990s, falling from its top 1980s ranking to last in the 1990s. Table 12 shows this expected shift in economic performance across BEA regions. Regional "winners" were named for their better than the national average performance over the decade, "losers" for their worse than national average performance, and "neutral" for their average performance.[3]

On balance, the 1990s will yield a new set of region winners and losers. The coastal regions of the country will likely pay a price for an excessive 1980s performance, while the interior regions of the country will do better. The Great Lakes, in particu-lar, are in a position to benefit from adjustments that are in store for the decade ahead. An almost uni-form move to diversify regional economies in the 1980s, however, will mitigate the magnitude of these differences between regions in the 1990s. Regional industry structures are now more similar to each other. In response to the stresses of the early 1980s, regions almost uniformly diversified in the 1980s—their employment coefficients moved toward unity. In addition to the shifts in regional performance that are expected, disparities in regional performance will be less pronounced.

NOTES
[1]For more detail see "Regional Winners and Losers", *Economic Issue Backgrounder*, May 1990, First National Bank of Chicago.
[2]Statistical results of Model A and subsequent models can be found in "Regional Winners and Losers", ibid.
[3]Ibid.

Epilogue

With all its diversity, strength, and common ground, the Great Lakes region is a remarkable and unique place. *The Great Lakes Economy Looking North and South* presents a contemporary portrait of an impressive economic region. Rich in resources —people, industry, natural resources and institutions—the Great Lakes region is challenged by the need to maintain its strengths and pursue new opportunities. Throughout the region's notable history, challenges were met and difficulties overcome. Now, the continual quest for economic growth and prosperity reckons with the realities of the international marketplace and environmental protection. Uncertainty, whether it pertains to personal economic circumstances, the welfare of community or the flux of national politics, is ever-present. Faith in the future may be an age-old expression, but for Great Lakes region residents, it is as fresh and forceful as the new day it heralds.

These fifteen chapters cover a lot of territory. The authors have set forth, in great detail, information and observations about the regional economy. The result is a noteworthy achievement in regional economic assessment. The strengths and weaknesses of the economy are explored and linkages among economic sectors are described. The complementarity and, in fact inseparability, of the economic and environmental attributes of the binational region is a common thread throughout the text. The authors successfully demonstrate that an integrated economic system, expressed in strong reciprocal trade flows, can flourish in a binational context. The recent U.S.-Canada Free Trade Agreement, even with its lingering questions, represents a political affirmation of the desire to improve on a bilateral economic relationship that is already the largest and one of the most barrier-free in the world.

The geographic boundaries of the Great Lakes "economic region" defy precise definition, as attested to by the authors of *The Great Lakes Economy Looking North and South*. In their use of economic data and region descriptions, various authors have identified six, seven, eight and nine states along with one or two Canadian provinces as comprising the "Great Lakes region." Irrespective of this divergence in description, which is partly due to economic data development and availability, the region is bound together by its natural resources and its developed infrastructure. The Great Lakes-St. Lawrence River system represents a common asset of the core region. This magnificent hydrologic resource, accounting for one-fifth of all fresh surface water on earth, divides the U.S. and Canada in a geo-political context, but unites them in an economic context. Different political jurisdictions within the region reflect facets of the attendant economic competition that characterizes neighboring economies. However, cooperative arrangements have emerged for appropriate endeavors such as resource management and region-wide promotion.

The Great Lakes region approaches the 21st century with an enviable record of long-term economic performance. Its legacy, though, may be a tough act to follow. *The Great Lakes Economy Looking North and South* identifies numerous important economic and public policy developments and trends that will be significant for the region's future. How we address these challenges and opportunities will indicate the level of progress and achievement the region can attain.

■ Regional population growth is slowing and a continuing pattern of suburbanization and relocation to rural "amenity" areas is evident. These population trends carry implications for labor availability, relative strength of political representation and economic viability for particular areas.

■ The binational Great Lakes economy has recently benefited from a period of restructuring. The manufacturing sector remains relatively important and productivity improvements have enhanced competitiveness, especially in the export sector.

■ Continued use and production of relatively high sulfur coal in the Great Lakes states is brought into question by new Clean Air Act legislation. Improved emission controls, clean coal technologies and importation of low sulfur coal will enhance the region's environmental quality while challenging its industrial cost competitiveness.

■ Substantial investment in infrastructure, (e.g. highways, telecommunications and electric capacity), will be necessary to keep the regional economy competitive in both the domestic and international marketplace.

■ Great Lakes region agriculture has been gradually diversifying in recent years and its status as a potent productive force for overseas markets will be solidified if the Uruguay Round of world trade talks succeeds in reducing agricultural product import barriers and export subsidies.

■ The U.S.-Canada Free Trade Agreement, intended to eliminate existing trade barriers and induce more two-way trade, will likely achieve its ultimate goal but a possible transition to a North American Free Trade Area with the inclusion of Mexico may be more difficult.

■ Economic dependence on the region's bountiful water resources will increase, adding new dimensions to the economic base but also increasing problems of competing and conflicting uses.

■ During the 1980s, a dramatic surge in the volume and nature of cooperative ventures between and among the states and provinces in the Great Lakes region took place. The challenge of the 1990s will be to build on this past success in collaborative governance and to integrate environmental and economic objectives in public policy.

A review of these and other trends identified by the authors, leads us to a set of inescapable conclusions. The Great Lakes region is but one component —albeit significant—of an international and global economy. Our destiny will be shaped in part by external forces, well beyond our control, with political, social and environmental characteristics as well as economic ones. Fortunately, we as a region are well-positioned to make use of the forces that are within our control. We speak of the building blocks for regional economic prosperity—a skilled labor force, a diversified economic base, an unequaled multi-modal transportation system, access to raw materials, and an infrastructure for production, distribution and use of goods, to name a few. Perhaps most significantly, this region can draw on an institutional infrastructure legacy of multi-jurisdictional, binational cooperation unequaled in any other region on the globe.

The Great Lakes region cannot afford to face its future with a "wait and see attitude." The global marketplace will "name the game" and "deal the cards" but the region will have every opportunity to "play its hand." Multi-jurisdictional cooperation— especially between the United States and Canada —will be the trump card in this high stakes game. Through the pages of this book, the Great Lakes Commission and Federal Reserve Bank of Chicago hope to strengthen this tradition of multi-jurisdictional cooperation—a tradition that has become a hallmark of this region's economic prosperity.

STEPHEN J. THORP AND MICHAEL J. DONAHUE

About the authors

DAVID R. ALLARDICE *is Vice President and Assistant Director of the Research Department at the Federal Reserve Bank of Chicago and an instructor at DePaul University. He has participated widely in economic programs and publications concerning the Midwest economy.*

CHRISTOPHER A. BAINES *is the Director of The Centre for the Great Lakes' Toronto office. Prior to joining The Centre, he was a market representative for Southham Business Information and Communication Group. His public service includes four years as Parliamentary Assistant to the Ontario Minister of Municipal Affairs and Housing. He is the president of the Georgian Bay Association and a former director of the Movement Against Acid Rain (Georgian Bay Chapter).*

ALBERT G. BALLERT, *a geographer, has focused his research on the Great Lakes since the 1940s and in 1956 he joined the Great Lakes Commission as Director of Research. Dr. Ballert presently serves as Director of Research Emeritus. While engaged in studies and analysis of all of the diverse aspects of the Great Lakes environment, his special interests concern the region's resources and waterborne commerce. Also, to provide a source of current references relating to the Great Lakes region, he has prepared periodically since 1959 a bibliography entitled* Great Lakes Research Checklist *which is published by the Great Lakes Commission.*

GARY L. BENJAMIN *is an Economic Adviser and Vice President at the Federal Reserve Bank of Chicago. In his current position, Mr. Benjamin supervises the Research Department's Agricultural and Rural Banking Section and is responsible for briefing Bank management on agricultural issues, directing research on agricultural and rural credit markets, and conducting special studies on economic trends and developments in the Seventh Federal Reserve District. Mr. Benjamin is also responsible for the Bank's biweekly economic publication,* Agricultural Letter, *and the Bank's quarterly survey of farmland values and agricultural credit conditions.*

ATHANASIOS D. BOURNAKIS *is a research economist at the Energy Resources Center of the University of Illinois at Chicago. He is the principal investigator in sponsored research for new energy technologies. He has conducted several studies in the field of energy conservation in large-scale buildings and in the area of residential conservation.*

MICHAEL J. DONAHUE *is Executive Director of the Great Lakes Commission, an eight-state agency providing a regional voice on resource management, economic development and environmental quality issues. He previously served as Director of the U.S. Office and Head of Research with The Center for the Great Lakes. He holds a doctorate in Urban, Technological and Environmental*

Planning from the University of Michigan and is an Adjunct Assistant Professor in its School of Natural Resources. Dr. Donahue has written numerous articles and book chapters, as well as a comprehensive study titled, Institutional Arrangements for Great Lakes Management: Past Practices and Future Alternatives.

ELEANOR H. ERDEVIG *is a Regional Economist with the Federal Reserve Bank of Chicago. She has written extensively on factors affecting the economies of Midwest states, including the impact of federal expenditures and taxation, federal spending on research and development, the importance of small businesses in economic development, and the outlook for future labor supply. Currently, she is engaged in research on human activities which affect the Great Lakes basin ecosystem.*

JOHN FRASER HART *has been a professor of Geography at the University of Minnesota since 1967. He received his Ph.D. from Northwestern University in 1950, and taught at the University of Georgia and Indiana University before he moved to Minnesota. He has published many articles on the geography of rural areas in the Midwest and South, is author of* The Land That Feeds Us (Norton, in press), *and is editor of* Our Changing Cities (Johns Hopkins, in press). *He was Editor of the* Annals of the Association of American Geographers *from 1970 through 1975, and served as President of that Association in 1980-81.*

ERIC B. HARTMAN *is an attorney and Senior Policy Analyst specializing in international trade and economic policy at the Northeast-Midwest Institute. The work of the Northeast-Midwest Institute focuses on policies affecting the economic strength of the northeastern and midwestern states that historically have formed the nation's industrial heartland. The Institute works closely with state and local governments in the 18 states of the region and with members of the U.S. House and Senate who make up the Northeast-Midwest Coalition. From 1986 to 1989, Mr. Hartman served as an aide on trade policy with U.S. Representative Sander Levin of Michigan.*

JAMES P. HARTNETT *is the founding Director of the Energy Resources Center at the University of Illinois at Chicago. In 1980, he organized the Midwest Universities Energy Consortium which includes the 20 major research universities in the Big 10 states. Widely-published in the fields of energy resources and in heat and mass transfer research, he has been the recipient of a Guggenheim Fellowship, a Fulbright Award, and other distinguished awards and honors.*

LARRY LEEFERS *is Associate Professor, Department of Forestry, College of Agriculture and Natural Resources, at Michigan State University. His research has centered on multiple resources planning, forest policy analysis, and the economics of Christmas tree management.*

TIMOTHY MCNULTY *is Executive Director of the Council of Great Lakes Governors where he previously held the position of Economic Policy Director. From 1986 to 1987, he directed the start-up of an economic develop-ment consortia of 30 communities surrounding Argonne National Laboratory.*

MADHU KAPUR MALHOTRA *is a partner in Kapur and Martin Associates, a Toronto consulting firm whose clients include Environment Canada and Environment Ontario. She was formerly a research associate for The Centre for the Great Lakes. She holds a Bachelor of Science from the University of Toronto.*

RANDEL A. PILO *is an economist with the Wisconsin Public Service Commission. Prior to his present position, Mr. Pilo was Lead Economist at the Division of Research and Planning, Wisconsin Department of Development. In addition to supervising a variety of research projects while at the Department of Development, he conducted research including a long-range economic forecast for Wisconsin, an analysis of the labor impact of mergers and acquisitions, and an economic assessment of environmental regulations on industries in south-eastern Wisconsin.*

DANIEL K. RAY *is the Head of Research of The Center for the Great Lakes and the director of its Chicago office. Prior to joining The Center, he worked as a program manager and analyst for California's Coastal Commission and Department of Water Resources. He holds a Master of Science in Ecology from the University of California, Davis.*

ROBERT H. SCHNORBUS *is Senior Business Economist and Research Officer at the Federal Reserve Bank of Chicago. He is also an Adjunct Professor at the University of Illinois and Research Fellow at the Regional Economics Applications Laboratory. Among his most recent projects, Dr. Schnorbus has been involved in research to develop regional production indexes, to analyze pricing behavior and efficiency in the steel industry, and to evaluate the financial performance of businesses in the Midwest. He is currently completing a detailed study of the Iowa economy that examines the economic perfor-mance of over 500 industries.*

STEPHEN L. J SMITH *is Professor of Recreation and Leisure Studies at the University of Waterloo in Ontario. Dr. Smith is the author of 3 books and 200 technical and scholarly papers on various aspects of recreation, leisure, and tourism. He also serves as a consultant for the Ontario and Canadian governments on a variety of tourism-related issues.*

DIANE C. SWONK *is the Regional Economist for the First National Bank of Chicago. At First Chicago, she designed and maintains the FNBC Regional Model, and authors the* First Regional Report. *She has provided testimony for both state and city governments and consulted for The Council of Great Lakes Governors. She received her masters degree in economics from the University of Michigan and an MBA from the University of Chicago.*

WILLIAM A. TESTA *is Senior Regional Economist and Research Officer in the Regional Section of the Research Department at the Federal Reserve Bank of Chicago. He has written widely in the areas of economic development, the Midwest economy, and state-local public finance.*

STEPHEN J. THORP *is Manager of the Transportation and Economic Development Program at the Great Lakes Commission. Prior to coming to the Commission in 1982, he was a waterways planner with the Minnesota Department of Transportation. He has also held positions in regional and city planning.*

DAVID D. WEISS *is an Associate Economist in the Regional Development Division at the Federal Reserve Bank of Chicago. He started at the bank after receiving a M.A. in Economics from Stanford University.*

HENRY P. WHALEY *is retired as Senior Vice President of operations for Cleveland-Cliffs Inc. He holds degrees in both metallurgical and civil engineering. Prior to his position with Cleveland Cliffs Inc., he was Group Vice President in charge of mining at Pickands Mather and Co.*

Acknowledgments

This volume was produced during 1990 and 1991 by the Research Department at the Federal Reserve Bank of Chicago under the direction of Karl A. Scheld, Senior Vice President and Director of Research, and David R. Allardice, Assistant Director of Research and supervisor to the Regional Section.

Concepts and organization were chiefly developed and carried out by Stephen J. Thorp of the Great Lakes Commission and William A. Testa of the Federal Reserve Bank of Chicago.

Coordination of design, layout, and graphics was conducted by Kathleen Solotroff with the assistance of Lynn Busby-Ward, Chris Cacci, John Dixon, Roger Thryselius, and Thomas O'Connell. Typesetting was coordinated by Nancy Ahlstrom and carried out by Yvonne Peeples and Rita Molloy. Communications assistance was provided by Velma Davis.

Editorial support and advice were contributed by Kathryn Moran, assistant editor. Editorial review was provided by analysts at the Bank including Linda M. Aguilar, David R. Allardice, Eleanor H. Erdevig, Rick Mattoon, William A. Testa, and David D. Weiss.

Thoughtful review of both the concept and contents was graciously contributed by a Board of Advisers. These advisers were drawn from public, private, and academic institutions in the Great Lakes region of the United States and Canada. The contents of this book do not necessarily reflect their views in any way. Members of the Board of Advisers included the following:

MARCUS ALEXIS
Dean, College of Business Administration
University of Illinois at Chicago

JAMES E. ANNABLE
Senior Vice President and Chief Economist
First National Bank of Chicago

SCOTT BAIR
Director
Office of Economic Policy, Planning and Research
Pennsylvania Department of Commerce

WALLACE BIERMAN
Manager, Division of Research and Analysis
Illinois Department of Commerce and
Community Affairs

DR. CHARLES F. BONSER
Director
Institute for Development Strategies
Indiana University

ANTHONY S. EARL
Chairman
The Center for the Great Lakes and
Partner, Quarles and Brady

GARY L. FAILOR
President
Toledo-Lucas County Port Authority

MARK HAAS
Chief Economist and Director of Business Research
Michigan Department of Commerce

DR. RON W. IANNI
President
University of Windsor

HOWARD KREBS
Chief, SEPH Analysis and Dissemination Section
Statistics Canada

LEE MUNNICH
Deputy Commissioner
Minnesota Department of Trade and
Economic Development

RICHARD MUNSON
Director
Northeast-Midwest Institute

G. DOUGLAS VALENTINE
Canadian Consul General, Chicago

RANDALL WADE
Administrator
Division of Research and Planning
Wisconsin Department of Development

SAUL J. WALDMAN
Vice President, Public Affairs
The Detroit Edison Company

HENRY G. WILLIAMS
Commissioner
New York State Public Service Commission

HONORABLE ROY WILT
State Senator, Pennsylvania